MIND WARP!

The *Fantastic* True Story of Roger Corman's

New World Pictures

Hemlock Books

England

PICTURE CREDITS:
New World Pictures, American International Pictures, United Artists, 20th Century Fox, Metro Goldwyn Mayer, John Hamilton, Dick Klemensen, Eric Hoffman, Bluewater Comics and Roger Corman.

Visit our website:
www.hemlockbooks.co.uk

First published in 2009 by
Hemlock Books Limited,
The Bristol Office,
2 Southfield Road,
Westbury-on-Trym,
Bristol
BS9 3BH

A CIP catalogue record for this book is available from the British Library.

ISBN 978-0-9557774-1-7

Design by Hemlock Books Limited.

Printed and bound in Great Britain by
CPI Antony Rowe, Chippenham and Eastbourne

Christopher T Koetting

acKNOWLedgemeNTS

This book would not have been possible without four individuals: first, my friend and publisher Denis Meikle, who supported the project; second, my beloved wife Valerie, who was a constant encouragement and constructive critic; third, my wonderful son Thomas, who gave up a lot of 'daddy time' and kept things moving by asking when I was going to be done; finally, Roger Corman, without whose creativity and vision, I would have had nothing to write about.

I am also indebted to the numerous writers and publications that have covered Roger Corman and New World Pictures over the years. I have done my best to give them due credit in the text, and I am grateful for the wealth of information that their efforts have provided.

CONTENTS

Foreword by Joe Ritter 7

Introduction 9

Chapter 1: *Angels, Demons and Nurses* 11
Chapter 2: *Cries, Whispers and Death Races* 49
Chapter 3: *Thrills, Chills and Spills* 93
Chapter 4: *Hollywood's Wild Angel* 125
Chapter 5: *Saints, Humanoids and Galaxies* 155
Chapter 6: *Harry, Larry and Larry* 203

Epilogue: *Life After New World* 235

New World Filmography 243

Bibliography 276

For my father,
in memory of our Sunday afternoon movie chats

Foreword: Roger Corman

by Joe Ritter

Working with Roger was a dream come true. I had grown up watching his films; my first nightmare that I can remember was brought on by watching Attack of the Crab Monsters *when I was a child.*

When I was a kid, there were funky ghetto theaters in downtown Brooklyn, all former movie palaces from the '20s with beautiful decor from the dim past: the RKO Albee, the Duffield, the Fox theatre and the Lowes Metropolitan, and I watched all Roger's films in that setting—me and my film-crazy friends. The fact that you could get your life threatened, ass kicked, and robbed just made the moviegoing experience more exciting.

Roger's films followed me as I grew up, and I began to seek them out, knowing that a great low budget movie was waiting for me. I became obsessed with the idea that one day Roger would call and I would make a film for him.

After Toxic Avenger *came out, I became friends with Barbara Boyle, a brilliant producer who used to be Roger's Lawyer at New World Pictures. She told me that I should make a film for him, and without telling me what she was up to, she called him to tell him to hire me. One day the phone rang: it was Roger. He invited me to come out to LA and make a film. Once I caught my breath, I dropped everything and moved to LA.*

I made Beachballs *in 1987, and it became a Roger Corman Comedy Classic, playing on Cinemax for 20 years.* Beachballs *is a silly little film; we shot it in 12 days, but it has its moments, including some of the cast from the* Toxic Avenger *playing the goofy bad guys. The* Beachballs *wrap party at his funky Venice studio was so wild and out of control, they banned wrap parties at the studio after that!*

My favourite memory of Roger was pitching low-budget ideas to him. He would let me come in to his office in the morning, and I pitched every wild idea I had, from Route 666, Samurai Women Unchained, Kiss me once, Kill me Twice, *and the cannibal comedy* Groupie Soup, *about a rock band that cooks and eats its groupies! Roger's eyes would light up or glaze over as I jumped around describing the crazy films I wanted to make. He never made any of them but it became a ritual, and I pitched him about fifteen movies while I worked for him. He always had time to listen to another one of my hair-brained ideas, and I loved talking to him about films and the people we had met and worked with.*

At that time, I was becoming known as a photographer and I was making portraits of famous Hollywood actors, actresses, and filmmakers. I called Roger and told him I wanted to shoot his portrait, and he was thrilled. The image we made together became the ultimate 'Roger Portrait', and it sums up his entire career in one image: a projectionist watching his favourite film from behind the glass in the projection booth. Helmut Newton saw the image when I was working on Dracula *with Francis Coppola, and told me it was one of the best portraits he had ever seen, next to my portrait of Isabella Rossellini.*

When I look at that image we made together, it reminds me of the man who loved films and filmmaking above all; he is a legend, and there will never be another filmmaker like him. He gave all of us a chance to chase our dreams and encouraged us to make them come true. I am honoured to be one of the young filmmakers Roger Corman chose to make films for him, and I was lucky enough to meet or work with three other Corman 'alumni': Francis Coppola, Martin Scorsese and Jonathan Demme.

Thank you, Roger.

(Joe Ritter wrote the screenplay to Troma's The Toxic Avenger **and directed the comedy** Beachballs. **He has served as assistant cameraman/steadicam operator on numerous films, including** Pulp Fiction, **Bram Stoker's Dracula, Godzilla, Starship Troopers and Barton Fink.** *He is a highly-regarded professional photographer and his 'Roger Portrait' can be found on page 235.)*

Mind Warp

INTRODUCTION

It was quite a sight: five long-haired hippies high-stepping their way through the streets at the 1969 International Film Festival in Cannes, France. They had cause for celebration—their low-budget existential biker opus *Easy Rider* had just been nominated for the coveted *Palme d'Or* prize for Best Picture. On the left was the film's writer/director/co-star, Dennis Hopper; in the middle, its writer/co-star Peter Fonda; on the right, its co-star and advocate Jack Nicholson. Little did they know it, but their labour of love was to become a watershed film which would herald the dawning of a new generation in Hollywood.

Tinseltown was in desperate need of new blood. The turbulent decade of the 1960s had seen a dramatic drop in movie attendance as the major studios—most of them in the hands of various corporate conglomerates by decade's end—proved themselves hopelessly out of touch with what the movie-going public wanted. Awash in red ink, Hollywood was ready to take a chance on America's own 'New Wave' of filmmakers, whose ranks included the likes of Hopper, Fonda, Nicholson, Francis Ford Coppola, Peter Bogdanovich, Martin Scorsese and Robert Towne.

Watching from the sidelines was the man who had given (or *would* give) all of these upstarts their break in the film industry: 43-year-old Roger Corman. By the end of the '60s, Corman had produced and/or directed some 65 films, including his extremely popular and profitable Edgar Allan Poe adaptations for James Nicholson and Sam Arkoff's American International Pictures (AIP). Corman had also produced/directed two AIP films which were important precursors to *Easy Rider*—the biker film *The Wild Angels* (1966), also with Fonda, and the LSD exposé *The Trip* (1967), again featuring Fonda alongside Hopper in a script by Jack Nicholson. Corman had actually tried to entice AIP to bankroll *Easy Rider*, but Nicholson and Arkoff balked at his insistence that Hopper direct the picture.

AIP's failure to make one of the most successful and influential films of its time was only one in a long line of setbacks which had Corman thinking seriously about a declaration of independence. The increasingly conservative Nicholson (his company was about to go public), concerned that the film might be taken as an endorsement of the drug culture, had altered the ending of *The Trip* to a 'cracked' freeze-frame on Fonda, thus implying that LSD can only lead to a bad end. Corman had subsequently travelled to Germany in 1968 to bail out AIP when director Cy Endfield's sexual hang-ups left its magnum opus, *De Sade,* high and dry. However, Corman's efforts went for naught when Nicholson's editorial scissors made mincemeat of the fabled Marquis's much-hyped *bacchanalia*.

Worse was to come. In 1970, Corman's counterculture epic *Gas-s-s-s!* (in which everyone over the age of 25 dies after a nerve-gas leak) proved to be his last directorial effort for AIP, as the picture lost most of its climax and barely saw release. Corman had a similar experience with United Artists the following year, when they redubbed all the German accents in his World War I aerial combat film *Von Richthofen and Brown* (aka *The Red Baron*), then cut out a nude love scene for good measure.

Enough was enough. Corman hung up his directing guns for what would turn out to be twenty years. Fortunately, he had seen the writing on the wall early enough to give himself a new lease on life. He was about to enter a whole New World..

US theatrical poster for House of Usher

aNgels, demoNs aNd NuRses

'Roger Corman was not an early mentor; he was the only mentor I ever had.'
—Stephanie Rothman, director of *The Student Nurses* and *The Velvet Vampire*

'I found him a very courteous and gentlemanly guy, but a very stern and tough customer who was quite polite as he explained these outrageous tactics of exploitation in cold, calm terms.'
—Martin Scorsese, director of *Boxcar Bertha*

It Conquered the World

Roger William Corman was born in Detroit, Michigan on April 5, 1926. He was the first of two children born to William and Ann Corman (his brother Gene was born 18 months later) and spent his early years as a child of the Great Depression. Like many who grew up during that time, the experience forged a lasting impression that made him both tight-fisted and highly suspect of *laissez-faire* capitalism.

When Roger was 14, the Corman family relocated to Beverly Hills, California. It put the youngster in touch for the first time with the film industry that was to become his future. Upon graduation from Beverly Hills High School, he enrolled at Stanford University in Palo Alto, California as an aeronautical engineering student. He would spend his second and third college years at the University of Colorado at Boulder, in a Naval officer training program. With the end of World War II, Corman's obligation to the Navy was waived and he returned to finish at Stanford in 1947 with a degree in Industrial Engineering.

The following year, Corman entered the film industry as a messenger and then a story analyst at 20th Century-Fox. The corporate politics put him off, however, and in 1950, he decided to award himself some time out of the US, first studying literature at England's Oxford University and then bumming around Paris. After a year, Corman's funds ran out and he returned to California, still determined to make it in the film business.

There were no jobs to be had at Fox, but he began reading scripts for different agencies around town, as well as writing some of his own. In 1953, one of his scripts called *The House in the Sea* was purchased by Allied Artists for $3,500. In exchange for the experience, Corman worked for nothing on the picture, which ended up being rewritten by five other people and coming out as *Highway Dragnet*. The film, which starred Richard Conte as a Korean War vet wrongly accused of murder, earned Corman his first professional credits, as co-writer and associate producer.

In the spring of 1954, Corman established his own production company, Palo Alto Productions. Along with his younger brother Gene, Corman operated out of a tiny office above the Cock 'n' Bull pub on Hollywood's Sunset Strip. They would subsequently produce the cut-rate ($12,000) sci-fier *Monster from the Ocean Floor* (1954), which was picked up by Robert Lippert for distribution, as well as the more ambitious $50,000 racing flick *The Fast and the Furious* (1955).

It was through *The Fast and the Furious* that Corman's path would cross those of Nicholson and Arkoff, who ran the small independent American Releasing Corporation. It was a marriage made in exploitation heaven, and Corman would end up becoming one of ARC's (soon to become AIP) top suppliers, both producing and directing such '50s' drive-in staples as *The Day the World Ended, Gunslinger, It Conquered the World* (all 1956), *Machine Gun Kelly, Teenage Caveman* (both 1958), and *A Bucket of Blood* (1959).

Corman was not yet beholden to AIP, however. Being his own man meant that he was free to ply Palo Alto's wares to other companies as well, whether it be another independent like Allied Artists (for whom he produced/directed the cult classics *Attack of the Crab Monsters* and *Not of This Earth* in 1958) or even the majors (he produced/directed *I, Mobster* for 20th Century-Fox and produced *Stakeout on Dope Street* for Warner Brothers, both also in 1958).

The majors largely ignored the drive-in market, and that fact helped AIP to become the nation's top supplier of exploitation product by the end of the 1950s. It was a cash bonanza, and Corman—who was as responsible as anyone for AIP's meteoric rise—began to wonder why he was not enjoying more of the spoils. He realised that to do so he

Roger Corman (right) on the set of House of Usher

12

would have to enter the distribution game, which he did in 1959 when he and Gene dropped Palo Alto and formed the Filmgroup Company.

Corman began by releasing double-bills of films that he had executive-produced (*High School Big Shot/T-Bird Gang*) or picked up (*High School Caesar/Date Bait*). He did reasonably well, and he decided to put some of his producing and directing energies into the fledgling outfit. His first effort for Filmgroup was the notorious black comedy *Little Shop of Horrors*, shot over a weekend for $28,000, utilising the stock company of players and technicians that he had now amassed. Although the film met with little interest when it was released on a double-bill with another Filmgroup picture, *The Last Woman on Earth* (which Corman also produced and directed), in 1960, its cult appeal grew over the years to the extent that it became an off-Broadway musical in 1982 and a major-studio remake in 1986.

Corman would produce/direct four more features for Filmgroup in 1959 and 1960, including *The Wasp Woman, Ski Troop Attack, Creature from the Haunted Sea* and *Atlas*. None cost very much or did very well. However, with the release of AIP's $300,000 Edgar Allan Poe adaptation, *House of Usher,* in 1960, Corman was suddenly catapulted into a whole new level of filmmaking. *Usher's* resounding success ensured Corman's directorial talents would no longer be confined to the also-rans. Utilising the iconic talents of silken-voiced screen horror legend Vincent Price, he would go on to produce/direct seven more Poe films over the next four years (although one, *The Haunted Palace*, was Poe in name only, having been based on a novella by H P Lovecraft)—and Filmgroup was essentially left to his protégés during this time. One in particular was Francis Ford Coppola, who in 1963 helmed an effective *Psycho*-type thriller called *Dementia 13* on location in Ireland, as well as shooting sexually-suggestive monster scenes for inclusion in a Soviet science fiction film (which resulted in *Battle Beyond the Sun*). Coppola also contributed to Corman's final directorial effort for Filmgroup—its most notorious production: *The Terror*. Mainly shot in three days in 1962 on sets left over from AIP's *The Raven*, and utilising the services of that film's co-headliner Boris Karloff, *The Terror* was essentially made up as it went along over the following year, with additional scenes being shot by Coppola, Jack Hill, Monte Hellman, Dennis Jakob and even co-star Jack Nicholson. The result was something of a mess when it was finally released in

Dementia 13 (Luana Anders)

1963, the year Gene Corman decided to head for greener pastures at 20th Century-Fox. It was Gene's contacts with theatre-chain owners which had kept Filmgroup relatively independent; when he left, Roger ceded distribution of Filmgroup pictures to AIP (he relinquished the right to collect distribution fees the following year).

Because the Filmgroup pictures were cheap and none-too-successful, Corman never bothered to copyright them, an oversight which has cost him untold millions in residuals over the years (*Little Shop of Horrors* and *The Terror* have been released by practically every public-domain video company in the world). His apathy also showed in the fact that Filmgroup soon became little more than a supplier of direct-to-television product for AIP, including two more Soviet sci-fi cut-and-paste jobs, *Voyage to the Prehistoric Planet* and its companion piece, *Voyage to the Planet of Prehistoric Women* (notable for Mamie Van Doren's scallop-shell bikini and Peter Bogdanovich's less-than-stunning directorial debut). After 1966, Filmgroup ceased to exist.

Corman gave the eulogy to Filmgroup to author Mark McGee for his 1988 book, *Roger Corman: The Best of the Cheap Acts*—'The Filmgroup made money every year but we never made much money. I finally just let it drift away because I realised I could not produce, direct and run a distribution company at the same time. It was too many things. My feelings at the time were that I wanted to produce and direct.' By 1970, however, his feelings would be a whole lot different.

In J Philip di Franco's book *The Movie World of Roger Corman*, actor David Carradine made the comment that 'Roger is an enigma, a very contradictory kind of person. He is extremely hip and at the same time very square.' In point of fact, Corman's contradictions bordered on the cynical. He somehow managed to be both a social liberal and a fiscal conservative: a diehard Democrat who nevertheless went out of his way not to hire union labour. He decorated his office with revolutionary posters from the May '68 student riots in Paris but required his young acolytes to work long hours for very little pay. He touted the accolades that he received from abroad, but writer/director Jack Hill told *Fangoria*, '[Roger] used to laugh about how critics in Europe always found these mysterious messages in his pictures which, if you knew the truth, was just done to save a nickel. They read things into the movies that are absolutely laughable. They would invite him to Europe and give him a first-class plane ticket. He would go to the airport and cash it in and travel cabin class, and pocket the rest of the money.'

Reflecting on his early days as a filmmaker, Corman told the *Los Angeles Times*, 'It was great fun. It was stimulating. It was creative. It was a great way to live.' Working in the horror genre also gave Corman the opportunity to play Freud: 'Good horror is like good sex. You build up tension then jolt your audience. With sex you also have [that] exciting climax.' As his 1990 autobiography *How I Made a Hundred Movies in Hollywood and Never Lost a Dime* made clear, the connection between sex and horror was of particular interest to Corman: 'The deeper you go into the dark hallways...the deeper you are delving into, say, an adolescent boy's first sexual stirrings. These are contradictory urges—an irresistible attraction and desire for sex and the fear of the unknown and illicit. The very ambivalence builds tension.'

As a filmmaker, Corman was often battling the equally contradictory urges of the artistic director and the spendthrift producer. Sometimes, this would lead to an opportunism which was beneficial, as when a forest fire in the Hollywood Hills provided the charred landscape that was used for *House of Usher*'s opening sequence. More often than not, however, the penny-pinching was detrimental: 'Roger is in fact a very talented guy,' said Hill. 'He used to be a very fine director. His biggest enemy was himself as a producer. He was so cheap that he wouldn't do things right.' When Roger Corman stopped directing and became a full-time producer, many of those who worked for him found themselves in agreement with Hill.

'I had read a book by an advertising man who said that the two most significant words in the ad business are new and free.. I was going to go with New World Films, but I had the feeling that film might someday be a transitory phenomenon, replaced by lasers or tape or something else. So I went with New World Pictures, figuring whatever they use to make movies, the result will always be pictures.'

—Roger Corman, 1990

Corman was due to fly to Ireland in August 1970 to begin shooting *Von Richthofen and Brown* for his brother Gene, who in turn had negotiated a distribution deal with United Artists. He was going back to the beginnings of aerial combat, which was appropriate, considering that he was also in the beginnings of an entirely new business venture. Earlier in the year, he had contacted his old friend Lawrence Woolner, a southern theatre owner and distributor for whom he had directed *Swamp Women* and *Teenage Doll* some 15 years earlier. Woolner, along with his brother Bernard, were specialists in low-grade fare like *Attack of the 50 Foot Woman* (1958) and *The Human Duplicators* (1965), but they were well connected, and with Gene Corman not wanting to pick up where Filmgroup left off, Roger decided the brothers Woolner were his best bet to help start a film production/distribution company.

'New World Pictures is an attempt to build a distribution company from scratch, built on my own savings,' Corman told the *Los Angeles Times*. 'I thought that since I backed all those people from money saved from pictures I directed myself, why not put it on an organised basis and form my own company—particularly at a time when the motion picture business is in flux. Production at the major studios is down and the major independent distributor, American International, is moving into a more expensive type of picture, so I felt the opportunity was right for a new production and distribution company.'

'There were business reasons to go into distribution,' Corman elaborated in his autobiography. 'One was that the film rentals go to the distributor first to cover his fee and expenses.. there was money to be made there. Another major justification was that you can determine with much greater control when and in what theatres you book your films. You decide how much money to spend on advertising your films. You control the negotiations for terms with the theatre circuits.'

'I mean, dig it. If you're like out trippin' on your own, man, you go over the high side; it's righteous, ain't it? But, I mean, when somebody helps you, man, it's got no class!'

—Deputy gang leader Tim (William Smith) in *Angels Die Hard*

Corman decided that the firm's first movie should be in a proven genre—one he himself had helped to establish, in fact. A rip-roaring biker movie would do the trick—this was, after all, only a year after *Easy Rider*. Fortuitously, a former member of his repertory company, Charles 'Beach' Dickerson, was looking to produce a biker movie but had raised only $65,000. Corman agreed to provide the remaining $60,000 on the condition that Dickerson make and deliver the picture in time for New World's inauguration that May. Dickerson took the bait and contacted his old friend Richard Compton to write and direct the none-too-subtly titled *Angels Die Hard.*

> *A group of Hell's Angels ride into the peaceful Sierra Nevada town of Whiskey Flat and raise hell—including the rape of a girl on a table piled with spaghetti. One of their number is killed and they kidnap the local undertaker to prepare a funeral, at which they turn their friend's grave into a communal urinal. The bikers temporarily redeem themselves when they rescue a child trapped in a mine cave-in, but when the sheriff's daughter takes up with the Angels' leader, the locals form an angry, torch-bearing mob and head to the hellions' camp-site to settle the score..*

Just two weeks before *Angels'* June 1970 release, Corman and Larry Woolner opened the offices of New World Pictures at 8831 Sunset Boulevard in Hollywood. New World occupied the penthouse suite of a four-story building situated across the street from a burlesque establishment and down the block from the famous Whisky a Go-Go. Given New World's product in its early years, they could not have picked a more apt location.

Despite *Angels Die Hard* being Compton's first time at bat (not counting a porn film that he and Dickerson had produced), he acquitted himself well—the film delivers the goods and features some impressive camerawork and a no-name rock soundtrack, though it is seriously marred by a lame rednecks-versus-bikers shootout and a real 'Huh?' ending. The picture benefits from a breakout performance by William Smith, who would go on to become B-cinema's answer to Charles Bronson, and features an early turn by *Grizzly Adams*'s Dan Haggerty. New World's maiden effort was a success, bringing some $700,000 in rentals (that part of the gross box office take which is paid to distributors by exhibitors) in to the rookie company, and giving Corman a huge return on his investment.

> *'It isn't synthetic to get beyond where you end and into where it all begins.'*
> —Amoral biker Les (Richard Rust) in *The Student Nurses*

New World's follow-on project came from a brainstorm of Larry Woolner, who suggested to Corman that they should make a sexy film about young nurses. Corman had an unlikely person in mind to direct it.

A graduate of the University of Southern California (USC) Film School, 25-year-old Stephanie Rothman had been the first female to win a Director's Guild of America Fellowship for her student film in 1964. She subsequently had been apprenticed to Corman, for whom she served as associate producer on *Voyage to the Prehistoric Planet, Beach Ball* (both 1965) and *Queen of Blood* (1966). Along the way, she was given her directorial stripes when Corman put her on one of his amalgamated litmus tests: handed a thriller called *Portrait in Terror* that had been filmed in Dubrovnik, Yugoslavia, along with beatnik footage shot by Jack Hill, Rothman was told to shoot new scenes, mix it all together, and come up with a horror film that could be called *Blood Bath.* She decided to turn it into an atmospheric vampire film and shot quite a bit at Venice Beach, California, to match the coastal scenes in *Portrait.* She also added an impressive sequence with Sandra Knight (Mrs Jack Nicholson at the time) dancing on the beach, filmed with distorting lenses to give it a kaleidoscopic look.

The lady clearly showed talent, but the only directorial assignment that had come her way was a Tommy Kirk-Deborah Walley AIP beach flick called *It's a Bikini World* (1967), produced and co-written by her husband, Charles S Swartz. Despite Rothman's efforts to add some feminism into the mix, the picture was a failure that pushed her out of filmmaking for three years, though she and Swartz had served as Corman's production executives on *Gas-s-s-s*.

Keeping up with Corman paid off: Rothman and Swartz were contacted by New World's president before he left for Ireland and hired to make what already had been titled *The Student Nurses*— Swartz would co-produce, Rothman would co-produce/direct, and they would collaborate on the story. 'We were free to develop the story of the nurses as we wished,' Rothman told interviewer Henry Jenkins, 'as long as there was enough nudity and violence distributed throughout.' Once things were in place, it was up to Don Spencer to mould the premise into script form.

Four student nurses meet four diverse guys who change their lives: Sharon becomes attached to a poet who is terminally-ill, Priscilla hooks up with a free-spirited hippie biker who makes her pregnant and then dumps her, Phred becomes another conquest of the hospital's sexy

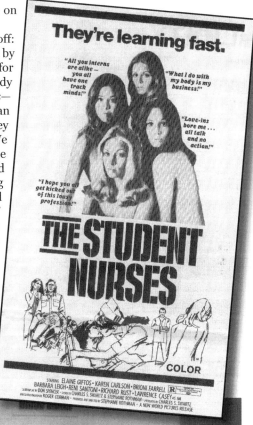

The Student Nurses/US theatrical poster

gynaecology intern, and Lynn sets up a free clinic with an armed Latino radical—under whose tutelage she becomes an urban guerrilla.

To say that *The Student Nurses* is an atypical exploitation film would be a major understatement. The sub-plot of Lynn (Brioni Farrell) becoming a militant radical and getting involved in a shootout with police is hardly the norm, but it is the film's depiction of Priscilla (played by newcomer Barbara Leigh, who would later become tabloid fodder because of her involvement with Elvis Presley and Steve McQueen) and her predicament which showcases Rothman's real talents. After Priscilla meets her wandering biker-man at a 'love-in', the two drop acid and, in a scene reminiscent of Hiroshi Teshigahara's *Woman in the Dunes* (1964) or Michelangelo Antonioni's *Zabriskie Point* (1970), they have sex on a beach in slow motion until Priscilla's trip turns sour and she imagines that a crowd is watching her. Subsequently pregnant and abandoned, she tries to convince an all-male medical board of her need for a so-called 'therapeutic abortion' but she is turned down (this was three years before Roe vs Wade made abortion-on-demand legal in America). Her girlfriend Phred (Karen Carlson) is dating the resident gynaecologist who, despite Phred imploring him not to, agrees to perform a home abortion. Rothman then cross-cuts between Priscilla's painful procedure (during which she suffers a nightmare about having the abortion on a beach while a whole crowd watch and condemn her) and Phred's vindictive, unsatisfactory sex with another doctor. Rothman makes it clear that promiscuity cn have unintended consequences—a message which one would hardly expect to find in a conventional drive-in sex picture.

'Once I paid my debt to the requirements of the genre,' Rothman told Jenkins, '[it] allowed me to address what interested me.. political and social conflicts and the changes they produce. It allowed me to have a dramatised discussion about issues that were then being ignored in big-budget major studio films.'

Variety was quick to take note of *The Student Nurses* as something altogether unexpected: 'Pic is an exploitation item to be sure, but beyond those angles, general audiences will find a surprising depth.' The *Los Angeles Times* damned with faint praise, saying the film was 'never quite as bad as it threatens to be. A taste prevails, holds it in check, and manages to make individual characters and relationships intermittently believable.'

Produced for $120,000, *The Student Nurses* was released in August 1970 and garnered over $1 million in rentals—another hefty return for a small investment. New World was two for two, and Woolner quickly signed Rothman and Swartz to write a follow-up, *The Student Teachers*.

'We're gonna get stoned and let the world blow over.'
—Apathetic hippie in *Gas-s-s-s*

The previous year had seen Commonwealth United score a considerable drive-in hit with the X-rated women's prison picture *99 Women*, directed by Jess Franco and featuring Maria Schell, Herbert Lom and Mercedes McCambridge. While New World could not afford names of that calibre, it certainly could borrow *99 Women*'s exotic prison locale (exteriors were shot in Brazil) and scantily-clad inmates. To that end, Woolner commissioned AIP alumnus James Gordon White (*The Glory Stompers*, *The Mini-Skirt Mob*) to write a screenplay that Roger Corman would direct in Puerto Rico in early 1971, entitled *The Big Doll House*.

Woolner liked the title but hated the prose, so *Student Nurses* scripter Don Spencer was assigned to pen a new draft. While the *Doll House* was being rebuilt,

Corman's AIP swan song was finally released that October (nearly a year after it was filmed), after receiving its world premiere two months before at the Edinburgh Film Festival, which happened also to be hosting a tribute to the director.

After a mysterious gas escapes from an Army testing ground in Alaska, everyone over 25 ages rapidly and dies, leaving the youth of the world in charge. Anarchy reigns, and lovers Coel and Cilla make their way out of the chaos of Dallas on their way to New Mexico in search of the so-called 'Oracle'. Along the way they pick up two other odd couples, and run foul of crazed cowboy used car salesmen, a psychotic football team, and a chapter of the Hell's Angels protecting their sacred golf course. The Oracle turns out to be a sham, but the couples find refuge on an Indian reservation just the same.

Painfully unfunny and instantly dated, *Gas-s-s-s* plays like a lame *Laugh-In* skit that goes on interminably. Its satirical shots at the establishment ring hollow (especially coming from a forty-something director) but, conversely, its portrayal of the counterculture is hardly sympathetic either (most of the youngsters are just strung-out, hedonistic losers). As a result, the film has no one to identify with. To make matters worse, some moments of *Gas-s-s-s* are downright tasteless (shots ring out when Coel and Cilla ride past the Texas School Book Depository; Cilla willingly and cheerfully submits to three rapists; God speaks with a mocking Yiddish accent) and what flashes of inspiration exist (such as having Edgar Allan Poe, his raven, and his 'lost love' Lenore serve as a kind of Greek chorus on a chopper) are few and far between. When AIP cut the final panoramic scene and abbreviated the divine dialogue, they were not subverting art; they were putting the film (and the audience) out of its misery.

Gas-s-s-s did not find good press in *Variety* ('Roger Corman, who has about as good a batting average in the low to medium-budget film field as any independent filmmaker, has struck out with this one') but it did receive a rave in *Rolling Stone*: 'Marvellously funny, relentlessly intelligent, truly hip. It is a dynamite flick.' Such was AIP's half-hearted attitude that the film was not released in New York until March 1971, and only then as the closing feature in The First Roger Corman Film Festival being held at the Kips Bay Theatre. It found a fan in Judith Crist of *New York* magazine ('There's a cool overlay and a serious undertone to the fun and games. It's worth seeing.') but Vincent Canby of the *New York Times* seemed to sum up the film's central flaw: 'To the extent that Roger Corman's *Gas-s-s-s* is an end-of-the-world movie, you might—if you were taking leave of your right senses—describe it as both his *Weekend* and his *Shame*, although it's far less funny than Godard and a good deal more pretentious than Bergman.'

'A girl on a bike with a gun—it's terribly phallic.'
—Op the Indian Witch (Angel Colbert) in *Bury Me An Angel*

Angels Die Hard had been so successful in relation to its cost that Beach Dickerson was quickly contracted to make a follow-up. He in turn went to the script supervisor on *Angels* to write and direct the new film and, by so doing, would continue the New World tradition of breaking new ground.

At age 27, Barbara Peeters already had extensive experience in the exploitation film world, having been costume designer on *The Fabulous Bastard from Chicago* (1969), the writer/co-star of *Caged Desires* (1970) and the co-writer/co-director of the lesbian-themed *Just the Two of Us* (aka *The Dark Side of Tomorrow*, 1970). With *Bury Me An Angel*, however, she would be the first and only woman to write and direct a biker film.

Bury Me an Angel

Haunted by the shotgun murder of her brother, Dag sets out with her biker friends Jonsie and Bernie to find the man responsible. After a journey filled with rednecks, bar-room brawls and an Indian witch who serves marijuana stew, they track the killer to a small town in the Sierra Nevadas. He tries to explain that the killing was a mistake—Dag's brother had stolen the man's bike and he wanted it back—but Dag will have none of it. Before he dies, however, the man forces Dag to confront the truth behind her obsession: an incestuous relationship.

Like Stephanie Rothman before her, Peeters took what could have been just a gimmick (as it was in H G Lewis's *She-Devils on Wheels*, 1967) and turned it into a powerful story of anger, guilt and revenge. Dixie Peabody, who had an uncredited bit part in *Angels Die Hard*, is terrific as Dag—a statuesque beauty who rides her own bike on her own quest that turns out to be more destructive to her than to her quarry. The collaboration of Peeters and Peabody to develop Dag's secret pain makes scenes which would normally be played for sheer titillation—a nude frolic in the river with her friends; lovemaking with teacher Dan Haggerty—into deeper revelations about Dag's past (the first reminds her of being in the bathtub with her brother; the second is interrupted when her brother's face replaces Haggerty's). There is also a shocking nightmare scene, replayed multiple times, in which Dag shoots her brother's killer repeatedly but he just laughs it off. Peeters subsequently explained her reasoning for this scene to the *Los Angeles Times*: 'I did that because it's a story about a girl who slowly goes insane looking for her brother's killer. How could I make the audience understand what she is going through unless they are shocked the same way she was?'

At the same time *Gas-s-s-s* was premiering in New York, *Bury Me An Angel* went into general release with little fanfare and no reviews. It managed to catch on, however, and played the drive-in circuit for the next seven years. Sadly, Peabody would only act in one more film—a small part in New World's *Night Call Nurses*

(1972)—before disappearing from the scene. For Peeters, though, her tenure at New World had only just begun.

Another filmmaker who was now co-opted to join the Corman bandwagon was John Ashley, an ex-AIP juvenile star who had been headlining a series of Filipino *Blood Island* horror films for Hemisphere Pictures. When Ken Lynn, head of Hemisphere, fell ill, Ashley seized the opportunity to go into business for himself, inviting *Blood Island* producer/director Eddie Romero and two others to join him as Four Associates Ltd. Their first production went before the cameras in Manila in September 1970—*Beast of the Yellow Night*. During filming, Ashley took a phone call from Corman, as he told author Tom Weaver: 'He called me and told me about this picture that they were going to do in Puerto Rico. I told him, "You ought to come down and take a look at the Philippines. I mean, it's all right here"—'cause the picture was set in a jungle, and in a women's prison. So he flew to the Philippines, took one look and asked me, "Would you stay around and exec-produce the show?" So two of my partners and I put up the above-the-line, Roger put up all the rest of it, and I stayed and supervised [*Big Doll House*].'

During his visit, Corman secured the American distribution rights to *Beast of the Yellow Night*, as well as putting in motion the gears to set *Big Doll House* before the cameras that November, but he would not sit in the director's chair as previously announced. The job was offered to Jack Hill, whose history with Corman included the aforementioned *The Terror* and *Blood Bath*. Hill had also done second-unit work on *The Wasp Woman* and *Dementia 13*, but he had had his biggest cult success with the offbeat horror film *Spider Baby* in 1968, before having the dubious honour of directing Boris Karloff in scenes shot for a quartet of unintelligible Mexican horror films immediately prior to the actor's death from emphysema in February 1969, at the age of 81.

In the Philippines, Collier is sentenced to 99 years hard labour for the murder of her rich, gay, playboy husband. She is put in a cell with five other women: Alcott, a pyromaniac, Bodine, a political prisoner whose boyfriend is a revolutionary, Ferina, who just wants to play with her cat, Grear, a black lesbian prostitute, and Harrad, a heroin junkie who killed her baby. When not engaged in field labour, muddy catfights or cockroach races, the women must endure various methods of torture overseen by a silent, hooded inquisitor. Eager to join the revolution raging outside the prison walls, the six determine to escape, but they must first contend with the prison's butch, sadistic captain and the seemingly-compassionate female warden, who is not all she appears to be..

For Hill, the experience of shooting in the Philippines was 'a fun nightmare.' 'The [Filipino] people are wonderful, and I love them, and they try so hard to please you,' he told *Fangoria*. 'You ask, "Can you do this and that?" "Oh yes, sure, no problem"—they like to see you smile. Then, of course, they can't do any such thing at all. They had stunt men who'd get up to take a fall, and cross themselves and jump. If they want to have a man on fire, they just set a guy on fire who'll try and jump into the water as quick as he can.'

The few critics who bothered to review *The Big Doll House* were uniformly unimpressed ('a trashy picture and strictly for the undiscriminating,' said the *Los Angeles Times*), but it hardly mattered—the picture was an astounding success, earning $3 million in rentals (against a cost of $150,000) and achieving overseas release through MGM, where it grossed an additional $4 million. It was also to introduce the world to an actress who would become a '70s icon.

'*Green, scared—and pretty!*'
—Jailbird Grear (Pam Grier) to newcomer Collier (Judy Brown) in *The Big Doll House*

Pamela Suzette Grier was born in May 1949, in Winston-Salem, North Carolina. The daughter of an Air Force mechanic, she and her two sisters lived on military bases until the family moved to Denver when she was 14. With a stunning 38-22-36 figure, Grier made something of a name for herself in local beauty pageants, then left for Los Angeles in 1970, hoping to enrol in the University of California at Los Angeles (UCLA) Film School. What she ended up doing instead was working all over town as a receptionist—everywhere from a mortuary to AIP—while waiting for in-state residency status that never came through. Fortuitously, she took a job

Pam Grier

at New World that called for her to be a receptionist during the day and an intern at night, which was a glorified way of saying that she got to clean up the editing room. 'After they'd finish cutting a film,' Grier told *Horse Connection*, 'they'd leave, and I would come in and clean up. Then they'd come back in to work some more and I'd say, "You all clean up!" I had an attitude, but they just trashed the place.'

It was this attitude that caught Corman's attention, and he suggested Grier try out for *The Big Doll House*. 'Corman had me try out for the part of a white girl,' Grier told the *Los Angeles Times*. 'He said he wanted someone who was aggressive and bouncy and I thought if I could show him how aggressive and bouncy I was, nobody would care about my colour. When [Jack Hill] told another actress to shove me, I shoved her back. Roger thought it was great.'

Grier was offered $500 a week to shoot for six weeks in the Philippines and she took the plunge, though the location shoot was a real trial-by-fire, as the actress told *The Onion A.V. Club*: 'You're always in danger of something exploding, or leeches

or cobras or snakes. You can get hurt at any time.. It's not the place to be arrogant.'
Arrogant, no—gutsy, yes, as Eddie Romero told *Film Comment*, 'Pam Grier was the
gamest actress I ever worked with. She was willing to do anything—jump off a cliff,
whatever! I'd be talking to a stuntwoman and Pam would say, 'Oh, I can do that!'

For producer Corman, Grier and the Philippines were a winning combination.
Along with co-stars Judy Brown and Roberta Collins, Grier was immediately placed
in a follow-up picture, *Women in Cages*, shot virtually back-to-back with *Doll House*
and directed by Ashley/Romero associate Gerardo de Leon.

On Saturday, December 26, 1970, Roger Corman married Julie Halloran, who
had served as his assistant on *Von Richthofen*. Just four months after this coupling,
New World's first double-feature was released, headlined by the aforementioned
Beast of the Yellow Night.

> *Philippines, 1946. Fugitive Joseph Langdon, starving in the jungle, meets the devil,*
> *who offers him food in exchange for his soul. Langdon agrees. Twenty five years later,*
> *after passing through several hosts, Langdon's spirit revives deceased businessman*
> *Philip Rogers, much to the shock of his doctors and his wife Julia. Langdon's mission*
> *from Satan is 'to awaken the latent evil in the people I come in contact with,' but when*
> *his passions are aroused, Langdon becomes a demon that roams the streets, killing*
> *randomly. Because of his satanic curse, Langdon cannot die, much to the chagrin of the*
> *local police and army, not to mention the confusion of Rogers's long-suffering wife.*

If one were to imagine a cross between *The Devil and Daniel Webster* and
The Wolfman (both 1941), shot on a shoestring budget of $50,000 and with lots of
bad makeup and fake gore, then one has the essence of *Yellow Night*. It would be
just another trashy John Ashley Filipino horror film were it not for the presence of
character actor Vic Diaz, soon to become a familiar face in New World's upcoming
Filipino production programme, who plays the part of the devil with fiendish delight,

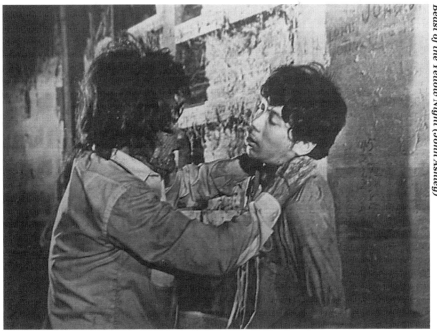

Beast of the Yellow Night (John Ashley)

23

given to dishing out such kernels of wisdom as, 'There's been a great deal said about the scarcity of truly good men. Why, truly evil men are just as hard to find,' while also assuring Langdon, 'Even I don't enjoy everything I have to do..'

US theatrical poster for Beast of the Yellow Night/Creature with the Blue Hand

Despite Diaz's amusing turn as Mr Scratch, Woolner had no faith in *Yellow Night*'s ability to go it alone, so he had contacted Sam Sherman at Independent International Pictures to secure a co-feature for it. As luck would have it, Sherman had just the ticket.

> *'This is ridiculous! First he's crazy, then he's not crazy! Can't you people decide once and for all?'*
> —An incredulous Sir John (Siegfried Schürenberg) in *Creature with the Blue Hand*

Beginning in 1959, West Germany's Rialto Films had produced a series of murder mysteries known as *krimis,* due to the fact that they were based on *taschenkrimis,* or pocket-sized crime novels. The author of all the books on which the films were based was Englishman Edgar Wallace, an incredibly prolific writer who penned some 170 novels, 17 plays and literally hundreds of short stories between 1905 and 1932, the year of his death. He had served on the board of directors of British Lion film studios and was in Hollywood at work on scripts for RKO when he died of pneumonia. His third and final screen treatment, *The Beast*, formed the story basis for what became *King Kong* in 1933.

Rialto produced some 32 *krimis* between 1959 and 1971, many of which were directed by Alfred Vohrer and featured Klaus Kinski and Harald Leipnitz. Such was the case with the film Sherman sold to Woolner: *Creature with the Blue Hand.*

> *Dave Emerson is found guilty of murdering his family's gardener and sent to an insane asylum, still protesting his innocence. With the help of an unseen benefactor, Emerson escapes and makes his way back to Greystone Hall. Meanwhile, a hooded assailant kills a nurse and prison guard with an armoured, spiked glove—the legendary 'Blue Hand'. Emerson tries to pass himself off as his twin brother Richard, but he is found out by Inspector Craig of Scotland Yard. His sister Myrna is attacked by the Blue Hand before being kidnapped by Dr Mangrove, head of the asylum, who imprisons her in the boiler room; he wants her to relinquish her claim to her late father's estate and has been using the Hand to frame Emerson for more murders. Inspector Craig and his boss Sir John raid the asylum and discover the identity of the Blue Hand, as well as the whereabouts of Richard Emerson, who has been mysteriously absent from the bloody proceedings.*

Ostensibly based on Wallace's 1923 novel *Blue Hand*, the film and its source are almost totally different. In the extremely convoluted novel, the title character is actually a woman, Lady Mary Danton. She is the benevolent protector of her long-lost daughter Eunice, who is about to inherit millions and become the target of a kidnapping by the nefarious duo of Jane Groat and her doctor son Digby.

Released in West Germany in April 1967, *Creature with the Blue Hand* is full of twists and turns, shady characters, fog-enshrouded countryside, secret passageways, humour (intentional or otherwise), a groovy jazz score by Martin Böttcher—and the inimitable Klaus Kinski in *two* roles. Though released as the bottom-half of New World's *Yellow Night* bill, it is definitely the superior picture: one of the few *krimis* to actually receive decent distribution in America.

Beast of the Yellow Night and *The Big Doll House* had proven to Corman that the Philippines was a good place to make movies. It was estimated that one could save as much as 45% in production costs by shooting in Manila over the States; plus, there were no unions to contend with or irritating labour regulations. There was plenty of local talent to be had, and the country itself offered a wealth of location opportunities ('We can fake many places here: Florida, Vietnam, South America.. we have jungle, desert, beaches.. it's all here,' Filipino producer/director Cirio Santiago commented to interviewer Erika Franklin.) For their next co-production, Corman, Woolner and Ashley decided on an unofficial remake of H G Wells's *The Island of Dr. Moreau*, to be called *Island of the Twilight People*. New World story editor Frances Doel produced a first draft script (later rewritten by Eddie Romero and Jerome Small), Pam Grier was offered one of the leading roles (that of 'Ayesa, The Panther Woman') and production was scheduled for the fall of 1971, which would coincide nicely with *Women of the Rice Paddies*, the planned sequel to *The Big Doll House*. New World's Filipino invasion was underway.

Von Richtofen and Brown (Don Stroud)

'I'll save my wine for the next gentleman your German knight blasts out of the sky.'

—Roy Brown (Don Stroud), refusing to toast the enemy in *Von Richthofen and Brown*

May 1971 brought the belated release of what would be Roger Corman's final directorial effort for nearly twenty years. The critics could smell the blood of *Von Richthofen* and, like Roy Brown before them, they went in for the kill: 'Extremely dull, at times ludicrous' (*Variety*); 'In short, a bore, and Roger Corman might be better off back in exploitation at AIP' (*Los Angeles Times*); 'The film is as hollow as its soundtrack' (*The Washington Post*). Only Roger Greenspun of the *New York Times* seemed clued as to what Corman, on the second biggest budget of his career, was attempting: 'Much of the film's material must have originated in the minds of Corman or his screen writers, but its major events appear to be fact—including the final, near magical landing of the red Fokker triplane almost intact, carrying the body of the dead baron. By this last most beautiful and mysterious transformation— in a film that rather specialises in mysterious, beautiful transformations—von Richthofen is made still in time, having become his own memorial.'

In the latter days of World War I, former cavalry officer Baron Manfred von Richthofen is transferred to the 10th German Fighter Squadron and quickly becomes an ace pilot, shooting down countless British and French fighters. At the same time, Canadian wheat farmer Roy Brown arrives to fly with the 24th British Fighter Squadron, where he too becomes an ace. While von Richthofen is a gentleman warrior, Brown is a pragmatic soldier, ready to do whatever it takes to win. The squadron raises the stakes by bombing the German airfield, forcing von Richthofen to follow suit. Eventually, the two men meet in the skies over France.. where only one can survive the encounter.

World War I saw the beginnings of trench, mechanised, and chemical warfare in addition to aerial combat, but it was in the air that the last vestiges of supposedly 'civilised' battle disported themselves, as personified by Richthofen and his British opponents. Ironically, Brown finds his modernising equal not in the Red Baron whom he ultimately shoots down but in von Richthofen's replacement as squadron commander—a young upstart named Herman Goerring, who shares Brown's scorn of the pretences of civility ('I make war to win,' Goerring tells von Richthofen after being upbraided for strafing nurses). While the film is an interesting character study of two men from different worlds, and features many impressively-photographed dogfights (utilising biplanes from *The Blue Max* and *Darling Lili*), it is his exploration of how WWI laid the groundwork for the rise of Nazism that makes Corman's film one of his best, albeit most unlikely, efforts.

'I've seen things here I've never seen before.'
—Lee Ritter (Michael Blodgett) in *The Velvet Vampire*

Vampires had always proven themselves to be box office, but the new decade had given rise to some daring experimentation, adding both lesbianism (*The Vampire Lovers*, 1970) and modern settings (*Count Yorga—Vampire* and its sequel, 1969 and 1970 respectively) to the mix. In Belgium, filmmaker Harry Kumel used both new wrinkles in his own film *Daughters of Darkness*, which saw French vampiress

Delphine Seyrig seduce modern couple John Karlen and Daniele Ouimet at an abandoned seaside resort. The film created quite a splash, both at the box office and with critics during its New York premiere in May 1971.

None of this had gone unnoticed by Larry Woolner, who laid aside Stephanie Rothman and Charles Swartz's script for *The Student Teachers* in favour of something else they had written: a modern vampire story entitled *Through the Looking Glass*. Production began in February, with the film being released that June under the new and more allusive title of *The Velvet Vampire*.

> *The Ritters meet the mysterious Diane LeFanu at an art gallery. Accepting an invite to spend the weekend at her ranch, the young couple find themselves individually seduced by their ethereal hostess, who happens to be a century-old vampire..*

As they had with *The Student Nurses*, Rothman and Swartz once again used the low-budget exploitation film to subvert conventions, both in terms of gender (*The Velvet Vampire* opens on a supposed 'damsel-in-distress', who calmly kills her attacker, washes her hands in a reflecting pool, and checks her makeup in a compact mirror) and genre (Diane is no ordinary vampire—she loves to tool around in her dune buggy in broad daylight). It is also a bravura exercise in technique, especially during three dream sequences in the desert, where Diane, in flowing red robe, first watches through then emerges from a mirror to interrupt the Ritters, who are making love on a huge brass bed. First, she steals Lee away, then she seduces and slices Susan while Lee is unable to stop her.

Nor is Rothman afraid to pay homage to the film's antecedents. Under her direction, the Mojave becomes a desert of abandoned mines, ghost towns and old graves, where the locals act just like frightened European villagers when asked the whereabouts of the LeFanu (as in J Sheridan LeFanu, Irish author of classic lesbian vampire story 'Carmilla') ranch.

Amazingly, critics at the time recognized none of this, regarding *Velvet Vampire* as just another schlock horror film: 'Will need a hard sell for fast sexploitation duals, where b.o. outlook is bleak' (*Variety*); 'Lots of arty effects, little credibility or terror—and no small amount of unintended humour' (*Los Angeles Times*); 'It is to be recommended only if you can see it at the New Amsterdam on 42nd Street, where audiences loudly, freely and obscenely associate with the action on the screen' (*New York Times*). It was left to New York's alternative paper, *The Village Voice*, to buck the trend and give credit where it was due: '*The Velvet Vampire* is a sexy little horror movie worth noting mostly because it was directed and co-scripted by a woman.. In spite of frequent articles demanding more women directors, this feminine effort has attracted no attention. A shame, because Rothman proves herself at least a craftsman—craftswoman, rather—while operating on a meagre budget, and even manages a few niceties with old conventions.'

Roger Corman himself had doubts about *Velvet Vampire* and determined that it, like *Beast of the Yellow Night* before it, needed a supporting feature to lean on. '[*Velvet Vampire*] did not turn out as well as I had expected,' he recalled to di Franco, 'and I felt that it could not stand alone as a top feature.. I called a friend of mine in Rome and asked him to find an Italian horror film that had been dubbed into English and that I could buy for no more than $25,000. He found one, and I bought it over the phone without ever seeing it.'

The film Corman bought was *Ivanna*, a Spanish-Italian co-production which had been released in Italy the previous fall. The price may have been right, but the title was hardly a come-hither, so he had Frances Doel come up with something else: *Scream of the Demon Lover*.

Biochemist Ivanna Rakowsky arrives at Castle Dalmar to assist in experiments seeking the elixir of life. Local villagers are convinced that the castle's handsome new Baron— Janos Dalmar—is responsible for the horrific deaths of six young girls. He shows Ivanna the embalmed, badly-burned body of his brother Igor and asks her help in reanimating him. Ivanna is plagued by nightmares in which she is stretched naked on a rack while burned hands caress her—hands that she believes belong to Janos, whom she offers to cure of his seemingly-murderous dual personality. The two fall in love and are married, but Ivanna discovers to her horror that the murderer is Igor, who is not really dead and who now wants Ivanna for himself..

For the most part, *Scream of the Demon Lover* plays like a Paul Naschy werewolf film without the transformation scenes. As with Naschy's Spanish Gothics, the film is liberally doused with nudity and sadism (usually combined), though Igor Dalmar makes an interesting precursor to Freddy Krueger, badly burned and murdering with a taloned glove. Carlos Quiney (billed as 'Jeffrey Chase') cuts an imposing, handsome figure as the tormented Janos Dalmar, while Erna Schurer (billed as 'Jennifer Hartley') is suitably pretty and feisty as Ivanna, a surprisingly liberated role which actually prefigures that in another New World Italian import—*Lady Frankenstein*.

In the summer of 1971, New World Pictures celebrated its first anniversary by reporting pre-tax profits of $3.2 million for the year, as well as announcing a new slate of films, to include *The Bombardier* (based on a novel by John Corrington, co-writer of *Von Richthofen*), *Captive Nurses, Co-ed Dorm, The Final Comedown*, and the aforementioned *Women of the Rice Paddies* and *Island of the Twilight People*. It also planned another 'women in prison' picture called *Sweet Sugar*, to shoot in Costa Rica and star *The Velvet Vampire*'s Celeste Yarnall, but she ended up in the Michael Winner-directed Charles Bronson-starrer *The Mechanic* (1972) instead.

New World also had three pictures in release during the summer, including its third and final biker film, *Angels Hard As They Come*, which served as the debut feature of a man who would become one of Hollywood's top directors.

'You call me kid again, I'm gonna kick your balls up around your ears!'
—Tough-guy biker Long John (Scott Glenn) in *Angels Hard As They Come*

Jonathan Demme was working for a commercials production house in London when he got the call to become unit publicist for *Von Richthofen*. His enthusiasm impressed Corman, who was in need of filmmakers for his new company. The director asked Demme to write a biker script; collaborating with his friend Joe Viola, Demme turned in a draft which had pretensions of being a motorcycle version of Akira Kurosawa's celebrated 1950 mystery, *Rashomon*. Corman gave it the once-over and quickly brought Demme back down to earth: 'Love the rape scene, love the murder, now let's throw the rest of this stuff out.'

> *Long John, Juicer and Monk, three members of the Hell's Angels, join a rival cycle group, the Demons, at a hippie commune in an abandoned ghost town. Beer, women, weed and racing are the order of the day until Long John breaks up an attempted gang-rape by the Dragons, resulting in a fight that inadvertently kills the rape victim. The Dragons put the three Angels on trial for murder and sentence them to be dragged through the streets and then kicked around in 'chopper polo'. Monk manages to escape and makes his way to the Angels' hideout, where he summons the cavalry to the rescue.*

After rewriting the script, it was agreed that Demme would produce and Viola would direct. In the lead role of Long John was cast future Hollywood heavyweight Scott Glenn (*The Hunt for Red October,* Demme's own Oscar-winning *The Silence of the Lambs*), while the supporting role of the commune leader went to an equally unknown Gary Busey, who was also to achieve fame some years later in *The Buddy Holly Story.*

Variety was unimpressed: 'Jonathan Demme and director Joe Viola have turned out a 90-minute offering that is without originality in any of its departments'. But the *Los Angeles Times* caught the hint that real talent was involved: 'Above all, it shows off a youthful cast to advantage and marks the filmmaking team of Jonathan Demme and Joe Viola as one to watch for in the future.' Corman agreed with the *Los Angeles Times*'s assessment and set the *Angels* duo to work on a new Filipino picture that would combine *The Student Nurses* with *The Big Doll House* to create what he originally entitled *Captive Nurses* before changing it to the more cerebral *The Prescription Revolution.*

> *'I'm black, but I'm also a woman—a woman of the whole world.'*
> —Nurse Lola (Joyce Williams) telling her boyfriend how it is in *Private Duty Nurses*

Next in line for a shot at the Corman factory was 28-year-old George Armitage, an alumnus of UCLA's motion picture program and co-star/associate producer/ writer of *Gas-s-s-s* (he also had a bit part as a German flyer in *Von Richthofen*). In true do-it-yourself fashion, Armitage would write, produce and direct *Private Duty Nurses*, a title that arrived in a rather roundabout way, as Corman commented to di Franco: '*The Student Nurses* was a great success, and it really surprised us all how well it did. We knew we were going to do a sequel, and we were casting about for a title when we got a letter from a group called the Private Duty Nurses Association saying that *The Student Nurses* was not a truthful statement of how nurses function and that they wished to protest. My sales manager got the letter and brought it to me and said, 'What are we going to do about this one?' I said, 'They have given us the title for the sequel—*Private Duty Nurses*!'

> *Three student nurses—one black, the other two white—are room-mates in Manhattan Beach, California: Lola is involved with a black doctor who runs an inner city clinic and joins him on a sit-in at her hospital to protest about its failure to hire black doctors, Spring cares for a Vietnam veteran with a plastic plate in his head who happens to enjoy the not-so-safe sport of motocross racing, and Lynn crusades against ocean pollution with a (married) intern who is ultimately gunned down by drug smugglers.*

Unlike Rothman's deft handling of the women's issues in *The Student Nurses*, Armitage loads his sequel down with everything but the kitchen sink. As the *Los Angeles Times* noted: 'Armitage proves he can dish out the soap suds with the best, leaving nothing from ecology to open-heart surgery unexploited.' He had been associate producer on the TV series *Peyton Place* and it shows—*Private Duty*

Nurses is little more than a top-heavy potboiler with none of the stylish interludes that Rothman had seen fit to include in her turn at bat.

> *'What kind of hell did you crawl out of?'*
> *'It was called Harlem, baby!'*
> —Jeffers (Jennifer Gan) to Alabama (Pam Grier) in *Women in Cages*

New World's final release of 1971 was the aforementioned *Women in Cages*. While it shared much of *The Big Doll House*'s cast and crew, Gerardo de Leon was no Jack Hill. Hill had given *The Big Doll House* several stylish touches (including a surrealistic torture room) as well as an edge; *Women in Cages*, however, was in the Jess Franco 'Eurotrash' mould—downbeat, dirty and rotten.

> *Southern belle Carol Jeffers is slipped heroin by her Filipino syndicate boyfriend and sentenced to ten years hard labour at the dreaded 'Carcel del Infierno'. The prison is presided over by black lesbian 'matron' Alabama, who operates her own private torture chamber, complete with guillotine. The syndicate wants Carol dead, so they try to have her junkie cellmate Stoke kill her. Meanwhile, the law wants Carol alive, so they arrange for her other cellmate Sandy to keep her safe. The trio escape, along with Alabama as their prisoner, and make their way to the sea, but they are taken aboard the syndicate freighter Zulu Queen, which also acts as a floating brothel..*

Critics were quick to notice the shoddiness: '*The Big Doll House* was mercifully silly from time to time, but there seemed no point in watching the unrelieved degradation depicted in *Women in Cages* beyond the first 30 minutes' (*Los Angeles Times*); 'The tortures and nudity roll on at a fast clip with occasional pauses that are unintentionally funny' (*Chicago Tribune*). As a result, Jack Hill was sent back to the Philippines to rebuild the Doll House, though this time it would be a Bird Cage.

In November 1971, it was announced that Roger Corman would be returning to the director's chair again for AIP on a Great Depression piece entitled *Boxcar Bertha*, to star Barbara Hershey and her common law husband David Carradine. As he contemplated returning the Nicholson-Arkoff fold, Corman had a bombshell dropped on him: Woolner had decided to leave, and he was taking two of New World's best talents—Rothman and Swartz—with him. 'I stopped working for Roger Corman because he did not pay me a living wage,' Rothman commented to Jenkins. 'In his opinion he didn't need to pay one to his directors, since he was giving them the chance to have their work seen widely, which might lead to more and better paid work.. My husband and I were offered a minority share in [Woolner's new company] and a living wage. In return, we were expected to make exploitation films that we co-wrote, he produced and I directed.'

Woolner moved right across the street and set up shop as Dimension Pictures. As part of his separation from New World, he had been given distribution rights to two films—*Island of the Twilight People* (released simply as *Twilight People*) and a Mexican softcore pickup, *The Sin of Adam and Eve*—and the whole of one property (*Sweet Sugar*), which became Dimension's first-ever production in January 1972 under the supervision of Swartz, now impressively-titled Executive Vice President of Acquisition and Production.

Rothman (now officially Dimension's Head of Project Development) and Swartz would write, produce and direct three films for Woolner—*Group Marriage* (1973), *Terminal Island* (1973) and *Working Girls* (1974). Swartz would also produce the cut-rate John Ashley Filipino fantasy *Beyond Atlantis* (1973) for Dimension, based on Rothman's story. In 1975, the couple's association with Woolner came to an end, as did their respective careers. Rothman wrote only one more film (*Starhops*) in 1977, on which she took the pseudonym 'Dallas Meredith' after she was replaced as director by fellow Corman acolyte Barbara Peeters. Swartz retired from producing and in recent years has been heavily involved in the promotion of digital cinema, serving as CEO of the Entertainment Technology Center at USC before his death in February 2007, at the age of 67.

For its part, Dimension Pictures had a string of drive-in hits during the 1970s, including *The Doberman Gang* (1972), *The Daring Dobermans* (1973), *Gator Bait* (1974), *Boss Nigger* (1975), *Dolemite* (1975), *Ruby* (1977) and *Kingdom of the Spiders* (1977). However, when the drive-in market effectively collapsed at the end of the decade, so did Dimension; Woolner declared bankruptcy in February 1981 and died four years later, at the age of 73.

In January 1972, the *Los Angeles Times* Calendar section ran a feature article by critic Kevin Thomas entitled 'Roger Corman—Director Who Changed the Face of Hollywood'. In it, Corman outlined his plans for New World's future, including films from the likes of Monte Hellman (who had started out on Corman cheapies like 1959's *Beast from Haunted Cave* but graduated to the major studio *Two Lane Blacktop* by 1971), Andrew Meyer (New York avant garde filmmaker) and Curtis Hanson (co-writer of Corman's 1969 AIP production *The Dunwich Horror*). An adaptation of French realist writer Alain Robbe-Grillet's 1965 novel *La Maison de Rendezvous*, a horror film called *Movini's Venom*, and a thriller called *Sweet Kill* were their respective projects; only the second two were to see the light of day at this time, but Hellman would direct a film for his former mentor two years later.

Corman also announced that he was going to make *One for the Gipper*, based on the life story of 1920s college football hero George Gipp, who previously had been portrayed by future US President Ronald Reagan in the Warner Brothers film *Knute Rockne All American* (1940). The project never made it past the announcement, but all of the hubbub surrounding New World gave one Frank Moreno, newly arrived as General Sales Manager, a lot to cope with in his first weeks on the job.

'I must warn you that my ideas are quite radical.. even more so than yours, father.'

—Tania Frankenstein (Sara Bay) in *Lady Frankenstein*

New World's first release of (March) 1972 was a reunion of sorts. Mel Welles, 'star' of Corman's *Little Shop of Horrors*, had since migrated to Europe to pursue a directing career. He had had a minor success with 1967's *Island of the Doomed*, but had mostly toiled uncredited on Spanish action movies starring Ray Danton, another actor who turned to directing. Welles had been approached by expatriate American millionaire Harry Cushing III to direct a film entitled *Lady Dracula*, in which Cushing intended Italian actress Rosalba Neri, with whom he was smitten, to play the lead. Welles went to work and booked the De Paolis Studios outside Rome, but discovered to his surprise that the property was in fact owned by *peplum* actor Brad Harris, who had no wish to part with it. To make matters worse, Cushing then refused to extend the monies necessary to keep the production going.

After a brief sojourn in England, where he retooled the script as *Madame Frankenstein* with Edward Di Lorenzo, Welles went straight to the offices of New World for Roger Corman's assistance. Corman, impressed that Welles had secured the services of former Mercury Theatre troupe member Joseph Cotten (who had just co-starred in AIP's art deco horror hit *The Abominable Dr. Phibes* with Vincent

Price) to play Baron Frankenstein, agreed to pick up where Cushing had left off. His generosity only went so far, however, as co-producer Dick Randall observed in *Variety*, '[Cotten's] price was a bit prohibitive for a film that cost under $200,000 to make, so we rewrote his part, cutting it to two weeks. In the final version, the monster turns on his creator and crushes him to death in the fifth reel. Either that or get a less expensive star.'

> *Tania Frankenstein returns home from university with a medical degree and a desire to help her father in his experiments with human organ transplants. Along with his assistant Charles Marshall, Baron Frankenstein creates a creature that is animated by lightning—it immediately crushes the Baron to death and sets off to terrorize the countryside. Tania wants to create another creature to salvage her father's reputation and convinces the crippled Marshall to let her transplant his brain into the handsome body of retarded field-hand Thomas. The operation is a success, but the first monster returns to the castle, looking to kill those who gave it life.*

Welles had two goals in mind with what was released as *Lady Frankenstein*, as he told interviewer Joe Meadows, 'We wanted to historically make it the first [horror] film with explicit sex in it.. Also, I wanted to get my shots at feminism. I was a pro-feminist at the time and I thought women had received a bad deal in education and everything.' The film missed the first mark by a long shot (the late '60s and early '70s had seen an avalanche of sex and nudity in horror films), and in fact it was not the first movie to add a feminine touch to the Frankenstein story either (besides 1935's *Bride of Frankenstein*, *Frankenstein's Daughter* had premiered in 1958 and the Baron's grand-daughter made her own debut in the mistitled *Jesse James Meets Frankenstein's Daughter* in 1966).

</p>*Lady Frankenstein* takes the worst of latter-day Hammer Horror (bad sets, rubber bats, unconvincing makeup, exploitative nudity) and performs the usual Italian Xerox job, which is supplanted only by Neri's (billed as 'Sara Bay') enthusiastic performance. Rosalba Neri had been acting since 1955, including appearances in a

Lady Frankenstein (Sara Bay)

number of Hercules films as well as spaghetti westerns (*Johnny Yuma, Arizona Colt, Johnny Texas*) and Jess Franco pictures (*99 Women, Justine, The Castle of Fu Manchu*). She had only used the 'Sara Bay' moniker once before (in the abysmal 1965 Franco and Ciccio spy comedy *The Amazing Doctor G*), but she would use it twice more—when she finally got to play Countess Dracula a couple of years later in *The Devil's Wedding Night* (released Stateside by Dimension), and in New World's own 1974 lady gladiator opus, *The Arena*.

(Corman cut ten minutes of footage from *Lady Frankenstein*, shortening or eliminating some twenty scenes. Contrary to popular belief, none of the deleted footage contained additional nudity or gore but was in large part expository scenes, many of which involved the investigation of police Inspector Harris (played by Jayne Mansfield widower Mickey Hargitay) into the Baron's death and the monster's murders. One cut which particularly irked Welles was a scene between Charles and Tania, in which he explains how the laboratory equipment works. As the director told Meadows, 'The film.. satisfied a number of my own pet peeves about horror films as I was growing up. One was that those films never showed you where the light came from when they performed these very delicate brain operations. Secondly, they never told you where the electricity was coming from to make all those little electric sparks and ladders going up and down in laboratories.')

> *'Did you ask me here because you wanted to be with me or because you wanted to get laid?'*
> —Eddie Collins (Tab Hunter) to neighbour Barbara (Nadyne Turney) in *Sweet Kill*

The Ides of March also saw the release of *Sweet Kill*, which had actually been produced more than a year before as *A Kiss from Eddie*. As he had with Rothman and Peeters, Corman had entrusted the production to a woman: 28-year-old Tamara Asseyev. Asseyev had been hired as a secretary by Corman in 1967, but, like many others, she instead found herself gaining immediate hands-on experience in film production. She oversaw the shooting of a prologue in an asylum with Luana Anders for the ABC-TV broadcast of Corman's AIP feature *The Pit and the Pendulum*, the second unit work on *The Trip*, and the budget for Peter Bogdanovich's *Targets*. She then went to Europe to co-produce *The Wild Racers* for Corman, which was directed by his long-time art director Daniel Haller. Asseyev and Haller hit it off, and she was invited to produce his next film, *Paddy* (which Corman financed), the story of a young Dubliner (played by Milo O'Shea) and his coming of age. At the same time, Haller and Asseyev collaborated on the Corman production of H P Lovecraft's *The Dunwich Horror* for AIP.

Cutting his directing teeth on *Sweet Kill* was 25-year-old Curtis Hanson, who had been editor of *Cinema* magazine and had served as an on-location rewriter for *Dunwich*, where he endeared himself to Corman, who was on the lookout for young (and cheap) talent. Hanson balked at doing motorcycle pictures or sex comedies, but when Corman suggested a 'modern horror film,' the young writer jumped at the chance. 'I wrote very quickly a script about an emotionally confused young woman who kills guys,' Hanson told *Ain't It Cool News*. 'Roger read it and his response was, 'I liked it, but it was a little too different having a woman be the killer.' So I then basically rewrote it and made the killer male.'

The role of the killer went to Tab Hunter, former '50s teen idol turned European expatriate who, at age 40, was looking for a change of pace. 'The film is about a very sick young man,' Hunter told the *Los Angeles Times*. 'The most sick character I've ever played. Different from all the other roles I've taken in the past.'

Eddie Collins is a good-looking physical education instructor living in a Venice Beach apartment who is irresistible to women. He is also a psychotic mama's boy, whose sexual hang-ups render him impotent and homicidal. A lonely female neighbour attempts to befriend Eddie, hoping to break down his air of indifference, but she discovers too late that no woman stays alive around Mr Collins for long.

'Beach Blanket Psycho' might have been a more fitting title for a thoroughly derivative Hitchcock rip-off, with the added 'hooks' of blood and nudity. What keeps the film afloat is the quality of the acting, with a bug-eyed Hunter effective in the 'Norman Bates' role and Nadyne Turney genuinely touching as the forever lonely next-door neighbour Barbara, who just wants Eddie to notice her (and is knifed in the shower for her trouble, as if the *Psycho* connection were not already obvious). Horror film buffs will spot a young Angus Scrimm (here using his given name of Rory Guy) as the landlady's handyman, several years before achieving cult status as 'The Tall Man' in Don Coscarelli's *Phantasm* franchise.

Critical response was surprisingly favourable: 'A horrifying suspense hit,' said the *New York Daily Mirror*; 'It has been made with a sensitivity and intelligence unusual for the normally lurid psycho genre,' observed the *Los Angeles Times*; 'Tab Hunter brings a high degree of conviction to a difficult part,' praised *Cinefantastique*.

35

Business, however, was far from stellar, and the film was soon pulled from circulation to be given a new lease on life as *The Arousers*—without the input of its producer or director.

In a new prologue, Corman added a sepia-toned flashback of a young Eddie (unseen except for his shoes) watching his mother undress, which then cuts to a modern-day stalker (ditto) watching a nubile young woman bathing. Another insert comes midway through the film, when Eddie goes out for a walk—then seemingly stops to watch a large-breasted woman washing her hair in a sink. A montage of the nude scenes late in the film was Corman's final addition. A new ad campaign was drawn up for a summer 1973 re-release which did not even mention Tab Hunter, but instead showed six photos of scantily-dressed women (not in the film) with the tag line 'They take on all comers!' Patrons were invited to test their 'Arousal Quotient' by taking a free 'Sexual Stimulation Test'.

Asseyev was not amused. 'That was pivotal for me,' she said in Mollie Gregory's book, *Women Who Run the Show*. 'I decided I'd work only on films that I had an emotional rapport with, that somehow reflected my sensibility as a woman, politically and creatively. I wanted to try to show a human condition, or show women coping in a positive way, that didn't denigrate them.' Asseyev subsequently partnered with another Corman alumnus, Alexandra Rose, and the two shared an Oscar nomination for Best Picture with *Norma Rae* (1979). In the 1980s, she produced several movies for television (including *The Penalty Phase* in 1986 and *The Hijacking of the Achille Lauro* in 1989) before becoming a best-selling author in the 1990s.

Hanson felt cheated as well. 'It actually was a very unhappy experience,' he recalled. 'It was one of many that I had on early pictures I did.. It was the first time I learned the lesson that I had the opportunity to learn multiple times after that which is: if you're going to risk being wrong, it's better to be wrong with your own mistakes than with somebody else's.' Hanson was scheduled to write/direct another film for Corman, the horror anthology *The Grave is Alive* based on stories by Clark Ashton Smith, but it never happened. He remained absent from the director's chair until the 1980s, when he made such films as *Losin' It* (1983) and *The Bedroom Window* (1987). In recent years, he has become the celebrated writer/director of such pictures as *L.A. Confidential* (for which he won a Best Screenplay Oscar, 1997), *Wonder Boys* (2000) and *8 Mile* (2002).

> '*I'm not bitter. I was bitter 350 years ago. I'm violent—you hear me, goddammit —violent!*'
> —Johnny Johnson (Billy Dee Williams), laying down the law in *The Final Comedown*

In March 1971, a revolution began in America's inner-city cinemas. It was heralded by the release of the independent, X-rated *Sweet Sweetback's Baadasssss Song*, a virtual one-man labour of love by 38-year-old Melvin Van Peebles. Full of violence, sex, humour and anger, it tells the story of Sweetback (Van Peebles), a black gigolo who goes on the run from the law after saving a Black Panther from racist cops. It connected with ghetto audiences like no other film before it and went on to make over $4 million in rentals. Three months later came the release of *Shaft*, a less outrageous, major-studio (MGM) black film that nevertheless caught the mood of the street with its 'black private dick who's the sex machine to all the chicks'. *Shaft* returned over $6 million in rentals, produced an Oscar-winning, mega-hit soundtrack for Isaac Hayes and made a star out of 28-year-old Richard Roundtree (who starred in two sequels, a short-lived TV series and a 2000 remake). Black exploitation—or 'blaxploitation' as *Variety* coined it—had arrived.

Watching all of this unfold was 32–year-old American Film Institute (AFI) intern Oscar Williams, who wanted in on the action. A fortuitous visit to the AFI by Roger Corman would give Williams that chance. 'Corman came to visit the school and speak,' Williams told *Shock Cinema*, 'and when he asked, "You guys have anything you want to do?" I said, "Yeah, I got a script." I gave it to him, and three days later, he called me back and said, "I'd like to do this. I'll put up $15,000 if you'll put up the rest." I had $11,500 promised to me by the American Film Institute to do a short film.. that was in the form of cameras, film, stuff like that—and Roger Corman gave me $5,000 at the beginning of the film, $5,000 while making the film, and $5,000 when I finished. That, plus the $11,500, made $26,500, and that's what it cost.'

'It' was *The Final Comedown*, which featured up-and-coming black stars Billy Dee Williams and D'Urville Martin (both of whom co-produced the film), along with cameos by Raymond St Jacques and R G Armstrong. Shot fast and loose on the streets of Watts, Los Angeles, Williams's film premiered at the Woods Theatre in Chicago in April 1972.

> *Leading a violent ghetto uprising, black radical Johnny Johnson is mortally wounded by the police. As he lies dying, he thinks of the things that led him to take up arms—the apathy of his put-down parents, the condescension of white liberals, job discrimination, constant police harassment, and a hopeless future for the young..*

'We were at the hotel—myself, Billy Dee Williams and D'Urville,' said Williams. 'And it started to rain. We were worried, but when we went down to the [Woods], there were lines around the block, and it scared the shit out of me!' The young director was not the only one frightened by *The Final Comedown*'s performance: 'A chilling film that should please both black and white militants and appal those who embrace a more moderate political stance' (*Variety*); 'It is a bad genre film—wholly exploitative of both its dramatic forms and its social situation' (*New York Times*); 'The movie is ugly and without intelligence. It is disturbing and wasteful of performers and talent whose charisma should be channelled into hope rather than gruelling negativity' (*Los Angeles Times*).

In *Final Comedown*, Williams is a writer/director who deals in absolutes—blacks are either angry militants or apathetic Uncle Toms, and whites are either racist bigots or naïve liberals. In Williams's world—as in Johnny's—there is no room for compromise. As the angry young (black) man, Billy Dee Williams' performance is powerful and shocking, especially to those used to the 'Black Clark Gable' image which he would cultivate in films like *Lady Sings the Blues* (1972) and *Mahogany* (1975). Williams would, in fact, disassociate himself from *The Final Comedown* in later years, as he did to the *New York News*: 'I swore I would never get caught in that again. I will no longer play in films that pit black against white. It just plays on the self-indulgence of ignorant people. We have to learn to serve each other in a beautiful way..'

'The film was not as successful as it might have been,' Corman told di Franco, 'because it was intensely political. It was a film of violence and of crime, but the political overtones were so heavy that they somewhat obscured the action.' As he had with *Sweet Kill*, Corman tried to overhaul *The Final Comedown* into something more saleable. He cut some of the film's more militant tirades and replaced them with new action footage shot by New World trailer editor Allan Arkush, retitled the result *Blast*, and released it in late 1976 with a retooled campaign to take advantage of Billy Dee Williams's new-found stardom.

Mind Warp

Oscar Williams, like Asseyev and Hanson before him, had no say in the matter and decided to use the pseudonym 'Frank Arthur Wilson' for his credit. He would go on to write and/or direct several films in the blaxploitation genre (*Five on the Black Hand Side, Black Belt Jones, Truck Turner*), though none were as aggressively political as *The Final Comedown*. His last film was *Death Drug* in 1978, featuring a pre-*Miami Vice* Philip Michael Thomas, and he has spent the recent years as both an actor and a teacher of film production at USC.

> *'Can't tell you what a trip it is to work in a place like this for three months!'*
> —American nurse Ellie St. George (Rickey Richardson) in *The Hot Box*

The month of May brought new announcements of upcoming films from New World, including *The Dune Roller, Snakes* (formerly *Movini's Venom*), *The Big Bird Cage* (formerly *Women of the Rice Paddies*), *Canyons* and another John Ashley-Eddie Romero Filipino picture, *The Woman Hunt*. It also saw the release of the latest effort from Jonathan Demme and Joe Viola, once known as *The Prescription Revolution* but now given the nitty-grittier title of *The Hot Box*.

Demme and Viola had sought to combine the elements from New World's two most successful genres by putting nurses into a Filipino women's prison movie. 'I've always loved cheapo movies,' Demme told *American Film*. 'And Corman uses one of my favorite formulas—action, nudity and a little social comment. What more can you ask for in a film?' What indeed?

US theatrical poster for The Hot Box

In the Republic of San Rosario, four American nurses are kidnapped by a guerrilla band under the leadership of peasant Flavio. The girls are charged with setting up a clinic and teaching the rebels first aid. After being involved in raids on a nearby government dispensary and a storage depot, they join with Renaldo, one of Flavio's disillusioned lieutenants, and escape. However, Renaldo is being blackmailed by sadistic Army Major Dubay and turns the nurses over to him. After being locked up, raped and tortured, the nurses have a change of heart, free an equally-recommitted Renaldo, and make their way to Flavio's camp to warn him of the coming army raid.

With *The Hot Box*, Demme could check off each part of the Corman formula that he admired: the action is bloody and sustained (including an impressive final battle between the guerrillas and the army), the women are pretty and often naked, and the political message is unmistakable. The dichotomy was not lost on the young writer/producer, as he told the *Daily Texan*: 'It was hilarious because we were doing a movie the theme of which was that in many repressed third world countries revolution is the only correct solution to the current problems. Meanwhile, we're cutting to the waterfall every five minutes so that the nurses can bathe nude and discuss their changing dialectics.'

Demme and Viola subsequently wrote another women's prison film that they called *Chains of Hate*, which was a feminised version of *The Defiant Ones*, wherein two troublemaking female prisoners, a white revolutionary and a black harem girl, are chained together and must brave *federales*, revolutionaries, and each other as they try to escape. Corman passed the script along to Ashley and Romero, who had it rewritten by H R Christian and produced it in the summer of 1972 with Pam Grier and Margaret Markov (also featured as a nurse-turned-revolutionary in *The Hot Box*). *Chains of Hate* was sold to AIP and released in early 1973 after undergoing two title changes, first to *Women in Chains* and then to *Black Mama, White Mama*. The Demme-Viola duo broke up after this, with Demme becoming a director for Corman while Viola went on to write and produce for television shows like *The Bionic Woman*, *T J Hooker* and *Equal Justice*. The two men were reunited in 2003 to produce the documentary *Beah: A Black Woman Speaks*.

The Big Bird Cage

'You can't rape me—I like sex!'
—American actress Terry Rich (Anitra Ford)
in *The Big Bird Cage*

The Big Bird Cage was finally opened for business in June, reteaming Pam Grier and writer/ director Jack Hill in the Filipino lock-up. For the first time, Grier had some real competition in the person of tall, sultry Anitra Ford (née Anitra Weinstein). The 30-year-old former model had done some TV work as well as an uncredited bit part in *The Love Machine* (1970) before landing the role of Terry Rich in *Bird Cage*; it proved a springboard to Ford becoming one of the first 'Barker Beauties' on the long-running TV game show *The Price is Right* and a brief but notable exploitation career that saw her co-star in no less than three 1973 drive-in hits: *Messiah of Evil*, *Invasion of the Bee Girls* and *Stacey* (for New World). She also secured a small but memorable role as Burt Reynolds' bitchy girlfriend in *The Longest Yard* (1974) and guested on several TV crime shows (*Baretta, SWAT, Starsky and Hutch*) before retiring from show business in 1977 and moving into real estate.

American actress Terry Rich is caught up in a Manila nightclub hold up engineered by local revolutionaries Django and Blossom. The authorities take her for an accomplice and send her to a women's work camp in the jungle. Meanwhile, the rebels decide that the way to encourage recruits is to add more women to their ranks; they decide that raiding the camp—known as 'The Big Bird Cage' in reference to the sugar mill that dominates the compound—is the best way to achieve both inspiration and recreation. Django and Blossom cheat their way inside as guard and prisoner respectively, to organize a revolt, but first they must contend with a vengeful Terry and her hardened camp-mates.

The Big Bird Cage is probably the world's first women's prison comedy, full of silly mud-fights, cat-fights, gang fights and fire-fights, not to mention priceless flirting between a moustachioed Sid Haig, as Django, the *laissez faire* revolutionary, and a hefty Vic Diaz, as Rocco, the effeminate guard. Another scene involving a seven-foot-tall blonde lesbian (Karen McKevic), a rub-down in lard, and a nude romp through the jungle has to be seen to be believed. Add blaxploitation princess Carol

Speed (*The Mack, Stud Brown, Black Samson, Abby*), a grossly overacting Andy Centenera as the megalomaniacal Warden Zappa, and a pyrotechnical conclusion worthy of Corman's Poe films, and you have what may be the penultimate WIP film—and the last movie that Hill would make for Corman for a decade. He would find greener pastures in the interim at AIP, where his *Coffy* (1973) and *Foxy Brown* (1974) were to make Pam Grier a household name.

'I don't want to steal your watch—I just want to smash your railroad!'
—Shelly (David Carradine) rebuking rail-boss Sartoris (John Carradine) in *Boxcar Bertha*

'Every two years I make my last picture for American International, and this is my current one,' Corman told the *Los Angeles Times*. The film he was referring to was *Boxcar Bertha*, which had originally been intended as a sequel of sorts to his AIP female gangster film *Bloody Mama* (1970) with Shelley Winters. He set his wife Julie to work researching the project and it was she who found the 1937 book, *Sister of the Road*, the autobiography of radical transient 'Boxcar' Bertha Thompson, as told to the anarchist crusader Dr Ben L Reitman.

Julie Corman became fascinated by the Thompson story, and although Reitman had died of a heart attack in 1942, Thompson herself was still alive. As Corman told Gregory, 'I did find Boxcar Bertha living in a kind of hotel in San Francisco. She was extremely reclusive. Though I never saw her, I got her release [to make the film]. I loved her story because it was about a woman living outside the system. In a way, at the time, I felt I was outside, too, looking at the social system pretty critically.. I felt her story was very much worth telling.'

Roger Corman engaged the writing duo of John and Joyce Corrington (scripters of *Von Richthofen*) to pen the screenplay of *Bertha*. Much to Julie Corman's chagrin, however, John Corrington had an entirely different take on the story: '[Corrington's] grandfather had been an IWW [Industrial Workers of the World] worker and he saw this as the story of union pioneer Big Bill Shelly.. I began to see that my brilliant idea about a woman outside the social norms was not going to stay pure. That was hard for me to deal with because by then I felt this was *my picture*.'

It was not to be Roger Corman's picture any more, either. Despite his previous pronouncements, Corman decided not to direct the film, handing the reins instead to a virtually unknown 28-year-old New York University (NYU) graduate/teacher named Martin Scorsese. Corman had been one of the few people to see and appreciate Scorsese's film debut, *Who's That Knocking At My Door* (1968), and was aware that the young Italian-American had also helped to shoot and edit Michael Wadleigh's *Woodstock* (1970). As soon as she arrived on the *Bertha* set in Camden, Arkansas, in October 1971, Julie Corman witnessed the beginnings of cinematic genius: 'Marty had already sketched every single shot in the picture and had tacked them all over the walls of his motel room in Camden. From that moment on, it was a Marty Scorsese film.'

During the Great Depression, young Bertha Thompson falls in with radical Big Bill Shelly and his crusade to unionize railroad workers. When Shelly is jailed, Bertha frees him and his two associates—card shark Rake Brown and black musician Von Morton. The foursome take to robbing trains and banks before holding railroad boss Buckram Sartoris hostage. In the ensuing melee, Brown is killed, Shelly and Morton are captured, and Bertha flees, only to be held captive at a bordello. She runs away, finds Morton, and they go looking for Shelly, who has escaped again. The reunion is cut short by Sartoris's men, however, who crucify Shelly to a boxcar while Bertha watches helplessly.

Boxcar Bertha (Barbara Hershey)

On its release via AIP in June 1972, critics were quick to notice that this was an exploitation film with a difference: 'The whole thing has been beautifully directed by Martin Scorsese, who really comes into his own here' (*New York Times*); 'What is most impressive about *Boxcar Bertha* is how.. Scorsese, in his first Hollywood venture, has managed to shape such familiar material into a viable film' (*Los Angeles Times*). Perhaps the critic who put it best (as was often the case) was the *Chicago Sun-Times*'s Roger Ebert, who wrote, 'I have the notion that Roger Corman.. sent his actors and crew South with the hope of getting a nice, simple, sexy, violent movie for the summer trade. What he got is something else, and something better. Director Martin Scorsese has gone for mood and atmosphere more than for action, and his violence is always blunt and unpleasant—never liberating and exhilarating, as the New Violence is supposed to be. We get the feeling we're inhabiting the dark night of the soul.. Scorsese remains one of the bright young hopes of American movies.'

One of the few naysayers was Ebert's rival (and future television partner), the perpetually clueless Gene Siskel of the *Chicago Tribune*, who commented, 'Director Martin Scorsese photographs the crucifixion from every possible angle to the extent that one gets the feeling that he is salivating with delight at shocking the audience. By the inclusion of such violence and a few tame nude scenes with Miss Hershey, who doesn't have a waist, *Boxcar Bertha* does not shock. It simply depresses.' He gave *Bertha* one star, in contrast to the three that he awarded the other film reviewed in the same column—Disney's *Now You See Him, Now You Don't*. Go figure.

> *'I just keep thinking that I shouldn't be thinking...but if I'm thinking that I should just be then I'm not being—I'm so mixed up.'*
> —Crazy mixed-up nurse Barbara (Patti Byrne) in *Night Call Nurses*

41

On her next film, Julie Corman was elevated to full-fledged producer and she immediately contacted Martin Scorsese to see who he might recommend to direct it. Scorsese suggested 24-year-old Jonathan Kaplan, one of his former NYU students, whose short film *Stanley, Stanley* had just won the grand prize in the National Student Film Festival. When Kaplan was called by Roger Corman, he thought at first that it was a prank and hung up, but on the second attempt, a rather annoyed Corman managed to convince Kaplan that the deal was legit. Kaplan was offered $2,000 and a round-trip ticket if he could be in Hollywood the following Monday.

On his arrival, Kaplan was handed a script that George Armitage had left behind called *Night Call Nurses* and then ushered into Roger Corman's office, where he was given a ten minute crash-course in real-world filmmaking, as he told di Franco: 'There was a male sexual fantasy to be exploited, comedic sub-plot, action/violence, and a slightly to-the-left-of-centre social sub-plot.. And then frontal nudity from the waist up and total nudity from behind and no pubic hair and get the title of the picture somewhere into the film and go to work.'

> *More drama in the lives of three pretty young nurses: Barbara tries to get over her sexual hang-ups by falling into bed with her group therapist (who is using her for an experiment), Janis becomes involved with a speed-freak trucker, and Sandy joins with a black revolutionary who needs her help to spring his captive leader from the hospital. Meanwhile, all three are being stalked by 'The Lipstick Maniac', who wants to punish them for their lack of chastity!*

The movie starts with a bang—literally—as a nude psychiatric patient pretends to jump from the hospital roof, but it is her china doll that explodes on the ground. *Night Call Nurses* then follows the Armitage mould, with everything from group encounters (including one that ends with nearly everyone, including *Bury Me An Angel*'s Dixie Peabody, stripping by a fireplace) to black militants, sky-diving nurses, tripped-out truckers, and a psycho orderly in nurse-drag (played by future director Dennis Dugan) thrown into the mix. There was little Kaplan could do with such a convoluted narrative but to keep things moving, and there is so much employment of still-frame montages and voiceovers that one is moved to wonder if they lost the original footage and had to make do as best they could.

Julie Corman had brought Barbara Peeters on board as production manager, and the two had given the film more of the feminine sensibility that was to be found in the earlier *The Student Nurses*. Advertised in the summer of 1972 as the 'Funniest Sexiest Comedy of the Year!' it did not impress the *Los Angeles Times*'s Thomas, who wrote, 'Alas, it's but mere ludicrous trash but at least has the decency to be funny.' But *Night Call Nurses* was another success, grossing $1 million (against a cost of just $115,000) and ensuring both Julie Corman and Jonathan Kaplan further work at New World.

> *'You mean that piece of whatever it is can think?'*
> —Scientist's girlfriend (Maria De Aragon) in *The Cremators*

The first New World release of fall 1972, *The Cremators*, was actually the project announced as *Dune Roller*, based on the 1951 Julian May (aka Judy Dikty) short story of the same name. In May's tale, Dr Ian Thorne, an ecologist studying tide-pools on the shores of Lake Michigan, comes across a small, drop-like object, similar to a marble with a tail. He discovers two more inside the body of a dead frog and another, larger one beside the charred body of a dead hobo. He makes the first into a charm and gives it to his girlfriend, who subsequently is chased in her boat by

a 15-foot-high glowing orb until she hurls the marble into the water. Thorne comes to realise that the objects are actually alien organisms, communicating with a host entity that lives at the bottom of the lake; when the organisms signal, the 'mother' rises to reclaim them, destroying anything and anyone in its path. Thorne collects a number of the marbles and sets a trap for the entity, which ensures that an explosive reception awaits it on its next appearance.

Screenwriter Harry Essex (*It Came From Outer Space, Creature from the Black Lagoon*) had acquired the property years earlier for a paltry $500, and the film that Essex wrote, produced, and directed follows May's narrative almost exactly. Produced in two weeks for $50,000, *The Cremators* substituted the rocky California coastline for the dunes of Lake Michigan (though it still inexplicably referred to the Pacific Ocean as 'the lake') and was one of the first efforts by visual effects artist Doug Beswick (*The Empire Strikes Back, The Terminator, Aliens et al*), whose superimposed alien fireball is comical but effective. Co-star Maria De Aragon, whose heavy blue eye shadow is more intimidating than the fireball, enjoyed a brief exploitation career in the early '70s (*Love Me Like I Do, Blood Mania, Wonder Women*) before achieving lasting fame under the mask of alien assassin Greedo in George Lucas's *Star Wars* (1977).

Essex produced the film independently but his agent had arranged distribution through New World—though the experience, as the director told Tom Weaver, was anything but pleasant for him: 'Corman and I didn't get along from the beginning—I mean, we just couldn't stand one another! He knew we were going to do the film for very little money, and I felt he just didn't give the picture a fair shake.. he'd put some of his own pictures as the main feature in a double bill, and put *The Cremators* in as a second. That meant that I'd get a flat fee.. while he played his own pictures on top for the percentage!'

Given the fact that *The Cremators* was very much a throwback, right down to former AIP composer Albert Glasser's score, Essex should have been grateful that it was released at all. As he himself said, 'The fact that anything came out of it was a miracle!'

'Defanging a snake is like castrating a man!'
—Snake goddess Lena Aruza (Marlene Clark) in *Night of the Cobra Woman*

Corman had become so committed to shooting in the Philippines that, earlier in the year, he had entered into a co-production deal with Premiere Productions, headed by Cirio Santiago, and agreed to help fund the construction of two new sound

ONLY THE COBRA COULD SATISFY HER UNEARTHLY DESIRES.

Starring JOY BANG · MARLENE CLARK · ROGER GARRETT
Produced by KERRY MAGNESS and HARVEY MARKS Directed by ANDREW MEYER
Screenplay by ANDREW MEYER Story by ANDREW MEYER and KERRY MAGNESS
A New World Pictures Release Metrocolor R

US theatrical poster for Night of the Cobra Woman

stages outside Manila. One of the strangest (and worst) films to take advantage of this new set-up was *Night of the Cobra Woman*, which was released in October after having been announced as *Movini's Venom* and *Snakes*. It was the mainstream directing debut of 29-year-old New Yorker Andrew Meyer, who had built a reputation as an experimental filmmaker in the 1960s, with films such as *Match Girl* (featuring Andy Warhol and The Rolling Stones) and *An Early Clue to the New Direction*.

The star of *Cobra Woman* was 25-year-old Joy Bang (née Joy Wener), who had appeared in Meyer's *An Early Clue*, as well as *Flower Child* (1967) and *The Sky Pirate* (1970). She had also worked with directors Roger Vadim (*Pretty Maids All in a Row*, 1971) and Woody Allen (*Play It Again, Sam*, 1972), and Paul Williams (*Dealing: Or the Berkeley-to-Boston Forty-Brick Lost-Bag Blues*, 1972), and she came across like a poor man's Goldie Hawn. Bang was at one point romantically linked with Keith Moon, drummer of rock group The Who, but she abandoned show business to take up nursing in the mid-1970s.

In occupied Philippines in World War II, nurse Lena Aruza is bitten by a rare firebrand cobra and transforms into an immortal snake woman. Thirty years later, a UNICEF researcher is working on vaccines and seeks out the still-youthful Lena for the fabled firebrand venom; she is turned away, but her boyfriend Duff arrives and has better luck—he becomes Lena's lover. The problem is that she has drained his youth and he has to have regular injections of venom to keep from aging. They strike a bargain: Duff will arrange discreet liaisons for Lena to drain young men and she will give him the venom. Lena's spirit becomes one with the snake god Dimballa and she is transformed into a pet that Duff is cursed to keep safe if he is to have his regular 'fix'.

Saddled with a confused story, terrible make-up and worse acting (even the usually reliable Vic Diaz is dismal as a mute hunchback), *Night of the Cobra Woman* proved that Meyer could not adapt his experimental style to the Filipino jungle. As Corman told di Franco, 'We were doing a number of scenes spontaneously.. and in my final meeting with [Meyer] before going to Manila, I pointed this out to him and said that upon his arrival on location he must have this straightened out, that he must solve these problems logically, but he did not.' *Variety* (which reviewed the film nearly two years after it premiered) seconded Corman's sentiments, referring to the 'muddied plot' and saying that 'Meyer's approach.. is deadpan and minus frills.' Corman would give Meyer another chance, although next time out, it was the usual cut-and-paste job that most would-be Cormanites were handed at the start.

In contrast to the cheap schlock that he was releasing, Corman was trumpeting his literary aspirations in the newspapers, boldly proclaiming that he had acquired four novels for production: Stewart Greene's *The Wild Political Prank*, Gordon Hiker's *High and Far*, Sherman Markenstein's *Dawn* and Marge Miller's *The Bad Joke*. Never heard of them? Neither had anyone else—because they never existed (or at least were never published). Adding more baloney to the sandwich was Corman's announcement that he was going to produce, and perhaps direct, a biography of famous painter James Whistler. R(obert) Wright Campbell (*Machine Gun Kelly*, *Masque of the Red Death*) had supposedly been commissioned to write the script, and Corman said he wanted Peter O'Toole in the lead and Angela Lansbury to play Whistler's mother (presumably the part, not the painting). Needless to say, Whistler never came near to being realised.

The third time proved to be lucky, however, as Corman did acquire the rights to the newly-published Charles Willeford novel *Cockfighter*. The boss of New World announced his plans to produce an adaptation of the novel in Florida in 1973, but it would actually be shot in Georgia in 1974, under the direction of Monte Hellman.

'I'm not a normal person.. I'm a star!'
—Roller derby queen Karen Walker (Claudia Jennings) in *Unholy Rollers*

Mary Eileen 'Mimi' Chesterton was born in Evanston, Illinois, in December 1949. She graduated from high school in 1967 as an honour student and top cheerleader and joined the Hull House theatre company in Chicago. In September 1968, while still at Hull House, she also took a job as a receptionist at the Chicago offices of *Playboy* magazine. Coming to the attention of staff photographer Pompeo Posar, Chesterton tested for and was awarded the November 1969 centrefold. To avoid any embarrassment to her family, she chose to use the name 'Claudia Jennings' for her layout.

Chesterton took her new name and the $5,000 check, packed her bags and her dog, and boarded the next plane for Hollywood. She had little immediate success, but all that changed when she was chosen as Playmate of the Year in June 1970. Soon, she was appearing in films like *Jud*, *The Love Machine* (both 1971) and *The Stepmother* (1972) and revealing to *Playboy* that she was excited about her prospects: 'The established studios are fading and lots of hip people are out here, trying to do exciting things. Films are entering a new era and I'm glad to be part of it,' she enthused.

One of the fading studios was MGM, which, in the summer of 1972, was heavily hyping its roller derby picture *Kansas City Bomber*, starring one of Hollywood's biggest sex symbols of the time, Raquel Welch. Metro's film was only moderately successful, but the hoopla surrounding its production attracted Roger Corman who agreed to produce a knock-off story for AIP. Howard Cohen and Vernon Zimmerman teamed up to write and direct the project, and fellow Chicagoan 'Claudia Jennings' was pegged to star.

After quitting her job at a cat food factory, roller derby fan Karen Walker tries out for her favourite team, The Avengers. She makes the squad and quickly establishes herself as the team's new number one star, much to the chagrin of her fellow skaters. She has an affair with a married team-mate and argues with the club's owner, who brings in another skater to replace Karen. But the feisty roller-rink queen is determined to go out with a bang—one that no one will ever forget.

Roger Ebert immediately picked up on what was to become the Claudia Jennings mystique: 'She plays a very tough broad, and turns in the hardest, most vicious female performance in a long time.' Likewise, the *Los Angeles Times* marvelled at how *Unholy Rollers'* supposed 'heroine' was portrayed: 'This rollette is no tart with a heart and a disappointing, sentimental love affair and a broken home to remind us that there are reasons for her hard exterior. No, indeed, Karen.. is a slut through and through, and as such she rings real.'

The movie itself rings real, from its locker-room taunting to the bar-room dirty jokes to the rowdy crowds to the cut-throat back-stabbing, both on and off the rink. It is crammed with violence, sex, nudity, four-letter words, sleazy promoters, cheesy endorsements, a wannabe '50s rock band called Louie and the Rockets, and a rapid-fire editing style, courtesy of none other than Martin Scorsese. *Unholy Rollers* was, as Ebert put it, 'a movie with the courage of its own lack of convictions.'

Lack of convictions had kept AIP from backing true talent in Dennis Hopper and Peter Fonda on *Easy Rider*, and now Corman would make the same mistake with Scorsese. The young director wanted Corman to produce his latest script, *Mean Streets*, but Corman offered support only if Scorsese rewrote it as a blaxploitation film. Scorsese wisely refused, formed his own company with producers Lee Perry and Jonathan Taplin, made the film his way and sold it to Warner Brothers. The rest is history—*Alice Doesn't Live Here Anymore* (1974), *Taxi Driver* (1976), *Raging Bull* (1980), *Goodfellas* (1990), *Casino* (1995), *Gangs of New York* (2002), *The Aviator* (2004) and *The Departed* (2006), for which he finally won the Best Director Oscar after being nominated five times previously.

US theatrical poster for The Woman Hunt

'There is no one here who does not tremble with delight at the thought of inflicting pain.'
—Millionaire host Spiros (Eddie Garcia) in *The Woman Hunt*

As New World was now in bed with Premiere in the Philippines, there was no more need for its former alliance with the team of Ashley and Romero. *The Woman Hunt*, Four Associates' final production for Corman, was a rather sleazy combination of the Filipino women's prison film and the oft-adapted Richard Connell short story, *The Most Dangerous*

Game. The only standout in the proceedings is former *Petticoat Junction* star Pat Woodell, who had also appeared in *The Big Doll House* and *The Twilight People.* As Spiros's lesbian henchwoman, Woodell is typically clad all in black (including her big black wig) and soft-spoken in her delight at the sadistic goings-on. Of her new-found exploitation career, Woodell told the *Chicago Tribune,* 'I'm aware that to a large extent I am a packaged good but I don't let it get to me and I try to enjoy it as much as I can. It's simply one of the means to reach my goals and I accept it as such.' As with so many other 'B' actresses, her goal was to get into bigger movies, but it failed to happen. Woodell made only one more film (*The Roommates,* 1973) and an appearance on TV's *The New Perry Mason* (1973) before fading into obscurity.

> *Four women are captured in the Philippines and taken to a jungle mansion. They are captives of millionaire recluse Spiros, who intends to use them to please his international clientele. When four captains of industry arrive, Spiros announces a new entertainment: the women will be set loose in the jungle for the men to hunt. Spiros' adoptive son Tony has a change of heart and decides to lead the girls in an escape. As the five flee into the jungle, Spiros declares the hunt to be on. Tony and the women must brave the hunters, Spiros's gunmen, cobras, and the treacherous terrain if they are to make it downriver to civilization.*

For his part, John Ashley would appear in three more Filipino movies (*Black Mamba, Savage Sisters* and *Sudden Death*) before chucking it all in to become a full-time producer. On Corman's recommendation, both he and Romero served as associate producers during Francis Ford Coppola's $25 million, 18-month Filipino shoot on *Apocalypse Now* in 1976-77, and Ashley went on to produce such TV shows as *The A-Team, Something Is Out There* and *Walker, Texas Ranger* before dying of a heart attack in October 1997, at the age of 62.

Fellini the Devil.
Fellini the Lover.
Fellini the Fantastic.

"'Amarcord' may possibly be Federico Fellini's most marvelous film...extravagantly funny. It is as full of tales as Scheherazade, some romantic, some slapstick, some elegiacal, some bawdy, some as mysterious as the unexpected sight of a peacock flying through a light snowfall. It's a film of exhilarating beauty."
—Vincent Canby, The New York Times

"What a film! Instantly one of the ten best movies of the year. Federico Fellini is a director that I admire above all others."—Gene Shalit, NBC-TV Today Show

"'Amarcord' is the most beautiful movie Fellini has ever made and a landmark in the history of film. It is a sprawling, hilarious, touching, evocation of life."
—Paul D. Zimmerman, Newsweek

"Fellini presents a beautiful carnival show of the sacred things in his life. He triumphs!"
—Stanley Kauffman, The New Republic

"'Amarcord' is an enthralling, marvelous and beautifully crafted film. Chalk up another triumph for Federico Fellini."
—William Wolf, Cue Magazine

"What a triumph! Fellini's new 'Amarcord' is even more beautiful than '8½'. It is a wonderstruck, affectionate work. One wants to shake someone by both his hands and say 'well done'."
—Penelope Gilliatt, The New Yorker

"Federico Fellini makes movies the way Picasso painted pictures. 'Amarcord' is an unforgettable dream machine, a masterwork, a cornucopia abrim with things to amaze and gratify any moviegoer still capable of responding to priceless sonnets."
—Bruce Williamson, Playboy

ROGER CORMAN Presents **FELLINI'S AMARCORD**

Produced by **FRANCO CRISTALDI**   Directed by **FEDERICO FELLINI**

Screenplay and Story by FEDERICO FELLINI and TONINO GUERRA • Director of Photography GIUSEPPE ROTUNNO • Film Editor RUGGERO MASTROIANNI
Music by NINO ROTA • PANAVISION® TECHNICOLOR® • AN ITALIAN-FRENCH CO-PRODUCTION F.C. PRODUCTIONS (ROME) P.E.C.F. (PARIS)
Distributed by NEW WORLD PICTURES

48

Chapter 2

CRieS. WhiSPeRS and deaTh RaceS

Cries and Whispers (Ingrid Thulin, Liv Ullmann)

'This odd dichotomy got us lots of publicity. It seemed hip, smart, rather amusing. We had exploitation and we had art and we were the leaders in both across the United States.'

—Roger Corman, from his autobiography

'The trouble with making a movie for Roger Corman is that he always insists on pissing on it before he releases it.'

—Angie Dickinson, star of *Big Bad Mama*

In the late 1950s and 1960s, the market for foreign films in America had exploded with the appearance of such European sex goddesses as Brigitte Bardot (*And God Created Woman, The Female*), Anita Ekberg (*La Dolce Vita, Boccaccio 70*), Gina Lollobrigida (*Beautiful but Dangerous, The Hunchback of Notre Dame*) and Jeanne Moreau (*The Lovers, Jules and Jim*). This revolution continued with a New Wave of French and Italian filmmakers who were willing to break with traditional film form and deal with previously taboo subjects, especially sexual. The vanguard of Francois Truffaut, Jean-Luc Godard, Federico Fellini and Michelangelo Antonioni not only made films with the actresses mentioned above, but created such international hits as *The 400 Blows* (1959), *Breathless* (1960), *8½* (1963) and *Blow Up* (1966).

However, the successful intrusion of subtitles onto American screens was on the verge of commercial collapse by the early '70s. One reason was that American cinema had caught up with its European counterparts and was recognizing a freer vocabulary and darker personal relationships in films like *The Graduate* (1967) and *Midnight Cowboy* (1969). As Emanuel Wolf, president of Allied Artists, told the *New York Times*, 'American movies, dealing with serious themes related to us, are more meaningful for audiences here.' Plus, the audience did not have to read the screen to understand what was happening.

Another major factor was economics. While many foreign-made films did well in America in the 1960s, only Fellini's *La Dolce Vita*, Costa-Gavras's *Z* and Claude Lelouch's *A Man and a Woman* made serious money. As prices on foreign films rose and the box office did not, the profit margin went down. There was also more competition from domestic product for screens which previously had shown foreign films. Bill Becker of Janus Films, a leading distributor of foreign films in America, told the *New York Times*, 'When there was a real 'art theatre circuit', films could be sent out inexpensively. Today a foreign movie, selling for more than the $10,000 of the early sixties—and purchased by a big company with operating costs—must earn about $500,000 to break even. And very few do.'

Yet another factor working against foreign films was the unexpected popularity of 'porno chic' in the major U.S. cities. Theatres that once enticed men with Bardot and Ekberg were now giving them all they could handle with the likes of Marilyn Chambers (*Behind the Green Door*, 1972), Linda Lovelace (*Deep Throat*, 1972) and Georgina Spelvin (*The Devil in Miss Jones*, 1973). Hardcore porn was cheap and highly profitable; foreign films had become expensive and a gamble.

The man who was to buck this trend was Roger Corman.

Despite the fact that New World expected to exceed its first year profits in 1972, Corman was concerned about his company's image. He did not want New World to be seen solely as *his* version of AIP, constantly taking on his former employer in the drive-in exploitation arena. Corman was both a filmmaker and a *cineaste*—he was being fêted again in December 1972 with a retrospective at Oxford University—and he wanted New World to reflect his own cinematic tastes. As Corman's long-time lawyer Barbara Boyle told author Ed Naha in *Brilliance on a Budget*: 'When New World first started, the drive-ins were the independent's exclusive realm. We could count on them. That's where we geared most of our product to.. It was Corman's foresight and all our efforts that led to our saying "No. We won't back off. We have to become a twelve-month company." And to be a twelve-month company, you have to be making and acquiring movies that are other than drive-in summer product.'

The opportunity presented itself in the form of *Cries and Whispers*, the latest film from celebrated Swedish director Ingmar Bergman, who had stunned the world with such artistic offerings as *The Seventh Seal* (1957, which Corman greatly admired and quoted in his own *Masque of the Red Death*), *Wild Strawberries* (1957) and *The Virgin Spring* (1960). Bergman's films had also fallen victim to the declining foreign film market, however, so much so that he had to produce his newest effort himself. He had been asking for a $75,000 advance for American distribution rights and had found no takers, until New World sales manager Frank Moreno was introduced to *Cries and Whispers* by Los Angeles theatre-chain owner Max Laemmle (nephew of Universal Pictures founder Carl Laemmle). It was love at first sight, and Moreno went ahead and bought the film without even talking to Corman.

Released to great critical acclaim in December 1972, *Cries and Whispers* became the most successful film of Bergman's career, outgrossing his previous five films combined. The engrossing and dreamlike study of four women drawn together by the terminal illness of one of their number was actually marketed by New World to both art houses *and* drive-ins and was equally successful in both, grossing $1.3 million in rentals. 'I've never met Bergman,' Corman told the *Los Angeles Times* in February 1973, 'but we have exchanged notes of mutual delight. He's invited us to Cannes, where the picture will be shown out of competition. We're going to discuss going into partnership.' Corman was beaten to the punch on that score by irrepressible impresario Dino De Laurentiis, for whom Bergman made *Face to Face* (1976) and *The Serpent's Egg* (1977). Corman continued to bathe in the prestige of *Cries and Whispers*, however, as the film was nominated for five Oscars in 1974 and won that for Best Cinematography.

Corman was ecstatic at the boost which Bergman's film had given New World, financially and aesthetically, and he tasked Moreno to begin looking for other foreign product. Their next attempt came in February 1973 with the release of the Jamaican film *The Harder They Come*, winner of the Silver Lion at the Venice Film

Festival. Starring reggae singer Jimmy Cliff, *The Harder They Come* was the semi-autobiographical story of a young would-be reggae star who turns to dealing dope to ́pay the rent, becomes an underground fugitive and subsequently a political hero. While it, too, garnered much acclaim (the *Los Angeles Times* called it 'one of the landmarks in black cinema'), it was not as successful initially as *Cries and Whispers*. But it eventually became one of the first 'Midnight Movie' cult hits (often playing alongside George Romero's *Night of the Living Dead* or David Lynch's *Eraserhead*) and even racked up an unbelievable eight-year run at the Orson Welles Cinema in Cambridge, Massachusetts.

When word eventually reached the street about New World's interest in buying art films, the company suddenly found itself bombarded with offers. 'You've really got to be careful before you take on the distribution of an art film,' Corman told the *Los Angeles Times*. 'Right now we're being offered them at least once a day and we're being very selective.'

> *'Just because you freaked out on your bosses don't turn you into no groovy dude!'*
> —Sassy Amanda (Carol Speed) to mercenary Jim (James Iglehart) in *Savage!*

In the wake of New World's new-found respectability, Corman outlined the company's new strategy to the *Hollywood Reporter* that April: 'We'll stay with the specialty markets, continuing our distribution of exploitation films and increasing our participation in the distribution of selected 'art' films. We will not try to compete with the major studios on middle-of-the-road pictures, where the majors have the strength to finance and book.' But in case New World's core audience had begun to worry that the company had gone 'legit', Corman offered his latest Filipino production, the blaxploitation film *Savage!*

US theatrical poster for Savage!

> In the banana republic of Baranca, black mercenary Jim Heygood helps the government to capture rebel commander Moncato, but he has a change of heart when the generals ruthlessly execute Moncato and his girlfriend. When he assaults those in charge, Heygood is thrown into prison but escapes during a transfer. He flees into the countryside with two female members of an American circus troupe and the trio

> *join the rebels. Heygood, now nicknamed 'Savage', becomes rebel leader in Moncato's stead and decides to take the fight directly to the capital city.*

Savage! was the first film that 36-year-old Cirio Santiago personally produced and directed for Roger Corman under the aegis of the New World-Premiere setup (it was also the first film that he had directed in English instead of his native Tagalog). Santiago had been making movies in the Philippines since the 1950s and had virtually grown up in the industry, as his father had founded Premiere Productions just after World War II. Santiago had been nominated three times for the FAMAS Award (the Filipino equivalent of the Oscar) and won it for his 1968 short *Igorota*. His relationship with Corman would be the most profitable of his career, spanning nearly 30 years, even though some of his cost-cutting methods did not endear him to Corman's employees: 'Cirio was so cheap that when he would send us the movies, they were only spliced on one side,' Allan Arkush told *Los Angeles Weekly*.

The action in *Savage!* is fast and furious—even though some of the stunts and fight-arrangements are poor—and showcases just how willing the Philippine Army was to cooperate with Western film production. As Corman told di Franco, 'You can really get the Philippine army to stage your battle sequences, and you can get really magnificent war sequences there in a low-budget film that you can't get in any other part of the world that I know of.' Apparently the army never read the scripts of the films it participated in, however, as they almost always advocated revolution!

While *Savage!* was no different, Corman had learned the lesson of his previous blaxploitation outing: '[*Savage!*] was a revolutionary film much as *The Final Comedown* was, but it was more successful because we kept the revolutionary concept— the radical political beliefs—in the background and concentrated on the straight action.' The fact that the film undressed Carol Speed and former *Hullabaloo* dancer Lada Edmund Jr at every available opportunity no doubt helped to obscure the 'message' as well.

> *'Our guests here are not exactly saints.'*
>
> —Prison warden in *The Big Bust Out*

Roger Corman has always maintained that his separation from Larry Woolner was an amicable one ('He walked away with a lot of money.. and we stayed good friends,' he wrote), but the story behind New World's next 1973 release raises some doubts about the nature of their parting. After *The Big Doll House* had played in Italy early in 1972 and fared well, an immediate Neapolitan knock-off was produced under the title of *The Crucified Girls of San Ramon*. Woolner knew about it, and so did Corman. Woolner needed product for his new company; Corman had several films already in the pipeline. Nevertheless, one-upmanship got the better of Corman when he heard that his former partner was going to Italy to buy *San Ramon*. As New World's boss told di Franco, '[Woolner] got on a plane to Rome before anybody could make the deal. I knew he had left. So while he was in the air, I bought the film by phone and telexed the money.. By the time [Woolner] landed.. the film had been sold to me—to his surprise.' Whether this was Corman's revenge for Woolner stealing Stephanie Rothman and Charles Swartz or simply a mischievous prank is hard to say, but his behaviour was strange for someone who knew first-hand what it was like to be screwed by a former employer.

> *Eight female convicts in a Turkish prison set out to work at a nearby convent. They overpower their guards and escape, heading to a supposed safe house, which turns out to be a front for a white slave ring. The slavers hustle the girls onto a freighter, but the*

captain helps them escape into the mountains, where they are attacked and raped by a group of bandits. The captain trains the women to fight and they make their way to the Iranian border. They stop over at a Muslim castle, only to be trapped by the slavers and the army unit for whom the women were intended as sex-slaves.

Corman really did a hatchet job on *The Crucified Girls of San Ramon*, cutting out nearly 20 minutes by shortening or eliminating some thirty scenes. As with *Lady Frankenstein*, all of the nudity and violence was left intact (naturally!), but character development and exposition suffered greatly. Retitled *The Big Bust Out* for American release, the film was marketed as yet another women's prison picture ('Soft skin bursting through hard prison walls!'), which was rather disingenuous: the prison scenes do not last past the first reel. It is, in fact, an adventure film that is well served by location work which features authentic castles, ruins, ancient villages and mountain vistas. While *The Big Bust Out* is humourless and revels in the constant degradation of its protagonists, it did at least offer a change of scenery from the over-used backdrop of the Philippines.

'Do you know you have a quite remarkable bone structure?'
—Young doctor (Richard Young) to sexy stewardess (Pat Anderson) in *Fly Me*

In July 1969, Louis K Sher's Sherpix put in distribution one of the most profitable films ever made: *The Stewardesses*. Costing just over $100,000, this story of an eventful 18-hour layover was released X-rated (it was subsequently cut for a more marketable 'R' rating) in 3-D, and it ended up making over $27 million at the box office. An obvious precursor to New World's 'nurses' movies, *The Stewardesses* had lots of sex and nudity, some drugs, a tragedy (the lead female character jumps off a 30-storey building), and some social relevance (one of the stewardesses has a relationship with a returning Vietnam veteran). The winning formula (sex + action + politics) that Corman had so often taken credit for ('We more or less originated this concept,' he told di Franco) can clearly be seen in *The Stewardesses* and it is difficult to believe that he and Woolner did not have the Sherpix film in mind when they commissioned *The Student Nurses*.

New World's low-rent rival Independent International joined in the aerial fun with *Bedroom Stewardesses* in 1970, and it would continue the hi-jinks in *Blazing Stewardesses* and *Naughty Stewardesses* in 1975, but Corman's company held off from flying the skies until Cirio Santiago decided to join the Mile High Club for his second production of the New World-Premiere deal. Since kung fu was big business in 1973 thanks to Bruce Lee and his many copyists, Santiago thought to spice things up even more by adding some high kicks to the mix and shooting parts of *Fly Me* in Hong Kong and Tokyo.

Three young stewardesses—Toby, Andrea and Sherry—head from Los Angeles to Hong Kong. Once there, Toby tries desperately to ditch her nagging mother (who surprised her on the plane) to be with David, a young doctor. Andrea's lover Donald has gone missing from their apartment and she is being courted by Len, who is secretly a narcotics agent. Sherry, meanwhile, has been kidnapped by a white slave ring for not turning over all of the drugs that she has been smuggling. Len comes clean with Andrea and tells her that Donald is actually the leader of the white slavers, who now have also kidnapped Toby and her mother. Len and Andrea confront Donald at his nightclub, while David takes it upon himself to free the captive girls.

Got all that? Mix in some pretty bad kung-fu fights (which were actually filmed, though not choreographed, by Jonathan Demme), a lot of nudity, a quick trip to the

Tokyo Ginza, the usual Manila digs and a typically overbearing Italian mother, and you end up one of New World's all-time worst. Unlike the nurses films, Santiago did not bother himself with left-wing sub-plots or attempts at style, settling instead for as much sex and violence as the 'R' rating could handle. *Fly Me* was the first New World release of summer 1973, and there would be three more.

> *'I don't like old men taking money from little girls.'*
> —P I Stacey Hanson (Anne Randall) to love-guru Rod (James Westmoreland) in *Stacey*

US theatrical poster for Stacey!

Andy Sidaris was an unhappy man. The 42-year-old had been, in his own words, 'the best television director that ever lived' for the work he had done with televised sports for the ABC Network—but it was the head of ABC Sports, Roone Arledge, who took the credit. Similarly, Sidaris had done a great deal of work (including directing the football game) on *M*A*S*H* (1970), but it was director Robert Altman who took all the credit on that one. Fed up with not being given his due, Sidaris had decided to make his own movie. As he told interviewer Jeff Young, 'I had an idea for a movie starring a female detective.. a female Raymond Chandler type character that lived in LA and who solved crimes. She was named Stacey, after my eldest daughter. I cast Anne Randall in the lead. Anne was a *Playboy* centrefold [Miss May 1967]. I interviewed a few Playmates and she was the one that was the most beautiful, the most athletic and had the most spunk to carry off the role.'

The budget for *Stacey* was announced at $175,000 and the production used Sidaris's sporting connections to its advantage by shooting on location at California's famous Riverside Racetrack (as well as borrowing all of Sidaris's existing equipment). In fact, the film cost $75,000, having been financed in a 50/50 split between Sidaris and Roger Corman, though the former was less than thrilled with his new business partner, as he told interviewer Rich Rosell: 'He was a pain in the ass to be in business with—"Here's the money, find it".'

> *Stacey Hanson, race-car driving private investigator, is hired by the matriarch of the Chambers family to dig the dirt on her nephew and niece. John Chambers is a closet homosexual who is being blackmailed by the chauffeur, who is not only John's lover but his wife's as well. Pamela Chambers is under the spell of the local cult leader, who*

specializes in love-ins and wants to ensure that Pam's inheritance comes his way. When the chauffeur turns up dead, Stacey must find whodunit while simultaneously trying to avoid attempts on her own life..

Stacey is the ultimate '70s 'with it' chick: independent, armed, drives a Corvette Stingray (when not racing), lives on a boat with her pilot lover, sports big bell bottoms and never wears a bra. Anne Randall, born Barbara Burrus in September 1944, had appeared in several films (*The Split, A Time for Dying, Hell's Bloody Devils*) and TV series (*The Monkees, The Mod Squad, Night Gallery*) in the late '60s/early '70s before her two-year stint (1972-73) as a 'Hee Haw Honey' on the long-running TV variety show *Hee Haw*. She followed her first and only starring role in *Stacey* with a bit part in *Westworld* (1973) and more television like *Love American Style* and *The Rockford Files*. Randall made her last appearance in an episode of *Switch* before she, like her co-star Anitra Ford, left the acting game for good in 1977.

Sidaris was clearly a fan of Sam Peckinpah, as witness the bloody, slow-motion shootout at the racetrack in the film's final act, which also features a chase through the desert with Stacey in a racing car trying to outrun the bad guys in a chopper. Loaded with action, sex and humour, *Stacey* set the stage for what would be a long-running career of so-called 'Bullets and Babes' films for Sidaris. Utilising primarily *Playboy* and *Penthouse* models, the director, with his wife Arlene and son Christian, made a small fortune from films like *Malibu Express* (1985), *Hard Ticket to Hawaii* (1987), *Do or Die* (1991) and *Fit to Kill* (1993); the series came to an end with *Return to Savage Beach* in 1998. Andy Sidaris died of cancer in March 2007, aged 76.

Originally released in June 1973, *Stacey* was re-released by Corman in January 1975 with a new title (*Stacy and Her Gangbusters*—which dropped the 'e' from her name) and a totally revised ad campaign which took advantage of Claudia Jennings's backwoods success, *Gator Bait*. Stacey went from being 'A Very Private Detective' initially to one of the 'Law-Breaking, Gun-Toting, American Girls!' as she posed on the posters with rifle and little else.

'Good morning Southland swinging students.. it's time to pack up your beach bodies and hit the books again!'
> —Los Angeles Deejay 'The Real' Don Steele in *The Student Teachers*

'We got letters from women's organisations,' Corman told di Franco, 'saying they had seen these films and were really surprised at how good and how pro-women's lib they were. We've even been written up in a number of women's magazines on these films.' So the beat went on with more young girls and their various professional and sexual adventures. Since their *Night Call Nurses* had done so well, Julie Corman and Jonathan Kaplan were called on to turn out another entry in the diaphragms-and-dialectics genre, *The Student Teachers*.

Three rookie high school teachers—Rachel, Tracy and Jody—each find unorthodox ways of reaching their students. Rachel teaches an after-school sex education class in which the kids make their own (hilarious) VD film; Tracy tires of cleaning brushes for her art teacher lover and joins with Mickey, the kid next door, to teach photography; Jody recruits former drop-out Carnell to help out at the local halfway house. No good deed goes unchallenged, however: Rachel's class is blamed when one of the students is attacked by a rapist in a clown mask, Tracy interrupts her lover in bed with his class model and finds nude photographs taken by Mickey, and Jody finds herself in the midst of a drug ring run by Carnell's former employer.

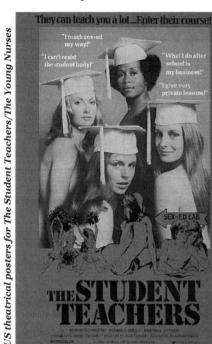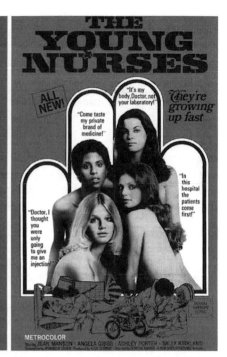

Rothman and Swartz had penned a draft of *The Student Teachers* in the Woolner days of New World, but it was rejected and Kaplan's friend Danny Opatoshu (son of actor David Opatoshu and another NYU student who had helped Kaplan on the script of *Night Call Nurses*) wrote a new version. Included in the usual exploitation highlights were two powerful and disturbing rape scenes, one in the women's locker room and the other (of Rachel) in an abandoned gymnasium. In the latter, Rachel does not resist in the hope that the rapist will not harm her (he does anyway). Afterwards, she straightens herself out, tries to clean up, drives home and immediately collapses in tears in Jody's arms. This sequence clearly bears the imprint of Julie Corman and Barbara Peeters (this time serving as second unit director), but Kaplan's treatment of the rape in the 1988 Jodie Foster hit *The Accused* shows that he, too, was just as sensitive to the destructiveness of the act.

Watching all of this, horrified, in a dingy theatre in San Francisco was a young father who had taken his family to *The Student Teachers* because he had worked on the film some time earlier. His name was Chuck Norris, World Karate Champion, who had shared a fight scene in the Roman Coliseum with Bruce Lee in the latter's *Return of the Dragon* (1972) and who ran a number of martial arts schools in southern California. When karate students had been needed for the scene in which Jody introduced Carnell to martial arts instruction at the halfway house, Norris was contacted. As he writes in his 2004 autobiography, *Against All Odds*, 'The producers told me that the movie was about a couple of teachers who were unhappy with the teaching methods in public schools, so they broke off with the system and created a different learning environment. It all sounded innocent enough, so I brought my two young sons, my brother Aaron, and about twenty other students to Inglewood.'

Norris had more or less forgotten about *The Student Nurses*, but now here he was with his wife and sons, watching the opening shot of Tracy (Brooke Mills), topless at the window of the apartment that she shares with a lover who is eagerly awaiting her in bed.. Norris' wife Dianne wanted to leave, but the karate champ was keen to wait for his big scene. 'We were constantly hiding the kids' eyes,' he writes. 'Finally our scene came on. There I was filling the screen in a gigantic close-up. Oh no, I thought, the one time I don't want to be on screen, and here I am, bigger than life!' That's show business, Chuck.. who went on from there to become one of the world's biggest action stars.

Jonathan Kaplan was to leave New World after this and direct blaxploitation films for Roger's brother Gene Corman (*The Slams*, 1973) and AIP (*Truck Turner*, 1974). He would go on to achieve great critical acclaim for *Over the Edge*, his 1979 drama of suburban juvenile delinquents, graduating to major studio films like *Heart Like a Wheel* (1983), *Project X* (1987), *The Accused* (1988), *Immediate Family* (1989) and *Unlawful Entry* (1992). His biggest successes in recent years have been in television, where he has served as a producer and director for hit shows *E. R.* and *Without a Trace*.

'When you get around to treating your nurses like human beings and your patients like people, then you give me a call.'
—Nurse Joanne (Ashley Porter) rebuking the authorities in *The Young Nurses*

With Kaplan gone, producer Julie Corman had to go searching for fresh talent. As a result, *The Young Nurses*, New World's final summer release, was a first for many behind the camera: director Clinton Kimbro (in his only outing) was actually the actor Clint Kimbrough (who had appeared in *Bloody Mama, Von Richthofen* and *Night Call Nurses*), while his rookie second-unit director was Pancho Kohner, who would produce ten Charles Bronson movies between 1976 and 1989. Likewise, newly-minted production designer Tim Kincaid was to become a specialist in direct-to-video schlock, as well as a prolific porn director (under the name of Joe Gage).

Kitty, Michelle and Joanne are nurses at La Mer Hospital in California. Kitty rescues Matt from a boating accident and becomes his lover, much to the chagrin of Matt's father who wants him to concentrate on the upcoming regatta. Michelle traces the overdose of an outpatient to a new drug called 'Quadrant' that is being pushed by Doc Haskell, her former mentor. Joanne exceeds her authority and gives an emergency transfusion to a hit-and-run victim, who later dies of scepticaemia—for which she is held responsible.

'By now New World has got its lucrative and mildly diverting formula down pat,' the *Los Angeles Times*'s Kevin Thomas said of Corman's business model. 'Cut back and forth between the exploits—sexploits might be the better word—of three nurses or stewardesses, get them out of their clothes as frequently as possible and throw in a couple of topical elements for relevance.' *The Young Nurses* was no different, though some amusement could be had spotting all the familiar faces in small roles, including director Sam Fuller (*Shock Corridor, The Naked Kiss*) as Doc Haskell, Corman stalwart Dick Miller as an indifferent cop, Allan Arbus (*M*A*S*H* psychiatrist Major Sidney Freedman) as an arrogant internist, and future Oscar nominee (*Anna*, 1987) and holistic priestess Sally Kirkland as a patient at the Women's Free Clinic where Joanne works.

'I'll make him lick the blade that cuts his throat.'
—Convict Lebras (Jim Brown) vowing vengeance in *I Escaped from Devil's Island*

The previous January, Gene Corman had entered into a deal with former football legend-turned-actor Jim Brown (*The Dirty Dozen, Slaughter*) to star in two prison

pictures, one set in period South America, the other a modern-day blaxploitation piece. The second was the aforementioned Jonathan Kaplan film *The Slams* for MGM, while the first was a co-production with brother Roger for United Artists: *I Escaped from Devil's Island*. Both ended up being released in September 1973.

I Escaped from Devil's Island was initially scheduled to be shot in Costa Rica by director Bernard Kowalski (*Night of the Blood Beast, Attack of the Giant Leeches*), but the location was changed to Acapulco in Mexico and the reins given instead to William Witney, veteran director of countless serials and TV westerns.

> *French Guyana, 1918. With the end of the war, all death sentences are commuted to life imprisonment and the prisoners are transferred to Devil's Island off the coast. Hardened convict Lebras decides to become the first man ever to escape from the island. Because of an old debt, he takes the communist Devert with him. They sail off on a raft covered in animal skins and make it to the mainland; once there, they head inland but are hunted by trackers, take refuge in a leper colony, are captured by Indians and become involved in a shootout with police at a village carnival. Ultimately, Lebras decides to return to his Indian captors (who had gifted him with a wife) while Devert sails on to Brazil.*

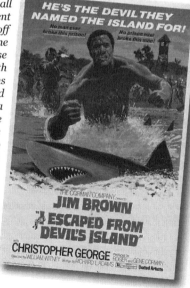

If all this sounds familiar, it should. *Devil's Island* is an outright steal from Henri Charriere's 1969 autobiographical novel *Papillon*, which, not too coincidentally, happened to be filming in Jamaica concurrently with the Corman production. Ted Richmond, producer of *Papillon*, sued the Cormans for copyright infringement but, as Roger told di Franco, his case was compromised: 'We were able to prove that there had been two previous pictures about Devil's Island plus a couple of novels and almost all of them had essentially the same story.. As a result.. the suit was dropped and never went to court.' Poetic justice prevailed, however: *Devil's Island* was barely noticed while *Papillon* (released that December), starring Steve McQueen and Dustin Hoffman, made over $50 million.

> *'I hear Li Kwei is reckless in his courage.. He is a nitwit.'*
> —'Young Dragon' Yen Ching (David Chiang) in *The Water Margin*

On July 20, 1973, one of the biggest cultural icons of all time died of a cerebral edema; he was just 32 years old. He was born Lee Jun Fan in San Francisco, but he became known the world over as Bruce Lee.

Lee had worked in Hollywood in the 1960s on TV shows like *Batman* and *The Green Hornet*, but his breakthrough came in 1971 when he went to Hong Kong to star in *The Big Boss* (aka *Fists of Fury*) for producer Raymond Chow. The film was a huge success and Lee starred in two more blockbuster hits for Chow (*The Chinese Connection, Return of the Dragon*) before returning to Hollywood to play the lead in *Enter the Dragon* for Warner Brothers. Sadly, what was to be his biggest triumph ended up being released posthumously in August 1973.

By then, however, the martial arts film which Lee almost single-handedly had put on the map was fast becoming an American movie-going phenomenon. Movies like *Chinese Hercules, Five Fingers of Death, Lady Kung Fu* (all 1973), *The Sacred Knives of Vengeance* and *The Street Fighter* (both 1974) all turned out to be big money-spinners, and Roger Corman was not one to miss out on a trend.

The biggest martial arts film producers were the Shaw brothers of Hong Kong, Run Run and Runme. Their studios were modelled on the old Hollywood system (even emulating the Warner Brothers 'shield' logo): they had their own stars, crews, and soundstages, and they controlled the distribution and exhibition of their films all over East Asia. In March 1972, the Shaws released one of their most ambitious films, *The Water Margin*, based on three chapters (66-68) of Luo Guanzhong's epic 16th century novel, a classic of Chinese literature. The brothers had in fact drawn from the novel five times previously and would adapt it again, four more times. The movie was directed by Chang Cheh, the undisputed master of Cantonese martial arts cinema, who previously had directed some 80 films for the Shaws. It also featured two of the studio's hottest young stars, David Chiang and Ti Lung, as well as Japanese actors Tetsuro Tamba and Toshio Kurosawa.

> *China, 1000 AD. The ruling Sung Dynasty is so corrupt that it inspires 'The Honorable 108', a band of outlaws who hide out on Mount Liang and dedicate themselves to ending the Dynasty's oppression. When their leader Chao Kai (Heavenly Father) is cut down by Sung militia headed by the ruthless Shih Wen Kung (Golden Spear), the 108 vow revenge. They ally themselves with Kung's noble brother, Lu Chun Yi (The Jade Unicorn) and his son Yen Ching (Young Dragon), and a series of confrontations with Kung climaxes in an epic battle on the provincial plains.*

The Water Margin is spectacularly staged and graphically bloody, something of a combination of Akira Kurosawa—whom Cheh greatly admired—and Sergio Leone (the soundtrack shamelessly apes Ennio Morricone's scores for Leone). The film features fights with arrows, swords, knives, poles, axes, spears and chains, as well as flying fists and somersaulting bodies. Huge armies with horses and banners meet on the field of battle while lovers plot, governments scheme, and brotherhood is betrayed—and upheld. It is a grand undertaking, but one that no American drive-in patron would sit through unedited.

Corman knew this when he bought *The Water Margin* and his solution was simple: 'We recut it and tightened it way down to emphasize the action,' he wrote in his autobiography. This was an understatement: Cheh's epic ran for 125 minutes; what Corman released as *Seven Blows of the Dragon* in September 1973 clocked in at 81. In addition to cutting a third of the film, Corman added an opening narration and had the Shaw Brothers film a sex scene between actors Ling Ling and Tien Ching (playing Lu Chun Yi's adulterous wife and her lover, respectively). His tampering paid off—*Seven Blows* became a drive-in hit (it initially opened with *I Escaped from Devil's Island*) that ran for several years.

'We have occasionally made cuts in films,' Corman told di Franco, 'but we always make them with the cooperation of the producer and the director. We never cut somebody else's film.' Mel Welles, Tamara Asseyev, Curtis Hanson, Oscar Williams, Ernst R von Theumer (director of *The Big Bust Out*) and now Chang Cheh begged to differ. The list would only grow larger in the years ahead.

> *'It's not bad to have pet Oms.. But all those wild Oms—they steal, they're dirty and multiply appallingly fast!'*
>
> —Racist Traag in *La Planète Sauvage*

French animator Rene Leloux began his career rather obliquely. Working in a psychiatric hospital in the 1950s, he used animation as a means of therapy for the patients. Two of the films that resulted from this strange collaboration were aired on French television and caught the attention of producer Andre Valio-Cavaglione. He felt that Leloux's unorthodox methods would mesh well with the avant garde ideas of some-time actor, illustrator and author of 'The Tenant' ('Le Locataire'), Roland Topor, and so he arranged a meeting.

Leloux and Topor teamed up for two animated shorts, *Dead Times* (1964) and *The Snails* (1965), in which they employed rostrum animation, a technique that utilises cut-outs of characters, props, and backgrounds from a variety of sources (the most famous practitioner of which was *Monty Python*'s Terry Gilliam). Valio-Cavaglione then suggested a full-length animated feature based on a science fiction novel. The novel he had in mind was 1957's *Oms en Serie* ('Oms by the Dozen') by Stefan Wul, the *nom-de-plume* of French dentist Pierre Pairault. But as there was no French animation industry to speak of, production had to be undertaken at the Jiri Trnka Studios in Prague. Although originally planned for the rostrum camera, Topor refused to take part in the animation process and the finished film was a mixture of cut-out and regular cell animation, with which the Czechs were more familiar. Production began in 1967 but came to a halt after the Russian invasion of Czechoslovakia in August 1968; it did not resume until 1971 and was curtailed by the Czech government again in 1973. In the process, four planned sequences had to be abandoned.

> *On the planet Ygam, the humanoid Traag giants rule. From the Planet Terra, they have taken the human Oms, which they keep as pets. One of the Oms, Terr, is raised by Tiwa in the Traag Grand Master's house. After learning all he can, Terr escapes and takes refuge with the wild Oms of the Big Tree. He has stolen the headphones that Tiwa used for education and is slowly bringing the other Oms up to speed. Horrified by this revelation—and the rapid Om reproduction—the Traags begin an aggressive extermination programme. Terr unites his tribe with the rival Oms of the Hollow Bush*

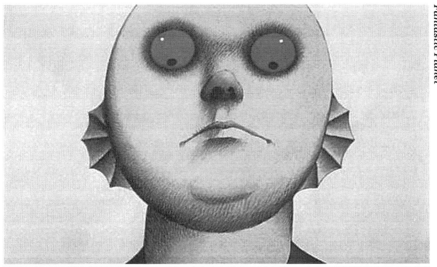

and they flee to an abandoned Traag rocket site. There they construct two rockets so they can escape persecution and fly to the so-called Strange Planet. On arrival, they discover the Traags' weakness and are able to effect reconciliation.

La Planète Sauvage ('The Savage Planet') has often been read as an allegory of the '68 Russian invasion but this is hard to sustain, given that the source-novel was written in the '50s and production on the film started a year before the Prague Spring. Its more obvious inspiration is the Book of Exodus, with Terr standing in for Moses, the Oms as the dislocated Israelites, the Traags as extraterrestrial Egyptians, and the journey to the Strange Planet being the equivalent of the flight to the Promised Land. Given that Topor was a Polish Jew who had experienced Nazi persecution, his attraction to the material is thereby obvious.

La Planète Sauvage was awarded the Special Grand Prix at the 1973 Cannes Film Festival. It was an unprecedented achievement—the first and only animated film ever to be so. Two of those who saw Leloux's film that May were Roger and Julie

Corman, who were enthralled by it and bought it on the spot for $125,000. New World dubbed it into English, changed the title to *Fantastic Planet*, and released it in December 1973.

'Highly engrossing science fiction,' said the *New York Times*. 'Disquieting, eerie and vastly imaginative,' raved the *Los Angeles Times*. 'Fascinating depth and imagination, humour and pathos underline a fine adventure story,' praised Judith Crist. 'Witty, trippy, politically and culturally subversive,' noted the *Los Angeles Weekly*. 'It should capture youthful interest, with enough workmanship and inventiveness to entice more adult audiences as well,' said *Variety*. Once again, the odd man out was the hapless Gene Siskel, who lambasted, '*Fantastic Planet* is really much more concerned with parading its grotesque line drawings of snapping lizards, jellyfish with jaws, trees that resemble modernistic floor lamps, space ships that look like hot dogs with shower heads, and a countryside strewn with small intestines..' Would that he had spent as much time watching the film as he obviously did trying to figure out what the drawings resembled.

Fortunately, the paying public saw the genius in Leloux and Topor's vision and *La Planète Sauvage* became an international success. It also served to further enhance New World's burgeoning reputation as a purveyor of fine foreign films.

'What can I do?—Find another Spartacus?'
—Frustrated Roman governor Timarchus (Daniel Vargas) in *The Arena*

New World's first release of 1974, *The Arena*, was a first in many ways. It was New World's first European co-production, filmed at Rome's Cinecitta Studios in the spring of 1973, and it was directed by first-timer Steve Carver who, like Oscar Williams before him, had come to Corman's attention via the AFI (he supposedly received uncredited help on *The Arena* from cinematographer Aristide Massaccesi, better known as porn director Joe D'Amato). It was also the first film produced by actor Mark Damon, who had starred in Corman's *House of Usher* and would go

The Arena (Pam Grier)

on to produce such international hits as *Das Boot* (1981), *The Never Ending Story* (1984) and *9½ Weeks* (1986). Finally, it was the first film to be edited by 27-year-old Joe Dante, who had been toiling away in New World's trailer department at the invitation of his friend Jon Davison, who had entered Corman's company via the Jonathan Kaplan bandwagon and became its publicity director.

In the Roman province of Brundisium, local governor Timarchus is trying to find new ways to entertain spectators at the arena. When a fight breaks out among the female slaves in his household, Timarchus decides to include women in gladiatorial combat. Two popular champions emerge—the Briton Bodicia and the Nubian Mamawi—and are pitted against each other on the promise of freedom to the winner. The two realise that this is a trick and give Timarchus a taste of his own medicine before rebelling and taking on the entire Roman army.

Pam Grier and Margaret Markov had already aped *The Defiant Ones* bit in the previous year's *Black Mama, White Mama*, but here they were again a few months later in a cut-rate feminised version of 1960's *Spartacus*. Like Timarchus, Corman had been looking for new ways to spice up the women's prison genre and had commissioned his favourite husband-and-wife writing team, the Corringtons, to come up with something different. Taking a giant leap backwards to ancient Rome not only afforded *The Arena* a different milieu but also an excuse to indulge in episodes of *bacchanalia*. The film serves as an interesting precursor to Ridley Scott's 2000 blockbuster *Gladiator*, particularly in its pairing of black and white slaves taking on the Roman Empire; things were to come full circle in 2001, when *Gladiator*'s success encouraged Roger Corman to remake *The Arena*—though this time in Russia.

Filmed side-by-side with Federico Fellini's *Amarcord*, *The Arena* gave the famed Italian director some welcome distraction, as Grier told *Horse Connection*, 'I came galloping onto his set, bareback and barefoot, wearing a leopard skin and big afro. Fellini stopped the shooting and yelled, 'My dream come true!' Little did he know it, but the incident would be an omen of things to come.

The Arena would turn out to be Grier's final film for New World. She had already been signed to a lucrative contract at AIP, where she was to star in a string of blaxploitation hits between 1973 and 1975: *Coffy, Scream Blacula Scream, Foxy Brown, Sheba Baby, Bucktown* and *Friday Foster*—on the completion of which she declared to the *Chicago Tribune*, 'Superchick is dead. I'm finished with being the black wonder woman.' After a brief run at the big time with *Drum* (1976) and *Greased Lightning* (1977), and a romance with co-star Richard Pryor, she fell into a professional slump; she had become too identified with the blaxploitation films that were no longer being made, despite her efforts to change her image. Grier had a few notable roles in the 1980s (*Fort Apache—the Bronx, Something Wicked This Way Comes*), but mostly stuck to television shows like *Miami Vice, Crime Story* and *Knots Landing*. In 1988, she was diagnosed with cancer but managed to beat the odds and put the disease into remission.

The 1990s heralded a major comeback for Grier, with her appearances in retro black films (*Posse, Original Gangstas*) and major-studio efforts (*Escape from LA, Mars Attacks!*). Her return to form was cemented in 1997, when director Quentin Tarantino (who professed to be one of her greatest admirers) cast her in the lead of *Jackie Brown*, an adaptation of Elmore Leonard's 1992 novel *Rum Punch*. Her performance as a flight attendant who gets mixed up in gun-running earned her a Golden Globe nomination. She then appeared in several flops (*Ghosts of Mars,*

Bones, The Adventures of Pluto Nash) before becoming a regular on the Showtime network's lesbian soap opera *The L Word* in 2004.

> *'We have a violent sorority here—and very strong ways of dealing with it.'*
> —Superintendent McQueen (Barbara Steele) in *Caged Heat*

New World's last women's prison picture took all of four months to shoot, edit and release (January-April 1974). However, its gestation was over 18 months, as it was first presented to Corman by Jonathan Demme in 1972 as the vehicle for his directorial debut. 'Soon after they wrapped [*The Hot Box*],' Corman recalled, 'Demme asked if he could direct a feature.. "Sure," I said, "come up with a women-in-prison picture." Demme spent a year working on the script [initially known as *Renegade Women*], getting a lot of guidance from Frances Doel. I decided not to finance the project because the cycle had peaked.. [Demme] got his own financing—$180,000—and I agreed to distribute the film.'

The financing came from a company called Artists Entertainment Complex, headed by Martin Bregman and Sam Gelfman, who stipulated that the picture had to be made in the States. Demme's wife Evelyn Purcell served as producer and the rookie director pulled off something a casting coup by persuading horror film icon Barbara Steele (who had co-starred of Corman's *Pit and the Pendulum* in 1961) to appear in her first feature since 1968. He also managed to squeeze in cameos from his former partner Joe Viola and the entire (George) Armitage family.

> *For drug-dealing and attempted murder, Jacqueline Wilson is incarcerated in the Connerville Institute for Women. The prison is filled with neurotics and hard cases and presided over by the crippled, sexually-frustrated Superintendent McQueen. Connerville employs a technique called 'CPT'—Corrective Physical Therapy—whereby troublesome inmates are involuntarily shocked, drugged and ultimately lobotomised. When Maggie, the toughest convict, escapes from work detail, Jackie joins her and the two steal a prison truck and a police car and make their getaway. They hook up with Maggie's wrestler friend Crazy Alice and decide to return to Connerville to rescue their friends from McQueen and her evil compatriot, Doctor Randolph.*

'This was before *One Flew Over the Cuckoo's Nest* [1975] came out,' Demme informed *Rolling Stone*. 'I thought, it may only be showing in drive-ins, but it shows what's going on in prisons. We are lobotomising patients to make them non-violent.' It was not the exposé element of the film, however, that encouraged the *Los Angeles Times*'s Kevin Thomas to lavish praise on what Corman had now retitled *Caged Heat*: 'With wit, style and unflagging verve, writer-director Jonathan Demme.. sends up the genre while still giving the mindless action fan his money's worth.' Thomas continued in the same vein: 'Demme evokes the rich, ironically but compassionately observed atmosphere of a Robert Altman film—and even throws in some well-done Felliniesque dream sequences for good measure.' Dreaming of a priest with a speculum did indeed invoke Fellini, but to say that a film full of gratuitous shower scenes, ridiculous shoot-outs, and a private wrestling clinic known as the Academy of Sexual Satisfaction was worthy of Altman was pushing things a little far.

Fifth-billed in *Caged Heat* was Cheryl 'Rainbeaux' Smith, who was to become a casualty of Hollywood's Boulevard of Broken Dreams. Born Cheryl Lynn Smith in June 1955, she acquired her nickname by hanging out at the Rainbow Bar and Grill in Los Angeles, a popular spot for musicians. Her acting career began at age 15, when she starred in the short film *The Birth of Aphrodite* (1971). From there, she spent the rest of the decade alternately starring in exploitation films (*Lemora the Lady*

Caged Heat (Barbara Steele)

Dracula, The Swinging Cheerleaders, The Pom Pom Girls) and softcore porn (*Video Vixens, Cinderella, Fantasm Comes Again*), and playing small roles in major studio pictures (*Phantom of the Paradise, Farewell My Lovely, The Choirboys*). She worked for Demme again in 1980 on his *Melvin and Howard* and appeared as Veronica Lake in the Steve Martin vehicle *Dead Men Don't Wear Plaid* (1982) before making her final screen appearance in Robert Mandel's drama, *Independence Day* (1983).

In 1975, Smith became involved with a rock musician who made her pregnant and got her hooked on heroin. Thus began a nearly 30-year struggle that saw her serve two prison sentences, lose custody of her son, destroy her career and become part of Los Angeles's large homeless population. In October 2002, at the age of 47, Cheryl Smith died of complications from hepatitis, brought on by her years of drug abuse. To many fans, she was the cheerleader version of Marilyn Monroe—right down to the tragic ending.

'I'm handled to train anything.'
—Tongue-tied nurse Sandy (Candice Rialson) in *Candy Stripe Nurses*

Candy Stripe Nurses was the first of four New World appearances by Cheryl Smith contemporary, 22-year-old Candice Ann Rialson, who was also to claim a special place in the hearts of exploitation fans. She had debuted as a bikini girl in *The Gay Deceivers* (1969) before her first credited role in Raphael Nussbaum's *Pets* (1974). In addition to her New World films (which would include *Summer*

65

School Teachers, Hollywood Boulevard and *Moonshine County Express*), Rialson appeared in other exploitation flicks, including a contemporary *Big Bad Mama* rip-off called *Mama's Dirty Girls* (1974) and the infamous *Chatterbox* (1977), in which she played a woman with a singing vagina. Like Smith, Rialson had small roles in major studio films (*The Eiger Sanction, Silent Movie, Logan's Run*) and showed up in various TV movies (*The Girl on the Late, Late Show, The Sam Sheppard Murder Case*) and series (*Shaft, Maude, Fantasy Island*) throughout the '70s. Her last performance was a bit part in the conspiracy thriller *Winter Kills* in 1979; after that, she retired from the business. She contracted liver disease and died in March 2006, aged 54.

US theatrical poster for Candy Stripe Nurses

At Oakwood Hospital, three 'candy stripe' (volunteer) nurses become involved with three different men. Marisa meets Carlos, who was shot in a gas station holdup and is falsely accused of being one of the robbers, Dianne meets Cliff, a star college basketball player who is being fed speed by one of Oakwood's doctors, and Sandy meets Owen Boles, an arrogant, impotent English rock star. Marisa tries to prove Carlos' innocence, Dianne tries to expose the malpractice and Sandy tries to resolve Owen's sexual dysfunction.

Candy Stripe Nurses was Julie Corman's third and final nurses film (though not New World's) but she felt that she had found her niche, as she told Gregory, 'I kept on producing because I realised that it was solving problems, my strong suit.' Another of her strong suits was finding untested filmmakers, like *Candy Stripe*'s Allan Holleb, a recent UCLA graduate. 'Looking at student films is my thing.. From a student film you can tell how the director works with actors and sets up shots.'

Corman was fortunate to have Barbara Peeters playing back-up on her films (she again served as second unit director on *Candy Stripe Nurses*). While Peeters shared Julie Corman's feminist sensibilities, she also knew the score as far as New World went: 'As long as you open big and close big and try to resolve three stories in the end, Roger lets you do what you want,' she told the *Los Angeles Times*. 'Just be sure you put in either a sex scene or an action sequence every 15 minutes.'

In July 1974, the *Hollywood Reporter*'s Hank Grant was the first to announce that Roger Corman had just secured the rights to distribute Fellini's *Amarcord* in America. Grant also reported that Corman and Fellini were mulling over a possible five-picture deal, to include a new version of *Casanova* with Jack Nicholson. Nothing came of this, however, and Fellini had to go through three other producers (including Dino De Laurentiis) before finally putting his *Casanova* (starring Donald Sutherland) before the cameras in the fall of 1975.

Acquiring *Amarcord* was not like acquiring *Cries and Whispers*. Unlike that of Bergman, Fellini's previous two films—*Satyricon* (1969) and *Roma* (1972)—were both successful and were distributed by United Artists. *Amarcord* itself was being distributed by Warner Brothers in Italy. 'The prices they were asking [for *Amarcord* at Cannes] were not realistic,' Frank Moreno told the *Los Angeles Times*. 'They wanted $400,000. We were prepared to pay $250,000 at the time but they still insisted on $400,000.' A compromise was reached once Fellini and Corman intervened. As Barbara Boyle said in Corman's autobiography, 'People wanted to go with us because of Roger's renown as a filmmaker in Europe.. Just to be with Corman's New World was perceived as a major plus.' The fact that it was a New World film which gave Fellini an eyeful of Pam Grier might also have helped.

A year in the life of a small Italian coastal town in the 1930s, as only Fellini could remember it, *Amarcord* was released in September 1974 and was a huge success. After premiering with the highest opening week in the history of New York's Plaza Theater, the film went on to take over $2 million in rentals, was lavished with critical acclaim, and was nominated for three Oscars, winning for Best Foreign Film. New World's schizophrenic strategy (exploitation and art) was clearly paying off.

> *'We ain't ever gonna be poor again...I swear to God!'*
> —Model provider Wilma McClatchie (Angie Dickinson) in *Big Bad Mama*

While it was continuing to rise in critical esteem, New World was also moving up in terms of its budgets. Corman was spending close to a half-million dollars on his latest production, *Big Bad Mama*, featuring Angie Dickinson, William Shatner and Tom Skerritt. The first New World film that he personally produced (probably because of the budget involved), *Big Bad Mama* was essentially a remake of *Bloody Mama*, only this time 'Mama' had daughters in tow instead of sons. After reading innumerable scripts for Corman, Frances Doel had taken a crack at writing one but found it less than rewarding, as she revealed in Corman's autobiography: 'I thought my draft was so bad and embarrassing that I pretended that Roger had given the script to one of our young film students who, I lamented so convincingly, had really mucked it up.' It was left to William Norton, scripter of *The McKenzie Break* (1970) and *The Hunting Party* (1971) to set things to rights. 'I urged Bill to feel free to totally revise it,' Doel said.

> *Paradise Texas, 1932. Wilma McClatchie and her two daughters, Billy Jean and Polly, are mixed up in a bank robbery in which they end up stealing both the money and the robber, Fred Diller. Their band is joined by Kentucky con man William J Baxter and they proceed to rob cash offices at a racetrack and an oilfield. Baxter replaces Diller as Wilma's lover, and the latter sleeps with both daughters in revenge and makes Polly pregnant. After robbing a wealthy industrialist, Wilma hatches a plot to kidnap the man's daughter and hold her for a $1 million ransom. Things begin to go awry when Baxter quits the gang and is arrested by the FBI. He leads the Feds to the gang's hide-out and a shootout ensues, from which only the daughters escape alive.*

Big Bad Mama became New World's biggest success to date (amassing almost $4 million in rentals), largely on the strength of Angie Dickinson's explicit sex scenes with Shatner and Skerritt. While neither Dickinson nor Skerritt had problems performing in the buff, 'Captain Kirk' did, as director Steve Carver recounted to *Shock Cinema*: 'Angie comes on the set and I'm going to clear it but she says, "No, I'm not shy and they're all nice people." OK, fine. Bill comes on and says, "You're not going to have all these people here are you?" I say we can clear it if he wants. So he goes and talks to Angie and I go over and Angie's laughing and says, "Look, Bill's got tape all over himself!" And he did. Angie says, "Bill, that's ridiculous", and

Big Bad Mama (Angie Dickinson)

she went in on him. Bill said he wouldn't do it if the people are here. Angie said *she* would and took off her robe right there. So Bill gave in and did it and took off the tape. But when doing coverage, it got progressively awkward because Bill's method, which wasn't directable, of coming on to Angie was not really sexy or believable and Angie would have to change the situation.'

When the film premiered at the AFI in July 1974, Dickinson's then-husband, composer Burt Bacharach, appeared to take his wife's on-screen cavortings and foul mouth in his stride, telling columnist Dorothy Manners, 'It's different from anything she's ever done. It's wild and different and gives her a character she's never played before. She's an actress, after all.' Dickinson's career received a big boost from all the publicity, and she found small-screen fame that fall when her TV show *Police Woman* premiered and ran for four seasons.

Critical opinion was divided, with *Variety* lamenting, 'The sheer predictability of all elements of this Roger Corman venture wipes out any substantive interest almost from the start, leaving a patina of gimmicks and style to carry the freight.' The *Los Angeles Times* thought differently, however: 'Unabashedly an exploitation picture with all the sex and violence an R rating can sustain, *Big Bad Mama* is nonetheless pretty good entertainment, lowdown and rambunctious.' The only opinion that mattered to Corman was the public's, and *Mama*'s bonanza led him to cast around for an immediate follow-up.

'Anything that can fight to the death and not utter a sound, well..'
—Professional cockfighter Frank Mansfield (Warren Oates) in *Cockfighter*

From the thrill of victory with *Big Bad Mama* came the agony of defeat with *Cockfighter*. Reuniting director Monte Hellman and star Warren Oates, who had worked together on *The Shooting* (1967) and *Two Lane Blacktop*, the film was based on Charles Willeford's 1972 novel, which tells the story of Frank Mansfield, a professional 'cockfighter' who has not uttered a word in three years—not because he cannot, but because he has chosen muteness as a way to avoid distractions in

Cockfighter (Warren Oates)

69

his quest for the ultimate prize: the Cockfighter of the Year medal. Pursuing his goal is not easy, however, as Frank sees his last remaining cock killed by 'Little David' owned by rich, arrogant Jack Burke, and also loses his car, mobile home, and girlfriend in a bet with Burke. The long road back begins with trying to collect old debts—including selling-off of the family farm from under the nose of Frank's ne'er-do-well brother—as well as briefly reuniting with his fiancée of eight years. Frank buys 'Icarus' from an old-time referee and forms a partnership with his ex-Madison Avenue neighbour, Omar Baradinsky. Together they strike out afresh on the cockfighting circuit, hoping to work their way to the Southern Cockfighting Tournament and a rematch with Little David.

In buying the rights to Willeford's novel, Corman had also committed to the author writing his own screenplay. Not surprisingly, it followed the book closely, though, as Willeford wrote in *Film Quarterly*, 'Writing a screenplay for the first time is like having a second haemorrhoid operation: it is not something I would willingly do again.' Willeford's first draft was 240 pages in length; his final draft was half that. During the scripting stage, *Cockfighter* went from being a film that Corman himself thought to direct to one that put Hellman in the director's chair. 'As a professional writer, I have worked with a good many different editors,' wrote Willeford, 'but never with anyone quite like Roger Corman..'

Willeford's script still needed paring down, and Hellman brought in novelist Earl MacRauch (*Arkansas Adios, Dirty Pictures from the Prom*) to do a re-write (MacRauch would go on to write the scripts for Scorsese's musical *New York, New York* in 1977 and the cult fantasy *The Adventures of Buckaroo Banzai* in 1984). From there, things moved fast, as Hellman told *Jump Cut*: 'I spent three weeks in Georgia before we started to shoot, and we spent four weeks shooting, and we spent an extremely short time editing—it was very fast. The editor [Lewis Teague] and I worked on it in separate cutting rooms so that he cut half the picture and I cut half the picture.'

According to Corman's autobiography, that was not the extent of Teague's involvement with the film, however. Corman wrote, 'Monte shot a good film.. but he pulled away from the action, the bloody stuff, and we never got the graphic close-ups that we should have had. I knew we'd have to shoot them second unit later.. Teague volunteered.. He and a cameraman had to go to Arizona, one of the states, like Georgia, where cockfighting is legal.. His stuff was so good, with such bloody close-ups of the action, that we had to cut back on it in the final cut.'

For his part, Hellman was more concerned with the cheap crew that Corman had hired than with the film's roosters tearing each other apart. As he told *Jump Cut*, 'They were really the most inexperienced crew that we could have had. They were fresh out of film school, and some of them were just incompetent.. We had less time to shoot because of the inefficiency of the crew. On a four-week schedule you have to be pretty damn efficient, and if you're losing two hours a day because of fuck-ups, that's a lot of time to lose.' To his credit, Corman *did* hire brilliant Spanish cinematographer Nestor Almendros.

The picture premiered in Georgia in August 1974 and immediately bit the dust. 'In Georgia it turns out that cockfighting is an embarrassment,' Joe Dante said in Corman's autobiography. 'It's like *child molesting*. It's not something people talk about. So no one goes to the movie. It gets terrible reviews and it's a disaster.' Corman thought at first that it was the title which was putting people off, so he promptly tried out two alternatives—*Wild Drifter* and *Gamblin' Man*. Neither spelled more dollars at the box office. Corman then conferred with his editors and decided on a rather disingenuous course of action, as Teague told the *Los Angeles Weekly*: 'I had a call from Roger saying, "We made a mistake. People in the South do not want to see cockfighting. We're going to change the title and make a new trailer. I want you to go through the footage and find every shot of sex and violence that you can." I said, "Roger, Monte didn't shoot any sex and violence." Roger said, "Hmmmm, I don't care where you get it." Allan [Arkush] and Joe Dante were cutting the trailer, so Roger said, "Give them the footage." I went through all these old nurses films and what-not and gave Joe and Allan all this footage of nurses' tits and police cars careening around corners. I called Roger back and I said, "Roger, I don't think it's right to put this footage in the trailer if it's not in the movie." He said, 'You're right, Lewis. Put it in the movie!' So, in that version [now entitled *Born to Kill*], Warren Oates falls asleep and dreams about student nurses.'

Unfortunately, *Born to Kill*, released in early 1975, ran straight into a brewing controversy over animal cruelty in films. That summer, both the *New York Times* and the *Chicago Tribune* had run articles decrying the inhumane treatment of animals in such recent films as *Bite the Bullet*, *The Day of the Locust* (which also featured cockfighting) and *The Wind and the Lion*. When she saw *Born to Kill*, *Tribune* critic Linda Winer wrote, 'Snipers I could have accepted. Even murdering bikers. But *Born to Kill* is an entire movie about killer chickens—which isn't funny a bit.' *Variety* called it 'an offbeat slice of grotesque Americana.. too slowly and cryptically developed to have much appeal.'

Even the usually reliable Kevin Thomas, while moved to call Oates's silent performance 'surely one of his finest,' could not come to grips with the material: 'The grisly sport itself is off-putting in the extreme, and there is not finally enough substance to sustain Hellman's relentlessly austere style and strong existentialist vision.' Aside from the gruesomeness of the cockfighting (which he did not shoot), Hellman felt that there was another reason why *Cockfighter* turned people off: 'We had a problem that was built into the script where the story didn't really get started until about forty minutes into it.. Consequently, everything that happened before that point seems slow.'

> *'I have it on very good authority that the world is coming to an end. I thought I'd go home and watch it on television.'*
> —Reluctant saviour Jerry Cornelius (Jon Finch) in *The Final Programme*

In the early-to-mid 1960s, writers like Brian Aldiss (*The Dark Light Years*), J G Ballard (*The Voices of Time*) and Harlan Ellison (*I Have No Mouth and I Must Scream*) stood at the forefront of a new wave in literary science fiction and fantasy. Standing alongside them was Michael Moorcock who, in 1968 at the age of 26, began a quartet of novels that over the next decade would chronicle the adventures of one of the genre's genuine anti-heroes: Jerry Cornelius. A Nobel-prize winning physicist, electric guitarist, mod, ascetic and hedonist, Cornelius was the very embodiment of the 'swinging' sixties. Cornelius had his first adventure in *The Final Programme*, in which he joins with a group of scientists and mercenaries led by the literal man-eater Miss Brunner to assault the fortress chateau of Cornelius's late father. Brunner's group wants a microfilm that holds the metaphysical secrets of Cornelius senior; Jerry wants to kill his drug-addicted brother Frank and rescue his strung-out sister Catherine, with whom he has had an incestuous affair. The mission is a total failure—Frank escapes with the microfilm and only Jerry and Brunner survive. They manage to track Frank to a vast cavern in Lapland, site of an old Nazi atomic research program, where they kill him and recover the film. With rockets and nuclear materials still at the site, Brunner is able to blackmail Europe's capitals into funding an army of scientists and technicians and, through the Cornelius secrets, she masterminds the creation of DUEL—a supercomputer. DUEL will synthesize the sum total of mankind's knowledge and transmit it into a single being, an hermaphrodite which will herald the beginning of a new era in evolution. Jerry and Brunner fuse together to become said superbeing—known as 'Cornelius Brunner'—which leads the populations of Europe to a mass drowning in the Atlantic..

The screen rights to *The Final Programme* had been acquired by Goodtimes Enterprises, a UK production company headed by David Puttnam, Roy Baird and Sandy Lieberson, which had made *Performance* (1970) with Mick Jagger and *The Pied Piper* (1972) with Donovan. In 1972, they approached Robert Fuest, who was enjoying great commercial success with his remake of *Wuthering Heights* and his *Dr Phibes* films (all for AIP), about directing a film version of Moorcock's book. 'It seemed to me that, having done *Phibes*,' Fuest told *Cinefantastique*, 'I didn't want to jump right into another horror film. Yet I wanted to do a film which extended the fantasy that was a prerequisite of the *Phibes* films and *Final Programme* seemed to possess all the necessary elements.'

Fuest was handed a 286-page script that Moorcock had written and he could make neither head nor tail of it. Subsequent drafts from other writers proved no better. Frustrated, and with time closing in on the proposed January 1973 start-date, he decided to write his own screenplay. In the meantime, rising young star Jon Finch (Polanski's *Macbeth*, Hitchcock's *Frenzy*) was cast as Jerry Cornelius, despite Fuest's preference for Timothy Dalton, who had played Heathcliff in the director's *Wuthering Heights*. 'The script was a very good compromise between what Michael Moorcock wanted and what [distributor] EMI wanted,' Finch told *Cinefantastique*. 'We altered Cornelius quite considerably so that he wouldn't be as esoteric as he is in the novels.. Moorcock isn't terribly satisfied. He feels the film is too commercial and that his books have been sold out in some way.' To film Moorcock's novel literally would have been prohibitively costly; Fuest's script is reasonably faithful to both the plot and the spirit of Cornelius's first outing. Fuest also handled the production design of the film, including a futuristic casino (where nuns play slot machines), the modernistic Cornelius mansion, a combination restaurant/mud-wrestling arena and the Lapland Nazi submarine base.

The film received some favourable reviews on its release in October 1973, including those of the *Daily Mirror* ('A film that could well become a cult') and *The Observer* ('An unqualified success'). But EMI marketed it inexplicably as an exploitation film (putting it on a double-bill with the softcore *Intimate Confessions of a Chinese Courtesan*) and effectively killed its chances of finding the more sophisticated audience for whom it was intended. 'The distributors didn't know what to do with this film,' Finch said in *Shock Cinema*. 'They didn't understand it.. We were going to do three of these Cornelius films. But we only did the one, because it was such a flop.'

'It falls between two schools,' Moorcock opined in *Cinefantastique*. 'Fuest's direction is shoddy and thick.. The film's performances are patchy, again the director's fault. I liked much of the casting, however.' He then put a caveat on any proposed sequel: 'It will only be made if I have more control over its realisation.' How must he have felt when he saw what Amicus did to his adaptation of Edgar Rice Burroughs's 1918 novel *The Land That Time Forgot*?

Into this dispute came Roger Corman, who, in typical fashion, decided that the best way to improve the film was to cut 13 minutes out of it, turning a tight 89-minute fantasy into an abbreviated, 76-minute pastiche. ('It was cut to rat-shit for its American release,' Finch told *Shock Cinema*.) Not only did Corman eliminate

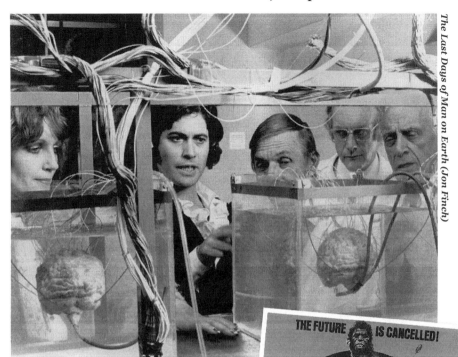

The Last Days of Man on Earth (Jon Finch)

all but a couple of minutes of Sterling Hayden's cameo as Major Wrongway Lindbergh but he also severely shortened the scenes in which Miss Brunner (Jenny Runacre) *explains* 'The Final Programme', first to the assembled scientists and then to Cornelius himself. He then decided, no doubt correctly, that *The Final Programme* was too esoteric a title for American audiences and had it changed to the more urgent *The Last Days of Man on Earth*.

Unfortunately, Corman was no more adept at handling the film than EMI had been. A case in point was its Los Angeles release in October 1975, more than a year after its American premiere in August 1974. *Last Days* had gained some good notices in publications as varied as *Time* ('A giddy, spectacular and sometimes quite funny fantasy') and *Cinefantastique* ('Fuest's film is most certainly the best science fiction fantasy film to appear since *2001*'), and it received a rave in the *Los Angeles Times* as well ('Savagely witty, supremely stylish and wildly imaginative'). On the strength of these, New World booked it for a limited run at an art theatre, where its high-brow advertising claimed, 'The Reality of *A Clockwork Orange*, The Infinity of *2001*'. It died a quick death, before returning in December as a mass-market drive-in piece on a double-bill with *Death Race 2000*. Little wonder that Kevin Thomas was moved to write, 'Far too sophisticated for an exploitation release and too far out

73

for a traditional foreign film presentation.. [*Last Days*] nonetheless surely deserves to be accessible to a wide audience.' It never was.

> *'Don't ever advertise what you can't produce!'*
> —'Superstud' Reno (Tim Taylor) in *Tender Loving Care*

New World's final release of 1974 came in October; it was also the company's last 'nurses' film. *Tender Loving Care* had been produced independently some 18 months earlier by the duo of writer/director Don Edmonds and Japanese former actress Chako van Leeuwen (née Hisako Tsukuba). By now, New World's 'nurses' formula was so familiar that they could outsource it to other producers, although in doing so the company apparently wished to remain anonymous. The movie was credited as being 'A Filmgroup Picture'.

> *Karen, a new nurse in town, moves in with two other nurses—Tracy and Lynn. Tracy is stealing drugs for her boyfriend David, a speed-freak resident, while Lynn becomes involved with Jackie, an injured boxer who has lost his nerve. Wasting no time, Karen starts dating 'Superstud' Reno, a motorcross racer who turns out to be a swinger, then opts for the conventional route with Ed, a handsome blonde doctor, who ends up dying in her arms.*

The Edmonds/van Leeuwen effort made a perfect *fin-de-siècle* entry by being essentially a patchwork of elements from all that had gone before. Though it did provide a welcome respite from the now overly-familiar women's lib and minority 'issues' sub-texts, the setting, characters and drama were all vintage New World. There are three nurses, two white and one ethnic, who co-habit. The first becomes involved with a no-good waster and then with a doctor—who is killed. The second has a junkie boyfriend and is raped by a blackmailing orderly; the mob guns down both she *and* her beau. The boyfriend of the third is recruited by a pusher, but she is able to save him from a life of crime. And everyone gets naked—frequently.

Where *Tender Loving Care* manages to rise above and become, almost by default, the best of the post-*Student Nurses* movies is that, unlike the 'nurses' in other New World movies, Karen, Tracy and Lynn are actually seen to *work* in the hospital. They are present in the emergency room helping to resuscitate flat-liners and assisting in bloody operations to save shotgun victims. They are there when patients die. They do not have the time to 'challenge the system' or 'fight the administration', because they are too busy working in the real world of medicine. The movie's final scene sums it up: her nurse's uniform stained with the blood of her dead lover, Karen is led away by Lynn and Jackie as the intercom rattles with paging-calls for nurses and doctors. No matter what the tragedy, the daily grind of the hospital goes on.

> *'You want it black—you got it black!'*
> —Diana 'TNT' Jackson (Jeannie Bell), turning out the lights in *TNT Jackson*

Actor Dick Miller, born Richard Miller in the Bronx in 1928, had been with Roger Corman almost since the beginning. Starting with *Apache Woman* in 1955 and continuing through *Big Bad Mama*, Miller had played supporting roles in no less than 30 Corman and New World films, which does not include his numerous appearances in other films (usually for AIP) and television shows. Beginning in 1970, Miller had begun to branch out, writing first draft scripts for the western *Four Rode Out* and the Jerry Lewis comedy *Which Way to the Front?*

After the huge success of *Cleopatra Jones* in 1973 (which featured model Tamara Dobson as a super-soul sister DEA agent kicking butt), and Pam Grier's *Foxy Brown* in 1974, Corman wanted his own sassy black heroine. He went to Frances Doel, and the two came up with a name for the character—Diana 'TNT' Jackson—and a quickie draft. Aware of his new-found screenwriting credentials, Corman hired Miller to write the screenplay for *TNT Jackson*. What happened next almost ended their 20-year friendship.

Corman was less than enthused by Miller's effort. According to Beverly Gray's excellent *Roger Corman: An Unauthorised Biography of the Godfather of Indie Filmmaking* (2000), a meeting between the two quickly dissolved into a shouting match that ended with Miller telling Corman what he could do with the script and Corman venting his frustration in turn on an innocent table-lamp. Needless to say, Miller was off the picture; the script was rewritten by actor Ken Metcalfe, who had appeared in several of New World's Filipino films, as he would in this.

US theatrical poster for TNT Jackson

In Hong Kong's notorious Yellow District, Diana 'TNT' Jackson is searching for her brother who, unbeknown to her, has been murdered by a drug cartel. She meets Joe, a nightclub owner, and with his contacts is able to infiltrate the organisation of crime lord Sid. Sid has been having problems: his heroin shipments are being ripped off and he is desperate to find the traitor responsible. Diana becomes the lover of Sid's enforcer, Charlie, who turns out to be the one in business for himself. Sid's problems mount when he discovers that his moll is a narc who has been trying to set up a bust. It seems that everyone wants a piece of Sid's hide, not least TNT Jackson.

The title role of *TNT Jackson* went to 31-year-old Jeannie Bell, *Playboy*'s Playmate of the Month for October 1969 and veteran of such blaxploitation films as *Melinda, Trouble Man, Black Gunn* (all 1972) and *Three the Hard Way* (1974); Bell had also appeared in Scorsese's *Mean Streets* (1973). However, the kung fu credentials required of the character were somewhat lacking. To make up for this, New World publicity director Jon Davison bestowed upon her the purely fictitious 'Ebony Fist Award'. But the Ebony Fist did not make Bell any more adept at the martial arts and producer/director Cirio Santiago was forced to enhance her fight scenes with jump-cuts, fast-motion and an obvious stunt double—though she did earn a place in cinema history with the first topless kung fu fight ever captured on celluloid. (Santiago got double value from Bell by shooting a companion piece—*Dynamite Wong and TNT Jackson*—simultaneously for the Filipino market.)

TNT Jackson would be a washout as a film were it not for the performance of 22-year-old Stan Shaw as Charlie, Sid's enforcer and secret competitor. One of the coolest villains ever to appear in blaxploitation, Chicagoan Shaw had a legitimate karate background in addition to having performed on Broadway. He would go on to a prosperous career with roles in *Rocky* (1976), *The Boys in Company C* (1978), *Roots: The Next Generations* (1979), *Billionaire Boys Club* (1987), *Harlem Nights* (1989), *Rising Sun* (1993) and *Snake Eyes* (1998). He would also make countless guest appearances on various TV shows, all the way from *Starsky and Hutch* in 1977 to *The X Files* in 2003.

Shaw or no, the critics were unimpressed with *TNT Jackson*. 'Dick Miller and Ken Metcalfe have created humourless, bitter characters who relate by fighting and killing. The script is excessively racist,' raged the *Los Angeles Times*. *Variety* was even more to the point: 'Bone-headed black chop-socky pic for grind houses.' Audiences did not seem to be similarly perturbed, and New World's first release of 1975 earned $1.3 million in rentals.

Running as second feature to *TNT Jackson* (as it had with *The Arena* and *Caged Heat*) was Melvin Van Peebles' *Sweet Sweetback* (minus his *Baadasssss Song*), which New World had acquired for re-release from Jerry Gross' Cinemation Industries. Corman's company cut *Sweetback* down from an X to an R rating, and sub-let the picture for the better part of two years.

> *'The only reason to turn her on was to turn her out.'*
> —Pragmatic pimp Irv (Paul Pompian) in *Street Girls*

In the dead of winter 1974, three men—Jeff Begun, Michael Miller and Paul Pompian—formed their own company (BMP Productions), raised $50,000, and shot a 16mm exploitation film called *Street Girls* in just six days in Eugene, Oregon. Miller had been a director of improvisational comedy with Chicago's Second City and San Francisco's The Committee; he had subsequently broken into filmmaking the old-fashioned way—by making a $12,000 porn film called *Teenage Fantasies* in 1971, featuring 'adult' star Rene Bond.

Miller co-wrote the script for *Street Girls* with one Barry Levinson, a comedy writer who had turned out sketches for the Carol Burnett, Tim Conway and Marty Feldman TV shows. The plot of the film was basically a steal from *Joe* (1970), with a concerned father trying to find his dropout daughter and encountering a whole seedy subculture which he never knew existed. Set mainly in a topless bar, Miller told *Film Comment*, 'I figured we'd try to get more tits per square inch than any other film and try to make it on the drive-in route. But it had too many tits per square inch and it was a little too tough.'

'Corman was the last distributor to see it,' Miller continued. 'He liked it and said he'd go with it. I don't think most of his people even liked it.' The film had to be cut for an 'R' rating, had trouble obtaining bookings in early 1975, and ended up featuring on triple bills (with other New World films like *The Arousers* and *Cover Girl Models*) for several years. One of the few who saw it was Charles Champlin, chief film critic of the *Los Angeles Times*. In a review entitled 'Cheesecake With Crumb of Dignity,' Champlin wrote, '*Street Girls* is a low, low budget, very, very quickie exploitation flick, soft-core and softheaded. The surprise and the slight exasperation is that it has a solid, sleety sense of place.. and two or three effective and attractive performances all but lost amid the amateurish other work.' Champlin's observation about Miller would be prophetic: 'It is clear that director Michael Miller had higher hopes than could be delivered and that he may well have better luck next time.'

Angel Anderson's parents think that she is going to college at the University of Oregon. She is not—she is a stripper involved in a lesbian affair with fellow dancer Sally, who is also a hooker. When Angel tires of Sally's side-line, she moves in with club bouncer Mario, but that is when her real problems begin. Club manager Irv wants Angel for his stable of prostitutes and has Mario hook her on heroin. Sven Anderson arrives in town in search of his daughter. Angel is now a virtual prisoner of Irv and Mario, who keep her on smack and only allow her out to turn tricks. Meanwhile, Sven is getting the runaround from everyone except Jimmy, the club's bartender, who has a change of heart and leads Sven to the strung-out wreck that is Angel.

While it is indeed amateurish, *Street Girls* nonetheless portrays the worlds of striptease and prostitution in a very raw, realistic way. There is wall-to-wall nudity in the picture, but none of it is erotic or titillating, nor is it intended to be. The dancers, for the most part, are awkward and embarrassed, while the male patrons are bored and crude. The world that Angel, Sally and the rest inhabit is one where men are users, abusers, pushers, perverts, or slobs—from the club manager to the bouncer to Angel's first 'trick', who gives her a pair of goggles and pushes her into the bathroom so that he can urinate on her. In many ways, *Street Girls* is far more effective than Paul Schrader's very similar *Hardcore*, which came four years later.

The film did little business, but Corman was impressed enough with *Street Girls* to give Miller a second chance. The director called his next proposed feature *Uptown Ladies*, in which he intended to focus upon, as he put it, 'the whores in Washington DC, who are servicing the senators and kings, a real international story with that funky street title. It's about Jacqueline Kennedy; it's about pussy brokering.'

Levinson, who was also assistant cameraman on *Street Girls*, went back to writing comedy, including two scripts for Mel Brooks (*Silent Movie, High Anxiety*). He would go on to become the celebrated writer/director of such films as *And Justice For All* (1979), *Diner* (1982), *The Natural* (1984), *Good Morning Vietnam* (1987), *Rain Man* (1988), *Sleepers* (1996) and *Wag the Dog* (1997). He would also produce the critically-acclaimed TV shows *Homicide* and *Oz* between 1993 and 1999.

In the early spring of 1975, New World announced its upcoming slate, which included *Big Bad Mama II* (to star Cloris Leachman), *Darktown Strutters, Death Race 2000, Fantastic Models Inc., Summer School Teachers* and the Japanese import *Tidal Wave*. Corman also announced that he had secured the American rights to the 1974 Australian film *The Cars That Ate Paris*. Despite its hokey title, this early work of writer/director Peter Weir (*Witness, The Truman Show*) centred on the small town of Paris in the Australian outback, whose entire economy is built around causing car crashes and stealing the valuables of the victims. For whatever reason—possibly because it was too similar in theme to the upcoming *Death Race*—Corman elected not to release the film and sold it instead to distributor New Line Cinema. New Line, in turn, cut it by almost 20 minutes, retitled it *The Cars That Eat People*, and released it as a straight exploitation piece in June 1976.

'*Now you know who owns this fucking town.*'
　　—Al Capone (Ben Gazzara), guaranteeing Chicago a free and fair election in *Capone*

Not surprisingly, the major studios in Hollywood had started to take notice of Roger Corman's highly profitable operation. In mid-1974, 20th Century-Fox,

Capone

for whom Corman had produced and directed *The St Valentine's Day Massacre* in 1967, came calling with an offer too good for him to refuse. '[Fox] wanted a series of films budgeted at about a million dollars—which was high for me but low for them—to fill out their distribution schedule,' Corman told di Franco. 'They made me a very nice offer.. They said they wanted to start right away and did I have any ideas, and I said, "Well, I made *The St Valentine's Day Massacre* a number of years ago, which did well, and one possibility to get this started would be to do [a movie about Al Capone]." They agreed immediately.'

The St Valentine's Day Massacre had been a first film script for Howard Browne, famous for his 1943 novel *Warrior of the Dawn* and a prolific television writer in the 1950s and '60s on such as shows *Cheyenne, Maverick, 77 Sunset Strip, Bus Stop* and *The Virginian*. When Fox agreed to another film about Capone, Corman immediately went to Browne, who drafted a screenplay entitled *The Big Fella*. Chicago-born Browne's interest in Al Capone dated back to his teen years as he told the Copley News Service: 'I was working as a collection man for a department store [in Chicago] when the St. Valentine's Day massacre took place. It fascinated me. What kind of man would line up seven people and shoot them like that? When I became a writer in 1941 it became a driving thing to learn about this.'

> *Brooklyn, 1918. Young Alfonse Capone helps out two members of gangster Frankie Yale's mob against the cops. For his pains, Capone receives facial scars and a spot on Yale's roster. A year later, Capone goes to Chicago to help Yale's friend Johnny Torrio set up a bootlegging operation to take advantage of Prohibition and by 1923, violent gang warfare has engulfed the city. In 1925, after an attempt on his life, Torrio leaves Chicago in Capone's hands. Capone spends the rest of the decade consolidating his rule through corruption, intimidation, violence and vice, culminating in the murder of rival Bugs Moran's gang on St Valentine's Day, 1929. Two years later, Capone is set up by enforcer Frank Nitti and convicted of tax evasion; he is fined and sentenced to 11 years in prison. At the close, he is shown as a raving lunatic, his mind ravaged by syphilis.*

Capone (Ben Gazzara)

Al Capone had been the subject of numerous films (*Scarface, Al Capone, The Purple Gang*) and TV shows (*Playhouse 90, Desilu Playhouse, The Untouchables*), even before the Browne-Corman treatment of 1967. Cast as Capone in their new version (released as *Capone* by Fox in April 1975) was Ben Gazzara, whose career had largely been in television (including his own series, *Run for Your Life*, in 1965-'68), though he had put in appearances in films like *Anatomy of a Murder* (1958), *The Young Doctors* (1961), *The Bridge at Remagen* (1969) and John Cassavetes's *Husbands* (1970). To make himself more convincing as Capone, Gazzara gleefully gained 20 pounds, as he told di Franco: 'It was wonderful—I ate spaghetti every day and I never had any guilt!'

In the role of Iris Crawford, Capone's mistress, was Susan Blakely, who had made her debut in 1972 in Merchant-Ivory's *Savages* and gone on to roles in *The Way We Were* (1973) and *The Towering Inferno* (1974). She had also appeared in *The Lords of Flatbush* (1974) with the young actor who would play *Capone*'s hit-man nemesis, Frank Nitti: 28-year-old Sylvester Gardenzio Stallone.

Born in New York in July 1946, Stallone made his screen debuts in 1970 with a porn film (*The Party at Kitty and Stud's*) and a thriller (*No Place to Hide*). He then had uncredited bit parts in Woody Allen's *Bananas* and Alan Pakula's *Klute* (1971) before appearing in *Flatbush* and Neil Simon's *The Prisoner of Second Avenue* (1975). *Capone* would be the first of three Corman productions in which Stallone would appear before achieving superstardom by writing and acting in the boxing drama *Rocky* in 1976.

The New York and Los Angeles critics were impressed with *Capone*—'Moves with cold efficiency, which is its style whether you like it or not'; 'Ben Gazzara may well be the best Capone ever'—but the Chicago duo of Ebert and Siskel were not. 'Sad to say, *Capone* isn't much fun,' said Ebert. 'There's one good laugh and a lot of violence.. During the chase scenes, the cars keep chasing each other around the same corners, because there are only about four corners in the whole city, and native Chicagoans will be amazed to see the lushly wooded California hills rising at the end of Wabash Avenue [the film is completely studio-bound except for some exteriors obviously shot in the Hollywood foothills].' Siskel wrote an entire article in the *Chicago Tribune* examining Capone's cinematic career and had this to say about Gazzara's interpretation: 'The three scars are accurately placed but look fake. As a matter of fact, the entire performance looks fake because it is obviously Gazzara as Capone.. [his] Capone is more thoughtful, more like a college graduate. It doesn't wash with the man or the myth.'

But *Capone*'s $2 million rental take meant a $1 million profit for Fox right out of the gate, which was good enough to greenlight three more films from Corman over the next two years.

'The world is waiting—once more, I give you what you want.'
—Mister President (Sandy McCallum), speaking to the masses in *Death Race 2000*

The September 1973 issue of *Esquire* magazine featured a short story entitled 'Roller Ball Murder' by University of Arkansas professor William Harrison. It was set in the not-too-distant future, when the world is controlled by corporations and the populace is kept entertained by a violent sport known as 'Rollerball', a macabre mixture of football, roller derby, motocross and hockey.

The following February, Harrison's story was optioned by producer/director Norman Jewison (*Fiddler on the Roof, Jesus Christ Superstar*) as a feature project for United Artists. Despite him having no experience, Harrison was encouraged by Jewison to flesh out his story into a screenplay; within a month, he had provided a harrowing vision of life in the year 2018. The plot of *Rollerball* revolves around Jonathan E, hero of the ultra-violent title-sport who, in the eyes of his corporate sponsors, has become a liability. His longevity in the sport and growing popularity pose a threat to corporate control of society and he is ordered to retire. Jonathan's competitive nature will not allow him to comply, however, and the powers that be determine that he must be exterminated..

Filmed in the summer of 1974 on a $5 million budget at Munich's Olympic City, *Rollerball* featured James Caan—famous for his portrayal of Sonny Corleone in Francis Ford Coppola's *The Godfather* and its sequel—in the role of Jonathan E; in support were John Houseman, Ralph Richardson, Moses Gunn and Bond girl Maud Adams, and extensive press coverage hyped Jewison's film to blockbuster proportions. When it was finally released in June 1975, it received mixed reviews and performed disappointingly (earning just over $6 million in rentals).

Ever the trend-follower, Roger Corman decided to capitalise on the advance publicity generated by *Rollerball* and shoot his own version of sport in a dystopian future. Like Jewison before him, Corman optioned a short story as the basis for his film. Written by novelist/screenwriter Ib Melchior (*The Angry Red Planet, Robinson Crusoe on Mars*) and published in 1956, 'The Racer' tells the story of Willie Conners, defending champ of a future America's premiere cross-country road race. To win this race, however, Connors must not only get from New York to Los Angeles in record time—he must also rack up points by hitting and killing pedestrians along the way (so-called 'Tragic-Accs'). Things go well until Connors is confronted by a woman carrying the body of a child whom he has run over. She calls him 'butcher', and the word haunts him to disaster.

Robert Thom had previously scripted films such as *The Subterranians, All the Fine Young Cannibals* (both 1960), *Wild in the Streets* (1968) and Corman's own *Bloody Mama*, so New World's boss hired him to write a draft screenplay for what was tentatively titled *The Race*. The draft that Thom turned in was unsuitable, as

Death Race 2000 (David Carradine)

Paul Bartel (director of Gene Corman's 1972 production *Private Parts* and second unit director on *Big Bad Mama*) found out when he was brought on board to helm the film. 'It was a really awful script,' Bartel told *Time Out*. 'It was very long and by the end of page 45, the cars still hadn't left New York City. All the characters were transvestites, and there was a lot of kinky fucking. It was very glitter-rock and very passé with everybody wearing chains and whipping each other. So I told Roger I didn't think it was practical, especially the scene where Grand Central Station was blown up.'

To try to shape *The Race* into something workable, Corman turned to writer/director Charles Griffith, his long-time friend and associate (whose professional relationship with Corman went all the way back to *It Conquered the World* in 1956). 'I looked at the script,' Griffith told Patrick McGilligan, 'and it was completely bizarre, unshootable and crazy, but it did have a lot of interesting things in it. "You're asking me to change this?" I asked Roger. He and I were always having trouble over the bizarre things in my screenplays. He told me that since the script had been written by a bizarre person, he figured it took another one to fix it.'

> *In the year 2000, the United Provinces of America is a dictatorship whose population is addicted to the Transcontinental Road Race from New York to New Los Angeles. The winner must not only reach New LA first, but also rack up points by running over pedestrians along the way. The hero of the race is Frankenstein, a two-time champion*

81

whose numerous accidents have supposedly made him a patchwork of plastic and steel plates; his new navigator is Annie, secret grand-daughter of the leader of the Army of the Resistance, who plan to overthrow the government and abolish the Death Race. Frankenstein and fellow racers Machine Gun Joe Viterbo, Calamity Jane, Matilda the Hun, and Nero the Hero must not only compete against each other but avoid attacks by the rebels to gain the ultimate prize—a meeting with Mister President.

'I met Paul Bartel,' Griffith continued, 'and we reached a mutual conclusion that the film had to be a satire, somehow a political satire, because there was nothing else we could do with [it].' But Corman saw things differently, as he told Mark McGee: 'What I wanted was something along the lines of *Dr Strangelove*: a serious comedy about violence.. I wanted to treat it with humour but what Paul and Chuck wanted to do was make it a silly comedy. A farce comedy. I wanted it to be a smart comedy.'

Not surprisingly, these conflicting points of view were headed for collision, as Chuck Griffith told *Senses of Cinema*: '[Corman] tried to make it serious. He was enraged with me for trying to make it funny, but he took me to see the cars and they were all goofy looking with decal eyes and rubber teeth. I said, "You can't be serious" and he tells me, "Chuck, this is a hard-hitting serious picture"!'

Over the years, Bartel, Griffith, Joe Dante and others have maintained that what was now to become *Death Race 2000* was, in Dante's words to Gray, 'a real pop art masterpiece before Roger got to it.' Corman supposedly 'ruined' the film in post-production by cutting down the humour and increasing the graphic violence. But an examination of the shooting script by Griffith puts the lie to this. Nearly all of the humour in the script is present in the film—and most of the acts of violence in the film are present in the script as well. In fact, there is actually *more* humour in the film than there is in the script, including things like Frankenstein's literal 'hand' grenade, Matilda shouting 'Blitzkrieg!' when running someone over, and Frankenstein making loud-mouth announcer Junior Bruce (played by 'The Real' Don Steele) the last casualty of the race.

While Jewison had James Caan as Jonathan E, Corman had David Carradine as Frankenstein; he initially had wanted Peter Fonda, but Fonda would not commit to shooting during the holiday season. Carradine, on the other hand, was anxious to parlay his small screen success with TV series *Kung Fu* (1972-75) into something larger. 'The main thing is, Roger gave me movie stardom—and when no one else was willing to do it,' he told di Franco. Carradine was the first of only two actors (Ron Howard being the other) with whom Corman negotiated a percentage deal with, giving the star 10% of the gross. Not that he did it with a smile on his face, as Carradine remarked to *Bright Lights Film Journal*: 'When he'd write me this cheque, he'd be so unhappy, I'd say, "Roger, don't you realise that when you're writing me a cheque for $30,000, you're still making $300,000 of your own?" But it didn't matter. He still just didn't like it.'

Critical response to *Death Race 2000* was decidedly mixed. On the pro side were Kevin Thomas ('*Death Race 2000*.. again demonstrates that imagination can overcome the tightest budget.. All told this is a fine little action picture with big ideas') and *Variety* ('Cartoonish but effective entertainment, with some good action sequences and plenty of black humor'), while the cons were represented by the *New York Times* ('An Orwellian vision of the American future, if you believe that Orwell was afflicted with blurred perception and an inclination toward the adolescent in satire') and the ever-antagonistic Gene Siskel ('It may be the goofiest and sleaziest film I've seen in the last five years').

But when it came to box office, *Death Race 2000* was a smash, earning nearly $5 million in rentals then adding to that total when it was re-released in 1977 to take advantage of co-star Sylvester Stallone's newfound fame in *Rocky*. Given that *Death Race 2000* took in nearly 17 times its cost ($300,000), whereas *Rollerball* barely broke even, one could say that David (Carradine) took on Goliath and won. Both films have since been remade and this time, both were losers: *Rollerball* took in just $19 million on a budget of $70 million in 2002, while *Death Race* (produced by Tom Cruise's company for Universal Pictures) took in $36 million on a budget of $45 million in 2008.

Death Race 2000 was the first New World release to be successful in Britain (*Big Bad Mama* had bombed there in January 1975 via EMI), where it grossed nearly £1 million via independent distributor Focus Films (a subsidiary of Brent Walker) in April 1976. Corman was so pleased that he published an open letter in *Variety,* where he commended Focus managing director Alan Kean for his 'flair for exploiting every cent out of a film through splendid public relations and publicity.' The film was subsequently re-released in the UK in January 1978 on a double-bill with another reissue, Bruce Lee's *Enter the Dragon*. *Death Race 2000* would go on to open in France in July 1976, after it had won the Grand Prize at the Paris International Fantastic and Science Fiction Film Festival.

(As a sidebar to this, *Death Race* was at the centre of the very first video game controversy, when an arcade machine inspired by it was released by Exidy in 1976. The object of the game was to run down 'gremlins' who were fleeing the player's vehicle; as they were hit, the victims would scream and be replaced by tombstones. Exidy denied that the intent of the game was to promote violence, but there was a huge outcry and *Death Race* became a target for The National Safety Council and several news programmes. In the end, it was pulled from the market after some 500 units had shipped (now highly collectable). In 1990, a domestic version of the game was released for use with the Nintendo Entertainment System.)

The month of May brought good news and bad for Roger and Julie Corman. The former was the birth of their first child, Catherine; the latter was the departure of Frank Moreno, who had been instrumental in upgrading New World's image. During his time as New World's general sales manager, Moreno had been dabbling in his own distributorship, Centaur Releasing. The company had commenced operations in 1973, releasing foreign sex films (*I Like the Girls Who Do, Naughty Nymphs, Teach Me)* as well as domestic product, like *Invasion of the Bee Girls*. Moreno then joined forces with Jack Hill, who wrote and directed Centaur's first hit, *The Swinging Cheerleaders*, in 1974.

With Centaur-Hill's second effort, *The Jezebels* (later known as *Switchblade Sisters*), locked into 1,200 playdates over the summer of '75, Moreno could no longer serve two masters and decided to go it alone. 'I learned double exploitation [at New World],' he told *Variety*. 'I exploited Roger Corman and he exploited me. But it was a great experience.'

'When that wave hits, 80 million people will be wiped out!'
—US Ambassador Warren Richards (Lorne Greene) in *Tidal Wave*

In March 1973, a publishing phenomenon swept Japan. Sakyo Komatsu's novel *Nippon Chinbotsu* ('Japan Sinks') became a runaway success, selling over four million copies in its first printing. The story begins off the southeast coast of Japan, where an island suddenly and inexplicably sinks. The DSV Wadatsumi is sent to investigate and at the bottom of the Japan Trench, the Wadatsumi finds the seabed covered in broad ruts, a sign of massive seismic shift. Volcanic eruptions and earthquakes point to one conclusion—the islands in the Japanese archipelago are in danger of sinking. The Japanese government sets about implementing 'Plan D',

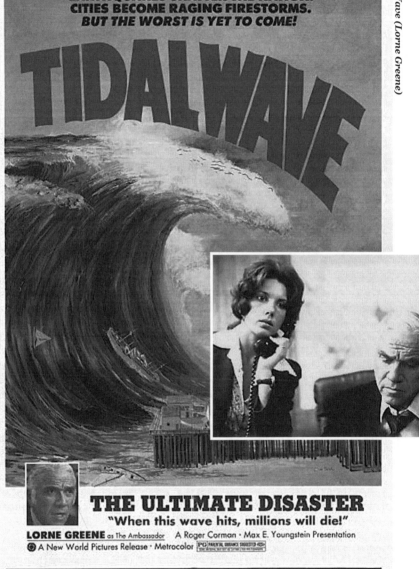

which involves the mass evacuation of the country and relocation of millions of Japanese to other nations. Meanwhile, parts of Japan are ravaged by earthquakes and tidal wave. The beginning of the end is reached when Mount Fuji erupts for the first time in 900 years—coincident with a prime ministerial address regarding the country's imminent demise. The biggest air and sealift in history manages to save two-thirds (70 million) of Japan's population before a cataclysmic geological upheaval sends the archipelago to the bottom of the Pacific Ocean.

The Toho Company, the house that Godzilla built, quickly bought the rights to Komatsu's novel and a screen version of *Nippon Chinbotsu* went into production in the summer. Released in December 1973, the movie was a smash hit, grossing over $7 million at the Japanese box office. With a running time of nearly two-and-a-half hours, the film was remarkably faithful to its source and caused quite a stir at the 1974 Cannes Film Festival.

The American rights to *Nippon Chinbotsu* were acquired by Max Youngstein, former United Artists executive and producer of *Fail Safe* (1964) and *Welcome to Hard Times* (1967). In November 1974, Youngstein partnered with Roger Corman to release the film the following spring—after the usual changes had been made for the US market.

The previous five years had seen numerous examples of Corman's tampering with other people's films, but Asian imports seemed to suffer the most. First was *The Water Margin*'s metamorphosis into the much-abridged *Seven Blows of the Dragon*, now *Nippon Chinbotsu* was about to suffer an almost complete makeover in its transition to *Tidal Wave*. 'I threw out everything but the good special effects the Japanese do so well,' Corman revealed to the *New York Times*. 'Then I got an American star, Lorne Greene [of TV's *Bonanza* fame], and I shot some additional footage with him. I made him an American delegate to the UN so that whenever the action got too complicated and you couldn't follow what was happening with this monster tidal wave killing all those people, we cut to Lorne at the UN and he made a speech which explained what was going on.'

'We shot Lorne in the studio looking worried, asking dumb questions,' Allan Arkush commented in Corman's autobiography. '[*Tidal Wave*] was dubbed into English by Joe [Dante], Jon [Davison], secretaries in the office, all doing Japanese accents.' The new scenes were written and directed by Andrew Meyer, in his first film since *Night of the Cobra Woman* (it would also be his last before his death in 1987 at the age of 43), and then spliced into what remained of *Nippon Chinbotsu*, which had been gutted from 143 minutes to a mere 82!

In the wake of *The Towering Inferno* and *Earthquake* (both 1974), the result managed to ride the crest of the disaster movie wave to the tune of a hefty $3.5 million in rentals on its release in May 1975. 'The movie made a fortune,' Dante remarked in *Brilliance on a Budget*, 'even though it was the kind of film that people leaving the theatre warned people outside the theatre not to go see.' The critics followed suit, including Vincent Canby of the *New York Times* ('*Tidal Wave* is occasionally very funny.. The cities that are destroyed would fit around your electric train'), Roger Ebert ('The movie never ends, but if you wait long enough it gets to a point where it's over') and *Cinefantastique*'s Bill Warren, who had also seen the original version ('What was done to [*Nippon Chinbotsu*] was nothing less than desecration'). Only the *Los Angeles Times*'s Linda Gross came to *Tidal Wave*'s defence, calling it 'authentic, informative and eye-dazzling.'

In 2006, *Nippon Chinbotsu* was remade by Toho (in collaboration with seven other companies) on a $25 million budget. It was once again a smash hit in Japan, but this time Roger Corman left it there.

> *'You give an inch, the guy takes two, you find out he only has three and you end up with zero.'*
> —Photography teacher Sally (Pat Anderson) in *Summer School Teachers*

Summer School Teachers, New World's first release of the summer of 1975, was Barbara Peeters's second time in the director's chair for the company; not surprisingly, the film has the least amount of sex and the most amount of action and humour of any of New World's three-girls-and-a-soap series. Peeters, who had handled the second unit direction on *The Student Teachers* and *Candy Stripe Nurses*, was well aware of the precariousness of her position, as she told the *Los Angeles Times*: 'Every woman who is allowed to direct in this town is a token.. Unless you come from a wealthy family or you're very well connected or unless you are married to a producer or distributor who can get you that money, you don't have a chance.'

Summer School Teachers

Three Iowa farm girls take summer high school teaching jobs in California. Conklin T, the PE instructor, encourages the girls to form a football team, while simultaneously romancing a naïve biology teacher; Denise teaches chemistry and becomes involved with a problem kid who is being set up by a car-theft ring. Sally teaches photography and encourages her students to shoot whatever they consider to be obscene.. After a brief fling with eccentric rock star, Sally takes up with a fellow photographer whom she has to teach a lesson in humility.

Peeters was fortunate enough to be in good with the boss's wife, and *Summer School Teachers* would be Julie Corman's sixth production in just three years. The fatigue of repetition was beginning to show, however—*Summer School*'s plot was mostly an amalgam of other 'nurses'/'teachers' films, though the inclusion of an all-female football team was a novel touch. The *Los Angeles Times*'s Linda Gross agreed: 'This oft-told tale of good teachers, rotten administrators, misunderstood kids and the all-important football game that brings them together has a spunky and decidedly female fantasy appeal. What girl wouldn't enjoy being beautiful—and a star football player?'

> 'What's the point of being an outlaw when you look like an in-law?'
> —Bertha (Merie Earle), the 85-year-old bank robber of *Crazy Mama*

What was first announced as *Big Bad Mama II*, then *The American Dream*, and ended up being released that July as *Crazy Mama*, had undergone numerous production difficulties. The film was originally intended to have been directed by Oscar-nominated (*Skyscraper,* 1960) documentarian Shirley Clarke, who seemed an odd choice, given her background, and the fact that she had not made a feature since *Portrait of Jason* in 1967. Ten days before shooting was due to begin, Clarke was fired and a rather dumbfounded Jonathan Demme was recruited to take her place. Corman's instructions to Demme were simple, as the director recalled for the *Austin Chronicle*: '"There's a casting session in half an hour, find all the locations and, by the way, the cast hates the script." I said, "Look Roger, I must read the script before I agree to do this." He said, "Absolutely not enough time for that." I said, "If Evelyn [Purcell, Demme's wife] can be second unit director, I'll do it." Corman said, "Okay, fine." And off we went and did it.'

Jerusalem, Arkansas, 1932. Daniel Stokes is shot by evictors in front of his wife Sheba and daughter Melba. Years later, Sheba and Melba Stokes are evicted from their hair salon in California. They decide to make the trek back to Jerusalem to buy the family farm, with Melba's pregnant daughter Cheryl and boyfriend Shawn in tow. En route, they team up with gambler Jim Bob, a hood named Snake, and an 85-year-old refugee from a nursing home named Bertha. The group takes to robbing chapels, racetracks and banks to get funds, but Jim Bob decides to blackmail his rich wife by arranging his own kidnapping. But the payoff goes wrong and he and Bertha are gunned down. Sheba, Melba and the others make it to Jerusalem, only to find that the farm has been turned into a country club; to make things worse, it is the scene of a wedding reception for the son of the man who shot Dan Stokes.

Crazy Mama was written by 'crazy' Bob Thom, another odd choice given the problems that Corman and company had encountered when presented with his draft for *Death Race 2000*. In any event, Demme was forced to make a number of changes to the script, especially towards the climax: 'It was supposed to end in a total bloodbath with everybody getting killed, the kids, Cloris [Leachman, star of the film], and I just couldn't handle that, somehow or other, but I was pissed off at Ann Sothern [Sheba] for being such an old kvetch so I let her get killed. Everybody else escaped. We had no ending. Roger said, "There's no ending here" so I came up with the idea of tacking on the flash forward [that shows the family running a burger stand in Miami in 1959].'

There were other problems as well. Julie Corman, the producer, was about to have her first baby. Showing admirable dedication to the company, she made sure that everything was hunky-dory before the delivery, as she told the *Los Angeles Times*: 'I happened to be out on location when labour pains began. I called in the staff to make sure film production wouldn't be interrupted during the following week. I signed a batch of cheques, talked with the auditor, filled out certain legal forms. When the pains began coming close together, two people helped me to a car and drove me to the hospital.'

Demme's film is basically a kinder, gentler version of *Big Bad Mama,* devoid of Steve Carver's emphasis on sex and graphic violence (*Crazy Mama* received a tame 'PG' rating). One could also say that it was the difference between how Julie Corman saw an 'outlaw' picture and how her husband saw one. The story being set in the '50s gave an excuse to pack the soundtrack with 'oldies'—*American Graffiti* style—as well as showcasing numerous landmarks of American pop culture, like Burma-Shave road signs, Las Vegas wedding chapels, pink Cadillacs, and even the Goodyear Blimp.

The critical reaction was tepid: 'This sadistic, sordid unveiling of wasted lives.. appears a waste of top talent in a mindless life of crime' (*Variety*); 'A ragged, witless attempt at an all-purpose rip-off from the Roger Corman organisation' (*Washington Post*); 'There's really too much that's contrived, too much that's patently derivative to take the film as a whole seriously' (*Los Angeles Times*). However, with *Young Frankenstein* (1974) and the role of Phyllis Lindstrom on the hit *Mary Tyler Moore Show*, Cloris Leachman was hot, and the box office rang to the tune of $2.3 million in rentals. The film's appeal was also helped by co-stars Donny Most and Linda Purl, both of whom were on the phenomenally-successful *Happy Days* TV show at the time.

'You'll never make it as a model until you learn to react as a woman.'
   —Fashion photographer Mark (John Kramer) in *Cover Girl Models*

Previously announced as *Fantastic Models Inc.* and released in August 1975, *Cover Girl Models* was the last of New World's female 'sex' soaps (though it, like *Tender Loving Care*, was released by Filmgroup); it was also the last film in the company's alliance with Premiere in the Philippines. As Corman told di Franco, 'We found the prices rising very heavily, and one of the reasons for shooting there was that it was economically suited to low-budget filming.. But as the prices rose, we retreated to the United States.'

> *Three fashion models, Barbara, Claire and Mandy, travel to Hong Kong for a fashion show. Barbara becomes involved with a travel agent who is a government operative, Claire tries to persuade a producer to offer her a role in his new film, Mandy becomes involved with a photographer. Flying on to Singapore, Barbara finds herself pursued by all and sundry for some microfilm which she has inadvertently transported, Claire is kidnapped by rebels who mistake her for the daughter of the American ambassador, and Mandy is offered $50,000 to switch agencies.*

Although Corman's contract with Premiere was finished, his relationship with Cirio Santiago would continue for many years. Even without New World, Santiago would hardly want for work and he churned out several well-known exploitation films during the remainder of the 1970s, including *Ebony, Ivory and Jade, The Muthers, Hell Hole, Vampire Hookers* and *Death Force*.

> *'Is this pimp or what?'*
> —Lady biker Syreena (Trina Parks), at the Casbah in *Darktown Strutters*

'I made only a few films on black subjects, largely for economic reasons,' Corman told di Franco. 'I felt it was foolish in the long run to be directing your films to only ten percent of the population of the United States and even less a percentage of the overseas market.' Gene Corman felt differently, however, and he produced such blaxploitation films as *Cool Breeze* (1972), *Hit Man* (a remake of the 1971 Michael Caine starrer *Get Carter*; 1972) and *The Slams* (1973), all for MGM. Gene and his brother's final blaxploitation film would be the outrageous *Darktown Strutters*, an unlikely black chopper movie/musical comedy directed by a man who had no experience in either of the above: 60-year-old William Witney, who probably had directed more TV westerns that anyone else in Hollywood, as well as the AIP-Vincent Price sci-fi opus *Master of the World* (1960).

> *Syreena, the leader of black ladies biker gang the Darktown Strutters, is trying to find her missing mother Cinderella. After being harassed by Marines, cops and the KKK, Syreena discovers that Cinderella is being held along with other prominent blacks in a dungeon underneath the mansion of barbeque magnate Commander Louisville Cross. Cross has perfected a machine that will replace black leaders with clones to further his political ends. Syreena manages to escape and assemble an army of bikers to assault the Cross mansion and free those held prisoner.*

Darktown Strutters is the black version of *Gas-s-s-s!* (they were both written by George Armitage) and it does not play any better. Deliberately over the top, the film is too lame to be funny, even when it takes on an American fast-food icon (Colonel Sanders of Kentucky Fried Chicken) and turns him into a cartoon villain plotting the demise of Black America. *Darktown* relies heavily on slapstick and sight-gags, but the level of the humour never transcends the adolescent, with a vendor selling 'potsicles', Syreena's kung-fu fighting brother accidentally knocking the house down, and everyone attired in goofy costumes.

US theatrical poster for Darktown Strutters

Press advertisement for
The Story of Adele H.

Gene Corman had produced the film for a company in Tennessee which was, unsurprisingly, unable to secure its release. He then took *Darktown* to his brother who, either out of pity or identification with his own failed satire, decided to put New World's name on it and schedule an August release. The critical response was blistering: 'An amateurish mishmash.. inept from start to finish' (*Variety*); 'The blatantly diffuse script, one-dimensional acting and artless directing only serve to make the frenetic business a lame, unfunny affair' (*New York Times*); 'A slapstick spoof with lots of energy that goes nowhere' (*Los Angeles Times*).

The film virtually destroyed the career of 28-year-old singer/dancer Trina Parks (Syreena), who had the distinction of being the first black woman to feature in a James Bond film when she played 'Thumper' in *Diamonds Are Forever* (1971). She would make only one more film, Cirio Santiago's *The Muthers* (1976), before disappearing from the screen forever. Co-star Roger E Mosley fared better, finding small-screen fame as helicopter pilot 'TC' in the '80s hit TV show *Magnum P.I.*

As if once were not enough, New World actually re-released *Darktown Strutters* in early 1977 under a new title of *Get Down and Boogie*, highlighting the film's

89

sole saving grace—some reasonably well-staged musical numbers, including The Dramatics' catchy performance of 'What You See is What You Get'.

In the fall of 1975, the President of New World trumpeted that he was going to begin to remake selected silent films, and he was starting with one of the biggest—D W Griffith's 1915 epic, *Birth of a Nation*. Given the inherently racist nature of Griffith's film (in its uncut form, it is decidedly pro-Southern, pro-KKK and anti-black), it seemed to be another odd choice for a man who proudly declared to the *New York Times,* 'I'm against racial injustice, corruption in government, pollution of the environment. I'm liberal to radical in my politics and I'm not afraid to put my message right up there on the screen.'

Corman was by no means the first producer to declare his intention to reshape Griffith's masterpiece to his own vision but, like those before him, he fell victim to the legal maze that surrounds the property. As was reported in *Variety*, '*Birth* is believed still protected by copyright in many foreign lands and it is believed that it would be hazardous to assume the film, derived from two novels of the late Rev Thomas Dixon, is in the public domain.' Corman came no closer to production on other silents that he had his eye on, either—*A Fool There Was* (1915) and *The Little Minister* (1921), the latter based on the James Barrie stage play.

To make up for all these non-starters, Corman put four films into production between October and December, though a scorecard was needed to keep up with the various title changes. The first was announced as *The Starlets*, then changed to *The Actresses,* then it was back to *Hollywood Starlets*. Second up was *Nashville Lady*, which in subsequent press releases was known as *The Girl from Nashville*. Third was *Harvest*, which quickly morphed into *Jackson County Jail*. Last but not least was *The Car*, which actually got in gear under the moniker of *Eat My Dust*.

Not that Corman was deterred from making his grand proclamations. He was soon touting *Wheel World*, to star Ann-Margret and her manager-husband Roger Smith, *Deathworld*, the sequel to *Death Race 2000,* to be written and directed by Robert Thom, and *Thunder and Lightning*, a car chase movie to star Susan George and tennis star Jimmy Connors. The first never made it past the press release, the second was delayed for three years, and the last saw production in 1977 with Kate Jackson and David Carradine instead.

On the foreign film front, New World's distribution arm released a triple-header, beginning in November with Joseph Losey's *The Romantic Englishwoman* and continuing in December with Francois Truffaut's *The Story of Adele H* and Volker Schlöndorff and Margarethe von Trotta's *The Lost Honor of Katharina Blum*. All three were received to critical acclaim, but it was the Truffaut film that was the breakout success, taking in over $1 million in rentals and earning an Oscar nomination for star Isabelle Adjani.

As New World celebrated its fifth anniversary in business, things were clearly going Roger Corman's way. The company had recorded a combined $11 million profit over those five years and in December, it held its first-ever sales convention at the Century Plaza Hotel in Hollywood, at which subsidiaries and salesmen were introduced to Robert Rehme, Frank Moreno's replacement as New World's general sales manager. That same month, Corman was profiled in the *New York Times Magazine*, in which he was crowned the 'King of Schlock'. He bragged to the *Times's* Bill Davidson about his new daughter, new house in Pacific Palisades, and the new offices which his company would soon be occupying in Brentwood. He spoke subsequently to the *Los Angeles Times* and reflected upon New World's standing in the industry: 'I would never apologise for the films I make because they are the best of their kind on the market.. [New World is] the most successful independent film company in the country—if you consider AIP to be a major. We are the best of the cheap acts.'

Chapter 3

Thrills, Chills and Spills

Publicity shot from Caged Heat

'The last couple of years I thought that a large proportion of the American public wanted to see blood or breasts. Now I think they want to see cars.'
—Roger Corman, 1977

'Roger used to refer to himself—and we heard this endlessly—as being 40 percent artist and 60 percent businessman. That was soooo Roger—to have a formula, even for that.'
—Jonathan Demme, director of *Caged Heat, Crazy Mama* and *Fighting Mad*

Hollywood had long turned the spotlight on itself and its often sordid history—from *Merton of the Movies* in 1924 to *Sunset Boulevard* in 1950, *The Bad and the Beautiful* in 1952 to *Inserts* in 1974. Between 1975 and '76, several films, including *The Day of the Locust, Hearts of the West, The Last Tycoon, Nickelodeon* and *The Wild Party*, followed in the tradition. As part of this latest self-reflexive craze, New World Pictures rang in the New Year by giving Bicentennial America what it had always wanted: a look inside Miracle Pictures, whose slogan, appropriately, was 'If it's a good picture.. it's a Miracle!'

'In this film, we are combining the myth of Romeo and Juliet with high-speed car action and a sincere plea for international atomic controls in our time.'
—Erich Von Leppe (Paul Bartel), 'Atomic War Brides' director in *Hollywood Boulevard*

First it was called *The Starlets*, then *The Actresses*, then *Hollywood Starlets*, then *Hello, Hollywood* then finally *Hollywood Boulevard*, the *pièce-de-resistance* of the Jonathan Kaplan Gang at New World—Allan Arkush, Joe Dante, Jon Davison and Danny Opatoshu. Kaplan himself would join in the fun, this time in front of the camera as a klutzy production assistant who gets to don the costume of 'Godzina'. Publicity head Davison had actually made the pitch to Roger Corman in the form of a wager, as he told the *New York Times*: 'I came right out with it and told Roger I'd like to make a bet with him that I could produce a film 50 percent cheaper than any that had been done at New World since he founded it in 1970. I said, "Your average picture takes 15 days to shoot, right? I'll do mine in 10 days." I saw a funny self-satisfied look come over his face and he said, "OK, you've got a bet. In order to win it, you'll have to do the picture for $80,000, but I'm only going to give you $60,000."'

Starstruck Candy Hope arrives in Hollywood from Indianapolis, looking to become an actress. She stumbles upon the office of agent Walter Paisley, who sends her to be a stuntwoman on Miracle Pictures' new film 'Queen of the Mob'. Candy does so well that Paisley dispatches her to the Philippines to feature in 'Machete Maidens' with clients Bobbi, Jill and Mary, Miracle's reigning star. During the shoot, Jill is killed by a real bullet in a staged firefight. On their return to the US, Candy, Mary and Bobbi are put into Miracle's 'Atomic War Brides', but Bobbi is murdered on set by a masked assassin. Candy comes to suspect that her boyfriend is responsible, but the real killer confronts the would-be starlet in the Hollywood hills.

Davison and Company won the bet—they brought in *Hollywood Boulevard* in ten days for the bargain price of $54,039.43. One reason that they were able to pull off such a feat was that the film was essentially built around stock footage: the prison bust from *The Big Bird Cage*, the skydiving scene from *Night Call Nurses*, roller derby scenes from *Unholy Rollers*, battle footage from *Savage!*, car crashes from *Big Bad Mama* and *Crazy Mama*, and chase scenes (as well as costumes and props) from *Death Race 2000*. As Dante stated in *Brilliance on a Budget*, 'Unless you were in on [the] joke, it was a complete nonsensical film. All these things happened—car crashes, the works, and the only reason they happened was that we had the footage.'

The film is crammed full of in-jokes. Paul Bartel's director 'Erich Von Leppe' was the name of Boris Karloff's character in *The Terror*, while Dick Miller's agent has the name of the crazed artist he played in *A Bucket of Blood*. Miller goes to a drive-in and watches himself in a scene with Karloff from *The Terror*. In addition to Bartel and Kaplan, Charles Griffith appears as a drunken pool cleaner, while Dante, Opatoshu, and Lewis Teague also make appearances as party guests (along with *Famous Monsters of Filmland* editor Forrest J Ackerman). Robby the Robot from *Forbidden Planet* (1956) makes his cinematic return, serving drinks to Miller and offering an impersonation of Rhett Butler, and the film ends with a send-up of Alfred Hitchcock's landmark climaxes (Big Ben in *The 39 Steps*; Mount Rushmore in *North By Northwest*) as the 'Y' in the famous 'Hollywood' sign crashes down on Mary (former Warhol groupie and *Death Race 2000* co-star Mary Woronov). For no reason other than novelty, *Hollywood Boulevard* features a musical number by country & western band Commander Cody and His Lost Planet Airmen, who had a Top 10 hit in 1972 with 'Hot Rod Lincoln' and who disbanded shortly after the completion of *Hollywood Boulevard*.

The advertising for the film was priceless, with satirical quips from Coppola ('I directed part of this picture but they re-cut and ruined it'), Corman ('The greatest ten-day picture of the decade!') and Martin Scorsese ('I haven't clapped so much since basic training films'). *Hollywood Boulevard* proudly proclaimed that it was 'Shamelessly loaded with sex and violence!' and its April 1977 opening in New York ran with the copy, 'In 1942, RKO premiered Orson Welles's *The Magnificent Ambersons* on a double bill with *Mexican Spitfire Sees a Ghost*. In 1977, New World Pictures continues in this tradition with *Hollywood Boulevard* on a double bill with *Cover Girl Models*.'

'There's never been anything quite like *Hollywood Boulevard*,' said Kevin Thomas, 'an outrageous, often hilarious spoof of the zany world of low-budget exploitation filmmaking. And what better company to produce such an effort than Roger Corman's New World Pictures?' *Variety* agreed: 'Roger Corman's New World Pictures has done as good a satire job on itself as anyone could in *Hollywood Boulevard*, a loving-hands-at-home tribute to the philosophy that a good piece of action footage deserves more than one usage.'

'In the right hand drawer of my desk,' Davison told the *New York Times*, 'I have a bus ticket back to New Jersey—if the picture bombs. In the left-hand drawer of my desk, I have three more scripts—if the picture takes off and it happens to me like it happened to Coppola, Bogdanovich and Scorsese.' Fortune smiles on the brave, and the left got the upper hand when *Hollywood Boulevard* became one of the most profitable films in New World's history, earning $1 million in rentals or nearly a 2,000% return on Corman's investment.

> *'I want to become what the public thinks I am.'*
> —Country singer Jamie Barker (Monica Gayle) in *The Girl from Nashville*

Gus Trikonis began his career as an actor in musicals, including *West Side Story* (1961) and *The Unsinkable Molly Brown* (1964), before directing his first film, biker flick *Five the Hard Way* (aka *The Sidehackers*) for Crown International Pictures in 1969—the same year that he married Goldie Hawn. They were divorced in 1974 and Trikonis directed his second film, the Filipino-lensed *Cockfighter* rip-off *Supercock*, the following year. He then directed the drive-in hit *The Swinging Barmaids* (aka *Eager Beavers*) from a script by Charles Griffith, before linking up with producer Peer Oppenheimer in 1975 to direct an original script by the latter, *Nashville Lady* (later to become *The Girl from Nashville*).

> *Having been raped by a neighbour and beaten by her father, 16-year-old farm girl Jamie Barker runs away to Nashville to pursue her dream of being a country singer.*

She finds that the town is run by men who are interested in only one thing, and it is not her singing. But Jamie has talent and is eventually discovered by country star Jeb Hubbard, who puts her under contract, rechristens her 'Melody Mason' and takes her on tour. As Jamie's popularity grows, it eclipses Jeb's, who beats and rapes her in a drunken rage. Tired of being used and abused, Jamie declares her independence and returns home to start again.

Appearing as Jamie Barker was Monica Gayle, who was not up to the required lip-synching but had managed to rack up quite an exploitation rap-sheet, working with the likes of Larry Buchanan (*Strawberries Need Rain*, 1970), Gary Graver (*Sandra, the Making of a Woman*, 1970), Edward D Wood Jr. (*Take It Out in Trade*, 1970), Harry Novak (*Southern Comforts*, 1971) and Jack Hill (*Switchblade Sisters*). She had also featured in the aforementioned *The Stewardesses* and had starred as 'Gepetta' in the softcore hit *The Erotic Adventures of Pinocchio* (1971). Gayle's appearance in *The Girl from Nashville* led to her being cast in the long-running TV soap *General Hospital* in 1976, but her tenure there was brief and she appeared in only one more film (*Love and the Midnight Auto Supply*, 1977) before fading into obscurity.

The film was the first New World picture to go into release under two different titles simultaneously; depending on which part of the country was hosting the screening, Jamie Barker was either the (abbreviated) *Nashville Girl* or the *New Girl in Town*. With the success of the Loretta Lynn biopic *Coal Miner's Daughter* (1980), Oppenheimer opted to re-release *The Girl from Nashville* independently in 1981, changing the title and ad campaign to *Country Music Daughter*.

'*This island is my only hope—if I stayed [in Europe] I'd die.*'
—Romanian Count Liviu (Peter O'Toole) in *Foxtrot*

At the age of 32, writer/director Arturo Ripstein was one of Mexican cinema's brightest young talents. He had begun his career in 1962 as assistant director to Luis Bunuel on *The Exterminating Angel*, and his first film as a director—1966's *Time to Die*—was co-written by none other than Colombian novelist Gabriel Garcia Marquez. In 1973, Ripstein was awarded the Mexican equivalent of the Oscar (the Golden Ariel) for *Castle of Purity*; the following year, he was nominated for the *Palme D'or* at the Cannes Film Festival for *The Holy Office*. In June 1975, the Corporación Nacional Cinematográfica (CONACINE), Mexico's national film office, placed Ripstein at the helm of its first-ever English language co-production (with Caravold Productions in the US), *Foxtrot*.

In 1939, with Hitler's armies on the march across Europe, Romanian Count Liviu, his wife Julia and servants Larsen and Eusebio, make their way to a deserted island in the Mediterranean. They try to isolate themselves from the horror of war by hosting high society parties, but when their supply ship is impounded, the foursome suddenly find themselves living like castaways. Old jealousies and accusations begin to surface and the group splits into two, with the servants at odds with their former masters in what becomes a battle for survival.

Filmed a year after the success of *The Great Gatsby* (1974), *Foxtrot* plays like an ad hoc combination of F Scott Fitzgerald and Daniel Defoe (with a dash of Jean Renoir's 1939 *The Rules of the Game*), which must have been part of the attraction for star Peter O'Toole who had just played Robinson Crusoe in *Man Friday* (1975). But Ripstein's film falls into the trap of other terminally dull '70s international co-productions (usually sired by such as Dino De Laurentiis, Carlo Ponti, Lew Grade or some combination thereof), which lost millions but gave extended vacations and huge pay-cheques to the likes of Richard Harris, Omar Sharif and Sophia Loren, in that there is little of substance beyond the glitz and the glamour. True to form, *Foxtrot* afforded O'Toole, Max Von Sydow and Charlotte Rampling a nice time of it on location in Cabo San Lucas, standing in for Majorca.

When New World Pictures purchased *Foxtrot* for American release, Ripstein was delighted. A spokesman for the director told the *Los Angeles Times*, 'He was concerned that it not be distributed by a major studio, fearing that it might just be thrown out to the public without the proper exposure.' It was Corman's intention for *Foxtrot* to be New World's first art film release of 1976, but when it found no takers after a brief test run in March, it was put on the shelf. There it stayed for 18 months until Corman decided to borrow the title of a 1953 French film—*The Other Side of Paradise*—and re-release *Foxtrot* under its new alias in November 1977, with a markedly more provocative ad campaign ('In Search of Pleasure They Went Too Far!'; 'A Garden of Sin and Seduction!') and some additional nude coupling between body doubles for O'Toole and Rampling. It was all for nothing, as the film languished in the also-rans. Arturo Ripstein, although he went on to a prosperous career, was greatly dismayed and never again made an English-language feature.

'The suspects are free and away and if you want to catch them, I suggest you call the Strategic Air Command.'
—Sheriff's deputy in *Eat My Dust!*

While many kids grow up in front of a television, 22-year-old Ronald William Howard of Duncan, Oklahoma had grown up *on* the television, first as little Opie Taylor in *The Andy Griffith Show* (1960-68) then as teenager Richie Cunningham in *Happy Days*, beginning in 1974. Howard's dream, however, was to become a director and, to that end, he had attended film school at USC for two years. But he realised that to make things happen, he would have to go where the action was—literally. Fortuitously, he had received an offer from New World Pictures to star in

Eat My Dust! (Ron Howard)

its upcoming production *The Car*. Howard disliked Charles Griffith's script, but he knew that opportunity presented itself in the form of Roger Corman. Accordingly, when Howard met with the New World boss, he brought along a script that he had written with his father (actor Rance Howard) called *'Tis the Season*. His proposal was simple—he would star in *The Car* if Corman agreed to produce his script. Corman was not exactly wild about what young Ron had handed him, but he made a counter proposal—do *The Car* and New World would back his first directing gig, provided that he could come up with something exploitable. A deal was done, and Ron Howard spent ten happy days over Christmas 1975 moonlighting as Hoover Niebold of Puckerbush County.

> *Hoover Neibold, son of the Puckerbush County sheriff, is deperate to impress blonde debutante Darlene Kurtz. At her insistence, he steals 'Mabel', the winning stock car of driver Big Bubba Jones, and the two go for a wild ride through the county. They are pursued by Hoover's father, his deputies, their friends and other stock cars, leaving a trail of wreckage and destruction in their wake. When the ride is over, so is Darlene's interest, but Bubba has found himself a new protégé..*

The Car was Charles Griffith's first directorial effort since *Forbidden Island* for Columbia in 1959, though he had acted as assistant director on several films, including *The Young Racers* (1963), *The Secret Invasion* (1964) and *The She Beast* (1966), as well as directing second unit on *Death Race 2000*. After Howard's ten days on set were up, *The Car* still required some three weeks of stunt work; in this, Griffith was assisted by Barbara Peeters, but the location grind took an unexpected turn. 'I was out shooting the country in the dust,' Griffith told *Senses of Cinema*. 'When I came back to the office.. I just said, 'They oughta call [this picture] 'Eat My Dust', and the heads in the sales department turned around and looked at me. I said I was just kidding, but too late; it became *Eat My Dust!*'

Released under that title in April 1976, *Eat My Dust!* drew a mixed reception from critics. '[It] starts slow, gets into high gear for a long stretch, and then begins running out of gas, but not before winning its stripes as a clever money-making vehicle,' said *Variety*. 'The cast.. acts as though *Eat My Dust!* matters,' observed the *New York Times*. 'It doesn't. It's simply another slick-looking Roger Corman time-killer for the summer kiddie trade.' A surprisingly hostile review from Kevin Thomas appeared in the *Los Angeles Times*: '*Eat My Dust!* suggests that all cops are morons, that anyone over 21 is a hypocrite or fool or both and, above all, that everything—but everything—is for the taking,' he ranted. 'What kind of values are these to feed the teenyboppers this film is so specially designed to attract?'

Profitable ones, apparently. *Eat My Dust!* attracted its audience to the tune of nearly $5 million in rentals. How much this had to do with Jon Davison's round of off-the-wall promotional gimmicks is anyone's guess, but New World encouraged theatre owners to put tongue in cheek when booking *Eat My Dust!* and:

- Hold a 'dust-eating' contest in the lobby, using wheat germ and awarding free passes to those 'consuming inordinate amounts.'
- 'Caution your audience that the action and thrills in *Eat My Dust!* are so intense that seat-belts have been deemed a necessary precaution in the theatre.. plant seat-belts in selected seats and offer a free soda to anyone who happens to sit in one.'
- 'Offer free passes to anyone who can prove that they can live up to this claim [the most speeding tickets] in your area. Passes can also be awarded to anyone who has incurred a traffic violation within the week. This kind of exploitation ploy is certain to garner attention.'

Fighting Mad (Peter Fonda)

'This is a free country.. everything's for sale.'
—Strip-mining tycoon Pierce Crabtree (Philip Carey) in *Fighting Mad*

Before he was sent in to rescue *Crazy Mama*, Jonathan Demme had been working for several months on a script for Corman entitled *Fighting Mad*. 'Roger wanted a movie in the *Walking Tall* [1973] vein and suggested strip-mining as a background,' Demme told *American Film*. 'The whole subject was galvanizing—I wrote a righteous, kick-ass movie.' He also wrote an identikit movie, as former New World staffer Beverly Gray recalled in her book, 'He used a large chart to analyse three low-budget hits of the day: *Billy Jack* (1971), *Walking Tall* and *Dirty Mary, Crazy Larry* (1974). Demme noted that these rural action thrillers had significant elements in common: a hero with an odd weapon, an offbeat mode of transportation, and an unusual sidekick. So, as Corman grinned appreciatively, Demme proposed his own screen project, in which his leading man wielded a crossbow, travelled on an old Indian motorcycle, and hung out with his toddler son.'

> Tom Hunter and his son Dylan travel from California to the family ranch in New Mexico for Thanksgiving. Upon their arrival, Tom discovers that Pierce Crabtree, the local strip-mining tycoon, has been pressuring everyone in the valley to sell their land and leave. The Hunter clan has so far refused, and is systematically being harassed by Crabtree's goons. After the death of his brother, sister-in-law and father, Hunter takes a crossbow and a magnum and heads for Crabtree's mansion to repay the land baron in kind.

Fighting Mad would be the second of four Corman productions for 20th Century Fox, which meant a somewhat inflated budget of $600,000 and a name actor (Peter Fonda) in the lead. Not that either helped; on its April '76 release, the box-office was poor and critical response was negative. *Variety* said that *Fighting Mad* 'doesn't waste time on such things as rounded characters and motivational development, but delivers its full quota of explosions, car chases, stabbings, and other turn-ons for the vigilante mentality that seems to have appeal today.' Kevin Thomas echoed that sentiment: 'Demme.. has allowed violence to outweigh ideas to such a degree that the picture becomes a turnoff, little more than a blatantly obvious play to the yahoo mentality.' The *New York Times* put it more succinctly: 'A film so determined to stir the viscera that it overlooks the nourishment of the brain.'

The film marked the end of Demme's work with Corman, as he subsequently graduated to the major league. He next directed *Citizen's Band* (aka *Handle with Care*) for Paramount in 1977, and *Last Embrace* for United Artists in 1979. Both were flops. But in 1980, he directed the quirky comedy *Melvin and Howard* for Universal, which won two Oscars (Best Actress for Mary Steenburgen and Best Screenplay for Bo Goldman). After the failure of his next studio film, *Swing Shift* in 1984, Demme spent the rest of the '80s concentrating on documentaries (*Stop Making Sense, Swimming to Cambodia*) and low-budget comedies (*Something Wild, Married to the Mob*), becoming moderately successful at both. His biggest commercial success came in 1991, with an adaptation of Thomas Harris's 1988 *The Silence of the Lambs*, which grossed over $100 million and won five Oscars, including that for Best Director. Demme had another big hit with the Tom Hanks-Denzel Washington AIDS drama *Philadelphia* in 1993, but his adaptation of Toni Morrison's 1987 novel *Beloved* (1998) and ill-advised remake of 1963's *Charade*, retitled *The Truth About Charlie* (2002), stumbled badly. He recovered ground in 2004 with a remake of *The Manchurian Candidate* and subsequently returned to making documentaries on subjects as varied as rock singer Neil Young and former US President Jimmy Carter.

Beginning with the role of the plant manager in *Swing Shift*, Demme paid his debt to Corman by casting him in several of his movies, including *The Silence of the Lambs* (as Director of the FBI), *Philadelphia* (a lawyer) and *The Manchurian Candidate* (a Cabinet member). In this, Demme was following the lead of Francis Coppola, who also had cast Corman as a senator in *The Godfather Part II* (1974).

> 'There's nothin' wrong with being a crook--everybody's crooked.'
> —Career criminal Coley Blake (Tommy Lee Jones) in *Jackson County Jail*

Michael Miller's proposed follow-up to *Street Girls*, the announced *Uptown Ladies*, had not been able to find a writer worthy of its salacious premise. But as fate would have it, rookie scribe Donald Stewart—who would go on to win an Oscar for co-writing Costa-Gavras's *Missing* in 1982—was about to suggest something different, as Miller told *Film Comment*: '[Stewart] said, "Why don't we do a whole movie on a rape?" and, bam, that was it. We put cars and trucks all around it and we had a movie.'

> *Dinah Hunter, a frustrated ad exec, leaves her job and her cheating boyfriend in LA to return to New York. Driving across country, her car and valuables are stolen by two junkie hitchhikers; she is then incarcerated as a trouble-maker when a local bartender accosts her. While being held in the cells, she is beaten and raped by a jailer whom she kills in revenge. Imprisoned along with her is career criminal Coley Blake, who steals the jailer's keys and together they flee the scene. But the pursuing cops dog their every move and eventually catch up with them at a smalltown Bicentennial parade.*

Filmed on a $500,000 budget over four weeks in late 1975, what started out as *Harvest* was released in April 1976 as *Jackson County Jail*, a title obviously

influenced by AIP's 1974 hit, *Macon County Line*. The film also borrowed *Macon County*'s innocents-caught-up-in-smalltown-violence theme, though its 36-year-old director had deeper meaning in mind: 'I was into making a Bicentennial film,' Miller said. 'I wanted the film to be a metaphor of where I felt the country was in 1976: there was a big struggle toward women's rights, there was understanding of criminal consciousness, and there were a lot of fools celebrating this July 4th and police were shooting down people in parades.'

Taut, tense and very well played, *Jackson County Jail* gave New World some of the best reviews in its history, from the likes of Vincent Canby ('Filmmaking of relentless energy and harrowing excitement that recalls the agit-prop melodramas of the 30s'), Roger Ebert ('As a statement on rape, this movie's about 10 times more powerful and honest than *Lipstick*' [a Dino De Laurentiis 'rape' film, released the same year]), and Kevin Thomas ('An example of exploitation filmmaking at its most creative, it turns back all the obligatory genre requirements.. to produce a harrowing image of Bicentennial America').

Not that the praise was unanimous, as *Variety* made clear: 'An annoyingly superficial pic.. that fails to follow through on what it starts, ending with minimum impact and a sense of missed opportunities.'

To mention the words New World and critical acclaim in the same sentence was, to some, an oxymoron; indeed, the company itself seemed at a loss as to how to market the film. On the one hand, exhibitors were advised, 'Effort should be made to tie in the picture's opening with local women's lib activities, particularly if there is a nearby campus.' Then, three points down the list, an entirely different approach was recommended: 'Have pretty girls dressed in prison garb (with name of film and opening date stenciled on) passing out handbills in heavy street traffic.. Theatre personnel can also be dressed in prison suits.'

Star Yvette Mimieux (who had burst sensuously onto the scene in 1960 with *The Time Machine* and *Where the Boys Are*) was furious at the ad campaign, which featured a still photograph of the rape scene with the tag line, 'What they do to her in Jackson County Jail is a crime!' As she commented to columnist Marilyn Beck: 'I was wary about making a picture for Corman, but I liked the script because it gave me a chance to play a woman of depth. As it turned out, I don't think he even realised this was a better property than most things he does. He was involved with six other projects at the same time and when it came to the ad campaign, he just took the easy way out, following his established formula for grabbing a guaranteed audience.'

The film earned $2.3 million in rentals; certainly, a tidy profit—but Mimieux thought it could have done better. 'I think the title is what discouraged a lot of people from seeing it,' she told UPI's Vernon Scott. 'I mean, *Jackson County Jail* just sounds like an exploitation film with a lot of heavy brutality, auto chases, shoot-outs and things like that.. *Harvest* would have attracted an entirely different sort of audience. It has, well, an artistic sound to it compared to *Jackson County Jail*.'

One person who saw *Jackson County Jail* was hairdresser-turned-producer and current boyfriend of Barbra Streisand, Jon Peters, who was so impressed that he signed Miller to direct Streisand's next project, a thriller called *Eyes* (from a pre-*Halloween* screenplay by John Carpenter). Over the next two years, the script passed through four other writers (including *Straw Dogs*'s David Z Goodman and *Nashville*'s Joan Tewkesbury), Streisand found herself replaced by Faye Dunaway (though she still sang the theme song 'Prisoner'), and Miller was given the boot in favour of Irvin Kershner. The result, released by Columbia as *Eyes of Laura Mars* in August 1978, was a flop.

In 1976, the month of May would bring much satisfaction to Roger Corman, both personally and professionally. The former was in the birth of his first son, Roger Martin (almost exactly a year after that of his daughter Catherine); the latter was in being profiled in print (in a series of ads by the Eastman Kodak Company) and on the CBS television program, *Camera Three*. 'The average run-of-the-mill film is something I'm definitely not interested in,' Corman stated for Kodak. 'We're working with some extremely talented young people, and feel that our best films are still to come.'

With that in mind, Corman announced in June that he was upping the budget ceiling on New World's films to $750,000. He was also embarking on a three-way co-production agreement with Edgar Scherick and Daniel Blatt of Fadsin Cinema Associates and Caravold's Gerald Green to bring novelist Joanne Greenberg's 1964 bestseller *I Never Promised You a Rose Garden* to the screen. The film was set to roll in the late summer on a $3 million budget, with Hungarian Peter Medak (*The Ruling Class*, 1972) directing and Charlotte Rampling (courtesy of Caravold, co-producers of *Foxtrot*) in the lead. Scherick and Blatt had acquired both the rights and Lewis John Carlino's pre-existing script from Columbia for $250,000, after the studio had tried and failed to mount a screen adaptation throughout the '60s with such directors as Mark Rydell and Jan Kadar and stars like Natalie Wood and Liza Minnelli. Not wishing to inherit bad karma, Corman hired Gavin Lambert (*Sons and Lovers*, *The Roman Spring of Mrs. Stone*) to rework Carlino's script.

New World also announced two other upcoming productions, both starring David Carradine: *Deathsport* (the sequel to *Death Race 2000*) and *Cannonball*. With its $1 million budget, *Cannonball* became a four-way co-production between New World, Gustave Berne's Harbor Properties, Sam Gelfman's Cross Country Productions, and Hong Kong mogul Run Run Shaw. With all of this wheeling and dealing, small wonder that Corman was moved to tell *Variety*, 'This is the biggest year we've ever had!'

However, in Corman's upping of the ante, other factors were at work beyond mere prestige. Like Fox before them, other Hollywood studios had taken notice of New World's stellar performance; unlike Fox, the rest of the 'big boys' did not want to partner Corman—they wanted to beat him at his own game. Accordingly, they

US theatrical poster for Cannonball

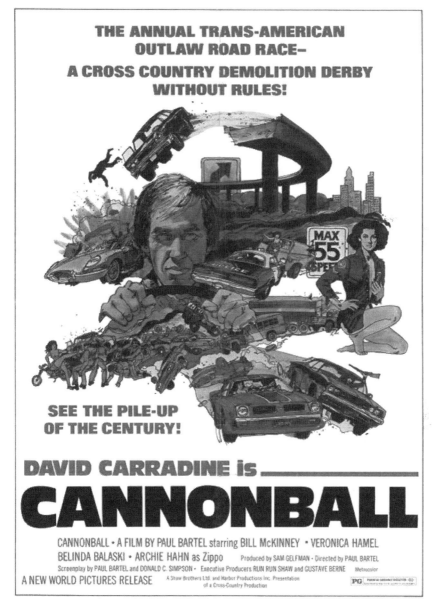

began to hire away his talent (even Julie Corman defected for a time to develop a $2 million disaster film for AIP about the sinking of California) and copy his films (with titles like *The Gumball Rally, Vigilante Force* and *White Line Fever*). They also exercised their considerable clout to out-book and out-promote New World, to the extent that lawyer Barbara Boyle and sales manager Bob Rehme threatened legal action in response. 'Small companies like us don't get lied to by exhibitors,' Rehme complained to *Variety*. 'If we've got a bomb, our customers tell us. But when we've got strong product they tell us that, too.. We've had customers apologise for cancelling or shortening playdates on grounds that the big distributors are forcing their own product.'

> *'Stupid American cars—they look like Tootsie Rolls on wheels!'*
> —German driver Wolf Messer (James Keach) in *Cannonball*

Producer Sam Gelfman, who had a percentage interest in both *Caged Heat* and *Cockfighter* when he was with Artists Entertainment Complex, had recently left that company and struck out on his own as Cross Country Productions. The name was inspired by Gelfman's first self-developed property—a cross-country road race movie called *Cannonball*, based on the real-life 'Cannonball Run', which had begun in 1971 as a protest against the imposition of a mandatory 55mph speed limit across the US. After the success of *Death Race 2000*, Gelfman had signed David Carradine to star and Paul Bartel to direct, and he had interested Fox, where the film had gone into development before being dropped. Undaunted, Gelfman had Bartel rewrite Don Simpson's script, then he secured financing from Gustave Berne, Run Run Shaw and finally New World. (Simpson would go on to partner Jerry Bruckheimer and produce such '80s megahits as *Flashdance, Beverly Hills Cop* and *Top Gun*, before dying of heart failure in 1996 at the age of 52)

> *An assortment of characters compete for the $100,000 prize in the third annual (and illegal) Trans America Grand Prix Auto Race, from LA to New York. The leader of the pack is Coy 'Cannonball' Buckman, in his first race since a fatal accident took the life of a female passenger. Buckman is accompanied on the trip by a female parole officer, but she winds up in a decoy car driven by Zippo, who imagines that he is Cannonball. Meanwhile, Buckman's brother, in debt to the mob, is engineering 'accidents' to ensure Cannonball's victory.*

'My films are analogous to Ritz crackers,' Bartel told *Newsday*. 'They are a low-cost entertainment staple.' But *Cannonball*, brought in at $780,000, actually cost nearly three times as much as *Death Race 2000* and made only $1.5 million in rentals. Nor did it impress the critics, as it started in Los Angeles ('Just another of New World's spate of mindless destruction derbies that feature mammoth car wrecks above all else'—*Los Angeles Times*), raced through Chicago ('Without the traffic copter the story would have been impossible to follow—but then why follow the story anyway?'--Roger Ebert), and ended up in New York ('Long on speed and the destruction of automobiles and short on logic and complexities of character'—*New York Times*).

Since nearly a quarter of the budget went to Carradine (and even more to a climactic demolition derby), *Cannonball's* casting allowance must have been slim: Bartel, Gelfman and Simpson all appear in their own movie, along with a host of other New Worlders, including Allan Arkush and Joe Dante (as two nerds running a junkyard), Jonathan Kaplan (as a gas station attendant), Martin Scorsese and Sylvester Stallone (as mafiosi munching fried chicken), and none other than Roger Corman himself as the (what else?) Los Angeles District Attorney. The ubiquitous Dick Miller is Bennie Buckman, while Mary Woronov and Louisa Moritz return from *Death Race 2000*.

Bartel had planned to make his own sequel to *Death Race*, called *Frankencar*, until Corman politely reminded him about a little detail called copyright. Corman might have been better off focussing on Hal Needham and Burt Reynolds, whose two biggest hits as director and star borrowed wholesale from *Cannonball*. The duo's *Smokey and the Bandit* (1977) featured Reynolds driving a black Trans Am, complete with reluctant female passenger, and car-jumping a dismantled bridge. *Cannonball* has Carradine driving a red Trans Am, with reluctant female passenger, car-jumping an incomplete overpass. Needham's follow-up *Cannonball Run* (1981) featured among its drivers an Englishman, two women in a sports car, a jock seconded by a country singer, and a motorcyclist who skydives out of a cargo hold. *Cannonball*'s drivers included a German, three women in a van, a hard-nosed racer seconded by a country singer, and a family man who flies his Jimmy cross-country in a TWA cargo hold.

In a sign of New World's growing respectability, *Cannonball* (with Scorsese's *Taxi Driver*) was chosen to open the Edinburgh Film Festival, which was hosting a mini-retrospective on the company that August. *Jackson County Jail, Nashville Girl, Hollywood Boulevard* and *Fighting Mad* were also on the Scottish marquee at a festival which had played host to one of the very first Roger Corman tributes six years earlier.

> *'C'mon.. let's get rich.'*
> —Bank robber Candy Morgan (Claudia Jennings) in *The Great Texas Dynamite Chase*

Back in 1973, Claudia Jennings had told the *Chicago Tribune*, 'I've done eight rotten roles in a row. If there's a bad girl in a B movie, I get the part.. But no more. I've just finished my last B movie [*Gator Bait*]. From now on I'm doing only A pictures or none at all. And I'm not uptight about it because you know what?

The Great Texas Dynamite Chase (Claudia Jennings)

I can afford to wait.' Unfortunately, the only A picture that came Jennings's way was Nicolas Roeg's *The Man Who Fell to Earth* (1976), in which she made a brief (and uncredited) appearance as Bernie Casey's wife. To keep her career moving, the resentful Queen 'B' took to guest spots on TV crime dramas like *The FBI, Cannon, Caribe* and *The Streets of San Francisco*. Three years after her defiant boast to the *Tribune*, Jennings swallowed her pride and enlisted in Yasny Talking Pictures' production, *Dynamite Women*.

> *After breaking out of a Texas prison, Candy Morgan uses dynamite to rob a bank and save the family farm; she is aided in the heist by fired bank-teller Ellie-Jo. Their paths cross again when Ellie-Jo hitches a lift from Candy. They decide to join forces and rob banks for a living, then head down to Mexico once their spree is over. Nicknamed 'The Dynamite Women' due to their modus operandi, they take a hostage in Slim, a petty thief who falls in love with Ellie-Jo and turns the duo into a trio. But the police are hot on their trail, and a trap is set for the girls that they cannot resist.*

New World's best outlaw film was the one it did not produce but only released (as *The Great Texas Dynamite Chase*). It features a showcase performance from Jennings as Candy, and good support from unknown Jocelyn Jones as Ellie-Jo and former child/pop star Johnny Crawford (best known for playing Chuck Connors's son on *The Rifleman* TV show) as Slim. It also has many elements that anticipate director Ridley Scott's better-known *Thelma and Louise* (1991), some 15 years off— two 'liberated' women fugitives heading for Mexico, picking up a young stud, and trying to stay one step ahead of a growing posse of cops.

Business was not so great, but the critical response was strong. 'The chases, fights and explosions are funny and spectacular. For a change, the friendship between two women is the heart of the story,' said *New West* magazine. 'A thoroughly entertaining role reversal romp. Claudia Jennings and Jocelyn Jones are dynamite,' raved the *San Francisco Bay Guardian*. 'A good example of a well-made exploitation film which works on two levels, providing kicks for the ozoner crowd and tongue-in-cheek humor for the more sophisticated,' praised *Variety*. 'A stylish and enjoyable fantasy about friendship among thieves,' commended the *Los Angeles Times*.

The accolades were something of a surprise to 26-year-old, first-time director

Michael Pressman, a former CalArts student, who confessed his reticence about making the film to the *Los Angeles Times*: '*Dynamite Chase* is not me. Perhaps the angle, bent and humour is but I want to make more personal films.. I'm semi-uncomfortable with the violence in my film. It's a mistake but I did it out of insecurity, to touch all the bases.' For Pressman, *The Great Texas Dynamite Chase* was simply a means to an end: 'Hollywood is a tough place that's going through a strong exploitation trend and I needed to get into the arena.' His gambit worked—he would go on to direct several major-studio films (*Boulevard Nights, Some Kind of Hero, Doctor Detroit*) before settling into television, where he has produced and directed for such hit shows as *Chicago Hope, Picket Fences, Law & Order* and *Cashmere Mafia*.

> '*All the authority I need is to blow their dirty, hippie heads off!*'
> —Crooked Sheriff Rankin (Lonny Chapman) in *Moving Violation*

Released in the same month as *Dynamite Chase* (August 1976), Corman's third production for Fox, entitled *Moving Violation*, was actually produced by his wife Julie, who turned the film into a showcase for stunt co-ordinator Barbara Peeters; in fact, several of her tricks (including a cop car having its roof sheared off when it slides underneath a trailer) were borrowed the following year by *Smokey and the Bandit*. Along with fellow New World veteran Teri Schwartz (who had been production manager, assistant director and/or associate producer on *Big Bad Mama, Capone, Hollywood Boulevard* and *Eat My Dust*), Peeters formed The Big Movie Company in 1977 with an eye to moving up the ladder: 'If I'm going to take the blame, then I want to make the decisions,' she told the *Los Angeles Times*. 'I consider real power

Moving Violation/US theatrical poster

107

the point when you're not afraid to fail.. I don't know any director who wants to spend his whole life making low-budget exploitation movies, just as nobody wants to spend their whole life in kindergarten. You look forward to graduating to high school.'

Drifter Eddie Moore meets Camille at an ice cream store. They drive to the mansion of an oil tycoon to skin-dip in his pool, but inadvertently witness the local sheriff murder a blackmailing deputy. Moore and Camille are accused of the crime, and thus begins a life on the lamb. One who believes their story is down-home lawyer Alex Warren, who makes a deal with the state to surrender them to the court in exchange for protection from the cops. On the steps of the courthouse, Alex is gunned down by the sheriff and his henchmen, Camille is put in hospital, and Eddie runs for his life..

Unlike Corman's two previous efforts for Fox, the talent in *Moving Violation* came almost exclusively from the small screen. Stephen McHattie and Kay Lenz had both won critical raves and huge ratings for their respective performances in *James Dean* (with McHattie providing an uncanny likeness in the title role) and *Rich Man, Poor Man* (in which Lenz's portrayal of Kate Jordache had earned her an Emmy nomination). Television was also the main claim to fame for supporting players Eddie Albert (*Green Acres*) and Will Geer (*The Waltons*). After directing *Mister Rock and Roll* for Paramount in 1957, the film's 57-year-old helmer Charles Dubin had worked exclusively in television, directing episodes of *The Defenders, The Big Valley, The Virginian* and *Ironside*, among many others. In 1965, he had produced and directed a critically acclaimed Rodgers and Hammerstein version of *Cinderella*, featuring Lesley Ann Warren and Ginger Rogers.

In September 1976, New World Pictures moved into its new, two-storey office block at 11600 San Vicente Boulevard, in the heart of LA's affluent Brentwood district. Constructed at a cost of $750,000 by Beach Dickerson—sometime actor, sometime building contractor—it was described by Beverly Gray as 'modest and utilitarian, to put it as kindly as possible.'

New World also continued with its foreign film pick-ups, including Francois Truffaut's *Small Change*, actress Jeanne Moreau's debut feature *Lumiere* and Akira Kurosawa's *Dersu Uzala* ('The Hunter'), which had already won the Oscar for Best Foreign Film. The American rights cost only $75,000, but because *Dersu Uzala* was a co-production between Japan and the Soviet Union, it became caught up in red tape to the extent that New World was unable to release it for nearly a year—though its eventual $400,000 in rentals made it worth the wait.

In its new surroundings, the company soon announced its biggest production ever, the disaster movie *Avalanche*, budgeted at $2 million. Gavin Lambert, who had already penned the script for New World's upcoming adaptation of *I Never Promised You a Rose Garden*, was engaged to write *Avalanche* as well. 'The great thing about an avalanche, unlike *The Towering Inferno* or *Earthquake*, is that it's over very quickly,' Lambert told *Variety*. 'Disaster movies nearly all have crummy scripts; that's the problem. If you were doing the first four or five films of that type, you didn't have to bother with character much, I suppose, but it's essential now, because the others haven't.'

'*People who are too religious make a lot of trouble for everybody.'*
—New York Police Commissioner (Mike Kellin) in *God Told Me To*

Larry Cohen was born in Kingston, New York, in July 1938. After attending the City College of New York in the early 1960s, he came to Hollywood and became a prolific writer for television shows like *The Defenders, Blue Light* and *Coronet Blue*; he also created the western *Branded* (1965-66) and sci-fi series *The Invaders* (1967-68). In the motion picture arena, he found time to write westerns (*Return of the Magnificent Seven, El Condor*) and psycho-thrillers (*Scream, Baby, Scream; Daddy's Gone A-Hunting*) before making his directorial debut with *Bone* for Jack H Harris in 1972. He then helmed a couple of blaxploitation films for AIP and Fred Williamson in 1973 (*Black Caesar, Hell Up in Harlem*) before hitting the jackpot with his killer-baby horror movie, *It's Alive*, for Warners in 1974.

Cohen's next film, shot in New York and London in the fall of 1975, seemed heavily influenced by the 'Ancient Astronaut' theories of Swiss author Erich Von Daniken, popularised in his 1968 book (and subsequent documentary) *Chariots of the Gods*. Von Daniken posited the theory that the technologies and religions of ancient civilisations were gifted to them by space travelers who were welcomed as gods. Two of his more controversial assertions were that the Bible was a history of alien encounters rather than divine ones, and that human evolution was advanced by sexual contact with extraterrestrials. Larry Cohen took these two hot-button issues and wrote, produced, and directed his fifth film: *God Told Me To*.

God Told Me To (Richard Lynch)

The people of this city are being terrorized.
The crimes have no motives.
The killers have one explanation...

GOD TOLD ME TO

IT WILL GIVE YOU NIGHTMARES FOREVER

"GOD TOLD ME TO"
Starring TONY LO BIANCO
SANDY DENNIS • SYLVIA SIDNEY • SAM LEVENE
ROBERT DRIVAS • MIKE KELLIN • RICHARD LYNCH
Guest Star DEBORAH RAFFIN • Music by FRANK CORDELL
Written, Produced and Directed by LARRY COHEN
A LARCO PRODUCTION • A LARRY COHEN FILM [R RESTRICTED]
A NEW WORLD PICTURES RELEASE • IN COLOR

In New York City, a sniper fires into a crowded street, killing and wounding dozens. When Detective Peter Nicholas confronts the shooter, he tells Nicholas, 'God told me to,' then leaps to his death. During a St. Patrick's Day parade, a cop goes berserk and begins shooting at the crowd before being shot himself. As he lies dying, he says the same—'God told me to.' After another man shoots his wife and children to the same refrain, Nicholas discovers that the perpetrators of these incidents were each visited by a mystery man with long blonde hair.. The stranger

109

goes by the name of Bernard Phillips, but he is not human—he is the hermaphroditic by-product of alien abduction. As well as willing people to kill, Phillips has assembled a cabal to assume control when mass hysteria takes over. To his horror, Nicholas learns of a bond that he shares with Phillips due to a sinister secret locked in his past; he must now confront his 'brother' if he is to put an end to the killings in God's name..

'Throughout history, any time a superior civilisation encounters a primitive society they are very often mistaken for gods,' Cohen told *Cinefantastique*. 'Almost every time this happens, the primitive people are destroyed, butchered violently by those they accept as God. I tried to put all these things together in modern form and hope that people will listen and try to make their own truth out of the film.' Unfortunately for Cohen, what people actually listened to were the universally negative reviews which *God Told Me To* received when New World released it in the fall of '76. After describing the film's convoluted plot, *Variety* commented, 'If all this sounds somewhat incredible, and confusing, it is; and it gets worse.. Larry Cohen has produced, scripted and directed a thriller with lots of loose ends.' Kevin Thomas was even harsher, dismissing Cohen's film as 'yet another gratuitous and nauseating bloodbath and, to the devout, a downright blasphemy.' *Cinefantastique*, while admitting the subject matter was 'groundbreaking', nevertheless took its director to task: 'Larry Cohen.. has a knack for hitting upon absolutely marvellous ideas which he then proceeds, with single-minded ineptitude, to drive straight into the ground.'

The critics were not the only ones turned off by *God Told Me To*. TV stations and newspapers refused to carry ads for the film, and star Tony Lo Bianco filed suit against Cohen, calling the film 'repugnant, objectionable, in poor taste and lacking in artistic merit.' The heat was on and New World pulled *God Told Me To* from theatres. When it returned in the spring of 1977, it had a new title (*Demon*) and a new ad campaign ('Conceived in a hell beyond our galaxy—destined to rule the world!') to make it appear to be some sort of extraterrestrial *Exorcist* movie. It made little difference at the box-office, however.

Cohen was upset that his movie had not received the hearing which he felt it deserved, and he blamed it on double standards. 'You make a film about the devil and that's acceptable,' he told *Cinefantastique*. 'The devil can do anything that's obscene or horrifying. The existence of the devil is a verification that there is a God. The church loves pictures about Satan, because by the very nature of his existence, there is a God on the other side. But when you start dealing with God, you run into people who are very touchy about it.' What people were touchy about had more to do with Cohen's approach to the material: 'We show that religion is probably the most violent form of amusement or entertainment or recreation.'

The failure of *God Told Me To* in no way deterred Cohen from continuing to court controversy, as he moved on from *God Told Me To* to tackle the sex-life of America's number one G-Man in *The Private Files of J Edgar Hoover* (1977) for AIP. When that film failed too, Cohen returned to a more commercial route with *It Lives Again* (aka *It's Alive II*, 1978), which set the stage for his almost exclusive tenure in the horror genre with films like *Q—The Winged Serpent* (1982), *The Stuff* (1985), *It's Alive III: Island of the Alive, A Return to Salem's Lot* (both 1987), the *Maniac Cop* trilogy (1988-1993), *Body Snatchers* (1993) and *Uncle Sam* (1997). More recently, he has written scripts for urban paranoia thrillers *Phone Booth* (2002), *Cellular* (2004) and *Captivity* (2007), as well as a remake of his own *It's Alive* (2008).

With the arrival of 1977 came more recognition for Corman the *auteur* (a two-month retrospective was hosted at London's National Film Theatre), a promotion for Bob Rehme (to Vice President) and the biggest slate of announcements yet from New World. Exhibitors were assured that the coming months would see a mix of acquisitions and in-house productions, including the previously announced *Deathsport 2020, Avalanche* and *I Never Promised You a Rose Garden*. New World would also be offering the latest from Andy Warhol (*Bad*), Ron Howard's directorial debut, *Grand Theft Auto*, the animated *Dirty Duck*, the documentary *Catastrophe* and several outlaw/action movies, such as *Blonde in Black Leather, Too Hot to Handle, Black Oak Conspiracy, Assault on Paradise* and *Shine*. New World also announced plans to produce a third film in AIP's *Dr Phibes* series, *Phibes Resurrectus*, to star Vincent Price and Roddy McDowall, though this on-off project (AIP also announced it as *Bride of Phibes*) was never a real contender.

Corman's most ambitious (or outrageous, depending upon how you look at it) announcement was a $12 million co-production with Japan's Toho Company, the war film *Iwo Jima*. An 'all-star cast' was promised, and while the film never made it off the drawing board, it nevertheless remained on New World's wish list for years to come.

Bob Rehme let it be known that New World was still in the market for foreign films, though the reasons now had more to do with profit margin than artistic merit. 'Ad costs are much lower,' New World's new VP told *Variety*, 'because we don't have to use TV much to reach the foreign film audience which is very aware of films being made and know what they want to see.' For Rehme (and Corman), there was legitimate reason to watch the bottom line: 'In New York last summer we had to pay $7,000 for a 30-second spot in [Ron] Howard's *Happy Days* rerun. Now that same time costs $10,000.'

> *'All my life I've wanted to be free—to be free as a bird.'*
> —Laundress Claudia (Claudia Cardinale) in *The Adventure Begins*

While still a teenager, Carlo Di Palma became involved in the seminal classics of Italian Neorealist cinema, pulling focus on Vittorio De Sica's *The Bicycle Thief* (1948), Roberto Rossellini's *Rome, Open City* (1945) and *Paisan* (1946), and Luchino Visconti's *Ossessione* (1943) and *The Earth Trembles* (1948). In the '60s, he graduated to cinematographer on Michelangelo Antonioni's *Red Desert* (1964) and *Blow-Up* (1966) and in 1972, he directed his first film, *Teresa the Thief*, featuring Monica Vitti (*Red Desert, Modesty Blaise*) in an acclaimed performance as a high-spirited young woman who steals to survive during WWII but is unable to stop once the fighing is over. Di Palma's second film, *Qui comincia l'avventura* ('The Adventure Begins') was made in 1975 and also starred Vitti, along with another Italian sex symbol—Claudia Cardinale.

> *In rural Italy, Claudia, a laundress, leaves her mundane life behind and hitches a ride with blonde cyclist Monica, dressed head-to-toe in black leather. Monica is headed for a rendezvous in Naples; along the way, she spins tall tales of her alleged adventures in America and Russia. The girls crash the motorcycle, pick up an adolescent card shark named Tex, and run foul of the mob by winning a fortune in a casino. At the end of the journey, Claudia discovers that it has all been a sham—Monica was on the way to her job as an usherette in a cinema, the real source of all her stories.*

Ironically, the one foreign pick-up that desperately *needed* some editing was the one that Corman left alone. At 100 minutes, Di Palma's film was much too long, but what New World retitled *Blonde in Black Leather* rode in and out of theatres so

111

fast in March 1977 that no one took any notice. The film plays like a comedy version of Jack Cardiff's *Girl on a Motorcycle* (1968), with Vitti in the Marianne Faithfull role, the problem being that Di Palma's picture is laborious and not particularly funny. The film contains elements which predate both *Cinema Paradiso* (1988) and *Thelma & Louise*, but neither they nor the beauty of the female leads can compensate for a total lack of narrative direction.

Di Palma would only direct one more film, *Mimi Bluette* (1977), again featuring Vitti along with Shelley Winters and Tommy Tune. He subsequently returned to cinematography and, in 1986, began a decade-long association with Woody Allen on the New York *auteur's Hannah and Her Sisters*. Di Palma shot his final film, the documentary *Another World is Possible,* in 2001, and died three years later at the age of 79.

'I never bet on anything but a sure thing...it makes life less complicated.'
—Seductive hitwoman Samantha Fox (Cheri Caffaro) in *Too Hot to Handle*

US theatrical poster for Too Hot to Handle

Born in Miami, Florida in April 1945, sultry blonde bombshell Cheri Caffaro was in many ways the 'white man's Pam Grier'—tough, liberated, and outrageously sexy. Caffaro came to drive-in prominence in 1971, playing undercover agent Ginger McAllister in the softcore actioner *Ginger*, which was written and directed by her then-husband Don Schain. The film was a smash hit and two sequels followed: *The Abductors* (1972) and *Girls Are For Loving* (1973). She also starred in the X-rated political drama *A Place Called Today* (1972), and the AIP Filipino women's prison movie *Savage Sisters* (1974).

Both *A Place Called Today* and the Ginger films had been produced by Derio Productions, headed by Ralph T Desiderio. At the Cannes Festival in 1974, Derio announced a new action vehicle for Caffaro— *Hit Woman*, to be distributed by Avco Embassy (which had also released *A Place Called Today*). However, that deal fell through and Derio's *Hit Woman* project sat on the shelf for two years before finally going before the cameras in the Philippines in January 1976.

Samantha Fox is a contract killer operating out of Manila. She suffocates a sadistic banker, drowns an art smuggler, and electrocutes the head of a white slave ring. Her righteous killings put Inspector De La Torres on her trail and the two become lovers. After setting up rival drug lords to kill one another, Samantha plans to head for Rome. The question is whether or not she will be going alone..

Hit Woman proved to be the ultimate Cheri Caffaro vehicle, as she designed her own '70s-chic costumes while also dressing up as a dominatrix and frequently appearing either nude or in the skimpiest of bikinis to show off her all-over tan. Samantha Fox's sexual liberation is never in question—she is always on top during bouts of lovemaking and even day-dreams about sex while watching a slow-motion cockfight. Like *Stacey* before her, Samantha is independently wealthy, drives a Corvette Stingray, and lives on a yacht—and like *Ginger*, *Hit Woman* was clearly designed to be the first in a series that never materialised.

Caffaro's commercial track-record convinced Roger Corman to pick up where Avco Embassy left off, and New World released *Hit Woman* as *Too Hot to Handle* in March 1977. But it became lost in the shuffle and found few viewers. Desiderio subsequently bought the film back, when Derio formed its own distributorship in 1979, and re-released it along with the sex comedy *H.O.T.S.* Caffaro co-wrote and co-produced *H.O.T.S.* but never again acted for the camera; she served as associate producer on *The Demons of Ludlow* in 1983, before retiring from the film business for good.

'People stink.. all they do is eat, fuck and watch TV.'
—'Old bag' Estelle (Brigid Polk) in *Andy Warhol's BAD*

In 1963, 35-year-old 'pop'-art superstar Andy Warhol began to make movies. Some, like *Blow Job* and *Kiss*, lasted for less than an hour; others, like *Sleep* and *Empire,* lasted anything from five to eight hours. Things began to move in a more commercial direction with *Chelsea Girls* (1966), which was co-directed by Warhol and 28-year-old Paul Morrissey and which became the first underground film to play in mainstream theatres. The Warhol-Morrissey collaboration continued with the trilogy *Flesh* (1968), *Trash* (1970) and *Heat* (1972), all of which received general releases and starred previously unknown Joe Dallesandro. While Warhol remained in his native New York, Morrissey and Dallesandro went to Italy in 1973 to shoot *Flesh for Frankenstein* and *Blood for Dracula*, both of which, with the Warhol name

Andy Warhol's BAD

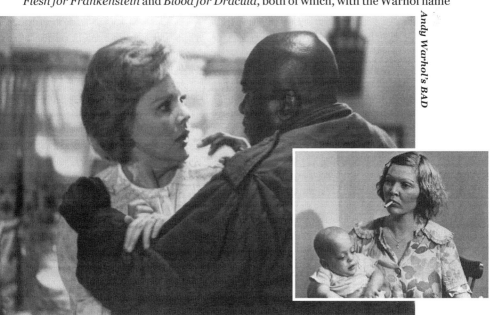

attached, became huge hits. The trio parted company in 1975, which opened the door for two new faces at Warhol's 'Factory': 24-year-old producer Jeff Tornberg and 26-year-old director Jed Johnson.

Tornberg had previously been with the Robert Stigwood Organisation, where he had optioned a new Warhol project called *BAD*. When he decided to strike out on his own, Tornberg took *BAD* with him, generating a large part of the film's $1.5 million budget (the highest ever for a Warhol production) via foreign pre-sales. 'It's the excitement of the unknown,' the young producer told the *Los Angeles Times*. 'Everyone wants to know what Warhol can do with $1 million!'

'We've always wanted to make a big movie,' Warhol told the *Times*, 'but we've never had the money.. we love the polish of the professional crew. If you can direct something like this, you can do anything.' That must have come as cold comfort to Johnson, who was making his directorial debut after having shot and/or edited Warhol's *Women in Revolt* (1971) and *L'Amour* (1973).

> *From her home in Queens, Hazel Aiken runs an electrolysis salon—and a murder-for-hire ring, composed entirely of young women. When not pulling hair or ordering hits, Aiken spends time with her deadbeat husband, terminally ill mother, weepy daughter-in-law and newborn grandson. A big money opportunity presents itself when the wife of the local newscaster wants her autistic son 'euthanised'. Aiken's assassin of choice is unavailable but she recommends a man, LT, who moves into the household and begins to take control. Meanwhile, Aiken has to deal with a crooked cop, who wants a bust in exchange for his continued protection of her business..*

A New York slice-of-life as only Andy Warhol could present it, *BAD* is full of dirty diapers, overflowing toilets, porn magazines, melted ice cream and flatulating women. Characters are at best neurotic and often complete sociopaths, who think nothing of setting a cinema on fire, robbing cripples, stabbing dogs, or dropping babies out of windows—though this is par-for-the-course in an environment where a news broadcast heralds a 'record' 13 killings in a single day.

In the lead role of Hazel was 46-year-old Carroll Baker, in her first American film since her battles in the late '60s with movie mogul Joseph E Levine (and a messy divorce) led to a self-imposed exile in Italy; Baker had found fame (and an Oscar nomination) at the age of 25, playing the title role in Elia Kazan's *Baby Doll* (1956), which she followed with parts in *Giant* (1959), *How the West Was Won* (1962) and *Cheyenne Autumn* (1964) before starring in Levine's productions of *The Carpetbaggers* (1964) and *Harlow* (1965). 'You can hardly call making an Andy Warhol movie a comeback,' she told the *Times*. 'It's more like going to the moon! The subject is totally unique. These characters are normal, sweet-looking people who are monsters without knowing they are monsters. It's an attack on middle-class morality. These people have no conscience whatsoever. Their god is money and anything is justified so long as it pays well.'

Shot in the spring of 1976 and released by New World a year later, *BAD* found both admirers and detractors for itself in the critical community. *Variety* said that watching *BAD* was 'a compellingly revolting experience. This is among the blackest of black comedies.. Don't see it after eating.' Vincent Canby was more eloquent, writing that '*BAD* is not only the most stylistically conventional Warhol comedy to date, it is also the most forthrightly satirical.. It is, indeed, as much an artefact of our time as a comment upon it.' Kevin Thomas, however, was not impressed—'All told, *BAD* is a pretty sick business'—and neither was Gene Siskel: 'Beware of Andy Warhol's *BAD*. It has very little of the artist's touch.. all there is to *Bad* is bad taste.' Perhaps the *New York Daily News* put it best, terming *BAD* 'A movie with something to offend absolutely everybody.'

'Art was never like this!' said the New World ads, but the fact that it was the company's first ever X-rated film severely limited its exposure, and it disappeared quickly from the scene. Corman felt that there was another reason why *Bad* did not reach its audience, as he told di Franco: 'It was a straighter commercial film than some of [Warhol's] earlier far-out pieces, and not as successful. I have a feeling that when the audience saw the name Andy Warhol they really wanted a more experimental-type film.'

Warhol only produced two more films—*Cocaine Cowboys* (1979) and *Blank Generation* (1980), both of which were directed by German Ulli Lommel—before dying of complications from gall bladder surgery in February 1987 at the age of 58. The lives of *BAD*'s producer and director were also cut short, as Tornberg died of AIDS in December 1994, and Johnson was a passenger on the ill-fated TWA Flight 800 that exploded in mid-air in July 1996.

> *'If you continue to irritate me you're gonna find out that I can be a very mean person.'*
> —Bad guy Harrison Hancock (Robert F Lyons) in *Black Oak Conspiracy*

In April 1974, AIP released *Macon County Line*, directed by Richard Compton of *Angels Die Hard* and produced by Max Baer Jr, formerly 'Jethro' of *The Beverly Hillbillies* TV show (they also co-wrote the film). Baer played a Southern sheriff in the 1950s, who is hell-bent on killing two brothers whom he wrongly accuses of the murder of his wife. A hybrid of *American Graffiti* and *Walking Tall*, the film was the most successful independent release of the year, earning over $8 million in rentals. (A name-only sequel called *Return to Macon County* was released in 1975 and starred unknowns Nick Nolte and Don Johnson.)

Chris and Wayne Dixon, the accused siblings, were played by real-life brothers Alan and Jesse Vint, who were natives of Tulsa, Oklahoma. They had guest starred in numerous TV shows like *Bonanza*, *The FBI*, *The High Chaparral* and *Mission: Impossible,* as well as featuring in *Silent Running* (1971), *Two Lane Blacktop*, *Badlands* (1973) and *Chinatown* (1974). The success of *Macon County Line* saw the duo cast as crazy Marjoe Gortner's room-mates in Universal's *Earthquake*, but Alan went back to television while Jesse continued on in films like *Bug* (1975) and *Bobbie Jo and the Outlaw* (1976). He then decided to produce his own version of *Macon County*, forming a company with Tulsa couple, Tom and Gail Clark. Vint found a treatment by Hugh Smith called *Black Oak Conspiracy*, rewrote it, and began to look for a crew for the $300,000 production. But in his hiring, he made a beginner's mistake, as he told *Shock Cinema*: 'I fell into the trap of using veterans who had been working in television forever. These guys, bar none.. they had no enthusiasm for the project. They were only waiting to pick up their cheques and get the hell home to figure out all the overtime and every other goddamn thing.'

> *Hollywood stuntman Jingo Johnson returns home to the town of Black Oak to find his mother in a nursing home and the homestead demolished by a strip-mining company. Jingo's old girlfriend Lucy is being wooed by town jerk Harrison Hancock, son of land tycoon Bryan. Together with the crooked pair of Sheriff Grimes and Doc Rhodes, the Hancocks have come up with a scheme to make all the town's old folks sign away their land in exchange for free care in the nursing home. When Johnson's mother dies of an overdose, he vows to discover the truth—and to make those responsible pay.*

As audiences had seen all of this umpteen times before, it was small wonder that Vint could find no enthusiasm among his crew. *Variety* said it best: 'Previous successes dictate the format of the Southern revenge meller. Essential elements include the corrupt sheriff, a hot-headed but good-hearted outsider with a strong right hook, at least three car chases and one final shoot out. It is helpful to give the sheriff a paunch along with a dumb deputy, dress the villains in leisure suits and the hero in down vests and faded dungaree jackets, explode no less than two new autos and coin a minimum of one clever wisecrack. *Black Oak Conspiracy*, the newest entry from the homeland for this genre, New World Pictures, follows the book'

New World ended up with *Black Oak* simply because, as Vint said, 'Roger was the guy we showed it to first. He released the film, and it played all over the world. It should've made me rich, but for some reason, it didn't. I'd have to say that Roger Corman made a lot more money off the film than I did.'

> *'We're not kissing anybody's rear end in this world.'*
> —Sassy moonshiner Dot Hammer (Susan Howard) in *The Moonshine County Express*

The early-to-mid 1970s saw a rash of Southern 'Good Ol' Boy' films, the most famous of which starred Burt Reynolds—*White Lightning* (1973), *The Longest Yard* (1974), *W.W. and the Dixie Dancekings* (1975), *Gator* (1976) and *Smokey and the Bandit*. Moonshine whiskey or 'hootch' played a supporting role in most of these movies, but it was the star of such drive-in hits as *Bootleggers* (1974) and *Moonrunners* (1975), the latter of which served as the basis for the inane but surprisingly popular TV series, *The Dukes of Hazzard* (1979-85).

In May 1976, New World rival Dimension Pictures made its own contribution to the genre: *Dixie Dynamite*. Ingénues Jane Anne Johnstone and Kathy McHaley starred as Dixie and Patsy, who inherit the family business when their moonshiner father is killed, along with a strong taste for revenge. Just as *Dixie* was released, the fledgling Universal Majestic put *Shine* into production—with almost the exact same story, the only difference being the presence of three girls instead of two.

Shine was the third time that independent producer Ed Carlin had worked with director Gus Trikonis, the two having made *The Swinging Barmaids* (1975) and *The Student Body* (1976) prior. Through his company Premiere International, Carlin had acted as New World's foreign sales representative, and he would soon be recruited to head Corman's international distribution operation. On that basis, New World took over distribution of *Shine* and rechristened it *The Moonshine County Express* for its April 1977 release.

> *When their father is killed and his moonshine still destroyed, the three Hammer girls, Dot, Betty and Sissy, learn that pappy had buried bootleg whiskey during Prohibition which is now worth a fortune. With the help of stock car racer J B Johnson, the girls plan to take revenge for their father's death by undercutting local liquor baron Jack Starkey. But Starkey plays rough, as Hammer found out, and the girls are soon in the middle of a turf-war.*

Despite featuring exploitation starlets Claudia Jennings and Candice Rialson, along with *The Brady Bunch*'s Maureen McCormick, *The Moonshine County Express* was a relatively tame PG-rated feature with little sex or nudity, and none at all from the principals—including Susan Howard, who went on to find fame as Donna Krebbs in the TV series *Dallas*; though featuring plenty of shoot-outs and stunts, it was more character-driven than its kissing cousins, as the *Los Angeles Times* noted: 'Hubert Smith and Daniel Ansley have written a poignant romantic relationship [between Dot and J B Johnson], which is a pleasant departure from most contemporary films, let alone an exploitation one. Their script also contains welcomed down-to-earth family scenes interspersed with the car chases and other routine action.'

Such praise, along with the presence of Jennings, McCormick, and *Cannon* TV detective William Conrad (as the evil Starkey), helped to make *Moonshine County* New World's first success of 1977, earning over $1 million in rentals. In addition to appreciating the film's box-office, Corman also appreciated its approach, as he told di Franco: 'I liked it very much because it was an action picture played in the South that did not put down the southerners. It tended to be very honest.'

Assault on Paradise (Oliver Reed)/Press advertising

'*Who will you send for? Who will stop the wind?*'
—Crazy extortionist Victor (Paul Koslo) in *Assault on Paradise*

Independently produced by Arizona financiers, *Assault on Paradise* was shot in the fall of '76 and released by New World in May 1977. Like *The Girl from Nashville*, it went out under another title simultaneously: *The Town that Cried Terror*. Neither proved a hook for audiences, so New World withdrew the film until the fall, when it was re-released as *Maniac!* with two completely different ad campaigns—the first, that of a conventional thriller; the second, that of a slasher film (a masked killer stalks a screaming woman, her dead boyfriend slumped over a steering wheel). Again, the movie found no takers and it was retitled once more (as *Ransom*) for its ancillary releases.

The exclusive community of Paradise finds itself under attack by a crazed extortionist who dresses as an Indian brave and calls himself Victor. He demands a ransom of $1 million or he will kill everyone in Paradise. Land baron William Whitaker summons soldier of fortune Nick McCormick to put a stop to Victor's shenanigans. A rendezvous is arranged in the desert, but Whitaker double-crosses Victor with counterfeit money. Enraged, Victor ups the ransom to $4 million and assassinates the mayor. Nick tires of Whitaker's games and decides to make Victor a personal crusade.

Despite its poor performance, *Assault on Paradise* had one of the strongest casts of any New World release up to then, including Oliver Reed, Stuart Whitman, Deborah Raffin, Jim Mitchum and John Ireland, and it marked the return to the company of its first director, Richard Compton. The intervening years had been good to Compton, as he had directed the well-regarded Vietnam war film *Welcome Home Soldier Boys* (1972) for 20th Century Fox, and the hugely successful *Macon County Line* films for AIP. He would soon become one of television's most prolific directors, both in the 1980s (*T J Hooker, The Equalizer, Miami Vice*) and '90s (*Babylon 5, Sliders, Charmed*). Compton continued to direct TV series well into the new millennium (*The Fugitive, The X-Files, JAG*), until his death in August 2007 at the age of 69.

'This is demeaning! What about my male ego, my moral ethics, my women's rights?'

—Insurance nebbish Willard Eisenbaum in *Down and Dirty Duck*

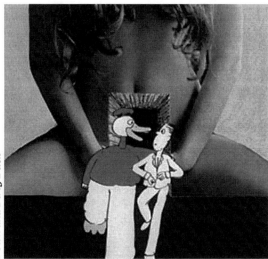

Down and Dirty Duck

In 1972, the world of animation was turned upside down, courtesy of the 'anti-Disney', 34-year-old Ralph Bakshi. With the backing of producer Steve Krantz, Bakshi wrote, directed and animated the first adults-only feature cartoon, *Fritz the Cat,* based on the underground comics of Robert Crumb. This 'X rated and animated!' tale featured the title character: an anthropomorphic college dropout who roams through the sex-and-drug-obsessed 1960s. The film was a huge success, grossing over $4 million in rentals for independent distributor Cinemation, which had also struck gold with Van Peebles's *Sweet Sweetback.*

Bakshi and Krantz returned the next year with *Heavy Traffic*, another X-rated wonder, this time combining animation and live-action to showcase the surreal fantasies of Jewish-Italian cartoonist Michael Corleone. Though the film was well reviewed, and received a major release through AIP, it was not nearly as successful as *Fritz the Cat*, earning only $1.5 million in rentals. Slightly more successful was Krantz's production of *The Nine Lives of Fritz the Cat* (1974), an R-rated sequel produced for AIP but without the participation of Bakshi (animator Robert Taylor took his place).

Bakshi returned in 1975 with the extremely controversial *Coonskin*, another animation/live-action combination that followed the exploits of a black fox, bear, and rabbit who rise to the top of organised crime in Harlem. It was initially made for Paramount, but the racial angle proved too strong for the studio, who sold it on to independent distributor Bryanston (which went bankrupt during its release). Bakshi subsequently turned his talents to PG-rated fantasy, animating films such as *Wizards* (1977) and a much-abridged adaptation of J R R Tolkien's *The Lord of the Rings* (1978).

The buzz surrounding Bakshi's films inspired animator Charles Swenson to collaborate with musicians Howard Kaylan and Mark Volman (of rock groups The

Turtles and Flo & Eddie, with whom he had worked on Frank Zappa's *200 Motels*; 1971) on their own 'adult' animated feature. In 1974, at the animation studio of Murakami-Wolf, the trio began production of *Cheap* —a reference to the new film's miniscule budget.

> *Willard Eisenbaum is a nerdy claims agent at the Big Time Insurance Company who is sent to investigate a claim from Painless Martha's Tattoo Parlor. His arrival causes Martha to suffer a heart attack; in her will, she stipulates that her son, Eddie the Duck, must 'take care' of the one who did her in. Since Willard is a virgin, Eddie makes it his business to have him sexually educated—in a brothel, in the desert, and in Willard's apartment, where Eddie takes matters under his wing by revealing himself to really be 'Daisy' the Duck.*

What became known as *Down and Dirty Duck*, with the exception of a few trial runs, had sat on the shelf for the better part of three years. It ended up with New World largely because one of its producers, Jimmy Murakami, had worked on *Gas-s-s-s!* and *Von Richthofen and Brown*, and Corman was interested in cashing in on the adult animation trend. Unfortunately for him, he was a day late and a dollar short and the film received relatively little play under the abbreviated title of *Dirty Duck*. It did, however, receive a rave in the *New York Times*, which called Swenson's film 'a rather zany, lively, uninhibited sexual odyssey that manages to mix a bit of Walter Mitty and a touch of Woody Allen with some of the innocence of Walt Disney, the urban smarts of Ralph Bakshi, the mysticism and psychedelic eclecticism of *Yellow Submarine* [1968] and the unabashed libidinous relish of the cartoonist Robert Crumb'!

This was actually a fancy way of saying that the film took from everything and came up with nothing. It is lewd, crude and smutty, with an adolescent snickering approach to sex, women, minorities, gays etc. Like *Fantastic Planet, Dirty Duck* is a combination of ink and cut-out animation, but the similarity ends there. It has absolutely no sense of original style, as it steals from Bakshi, Crumb, Gilliam and the cartoons of Jules Feiffer, all without capturing their wit or creativity. In the words of *Dirty Duck*'s title theme, easily the best thing about the entire enterprise, 'This whole movie is a great big hunk of.. *shit*, yeah!'

Amazingly, Swenson was able to recover from this error and become a partner in Murakami-Wolf, and the company went on to produce such TV cartoons as *Puff the Magic Dragon, Strawberry Shortcake, Alvin & the Chipmunks*, and *Teenage Mutant Ninja Turtles* between 1978 and 1992. Charles Swenson also co-wrote and co-directed the Lucasfilm animated feature *Twice Upon a Time* (1983) and served as a producer on Nickelodeon's hit animated series *Rugrats* in 1994.

'Judd knows.. he knows what he knows.'
—Crazed hotel proprietor Judd (Neville Brand) in *Starlight Slaughter*

What *Fritz the Cat* did for animation, *The Texas Chain Saw Massacre* did for horror. In September 1973, 30-year-old Texan college professor and documentary filmmaker Tobe Hooper joined forces with some fellow teachers and students and, with just $140,000, made a film which became a permanent part of the Museum of Modern Art, was honoured at the Director's Fortnight at Cannes, and was hailed by critic Rex Reed as 'The most terrifying motion picture I have ever seen.' Like Hitchcock's *Psycho,* it was inspired by the true story of 'Plainfield Butcher' Ed Gein and told a tale of five teenagers who are systematically stalked and murdered by a family of cannibals, the facilitator of whom is the chainsaw-wielding Leatherface, who sports a mask made of human skin. While nothing like as gory as its title and subject matter suggested, *Chain Saw*, like *Night of the Living Dead* before it, was a thoroughly visceral experience.

Released initially by Bryanston Distributors in 1974 and subsequently by New Line Cinema (who took on the rights after Bryanston's 1976 bankruptcy), the film proceeded to earn over $14 million in rentals, making it one of the most successful independent movies ever. Hooper's film inspired countless others in similar vein and was itself sequelled three times between 1986 and 1994, remade in 2003, and prequeled in 2006.

Hooper's eagerly-awaited follow-up, *Death Trap*, started production in March 1976. Unlike *Chain Saw*, it was not a project that he instigated but one that he was hired to direct by the Rustam brothers—Mohammed, Mardi and Samir—who had been responsible for such cinematic treasures as *Dracula vs Frankenstein* (1971), *Lash of Lust* (1972), *Psychic Killer* (1975) and *Nigger Lover* (1976). However, the film's advertised budget of $600,000 bought a once-in-a-lifetime cast, including Neville Brand, Mel Ferrer, Stuart Whitman, Carolyn Jones (then 'Morticia' of *The Addams Family*), William Finley (*Phantom of the Paradise*), *Chain Saw*'s Marilyn Burns and future 'Freddy Krueger', Robert Englund. *Death Trap* was also peopled by New World starlets such as Roberta Collins (*The Big Doll House*, *Death Race 2000*),

US theatrical poster for *Eaten Alive!*/Neville Brand

Janus Blythe (*Black Oak Conspiracy*) and Cryotin Sinclaire (who, under the alias of 'Lynda Gold', had been Crazy Alice in *Caged Heat*).

Filmed entirely at Producer's Studio on Melrose Avenue in Hollywood, *Death Trap* 'has a lot to do with lights and shadows,' Hooper told *Variety*. 'It takes place in a single night, from dusk to dawn. And all the characters bring with them some sort of history, they're not just cardboard characters walking into a slaughterhouse..'

> On a lonely bayou sits the dilapidated Starlight Hotel, run by crazed Vietnam veteran Judd, who happens to keep a pet crocodile in the swamp next door. The reptile comes in handy, as Judd''s hobby is murdering his guests with pitch-fork or scythe (including a runaway hooker and her dying father, a neurotic traveler, and a young punk) then disposing of the bodies in the swamp. But Judd's mania causes him to make mistakes, which eventually land him in the jaws of his amphibious companion.

'Hate Surprises at Strange Hotels?' asked the ads, when the Rustams premiered the film at Texas theatres in August 1976 under the new name of *Starlight Slaughter*. The allusion to *Psycho* was obvious, but not totally unfounded: if Norman Bates had been a long-haired Vietnam vet and the swamp next to his motel inhabited by a huge crocodile, then *Psycho* would have been *Starlight Slaughter*. Such was the ambience of Hooper's second rural gothic, though the studio-bound production allowed the Texan to stage a *grand guignol* from the outside in, as the mist-shrouded bayou is no more welcoming than the interior of the decaying hotel: everything is bathed in hellish red light, the deafening sound of crickets and frogs compete with plaintive country & western numbers on the radio, and a young girl (a pre-*Halloween* Kyle Richards) spends most of the film under the hotel's porch in a dusty, dank maze of cobwebs, junk and rats. Were it not for Brand's scenery-chewing turn as Judd and a general air of compromise, *Starlight Slaughter* might have been seen as a worthy successor to Chainsaw Massacre.

As it was, the film never received a general release, though it played under five

Eaten Alive! (Robert Englund)

different titles over a period of seven years. In the spring of 1977, it was rechristened *Eaten Alive!* and distribution was taken over by New World, which also released it in some markets under its original title of *Death Trap* (with the hasty revision pasted over *Eaten Alive!* on the posters). In early 1981, it was reissued regionally as *Horror Hotel*, this time by M&M Films. Hooper's opus had its last theatrical bookings in late 1983, when Motion Picture Marketing put it out as *Legend of the Bayou*.

Under any name, *Starlight Slaughter* failed to impress the critics. 'The lack of work has forced many top actors to turn to demeaning films for a pay-cheque,' said the *Syracuse Herald-Journal*. 'However, none should become so desperate as to latch on to such a waste as this film.' *The Los Angeles Times* called Hooper's film 'one horrendous and ludicrous movie where bondage, brutality and sadism are rampant.' *Cinefantastique* was equally dismissive: 'The film is predictable, well beyond the tiresomeness of clichés; the mechanical alligator doesn't work at all; and the film totally lacks the kind of nerve-wracking aural assault of *Chain Saw*.'

As far as Hooper was concerned, *Starlight Slaughter* was only the beginning of a long line of disappointments and missed opportunities. In July 1976, he and Kim Henkel (who had co-written both *Chain Saw* and *Eaten Alive!*) were signed to a five-picture contract with Universal, to begin with the horror film *Bleeding Hearts*. The deal quickly fell apart and Hooper subsequently signed on with Dick Clark and Edward Montoro to direct *The Dark* in 1977; after just three days of filming, he was fired and replaced by former stuntman John 'Bud' Cardos. Hooper directed the highly successful made-for-TV adaptation of Stephen King's *Salem's Lot* in 1979, but his 1981 big screen return, *The Funhouse*, was plagued with production problems and was a flop at the box office. That same year, he was hired to direct the British thriller *Venom* but was again fired and replaced (this time by Piers Haggard). In 1982, Hooper had his biggest commercial success with Steven Spielberg's production of *Poltergeist*—though rumour had it that he took more direction on the film than he was allowed to give.

Between 1984 and 1986, Tobe Hooper made three films for Menahem Golan and Yoram Globus's Cannon Group, including the $25 million adaptation of Colin Wilson's 1976 novel *The Space Vampires* (released as *Lifeforce*), the $12 million remake of 1953's *Invaders from Mars*, and the long-awaited sequel *The Texas Chainsaw Massacre Part 2* (which he had almost made with John Milius in 1980); all three were failures. During this time, Hooper was also attached to films that either were never made (*Pinocchio the Robot*) or were eventually made by other directors (*King Solomon's Mines*, *Return of the Living Dead*, *Spider Man*). He subsequently returned to television, where he has remained for the better part of 20 years, directing episodes of Spielberg's *Amazing Stories* and *Taken*, *Freddy's Nightmares*, *Tales from the Crypt*, *Nowhere Man*, *Dark Skies* and *Masters of Horror*.

As New World approached its seventh anniversary that June, things were not looking good. The company had released eleven films during 1977, but only one of them (*The Moonshine County Express*) had made an impact at the box office. To make matters worse, the landscape of cinema was about to be changed forever by the release of George Lucas's blockbuster *Star Wars* which, along with Spielberg's *Jaws* (1975), clinched summer moviegoing as the exclusive domain of the major studios—a fact which holds true to this day.

Star Wars set another precedent that spelled trouble for New World. When a Chicago drive-in chain managed to play two major first-run releases—*Star Wars* and Columbia's Peter Benchley underwater thriller *The Deep*—during the summer of '77, it marked a first for the industry. Until that time, drive-ins had been seen as also-rans in which to dump product which was played out at the hardtops. But the studios began to realize that drive-ins catered to a completely different audience from traditional theatres and that a booking for one did not necessarily mean competition for the other. What had once been a guaranteed market for Corman's product was suddenly up for grabs, and by companies with far greater financial resources than New World Pictures.

Rabid

hollywood's wild angel

'We live in a compromised society, and I would think of myself as something of a compromised artist.'

—Roger Corman, 1979

'To us, Roger was an iconoclast with his left-wing posters all over the office as he counted his money.'

—Joe Dante, director of *Hollywood Boulevard* and *Piranha*

On March 1, 1977, Ron Howard turned 23. On March 2, he set about directing his first film. True to his word, Corman was giving Howard his chance behind the camera—with the following conditions: it had to be action comedy centring around a car chase, it had to involve young people on the run, Howard had to star, and it had to be called *Grand Theft Auto,* simply because that title had tested well with potential audiences.

'How dare you call Sam Freeman a fortune hunter! He's an environmental research major!'

—Irate heiress Paula Powers (Nancy Morgan) in *Grand Theft Auto*

GTA was a Howard family affair—Ron had co-written the script with his father Rance, who was also associate producer and played a detective hired by Bigby to find his daughter. Ron's brother Clint is featured as one of the many pursuers, and Marion Ross, Howard's screen mom in TV's *Happy Days*, co-stars as another crazy mother (Garry Marshall, creator/producer of *Happy Days* has a cameo as a Vegas underworld boss). Ron's wife Cheryl Howard was also pressed into service as an on-location caterer when the crew complained about the quality of food that New World was providing in the California desert.

Sam and Paula want to get married. Unfortunately, Paula comes from the well-to-do family of political candidate Bigby Powers who wants her to marry flaky rich preppie Collins Hedgeworth. Sam and Paula decide to elope; they steal Bigby's Rolls and head for Las Vegas. Bigby calls on Vegas muscle to intercept the couple, but he also calls up deejay Curly Q Brown and offers $25,000 to anyone who can stop the young lovers. Curly sees this as the story of his career and takes off in hot pursuit, broadcasting live from a chopper. Soon everyone is after Sam and Paula, and Sam begins to wonder if Paula is more interested in defying her father than marrying him.

125

A wild combination of *Romeo and Juliet* and cult car-chase movie *Vanishing Point* (1971), *GTA* wrecks Ferraris, Porches, Beetles, Dodge Chargers, any number of stock cars and, finally, a Rolls Royce. Shot in four weeks on a $602,000 budget, Ron Howard and his crew (which included cameraman Gary Graver and second unit director Allan Arkush) worked at such a breakneck pace that they broke New World's record for the most shots in a single day—91 (the previous record holder

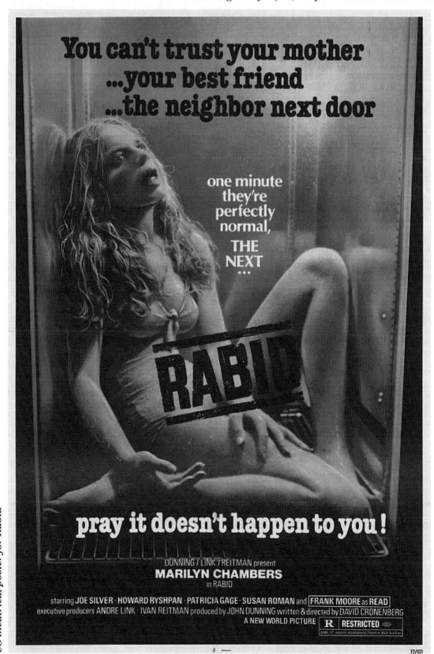

was *Hollywood Boulevard* with 82). 'I never really understood the feeling of being totally wiped out before,' Howard told the *New York Times*. 'I didn't know how exciting it could be to solve the problems involved in making a movie. If I had a choice right now, acting or directing, I would direct.'

'Nobody knows how completely boring it is to be an actor,' Howard went on to Roger Ebert. 'You wait around for hours for the next scene, and then you get your energy up, and then it's over, and you're down again, and waiting again.. by the end of the day, you're exhausted, and it's mostly mental. As a director, from the first moment I was up in the morning, I had all these decisions to make, all the cast and crew to deal with, the problems of the locations.. my energy was up all the time. It was a natural high.'

Critics generally approved of the new kid on the block. 'Howard has directed with a broad but amiable and well-disciplined touch in this screwball comedy,' said *Variety*. 'As a director, Howard efficiently keeps the action fast, the comedy farcical and the youngsters sympathetic,' observed the *Los Angeles Times*. The strongest praise came from the *New York Times*, which noted, 'Mr. Howard need take a back seat to no one when it comes to competence in the genre. His debut as a director of feature films may not mark him as an innovator, but neither does it suffer from comparison to its many predecessors.'

New World's first release of the summer of '77 earned $2.5 million in rentals. Although this was half of what *Eat My Dust* had made a year earlier, it was still respectable enough for Corman to offer Howard a two-picture directorial contract. The youngster politely declined, completed his obligation to *Happy Days* in 1980 and set off on the road to becoming one of Hollywood's most successful directors. He began with comedies and fantasies in the 1980s (*Night Shift, Splash, Cocoon, Willow*) before moving on to star-studded dramas in the '90s (*Backdraft, Far and Away, Apollo 13, Ransom*). In 2002, he won his first two Oscars, for co-producing and directing *A Beautiful Mind*; he followed that up with international smash *The Da Vinci Code* in 2006, based on Dan Brown's controversial 2003 bestseller.

> *'I have to have blood. It's all I can eat. It's not my fault.'*
> —Bloodsucker Rose (Marilyn Chambers) in *Rabid*

While Tobe Hooper was hacking his way through the south, 32-year-old David Cronenberg was doing the same in the Great White North. In 1975, his gory debut feature, *The Parasite Murders*, grossed over $5 million worldwide against a cost of just $185,000; it earned the distinction of being one of the few films financed by the Canadian Film Development Corporation that actually turned a profit. In the US, the film was picked up by AIP, who retitled it *They Came from Within*, cut the gore to an 'R' rating, and put it out via subsidiary Trans American Films.

The Parasite Murders was produced by Cinepix, a Montreal company headed by John Dunning, Andre Link, and Ivan Reitman which had specialised primarily in porn. After the success of Cronenberg's first film, Cinepix wanted a follow-up; the director obliged by dusting off a script which he had written some time before called *Mosquito*. Cronenberg revised the story as *Rabid*, and in November 1976, it entered production on a budget nearly three times that of *The Parasite Murders*.

After a motorbike accident, Rose and boyfriend Hart are taken to the Keloid Cosmetic Surgery Clinic; Hart only has minor injuries but Rose has suffered critical trauma. Dr Keloid decides to try an experimental skin-graft treatment on Rose which theoretically will result in the formation of new organs. Instead, Rose develops a needle-like organ under her arm that sucks the blood of unsuspecting victims, then turns them into rabid

127

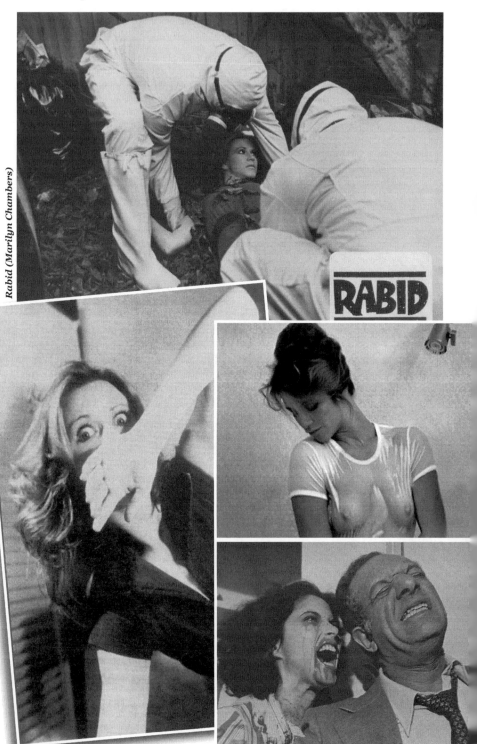

Rabid (Marilyn Chambers)

killers. Montreal is put under martial law as the disease reaches epidemic proportions and Hart tries desperately to find Rose and stop her reign of terror.

Cronenberg had wanted Sissy Spacek for the role of Rose, having been wowed by her performance in Terrence Malick's *Badlands* (1973). Cinepix vetoed the idea and instead cast porn queen Marilyn Chambers, who managed to acquit herself surprisingly well as a reluctant Typhoid Mary. It must have been a source of some amusement to Chambers to be armed with a phallic weapon, though Cronenberg was aware of the potential problems in putting his concept across. 'I knew it was going to be one hell of a challenge to make people believe that premise,' he told *Cinefantastique*. 'I like to show people something absolutely amazing and make them believe it by the time the film is finished.'

Cronenberg's original screenplay had gone to some pains to explain how the vampiric organ has come into existence, as Keloid explains the procedural details to both his colleagues and Rose. But much of this material was deleted as shooting went along and what was filmed ended up being abbreviated for the sake of running time. Only later would he come to realise that this expediency had seriously compromised the verisimilitude of the piece: 'It was a mistake. It would have provided a simple rationale in terms that people could understand. Even those who liked the movie have asked, "But what *was* that thing?"'

Released in Canada in April 1977, *Rabid* earned over $1 million and took its place beside *The Parasite Murders* in the Top 10 Canadian box office performers. Roger Corman immediately snapped up the American rights and released *Rabid* that June to $2.2 million in rentals and a decidedly mixed critical reaction: 'Highly exploitable, extremely violent, sometimes nauseating..' (*Variety*); 'As a director, Cronenberg displays talent and sustains gruelling tension, but his storytelling is slothful and haphazard. Instead of narrative cohesion, he assaults with graphic bludgeoning, bloodletting and skin grafting' (*Los Angeles Times*); 'Cronenberg has a sense of tastelessness that makes Peckinpah films look like Sunn Classic nature reels' (*Cinefantastique*).

Rabid owes much to George Romero and his 1973 opus *The Crazies*, but in its assault on a major metropolis by legions of flesh-eating nasties, Cronenberg's film actually forecasts Romero's own *Dawn of the Dead* (1978). Cronenberg followed up his two horror hits with a racing picture called *Fast Company* (1977), in which exploitation greats William Smith and John Saxon lock horns, but it was a flop. The director found himself drifting for a time before landing in the arms of Pierre David and Mutual Films, who were about to create a new Canadian distributorship with an American company called New World Pictures.

> '*She* is *tuned up! She's just temperamental.. like some other people I know!*'
> —Harley Thomas (David Carradine) joking about his Chevy in *Thunder and Lightning*

After the relative failure of *Cannonball,* David Carradine had made up ground by playing folk singer Woody Guthrie in Hal Ashby's celebrated *Bound for Glory* (1976), for which he was nominated for a Golden Globe. Carradine would soon be working for Ingmar Bergman in *The Serpent's Egg* (1977), and also with Charlton Heston in the Universal disaster flick *Gray Lady Down* (1978).

Kate Jackson first appeared in American living rooms as Daphne Harridge on Dan Curtis's horror 'soap' *Dark Shadows* in 1970, then she moved on to play nurse Jill Danko on the cop show *The Rookies* for Aaron Spelling in 1972. Her stock rose sharply in 1976 when Spelling cast her as Sabrina Duncan, one of the three original *Charlie's Angels*, a role that she played until she left the show in 1979.

In the summer of '77, both stars were hot, and Roger Corman united them as *Thunder and Lightning*, scripted by William Hjortsberg, who would go on to write the supernatural *noir* novel *Falling Angel* (1978, on which Alan Parker would base his 1987 film *Angel Heart*), as well as the Ridley Scott fantasy *Legend* (1985).

> *Everglades bootlegger Harley Thomas is engaged to Nancy Sue, the daughter of soft-drinks king Ralph Junior Hunnicutt. Nancy Sue disapproves of Thomas's line of work but is shocked to find that her father's soda-pop plant is actually a front for a mob-run moonshine factory. When Hunnicutt sends out his latest shipment of rotgut, Thomas and Nancy Sue decide to stop it. Hunnicutt's goons and two mob hit-men are ordered to apprehend the couple, and a chase ensues throughout the state.*

Like the Ron Howard films, the last of Corman's productions for Fox was a comedy car-chase movie. It was also the most successful of the quartet, earning over $3 million in rentals. The Carradine-Jackson combo was a big draw at the box-office but the critics also seemed to appreciate director Corey Allen's screwball approach: 'Every time a chase picture finally has had its day, along comes another to prove that imagination and a fresh approach can still snag an audience.. *Thunder and Lightning* has just about everything in the action department but Dracula loping after Frankenstein's monster' (*Variety*); '*Thunder and Lightning* is less like a live-action movie than a 95-minute Bugs Bunny cartoon—which is one of the nicest things about it' (*New York Times*). As with *Eat My Dust*, however, Kevin Thomas was once again indignant: 'The movie.. is not merely utterly mindless but is also yet another increasingly disturbing instance of making a joke out of the law and celebrating vandalism.'

Corey Allen started out as an actor, perhaps best known for his performance as Buzz Gunderson in the James Dean picture *Rebel Without a Cause* (1955), and he began directing for television in 1969. He concentrated mostly on crime shows (*Mannix, Ironside, Hawaii Five-O, The Streets of San Francisco*) but gained good notices for his work on made-for-TV movies like *Cry Rape* (1973) and *Yesterday's Child* (1977). The commercial success of *Thunder and Lightning* led to him being chosen to helm New World's most expensive movie to date, *Avalanche*.

> 'You want to make me friendly, fill me with happy lies, take away my symptoms, send me home.. then what will I have left?'
> —Schizophrenic Deborah (Kathleen Quinlan) in *I Never Promised You a Rose Garden*

At the tender age of 16, Joanne Greenberg went crazy. She spent three years in a mental hospital but lived to tell about it, which she did in 1964 in a book titled *I Never Promised You a Rose Garden*. Greenberg sought to retain her anonymity, however, so she employed a pseudonym: Hannah Green. The book failed to sell at first but, gradually, it developed a following, largely among teenage girls who could identify with the main character of Deborah Blau and her struggle to distinguish fantasy from reality. By 1977, *I Never Promised You a Rose Garden* had sold over four million copies.

In Greenberg's novel, Jacob and Esther Blau reluctantly have their 16-year-old daughter Deborah committed to an asylum after a suicide attempt. Deborah is a schizophrenic who believes herself to be 'Januce' and living in the Kingdom of Yr, in the midst of gods and demons. Deborah is cared for by Clara Fried, whom she christens 'Furii', and over time, Fried begins to unlock what drove Deborah to the edge—a traumatic operation for a tumour when she was five, jealousy at the birth of her sister, anti-Semitism in her neighbourhood, school and summer camp—and

the slow process of bringing her back to reality begins. Over three years, Deborah becomes a beacon of hope for the outcast patients of the Disturbed Ward, as well as earning the privilege of out-patient status and returning to school. With Fried's help, she irrevocably casts her lot in with the real world.

I Never promised You a Rose Garden had been a Hollywood property for over a decade without making it to the screen, but the success of 1975's *One Flew Over the Cuckoo's Nest* suddenly turned the novel into a viable project. However, by the time *Rose Garden* finally went before the cameras in February 1977, director Peter Medak and star Charlotte Rampling were out, to be replaced by British TV director Anthony Page (*The Missiles of October, The Adams Chronicles*) and 22-year-old Kathleen Quinlan, a former champion gymnast who had a small part in *American Graffiti* and a larger one as a troubled teen in *Lifeguard* (1976). On being offered the lead role, Quinlan told the *Los Angeles Times*, 'It frightened me—a lot—at first, but out came the Irish in me. I decided to find out what it feels like to be crazy. I mean *really* crazy.' (In addition to Quinlan, *Rose Garden* proved to be a training ground for three other famous names of the future—composer Danny Elfman and actors Dennis Quaid and Mel Gibson.)

'Everyone thinks they know what a schizophrenic is,' Quinlan continued. 'I did. Then I did all my research, you know, at hospitals and reading. Then I played Deborah. Now I'm not so sure.' As Dr Fried, Swedish Ingmar Bergman veteran Bibi Andersson also took her role seriously, to the point of questioning the veracity of the script. 'This is a serious subject,' she told Roger Ebert, 'and one shouldn't be careless with it. I asked Gavin [Lambert] what authorities he's used in gathering the information about schizophrenia for the film. It turned out the screenplay was very technically accurate, and so now I trust it.'

Critics fell over themselves to praise Quinlan's performance, which earned her a Golden Globe Award nomination. 'She is terribly convincing in this impossibly demanding role,' wrote Kathleen Carroll in the *New York Daily News*. 'She takes a no-holds-barred character and manages almost to underplay the role,' enthused Janet Maslin of *Newsweek*. 'Kathleen Quinlan is nothing short of brilliant,' cooed

Rex Reed. Reviews were more muted when it came to the film itself, however. 'Good intentions and sensationalism compete for viewer interest.. Unfortunately, both lose,' said *Variety*. Vincent Canby admitted, '*Rose Garden* is something I can say I admired much more than I really liked.' Gene Siskel also concluded that 'one too many stories get in the way of one fine performance in the film.' An exception was Charles Champlin of the *Los Angeles Times* who, after a highly literate essay on the film, summarised by saying, 'It is a well-made, sensitive and splendidly acted psychological drama.'

Though rentals of $3.2 million made *I Never Promised You a Rose Garden* New World's biggest success of the year, that was small potatoes compared to the $56 million which United Artists had reaped from *Cuckoo's Nest* (although to be fair, the UA production benefited from the star-power of former Corman protégé Jack Nicholson). But producer Edgar Scherick, for whom Greenberg's novel had become something of a *cause célèbre*, was pleased. 'This picture was destined to be made,' he told the *Chicago Tribune*. 'We made it as it should be done, with the right people and the right script.' (Aside from changing the family's name to Blake, the fantasy world to Yri, and other narrative condensations, Carlino and Lambert's Oscar-nominated script is very faithful to the novel.)

Corman, who functioned as co-executive producer, saw the film as a turning point for New World—as he told di Franco, 'This picture was my attempt to make an American film of somewhat more artistic significance.. I believe that this film will be as important for the company as *Cries and Whispers* was previously.'

The period between August and December 1977 was one of great expansion, both for Corman's family and for his company. The Corman household increased to five in number that August with the birth of his second son, though father and mother were deadlocked as to a name. 'I have to name my son before I start my next production,' Corman jokingly revealed to the *Los Angeles Herald Examiner*; Brian William Corman was the eventual outcome.

On the projects front, New World was never busier or bolder. It announced that it was negotiating to film *The Plot to Kill Castro!* in Cuba the following spring (though nothing would come of it), as well as gearing up to produce yet another southern-fried pot-boiler entitled *The Night the Lights Went Out in Georgia* and based on the Vicki Lawrence chart-topper from 1973. (This latter of the two ended up in development hell for four years, until Avco Embassy produced it in 1981.)

At New World's third annual sales convention in November, Corman took the mike at the Century Plaza Hotel and announced to his salesmen and the attendant press a $30 million, 20-picture production/distribution slate for the coming year. Holding pole position on this list was a film by Hollywood's current *enfant terrible* Peter Bogdanovich (who was *persona non grata* in Tinseltown after too much lip and too many flops)—a $2 million adaptation of Paul Theroux's 1973 novel *Saint Jack*, to star Ben Gazzara. Corman also announced the most expensive acquisition in New World's history (somewhere between $6-7.5 million, depending on which report you read): the Stephen Sondheim musical, *A Little Night Music*, featuring Elizabeth Taylor and Diana Rigg, which had been produced in Austria in the fall of 1976 and been stuck in a holding pattern since then.

More class for the masses was added by the further acquisition of *A Hero Ain't Nothin' But a Sandwich*, a co-production of Robert Radnitz and the Mattel toy company, and based on Alice Childress's popular 1973 ghetto-speak novel. At the same time, New World took over distribution from Fox of two previous Radnitz films, *A Dog of Flanders* (1960) and *Misty of Chincoteague* (1961).

The most ambitious of New World Pictures' new business ventures was a co-production arrangement with the world-wide leader in 'supermarket' romances, Harlequin Books. New World was lined up to distribute the publisher's first foray into motion pictures, an adaptation of Anne Mather's 1974 tear-jerker *Leopard in the Snow*. If successful, the plan was for Harlequin to follow up *Leopard* with four more films for New World over the next three years.

In addition to the already announced *Deathsport* and *Avalanche*, New World also planned to produce seven other films:

- *The Bees*, Corman's answer to Irwin Allen's upcoming disaster film The Swarm (1978), to star John Saxon and mark the return to New World of director Jack Hill.
- *Cheerleaders*, a mystery about three kidnapped cheerleaders to be produced in the Philippines by John Ashley and Don Schain.
- *Claws*, a remake of the 1942 Val Lewton classic Cat People, to be produced by TV veteran Charles Fries and ex-Amicus Films chairman Max J Rosenberg.
- *Hard Time Aces*, a $1.5 million revolutionary adventure set in South America, to star The Wild, Wild West's Robert Conrad and be produced by Ashley.
- *The Horse is Dead*, an original comedy to be directed by Ernest Pintoff (Dynamite Chicken) and produced by Cannonball's Sam Gelfman.
- *The Moviegoer*, a $1.5 million adaptation of Walker Percy's famous 1961 novel, to be directed by Jim McBride (David Holzman's Diary, Glen and Randa) on location in New Orleans. Written by McBride and L M Kit Carson, it was to star Carson's wife Karen Black and Sam Waterston.
- *Piranha*, a $1 million co-production with United Artists to be produced and directed by Hollywood Boulevard's bet-winning duo of Jon Davison and Joe Dante.

In the final analysis, New World produced only two of these films—*The Bees* and *Piranha*. *Claws* became *Cat People* (made in 1982 by Universal and directed by Paul Schrader), and the rest were never made at all.

Rounding out the bumper crop of new titles were four pick-ups, including *The Force Beyond,* a haunted house movie from *The Moonshine County Express* duo of Ed Carlin and Gus Trikonis, and *Jokes My Folks Never Told Me,* an episodic sex comedy in *Groove Tube/Tunnelvision* vein. New World also acquired two from Canada's Cinepix: *Blackout,* an all-star look at the July 1977 New York City power failure, and *The Tigress*, the second sequel to 1975's *Ilsa, She Wolf of the SS*.

In assessing all these announcements, *Variety* commented, 'With New World Pictures' declaration last week.. the already vague distinction between the so-called major and independent film companies has become even further clouded.' The trade paper concluded: 'The planned and complete items cover such a range and are so numerous that it may be time to throw away the old definitions.'

The final piece of the expansion jigsaw came in December, when New World formally joined forces with Pierre David's Mutual Films of Canada to create the new distributorship of New World Mutual Pictures. In so doing, New World not only gained an interest in a foreign distributor, it also acquired a piece of David Cronenberg's upcoming horror film, *The Brood*.

'My momma didn't raise no chickens.'
—Teenage heroin addict Benjie (Larry B Scott) in *A Hero Ain't Nothin' But a Sandwich*

Producer Robert Radnitz and the Mattel company had teamed up previously in 1972 to bring William Armstrong's 1969 novel for young adults, *Sounder*, to the screen; it featured newcomer Kevin Hooks as a black youngster in 1930s Louisiana who undertakes a personal odyssey to visit his incarcerated father. The film was a huge success, was nominated for four Oscars—including Best Actor and Actress for

Paul Winfield and Cicely Tyson, and it spawned a sequel in 1976. That same year, Radnitz and Mattel had reunited Winfield, Tyson, and Hooks in an adaptation of another young adult novel about a black teenager's personal journey, *A Hero Ain't Nothin' But a Sandwich.*

The Alice Childress novel told the story of Benjie, a 13-year-old heroin addict. Childress herself was commissioned to write the screenplay and she kept things essentially the same—although in contrast to the book, she gave the film a happy ending. After the movie won Best Film, Best Actor, and Best Actress awards at the Festival of the Americas, Corman acquired it for distribution. 'I wanted to release this film because it was intelligent and well made,' he told di Franco. 'There was a time when only lurid, action-oriented films were being made for black audiences. We now have the opportunity to present films of a better calibre which are intended primarily for black audiences but which have also the substance and quality to appeal to changing tastes in both black and white audiences.'

New World premiered *A Hero Ain't Nothin' But a Sandwich* in Los Angeles in December in a limited run, so as to qualify for Oscar consideration (which it failed to receive). As with Kathleen Quinlan's performance in *I Never Promised You a Rose Garden*, critics were beside themselves in praise of 16-year-old newcomer Larry B Scott, who had played Benjie. 'The central performance by young Larry Scott is professionally dazzling and uncommonly moving,' said Charles Champlin.

'Vulnerable, tough, young Larry Scott is nothing short of extraordinary,' effused the *Hollywood Reporter*. *Playboy*'s Bruce Williamson called him 'phenomenal' and *Parent's Magazine* declared him 'incredible'.

When the film entered into general release early in 1978, however, response was not so enthusiastic. 'The 107-minute film ultimately becomes a series of static dialogue sequences between assorted characters,' observed *Variety*. 'There's little sense of movement, instead just talk, talk, talk.' Janet Maslin of the *New York Times* likewise found fault, commenting, 'This is a tragic tale told by filmmakers who don't seem able to believe that such things are really possible.. [it is] a movie that spells out everything but never manages to be entirely lucid.' The *Chicago Daily Herald* was of the opinion that the film was 'unlikely [to] have much appeal outside the black community' and decried its 'oppression mentality'.

Despite being hailed by civil rights leaders like Jesse Jackson as 'a film that *all* Americans must see,' few actually did. This despite the fact that the marketing of the film included a reprinting of the book and the issuing of a soundtrack album by the Hubert Laws Group. *Variety* was right when it said, 'New World Pictures faces a marketing problem.. in its admirable attempt to avoid seamy exploitation, [the film] becomes instead pedantic and preachy.'

> *'A civilised man can tolerate his wife's infidelities, but when it comes to his mistress, a man becomes a tiger.'*
> —Count Mittelheim (Laurence Guittard) in *A Little Night Music*

Hero was not the only film that New World had vying for Oscar attention in Los Angeles that December. The company had also arranged a special engagement for the screen version of Stephen Sondheim and Hugh Wheeler's smash Broadway musical *A Little Night Music*, which had been based on Ingmar Bergman's *Smiles of a Summer Night*. The film was actually completed more than a year earlier, as an attempt by the state-run Wien Film to jump-start the moribund Austrian film industry (Ken Annakin's *The Fifth Musketeer*, with Rex Harrison and Olivia de Havilland, had been another such). Featuring Elizabeth Taylor, Diana Rigg, Lesley Ann Down, Len Cariou, and Hermione Gingold (the latter two having appeared in the stage version), *A Little Night Music* was a sumptuous, old-style, multi-million dollar production that, given the cast and popularity of the musical (especially the song 'Send in the Clowns'), seemed a sure-fire winner. In fact, New World was so emboldened by the prestige of the piece that it asked exhibitors for a $100,000 non-refundable guarantee to book the film for Easter 1978, something unheard of from an independent distributor.

> *Vienna, 1905. Frederick Egerman and Carl-Magnum Mittelheim are both engaged in clandestine affairs with famous stage actress Desiree Armfeldt. Tired of being used as a whore, Desiree decides to force the issue by inviting both men and their wives to her mother's country estate for the weekend. The soirée ends with the two wives swapping their husbands for alternative partners and Count Mittelheim challenging Frederick to a duel, as a result.*

At first, New World's gambit seemed to be paying off. *A Little Night Music* was nominated for two Oscars (Music and Costume Design; it won the former) and received a good deal of critical acclaim in advance. Rex Reed called it 'The most consistently stylish, intelligent and enchanting movie musical since *Gigi*.' The *Los Angeles Examiner* declared it '..Inventive, saucy, beautiful.' *New West* magazine said that it was 'A remarkable achievement-witty, stylish, breathtaking.' Charles

Champlin proclaimed it 'A superior entertainment, with uncommon qualities and quantities of charm, style and sophistication.'

But when the film received a wider release early in 1978, it met with the same negativity that had greeted *Hero*. 'Uneven and sometimes slow.. Director [Hal] Prince has been too cautious and has failed to give the film sufficient visual flair and movement,' said *Variety*. Vincent Canby was even more dismissive, stating, 'It's something more than a shock that the film.. not only fails to raise the spirits; it also tramples on them. The more kindly disposed will leave the theatre depressed, a lot of others may be in a rage. Though it's possible to fail with intelligence and grace, the movie.. pursues disaster in the manner of someone who, with mindless self-confidence, saws off the limb he's sittin' on.' Gene Siskel, as ever, joined the chorus of disapproval: 'As far as entertainment value is concerned, the film is stiff, awkward and dated. Taylor is not attractive on the screen. She may be courageous in playing some of her scenes without makeup, but in so doing, because of her 'star' status, her weathered face dominates the screen and the story.'

A Little Night Music was a resounding flop. One of the main charges against it were the changes which had been made in its transition from stage to screen, particularly the switch of setting from Sweden to Vienna. Harold Prince, director of both the musical and the movie, tried to explain the rationale to the *Los Angeles Times*: 'On the stage it was what we called our Chekhov musical. The Chekhov didn't seem appropriate in the film. The characters in the film are more accessible, the emotions are more Middle European and recognisable.' Of course, the fact that the Austrian government had stumped up a chunk of the budget probably had something to do with it, also.

Executive Producer Heinz Lazek, the head of Wein Film, blamed the movie's failure on absentee producer Elliott Kastner (of *Where Eagles Dare* and *The Long Goodbye*). Others put the blame on the inability of Elizabeth Taylor to sing. Still more felt that New World had lacked the resources to market and release the film properly. Whatever the reason, Prince was defiant, telling the *New York Times*, 'The only thing I care about is that I like this movie, and so do the producers, and so does Steve Sondheim.'

> '*We* will *make some changes. You can't stand still; you must change. Change for us will be and is a matter of spending a little bit more money on our pictures and hopefully making slightly better films. Although we're happy with what we're doing at the moment.*'
> —Roger Corman, interviewed in *Hollywood's Wild Angel* (1978)

At the beginning of 1978, Corman found himself the subject of a documentary. As part of the Museum of Modern Art's New Films/New Directors series, Corman and New World were profiled by Christian Blackwood in the one-hour film *Roger Corman—Hollywood's Wild Angel*. It was a flattering portrait of the man and his career, highlighted by numerous clips and trailers, and it featured revealing interviews with Corman, David Carradine, Allan Arkush, Joe Dante, Peter Fonda, Ron Howard, Jonathan Demme, Jonathan Kaplan, Paul Bartel and Martin Scorsese.

Corman had not directed a film in almost a decade and, in the documentary, he appeared to throw cold water on the notion that he would do so again anytime soon: 'When I was directing a great deal a number of years ago.. I had a lot of energy. I don't have that energy anymore. Maybe directing is a young man's game. There is still a certain excitement in making films but I find most of the excitement now in the planning stage.. At this stage of my life, I'd just as soon ease back as for the energy to get out there every day.'

But Corman's reputation as a director continued to appreciate. In February, the Fox Venice Theatre in Los Angeles hosted a week-long tribute to the *auteur*, screening his films as both a director and producer. That May, he was honoured at Los Angeles' annual Filmex festival; after a midnight showing of Corman trailers and Blackwood's documentary, its guest of honour, along with recent protégés like Demme, Arkush, Kaplan, Bartel and Dante, took questions from the audience.

The accolades were having an effect. Within a year, Corman would be talking seriously about seating himself in the director's chair again.

'You really are an endless source of amusement.'
—The Devil (Victor Buono) taunting sceptic C J Arnold (Richard Crenna) in *The Evil*

Scientists or academics investigating alleged 'haunted' houses was hardly new in films—the premise had been handled effectively in *The Haunting* (1963) and in *The Legend of Hell House* (1973), though neither thought to confront their sceptics with Satan personified. That was left to writer Donald Thompson and director Gus Trikonis, whose film *Cry Demon* had gone into production in May 1977, had its title changed to *The Force Beyond*, then wound up as New World's first release of 1978 that March under the more generic badge of *The Evil*.

After the Civil War, Emilio Vargas captured the Devil and locked him in a sulphur pit beneath his mansion. A century later, psychologist

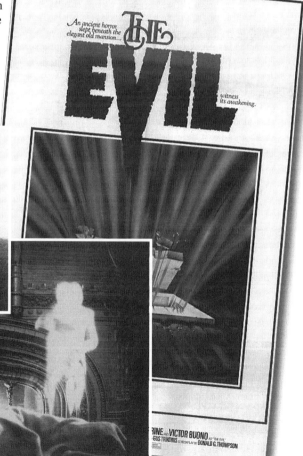

137

C J Arnold and his wife buy the Vargas estate to use as a drug rehab centre. Several students volunteer their services to help fix the place up. While exploring in the basement, Arnold removes a cross that bars a pit beneath the manse; in so doing, he releases an evil force that seals the house and begins to pick off the students one by one. Arnold and his wife descend into the pit where they come face to face with the Devil himself..

Producer Ed Carlin had assembled a strong cast, including Richard Crenna, Joanna Pettet, exploitation veteran Andrew Prine, and newcomer Mary Louise Weller, who would go on to *Animal House* (1978) and *The Bell Jar* (1979). But *The Evil* really belongs to corpulent character actor Victor Buono, Oscar nominee for *Whatever Happened to Baby Jane* (1962) and veteran of many a guest-spot on TV shows such as *Batman* and *Fantasy Island*, who turned his brief cameo as the Devil into the most amusing slice of monstrous villainy since Vic Diaz in *Beast of the Yellow Night*.

Variety felt that the gimmick worked—'Crenna and Pettet confront the devil himself, played with sinister angelicism by Victor Buono. A silly idea? Maybe, but Trikonis and Buono make it click'—but both the *Los Angeles Times* and *Cinefantastique* were of a different mindset. 'Surrealism doesn't fuse well with exploitation and Victor Buono has a lame role as evil incarnate,' said the former. 'Trikonis makes a fatal mistake imposing a literal interpretation of the Evil,' observed the latter. Corman evidently agreed, and some later prints of *The Evil* exorcised Buono altogether.

> *'Being fond of someone is not good enough reason to marry them.'*
> —Helen James (Susan Penhaligon) on arranged marriage in *Leopard in the Snow*

Before *I Never Promised You a Rose Garden* went into production, producer Edgar Scherick and his Palomar Productions, which had a big hit in 1975 with *The Stepford Wives*, announced plans early in 1976 to film a Harlequin romance, Anne Mather's *Leopard in the Snow*. It was to be filmed in England as a co-production between Palomar, EMI, and ex-Amicus co-founder Milton Subotsky. Julia Smith, veteran director of such British TV shows as *Doctor Who, The Railway Children* and *Dr Finlay's Casebook,* was scheduled to helm the film. But plans fell through, and the project reverted back to Harlequin.

For its part, Harlequin Books wanted in on the movie game, considering that its worldwide best-sellers were naturals for screen treatment. In January 1977, the Toronto-based company took advantage of an Anglo-Canadian film co-production pact to finance the $1.1 million *Leopard* on its own. To qualify for a tax break, the production had to be part-British, so producer John Quested and director Gerry O'Hara were brought on board. Quested had been the production manager on *The Running Man* (1963) and *The Lion in Winter* (1968), while O'Hara had worked with Otto Preminger on *Exodus* (1960) and *The Cardinal* (1963), as well as with Tony Richardson on *Tom Jones* (1963). As a team, however, the duo had made only routine exploitation films (*All the Right Noises, The Brute*).

Mather's novel tells of London socialite Helen James, who runs away from her domineering father. Stranded by a snowstorm in the Lake District, she is found by Dominic Lyall and his pet leopard, Sheba. In his Hawksmere estate, she discovers that Lyall was a famous racing driver who is now in self-imposed exile. Helen and Lyall fall in love, but he shuns her offer of undying devotion and sends her on her way. When she returns to Hawksmere, Lyall is gone. Helen finds him in hospital, where he has undergone an operation to repair his damaged hip; the operation is unsuccessful, but her desire to be with him despite his condition convinces Lyall that Helen loves him. They are married, and live happily ever after.

Mather's screenplay (co-written with Jill Hyem) not surprisingly did not stray very far from its source. Starring as Lyall was *2001*'s Keir Dullea, while Helen was Susan Penhaligon, who had appeared in *No Sex Please, We're British* (1973) and *The Land That Time Forgot* (1975) and would go on to feature in the BBC's version of *Count Dracula* (with Louis Jourdan) and director Paul Verhoeven's *Soldier of Orange* (both 1977). Support was provided by the likes of Kenneth More, Billie Whitelaw, and Jeremy Kemp.

Leopard in the Snow received its world premiere in Japan in January 1978, followed by Canada in February, and England and the US in March. New World's marketing left something to be desired ('Remember when a good love story made you feel like holding hands?') and the company's half-hearted distribution strategy effectively torpedoed the pact with Harlequin. Undaunted, the head of Harlequin Films, Chris Harrop, announced plans to film *Island of Dreams* the following year in Antigua, on a budget of $5 million. It was not to be, and the movie division was folded, although several made-for-television films were produced during the 1990s bearing the Harlequin name.

> *'Man is like a candle--he must radiate life by burning himself. I have a destiny to meet.'*
>
> —Bad guy Ankar Moor (Richard Lynch) in *Deathsport*

After several false starts, New World finally put *Deathsport*—ostensibly a sequel to *Death Race 2000*—before the cameras in October 1977. Produced by Corman, it was to be directed by yet another film school graduate, Nicholas Niciphor. For the first time, two of the biggest drive-in names in the business, David Carradine and Claudia Jennings, would be brought together, along with cult exploitation villain Richard Lynch (from *God Told Me To*). 'It is less satirical in tone than *Death Race 2000*,' Corman told di Franco, 'since it is less a sly comment on the escalation of violence in our time than a speculation about the polarities of society in the future.'

> *In the year 3000, after the Great Neutron Wars, there exist only two City States, the peaceful Tritan and the violent Helix, ruled by Lord Zirpola and his henchman, Ankar Moor. Zirpola plans to attack Tritan using a fleet of specially-equipped motorcycles called 'Death Machines', but he first tests them in the gladiatorial game of Deathsport by capturing two Range Guides, Oshay and Deneer, and making them fight for their lives. The two manage to escape and make their way to Tritan with Moor and his men in pursuit. Eventually, Oshay and Moor meet mano-a-mano on the plains of Tritan, in a sword-fight to the death..*

Hiring untested directors had worked for Roger Corman in the past, but with Nicholas Niciphor, the producer of *Deathsport* got more than he bargained for. 'In [Niciphor's] discussions, his mind kept going back to Vietnam,' co-star Jesse Vint told *Shock Cinema*. 'He would talk about the most grisly and gruesome things imaginable, and I could see that he was carrying a lot of baggage around with him. It was very difficult for him to relate to people, much less actors and actresses.. Nick was screaming at [Claudia] one day, and I could hear it from my dressing room. I stepped out and heard some kind of commotion going on. By the time I got there, David Carradine had done one of his karate kicks and sent Nick flying through the air. So there was a big disruption, [and] Nick was off the picture.' Niciphor's work on the film was attributed to 'Henry Suso' and he never directed again; he did, however, become the successful screenwriter of such films as Joseph Ruben's *Our Winning Season* (1978) and Alejandro Jodorowsky's *Tusk* (1980).

Deathsport (David Carradine)

In the same way that Jonathan Demme had been called on to bail out *Crazy Mama*, so Allan Arkush was put in charge of salvaging *Deathsport*. 'There had been lots of trouble on set,' he recalled for Corman's autobiography. '[Niciphor] had been threatening [Jennings], calling her in the middle of the night, getting paranoid, carrying a .45 under a ski parka in the desert. Plus they were trying to do stunts with street Yamahas. I spent four months 'fixing' this movie. I completely recut it, planned new stunts, straightened out the plot.'

As far as Jesse Vint was concerned, Arkush was simply wasting his time. 'It was David Carradine's contractual obligation to Roger.. Unfortunately, there was nothing in the contract that said Roger had to spend X-amount of money or make a quality film. It looks like he went out in his backyard and shot the damn thing. And using David's name, he was able to sell it all over the world. So he made it for nothing and sold it for a lot. We all knew that's what was happening, but we knew there was nothing to fret about because nobody was going to see the movie anyway.'

In its review, *Variety* seemed to concur. 'The best thing that can be said about [Carradine's] acting and his part is that he doesn't say much.. The best thing that can be said about [Jennings's] performance is that she gets to take off her clothes, twice.' Kevin Thomas, conversely, found the experience a pleasurable one: 'Longer on imagination than money, *Deathsport* plays like a parable for today's world.. [it] may be too impersonal to transcend its exploitation genre, but sure is lots of exhilarating fun.'

The film had a successful opening in Los Angeles in May 1978, earning over $400,000, but it quickly ran out of gas and never came close to approaching *Death Race 2000*'s numbers. At the same time, a third film in New World's future shock cycle, *Deathworld*, was announced as being 'in preparation for spring '78 release.' How New World intended to release an unmade film in the spring when summer was just around the corner was a conundrum which was never solved.

Deathsport was also the last film that Claudia Jennings would make for Roger Corman—and it was the last film that she would *ever* make. On October 3, 1979, the 29-year-old actress was killed in a head-on collision with a pick-up truck on California's Pacific Coast Highway. What made her death the more tragic was that Jennings was on the verge of the mainstream stardom that she had craved for so long. She had been producer Aaron Spelling's first choice to replace Kate Jackson on *Charlie's Angels* and had lost the part to model Shelley Hack only after network suits became nervous about her CV. She was also in line for roles in the Robert Zemeckis comedy *Used Cars* (1980) and Bob Rafelson's remake of *The Postman Always Rings Twice* (1981). She was not turning her back entirely on exploitation, however; had she lived, Jennings would likely have appeared in horror films *Blood Beach* and *Fade to Black* (both 1980).

Despite the failure of *Leopard in the Snow*, plans were afoot for Julie Corman to produce the historical romance *Love's Tender Fury* (based on the 1976 novel by Jennifer Wilde, alias Tom Huff) as a TV mini-series, a first for New World. 'I went to a television network and showed them.. a five-year collection of sales figures on this particular category of books. In something like 15 minutes, the network gave me the green light to develop *Love's Tender Fury* into a mini-series,' she told the *Los Angeles Times*. 'My involvement with romantic novels goes back to teenage years,' she continued, 'when I first read *Wuthering Heights*.. Heathcliff leapt off the pages as a most intriguing character, and when I grew up I married a dashing romantic figure. Persistence, you see, is practically the story of my life..' *Love's Tender Fury* never made it off the pages either, but Julie Corman's tale of persistence was far from over.

'You will see how fantasy becomes reality.'
—Ilsa (Dyanne Thorne) playing on a captive's fear of castration in *Ilsa, Tigress of Siberia*

The Nazis were commonly held to have a kinky streak, but Dirk Bogarde and Charlotte Rampling had made their perversions seem sexy as well. In 1969, the two were featured in Luchino Visconti's *The Damned*, the story of a wealthy family in the early days of the Third Reich. Because of its depiction of 'aberrant sexual behaviour', the film was rated X in the US; because it was an 'art' film, however, it was afforded major distribution through Warner Brothers and was nominated for an Oscar for Best Screenplay. Five years later, Bogarde and Rampling returned to the theme with an even more scabrous look at fascist sexual depravity, Liliana Cavani's *The Night Porter*. This time art had nothing to do with it, and a hard sell by master showman Joseph E Levine of *Hercules* fame ('The most controversial picture of our time!') turned it into a huge success.

David Friedman, the Joe Levine of sexploitation, had been involved with one of the first of the so-called Naziploitation films—*Love Camp 7*—in 1969. Likewise, Canada's Cinepix had imported the German Naziploitation film *Fraulein Without a Uniform* in 1975 and had a hit. That same year, the two decided to join forces to make their own Naziploitation epic, and one that would trump all others: *Ilsa, She Wolf of the SS*.

Ilsa was based on a real person: Ilse Koch, the so-called 'Bitch of Buchenwald'. In the film, Ilsa is the commandant of Medical Camp Nine, where she is attempting to prove to her Nazi superiors that women can withstand more pain than men. She

delights in torturing her female prisoners but she is also a nymphomaniac, who beds her male prisoners before castrating them. An American POW arrives who is able to give Ilsa unending sexual satisfaction, but the new stud proves to be her downfall when he ties her up and leads an escape, just as German forces destroy the camp to prevent its discovery by the Allies.

Full of softcore sex and hardcore gore, *Ilsa, She Wolf of the SS* was a worldwide hit, grossing $2.5 million in America, $1.5 million in Japan, and another $1 million in Europe (it was banned in the UK). The film made a star out of the well-endowed Dyanne Thorne who, at age 43, had been toiling away in nudies for fifteen years. But she had done her homework on Ilse Koch and clearly enjoyed playing the part. 'Ilsa is a very strong character,' she told the *Washington Post*. 'She is the whole cake, not just the icing. Men go on her arm, not the other way around. She is a woman without love, a woman without humanity. Ilsa is anti-life.'

US theatrical posters for Ilsa, She Wolf of the SS/ Ilsa, Harem Keeper of the Oil Sheiks

One outing was not enough for such a wicked lady, and although she had her head blown off in *Ilsa, She Wolf of the SS*, Ilsa was back in 1976 as *Harem Keeper of the Oil Sheiks*. Though not as grotesque as its predecessor, *Harem Keeper* was another success which solidified Thorne's popularity with the exploitation crowd. As a result, a third *Ilsa* film was planned, which was announced to the trades in May 1976 under the ridiculous title of *Ilsa Meets Bruce Lee in the Devil's Triangle*. When that went nowhere, Cinepix loaned Thorne out to German producer Erwin C Dietrich for controversial director Jess Franco's vile women's prison picture, *Greta the Mad Butcher* (erroneously advertised in some territories as *Ilsa the Wicked Warden*). On her return to the US, Thorne started work on what would be Ilsa's final chapter—*The Tigress of Siberia*.

Siberia, 1953. Ilsa is commandant of Gulag 14, charged with 'rehabilitating' political prisoners. She meets her match in Andrei Chicorin, who refuses to succumb to torture or Ilsa's feminine wiles. Before Chicorin can be executed, the gulag receives word that Stalin is dead and a purge has begun. Ilsa and her guards torch the camp and flee, leaving everyone for dead—but Chicorin survives.. Years later, he is a trainer with the Soviet hockey team at the World Cup in Montreal. When two of the players pay a visit to a brothel, he accompanies them to find that it is run by an exiled Ilsa, who is taking over the city's vice-dens. Ilsa recognises Chicorin and restrains him, so she can finish what she started almost a quarter of a century earlier.

The director of the first two *Ilsa* adventures had been *Tender Loving Care*'s Don Edmonds, but with *Tigress*, Cinepix gave the baton to Canadian Jean LaFleur, who had edited and directed second unit on *Rabid*. Working with LaFleur in the frozen north gave Thorne the happiest of her *Ilsa* experiences, as she revealed in *The Ilsa Chronicles*: '*Tigress* was a lot of fun to do. I love snow country anyway, anything that's cold I love. I really enjoyed that.'

The Tigress of Siberia opened strongly in Canada in October 1977 and in Japan in January 1978, but New World was forced to cut the film for its American release to obtain an 'R' rating, eliminating much of the gore (including the gruesome end to an arm-wrestling match over chainsaws!) and either shortening the sex scenes or replacing them with less explicit alternate takes. *Tigress* was given a trial run in the US in May 1978 but it never achieved a general release. It did, however, go on to a four-year engagement at US military bases overseas, at which it premiered in May 1980.

Dyanne Thorne had her moment in the sun, and she effectively retired after this last outing to become a minister of Religious Science, conducting wedding services in Las Vegas. She would still pop up in public from time to time, appearing briefly in the women's prison throwback *Hellhole* (1985) and in Franc Roddam's segment of *Aria* (1987), but the *Ilsa* films would always be her main calling card.

Press advertising for Avalanche

6 million tons of icy terror!

AVALANCHE

ROCK HUDSON
MIA FARROW

SCREENPLAY BY CLAUDE POLA and COREY ALLEN   DIRECTED BY
STORY BY   PRODUCED BY   COREY ALLEN   A NEW WORLD PICTURE
FRANCES DOEL · ROGER CORMAN · COREY ALLEN

'I want people to enjoy this land, not bury them in it.'
—Developer David Shelby (Rock Hudson) in *Avalanche*

After two years in development, New World's much-heralded 'event' picture, *Avalanche*, finally got underway in February 1978 with an eight week shoot at the Tamarron Ski and Golf Resort in Durango, Colorado. The film's budget had supposedly been upped from $2 million to $4 million (before filming was over, $6.5 million would be quoted), enough to buy the star-power of Rock Hudson and Mia Farrow. 'I don't mind calling it a disaster movie,' Corman told the Associated Press, 'since disaster movies have never failed to make money.' Unfortunately for its producer, *Avalanche* would be one of the first.

Developer David Shelby has spent years building a grandiose ski resort, greasing the palms of politicians and ignoring warnings from environmentalists. For the grand opening, he invites his ex-wife to what he hopes will be a reunion. Tragedy strikes when a small plane with his accountant onboard crashes into a mountain during a snowstorm and causes an avalanche. Shelby and his wife join the rescue teams in a race against time to save those buried beneath the snow; he gradually becomes aware of the part that he has played in the disaster, but it comes too late for reconciliation with his wife.

'*Avalanche* cost more than ten times the budget of the first film produced by New World,' Corman told di Franco. 'We hope there is a corresponding increase in quality. It marks a turning point for the company, as we hope it is but the first of more productions which will be bigger in budget and scope.' What Corman failed to realise was that the disaster movie genre had hit a peak some three years earlier, and that after *Star Wars*, no one was going to be fooled by 'special effects' which were a mixture of scratchy stock footage, obvious miniatures, and unconvincing mattes.

Apparently, no one who worked on the film was fooled by it either. Gavin Lambert was angered that director Corey Allen had, in his words, 'dewritten the script', and he was forced to employ the pseudonym of 'Claude Polla' for his credit. Allen himself told the *Los Angeles Times* that he 'didn't feel the aims of the film were fulfilled' and that he and executive producer Paul Rapp 'weren't working toward the same end.' Both Hudson and Farrow refused to promote the film, and Farrow did not even attend the July 1978 premiere in Denver (she was too busy pushing her Robert Altman movie *A Wedding*).

According to Allen, *Avalanche* fell victim to Corman's typical cost-cutting and schedule-changing. 'Essentially, [Paul] Rapp was acting as Roger's agent.. There were heavy pressures on Paul to bring the film in ahead of schedule, and these, I feel, were detrimental to the film.' The only person to come out of *Avalanche* with anything to brag about was second unit director Lewis Teague, who had managed to stage some impressive action sequences despite obvious budgetary limitations.

On its general release in August, *Avalanche* was comprehensively trashed by *The Washington Post*, which warned: 'After theatre managers add up the receipts, *Quarantine* may seem a more appropriate title for *Avalanche*, an inept disaster melodrama now at several obliging, unlucky locations. This fizzled brainstorm from New World.. looks like a cinch for the first supplement to The 50 Worst Films of All Time.' But not every critic felt the same. 'Although *Avalanche* is a formula disaster picture, its well-drawn, credible people and swift pacing combine to make it a satisfying diversion,' opined Kevin Thomas. *Variety* was similarly charitable in its view: '*Avalanche* combines all the familiar ingredients into a rolling, rushing thriller that will quickly capture its intended audience.'

During the dog days of summer, there was little enough audience for the film to capture in any event. Hudson and Farrow were hardly box-office gold at this point, and even the so-called 'Master of Disaster', Irwin Allen, had fallen on hard box-office times (his all-star production *The Swarm* had been a huge flop only the month before). Tellingly, New World did not report *Avalanche*'s rental figures, but it is doubtful that the film did anything more than break even.

'*They breed like flies.. there will be no way to stop them!*'
—Mad geneticist Dr Robert Hoak (Kevin McCarthy) in *Piranha*

When Steven Spielberg's screen adaptation of Peter Benchley's 1974 novel *Jaws* went into the box-office stratosphere in the summer of '75, it did not take long for other producers to follow suit. Whether they were Mexican (*Tintorera*), Italian (*Orca, Shark's Cave, Tentacles*), or American (*Barracuda, Evil in the Deep, Mako: Jaws of Death*), all of them wanted to make sure that people stayed out of the water and sought shelter in cinemas.

Jeff Schechtman was no different. He had been a producer's assistant to Fred Weintraub but in August 1975, he formed his own company, Terrapin Productions,

US theatrical poster for Angels Die Hard (1970)

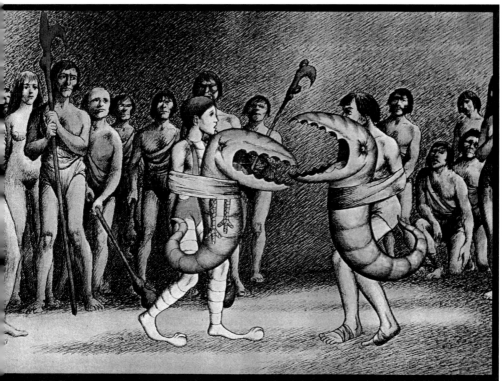

ROGER CORMAN
PRESENTS
A NEW WORLD PICTURE **FANTASTIC PLANET**

WINNER
GRAND
PRIX
CANNES FILM FESTIVAL
1973

DIRECTED by RENE LALOUX · SCREENPLAY by ROLAND TOPOR · RENE LALOUX
BASED ON THE NOVEL by STEVEN WUL · MUSIC by ALAIN GORAGUER · METROCOLOR · LES FILMS ARMORIAL

PG PARENTAL GUIDANCE SUGGESTED

The Last Days of Man on Earth (

Capone (1975)

Death Race 2000 (1975)

Fighting Mad (1976)

HE DRIVES THE FASTEST CAR IN THE STATE!
SHE HAS THE BEST SHINE IN THE WORLD!
TOGETHER THEY MAKE...

100 Proof Women

Runnin Shine Cross The County Line!

THEY MAKE IT EVERY NIGHT.

US theatrical poster for Moonshine County Express (1977)

starring JOHN SAXON · SUSAN HOWARD · WILLIAM CONRAD
MAUREEN McCORMICK · JEFF COREY · CLAUDIA JENNINGS

UNIVERSAL MAJESTIC, INC. and SUNSHINE ASSOCIATES present A DORO VLADO HRELJANOVIC and PAUL JOSEPH picture
"MOONSHINE COUNTY EXPRESS" · Produced by ED CARLIN · Directed by GUS TRIKONIS · Screenplay by HUBERT SMITH and
DANIEL ANSLEY · A NEW WORLD PICTURES RELEASE   color by Movielab

PG PARENTAL GUIDANCE SUGGESTED
SOME MATERIAL MAY NOT BE SUITABLE FOR PRE-TEENAGERS

77/85

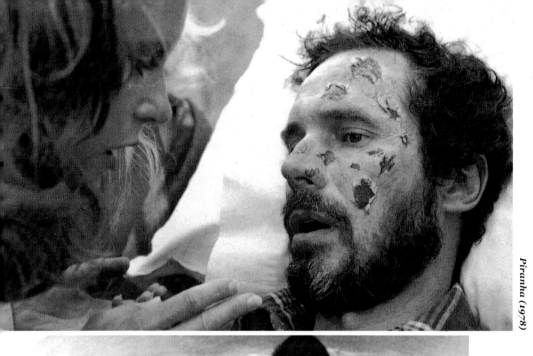

Piranha (1978)

Starcrash (1979)

Humanoids from the Deep (1980)

Android (1984)

and began peddling a script that he wanted to produce himself: *Piranha*. Written by Wilyam Eledge, it told the story of a crazed ichthyologist who put hundreds of deadly piranhas into Los Angeles swimming pools to avenge the death of his twin brother. When no one bit, Schechtman had Richard Robinson pen a second draft; this time, the piranhas were loosed into a river to attack merry-makers at the Kern Lake resort. In October, the reworked *Piranha* was announced as a co-production between Schechtman, Skip Steloff (who produced Sam Fuller's *Shark* with Burt Reynolds in 1969) and James Cullen (*The Devil's Rain*), with an expected release in the spring of 1976. In the event, nothing happened until Schechtman teamed up with *Tender Loving Care* producer Chako van Leeuwen, who brought Robinson's script to New World in 1977.

Roger Corman's interest in a waterlogged horror film was piqued primarily because *Jaws 2* had entered production in the summer of '77 with a planned June 1978 release date. Desirous of capitalising on the publicity that would be generated by the $20 million Universal production, Corman tasked Frances Doel with finding someone who could redraft Robinson's script into something usable. She turned up 27-year-old novelist and short story writer John Sayles.

'It was kind of the opposite of the kid sitting in class reading his comic book inside his geography book,' Sayles revealed to *Ain't It Cool News*. 'Frances used to read serious fiction and kept comics on the outside of them. So, when the agents called up and said, "I got this new writer, John Sayles," she went, "Oh, the one who writes the short stories!" The agent went, "Yeah, yeah, yeah. So, you've heard of him?" She went, "Oh, yeah. He's a good writer." The agent said, "Well, do you have anything over there?" And she said, "Well, we need a rewrite on a thing called *Piranha*." I said, "Sounds fine to me. Sounds like a *Jaws* spin-off." And that's exactly what it was.'

> *On the trail of two missing campers, 'skip tracer' Maggie McKeown and recluse Paul Grogan discover a seemingly-abandoned Army test site with a huge pool. They drain the pool and inadvertently release a shoal of piranha into a nearby river. The piranha were bred as part of a plan to infest the river systems of North Vietnam and the Army is alerted; they dump poison into the river but the piranha escape along a tributary and head towards to the newly-opened Lost River Lake resort. Maggie and Paul try desperately to warn the resort management but are dismissed as crackpots—that is, until the piranha show up for the festivities..*

Producing and directing *Piranha* would be the *Hollywood Boulevard* duo of Jon Davison and Joe Dante. '[Robinson] couldn't figure out how to get the people into the water once they were aware of the piranha infestation,' Davison explained to *Filmmakers Monthly*, 'so he had a giant bear chasing the people into the water to get eaten by the fish. But there was nothing really motivating the bear, so he came up with the idea of a forest fire driving the bear into chasing the people into the water to be eaten by the fish..' Dante picks up the story from there: 'The piranhas were originally called 'catranhas', a hybrid breed of catfish crossed with piranhas. Needless to say we refused to do Robinson's script, so Roger had John Sayles do a rewrite—although there was really nothing to rewrite. The only things that still exist from the original material are the piranhas and [Paul's daughter]. But there was a Writer's Guild arbitration and Robinson ended up with a story credit, which is certainly a tribute to his agent.'

'I decided that given a 90 to 100 minute movie, there should be a piranha attack every ten minutes,' Sayles told *Film Quarterly*. 'You open the picture with one and then every ten minutes you have another attack or some kind of action sequence. The basic problem with the story was, how do we get the piranha into the river? The first part of the story was about this but then I asked, why doesn't everyone just stay out of the river? They wanted the piranhas descending on the summer camp at the end so I had the end point. I drew a picture of a river and a lake and I said, okay, here's a schematic, visual thing of what happens but there's no point where the people are going to have a rest. So I drew a dam in the middle of it: the first half of the movie is getting to this dam; the second half of this movie is the piranhas getting around this dam, and then it started taking shape and incidents started taking shape before I had any characters.'

Filming began on March 15, 1978, at Aquarena Springs near San Marcos, Texas. It was a tight, 22 day-schedule, not helped by the last-minute cost-cutting that reduced the budget from $970,000 to $770,000. When asked by *Filmmakers Monthly* about whether or not Corman had any direct influence on *Piranha*, Davison commented dryly, 'Yeah, he cut the budget $200,000.' This despite the fact that the film was a co-production with United Artists, which put up half the cost in exchange for foreign distribution rights.

'Basically, the movie was a pain to film,' Dante told *Starlog*. 'It was a very ambitious picture for the small amount of money we had. Initially, we wanted to use all stop-motion [animation for the piranha effects]. When we approached Jon Berg, who worked on *Star Wars*, with the idea, he was horrified. We had to throw that idea out.. We didn't have much time to experiment with the special effects. We tried using rubber fish that [animator] Phil [Tippett] came up with but that didn't work. It was frustrating. Finally, Jon came up with a fish on a rod that was controlled by hand off-camera. We shot it at eight frames per second and it looked pretty good on screen, thank God. That was a lucky break because even if they had looked terrible, we would have had to use them.' 'The illusion of movement was created by the camera going by the fish,' Berg told *Filmmakers Monthly*, 'similar to what we were doing on *Star Wars* with motion control equipment. In fact the 'fish-bys' were done by Peter Kuran, who also worked on *Star Wars*.. The chief difference between us and *Star Wars* was that we didn't have rockets hanging on strings!'

Davison and Dante nevertheless were fortunate enough to be able to afford a cast of experienced professionals, including Bradford Dillman, Heather Menzies, Kevin McCarthy, Keenan Wynn, Barbara Steele, and Richard Deacon, along with Corman regulars Dick Miller and Paul Bartel. 'Going with a good cast is the only way to increase your odds of having a decent film,' Davison said.

The gamble paid off handsomely. Released in August 1978, *Piranha* became New World's highest grossing picture to date, earning over $6 million in domestic rentals and almost $10 million for United Artists overseas. Despite its commercial appeal, critical reaction was unenthusiastic. 'The title characters are never actually seen,' said *Variety*. 'Pic utilises a lot of red dye in the water, and an auditory effect for the gnawing that sounds like an air conditioner on the fritz.' *Cinefantastique* dismissed *Piranha* as a 'crude, exploitation horror movie, the kind Roger Corman used to personally direct, but now passes-on, baton-like, to a new generation of filmmaker.' When the film played in Chicago on a double-bill with *Dogs* (1976), Gene Siskel was beside himself: 'The box-office success of this disgusting double bill should give us all pause, pause to consider the public taste.. If you like seeing pre-teenagers yelp with pain, you'll love *Piranha*.' The one critic who came to the movie's defence was Charles Champlin, who wrote, '*Piranha* is what it is: a swift, efficient program picture which squeezes the most out of its dollars to squeeze delicious chills from the audience.'

'Roger asked me to get a couple of piranhas into the ocean at the end so they could breed and we could have a sequel,' Sayles told *Twilight Zone* magazine. The sequel rights did not rest with Corman, however, but with Schechtman and van Leeuwen, who cast in their lot instead with Italian producer Ovidio Assonitis (who had made the killer-octopus movie *Tentacles* in 1977) to make *Piranha 2: Flying Killers* in 1981. 'They had flying piranhas,' said Sayles, 'so that even if you stayed out of the water, they could fly through the air and grab you. Guys on oil rigs were being eaten..' A major overseas release through Columbia Pictures, the Jamaica-set *Piranha 2* was retitled *The Spawning* for its brief 1982 American run, which was handled by the independent Saturn International Pictures. In 1991, Assonitis announced a second sequel, *Piranha 3*, to be produced for Cannon Films, but this was never made.

In 1995, Corman remade *Piranha* as part of a *Roger Corman Presents* series on the Showtime network, utilising much the same script and effects. Yet another remake—*Piranha 3-D*, directed by Alexandre Aja (*The Hills Have Eyes* remake)— was promised for release in 2009.

In the way that he had done with his newly-formed Canadian distributorship, Corman established New World Pictures Limited in September 1978 to handle the release of the company's product in Britain. Distribution of New World's films in the UK had always been spotty (the last British release was *Jackson County Jail*, which was handled by Warner Brothers in March 1977) and only *Death Race 2000* had made anything of an impact. Tapped to head up the new sales operation, with its offices in Soho Square in London, was Bev Pearman, the former general manager of EMI Films. New World had a backlog of some two years' worth of movies, and

Blackout (Jim Mitchum)

the first scheduled release for the new distributor was to be *I Never Promised You a Rose Garden*, followed by *Deathsport* and *Avalanche*.

The move came at a time when New World was increasingly aware of the need to expand into new markets. By the end of the '70s, the drive-in was in decline. A combination of higher film rental rates, the introduction of daylight savings-time (which was delaying start times by as much as an hour, effectively killing family business), and escalating land prices (which made it much more lucrative to sell drive-ins than to modernise them), all conspired to put the future of the 'ozoner' in serious doubt. Another factor was the increasing number of suburban shopping malls, nearly all of which featured multiplexed, indoor cinemas.

Ed Carlin, now ensconced as New World's head of international sales and distribution, told *Variety*, 'Our operations have been squeezed by the majors' "discovery" of the drive-in market, and that, added to the rising cost of production, makes the foreign market a very relevant factor in our life.' In addition to the British set-up, Carlin said that New World was looking into establishing long-term distribution arrangements with companies in Europe.

> *'Someone's always asking for charity. I don't understand why I have to give charity.'*
> —Escaped convict Christie (Robert Carradine), terrorising the citizenry in *Blackout*

During the evening hours of July 13, 1977, three lightning strikes took out the power grid in New York City, rendering it useless for the next 24 hours. For a city enduring hard economic times, on edge over the 'Son of Sam' serial killings, and boiling in the summer heat, the blackout lit a powderkeg. In contrast to the festive spirit which had greeted the 1965 New York blackout, this one had been an excuse for widespread looting, arson, and vandalism. Some 1,600 stores were looted and over 1,000 fires set. The largest mass arrest in the city's history netted over 3,700 people and damages topped $300 million. The fallout from the blackout was so bad that it cost Mayor Abraham Beame his job.

148

Surprisingly, it was to be over 20 years before an indigenous filmmaker, New Yorker Spike Lee, would make a movie about the event: *Summer of Sam* (1999). For the Canadians at Cinepix, however, it was too good an opportunity to pass up. Just four months after it happened, *Blackout* began filming in Montreal.

> *A freak storm plunges New York City into darkness. A police van carrying dangerous criminals crashes and the gang are set free. Led by the psychopathic Christie, the four invade a nearby high-rise and begin to terrorize and rob the inhabitants. Off-duty cop Dan Evans comes across the wrecked van on his way to headquarters, then hears cries for help from the apartment block. He runs to the scene, and embarks upon a game of cat-and-mouse with the crooks in the building's darkened corridors.*

Gallic writer/director Eddy Matalon had scored a hit for Cinepix in 1977 with the sub-*Exorcist* movie *Cauchemars* (aka *Cathy's Curse*), a French-Canadian co-production. The same production companies joined with Cinepix to give Matalon a much larger budget (nearly $1 million) on *Blackout*; enough to buy a cast headed by Jim Mitchum, Belinda Montgomery and Robert Carradine, with guest stars Ray Milland, June Allyson and Jean-Pierre Aumont.

The resultant film was inspired as much by claustrophobic thrillers like *The Penthouse* and *Wait Until Dark* (both 1967) as by the actual New York blackout. The film's September 1978 release via New World, unlike its subject-matter, was a non-event—though it received a decent notice from *Variety*: 'A neat combination of comedy and terror make *Blackout* a refreshing and sturdy pic for audiences looking for a quick escape.' Among the few who sought it out was Kevin Thomas, who ended up looking for a quick escape from the theatre: '[*Blackout*] suffers from a power failure itself, having been short-circuited by a decided lack of energy, tension and imagination.'

The month of October brought a major management reshuffle at the House of Corman. Barbara Boyle, New World's executive vice president and legal adviser since 1974, took on the additional title of operations manager. Both Ed Carlin and Lois Luger (of the company's newly-created non-theatrical and TV sales division) were promoted to the role of vice president, and Paul Almond of Warner Brothers Records joined the company as vice president of business affairs. Frank Moreno, who had left New World in 1975, returned to fill the general sales manager post vacated by Bob Rehme, who had resigned earlier in the year to join Avco Embassy Pictures, of which he became president in 1979.

In the wake of the reorganisation, Boyle announced a whole slew of expensive new pictures, including the $15 million *World War III*, the $9 million *Iwo Jima*, the $4.5 million *Battle Beyond the Stars*, the $2.7 million *Lady in Red*, and the $1.2 million *Disco High*. Other projects being bandied about were *Robert E Lee*, a biopic that Corman had wanted to make originally for United Artists in the '60s, as well as another disaster film, *Volcano*. Boyle said that New World's green-lighting of a project was now contingent on marketability in three areas—theatrical, TV and pay-cable. 'In general,' she told *Variety*, 'if two of those three markets commit themselves, the picture is made.'

October also saw the release of New World's second and last Ingmar Bergman film, *Autumn Sonata*. It had been produced by Lew Grade's ITC Entertainment, but the British impresario had yet to establish an American distributorship (as he would in 1979 with Associated Film Distributors), so Corman took on the film's US release. It was a wise move, as *Autumn Sonata* earned over $2 million in rentals and garnered two Oscar nominations, including Best Actress (Ingrid Bergman) and Best

The Bees (John Saxon)

They Prey on HUMAN FLESH!

the BEES

Starring JOHN SAXON · ANGEL TOMPKINS · JOHN CARRADINE
Music by RICHARD GILLIS · Director of Photography: LEON SANCHEZ
Written, Directed and Produced by ALFREDO ZACHARIAS

Screenplay. It also won a Golden Globe Award for Best Foreign Film.

'You want us to conduct peace negotiations with bugs?'

—UN official in *The Bees*

Having already produced two archetypes of the disaster film, *The Poseidon Adventure* (1972) and *The Towering Inferno* (1974), Irwin Allen embarked in 1977 on his biggest production ever, the $21 million *The Swarm*. This time, cinematic catastrophe arrived in the form of African killer bees, invading Houston to put the sting on an all-star cast that included Michael Caine, Katharine Ross, Richard Chamberlain, Richard Widmark, Olivia De Havilland and Henry Fonda. Released by Warner Brothers in July 1978, the movie was savaged by the critics, ignored by audiences, and it ended up losing over $13 million.

Six months earlier, Roger Corman, like everyone else in the industry, had expected *The Swarm* to be another monster hit for Allen, and planned accordingly. He sent John Saxon, Angel Tompkins, and John Carradine south of the border to Mexico City with writer/director Jack Hill to film *The Bees*. Mexicans Michel and Alfredo Zacharias had brought the project to Corman and consequently were acting as its producers; once shooting was underway, Alfredo took it upon himself to supplant Hill as director. 'I walked off the set and didn't come back,' Hill told *Fangoria*. 'I went home and got my lawyers.'

At a remote UNESCO research station in Brazil, Franklin Miller is researching African killer bees. When a local boy is stung to death, the villagers attack the station and let loose the bees, which kill Miller. Cosmetics companies hear of the jelly produced by the bees and begin to illegally import them into the US. In doing so, they unleash swarms of the pests to attack cities. Researchers Hummel and Norman discover a pheromone that neutralises the bees and the Air Force sprays it country-wide; at first, it seems to work, but a mutant strain emerges that is resistant to the pheromone and capable of communication! Using a device developed by Hummel, the bees' message is conveyed to the United Nations—stop destroying the environment or face extinction.

With *The Bees*, Corman showed that he could make a movie every bit as silly and dumb as Irwin Allen's, but for a fraction of the cost. Money was saved through the liberal use of stock footage, from plane crashes and military manoeuvres to shots of ex-President Gerald Ford at the Pasadena Tournament of Roses Parade. The special effects were no worse than those in Allen's film, and Saxon, Tompkins, and Carradine (sporting a ridiculous German accent) were no less embarrassing than Caine, Ross, and Fonda. But while *The Swarm* was unintentionally hilarious, *The Bees*, in keeping with Jack Hill's approach, was humorous on purpose, though its notion of insects communicating ultimatums was a direct steal from *Phase IV* (1974) and *Bug*.

Released to non-existent business in November 1978 (Warners supposedly paid Corman a huge sum to delay the film's distribution), *The Bees* was given the same critical reception which had been afforded *The Swarm*. 'The movie.. doesn't work,' said the *Los Angeles Times*. 'There are too many ideas, which are not well woven together, and the disaster scenes are too low-key. In addition, the film has all the other earmarks of low-budget exploitation: sloppy execution, spotty special effects, poor colour and uninspired opticals.' *Variety* was similarly dismissive: '[Saxon and Tompkins] take their case to what appears to be a United Nations meeting being conducted in somebody's basement. It's all rather silly, although the film has its campy moments. It's never scary.' 'The film is one more entry in a tested and clichéd field,' said *Cinefantastique*, 'its commercial merits disguised in Zacharias's unflinching instability as a film director.'

'*We're the people our parents warned us to stay away from.*'
—Prison inmate Clair (Beverly Hope Atkinson) in *Outside Chance*

The month of December saw the premiere of New World's first made-for-TV production—*Outside Chance,* on CBS. The project had come about in the wake of CBS's airing of *Jackson County Jail* in September 1977, as director Michael Miller told *Film Comment*: 'It did pretty well, even though they put it up against *Charlie's Angels*. But they liked the picture. I was at the Century West Health Club and some guys were talking about doing *Where's Poppa?* [1970] as a television series. On my way home I was thinking, if they can do *Where's Poppa?* as a television series, we can do *Jackson County Jail* as a television series. So I got to the office and I told [producer] Jeff Begun to call Al Wagner [CBS vice president in charge of programming] in New York and tell him we have an idea to do *Jackson County* as a female *The Fugitive*. I was sure [CBS was] going to say yes, and they said yes.'

Because the rights to *Jackson County Jail* resided with Roger Corman, he was brought in as executive producer for the $1 million *Outside Chance*, which made history as the first independent, non-union movie shot for television. Despite her misgivings about how New World had handled *Jackson County*, Yvette Mimieux returned to reprise her role as Dinah Hunter. The first 15 minutes of the TV movie were simply abridged footage from *Jackson County*, with the new material coming after Hunter kills her rapist jailer. Apparently, she found the time to have a perm between committing the murder and being hauled before the court.

> *Dinah Hunter, a frustrated ad exec, leaves her job and her cheating boyfriend in LA to return to New York. Driving across country, her car and valuables are stolen by two junkie hitchhikers; she is then incarcerated as a trouble-maker when a local bartender accosts her. While being held in the cells, she is beaten and raped by a jailer whom she kills in revenge. An inmate sets a fire, and Dinah manages to flee the jail along with pregnant Lola; first they hide-out with Lola's cousins, who are illegal fur traders, then they wind up at the home of concert pianist Bill Hill. Lola has her baby but dies in the process. Hill and Dinah fall in love, but their solace is shattered by Lola's cousins, who want the money that she and Dinah stole from them..*

Jackson County Jail (Yvette Mimieux)

Corman felt that *Outside Chance* was strong enough to be released first as a theatrical feature and then air on CBS. 'We'd like to take this and see if we can run off a quick couple of million dollars,' he told *Variety*. 'We'll spend a minimum of $700-800,000, and up to $1.5 million on promoting and advertising the picture. The network gets the benefit of all that. All the arguments are on the side of doing it, other than inertia. CBS says they've never done this. Well, neither have we. But this project warrants it.'

The film was delivered to CBS in June, but inertia took over and the network sat on it, unable to decide whether or not to accept Corman's offer to release it theatrically. During the summer, New World placed the film in the Deauville and Edinburgh film festivals, where it received good notices, including one from *Variety*: 'This film is as adept as the first one, and a well made programmer that could find okay playoff.' Such prognostication was not enough to convince CBS, though, and it decided against a theatrical release for *Outside Chance*.

Despite having had to tone down his original concept, director Michael Miller remained upbeat about the whole experience. 'With the combination of CBS and Roger, we were given enough rope to hang ourselves, which was surprising and pleasing to us.. In the beginning there were a lot of guns and violence, stuff I didn't really care about, but then we got notes from the censors saying, "Please delete". Which was fine with me.' Miller would subsequently helm two more features—the Chuck Norris actioner *Silent Rage* and National Lampoon's *Class Reunion* (both 1982), before becoming a successful director of TV movies. (Never one to give up a winning formula, Corman remade *Jackson County Jail* yet again in 1997 as *Macon County Jail*, with Ally Sheedy and David Carradine.)

As the decade neared its end, Roger Corman and New World Pictures were at a crossroads. In only eight years, the company had become, as its notepaper proudly proclaimed, 'America's Largest Independent'. But this achievement had come at a price: Corman had established New World Pictures as a bid for freedom; now, he was a slave to the day-to-day running of a major film company, which was greatly impeding his creativity.

Corman had other worries also. Much of the young talent that had made New World's most successful films either had, or would, move on to bigger things. The foreign films that had given New World both profits and notoriety were becoming more expensive as the majors—particularly United Artists—took note of Corman's achievement in that area; serious competition was also raising its head in the form of Israeli cousins Menahem Golan and Yoram Globus, who had bought the Cannon Group in 1978 and since sought to claim New World's crown for their own. With the advent of home video and cable, as well as the disappearing drive-in, the whole landscape of cinema was changing. New World remained unrecognised overseas, despite making inroads in Canada and Britain. Last but not least, its attempts at in-house prestige films and blockbusters had yielded little fruit. It was not time to write New World's eulogy—its biggest hits were still ahead of it—but it *was* time to reflect upon which way to go.

Like the rest of Hollywood, Corman received a shock to the system in October 1978 when his chief competitor and former employer Samuel Z Arkoff announced that he was selling American International Pictures to Filmways. In less than 18 months, Arkoff would be gone and AIP would cease to exist, becoming the short-lived Filmways Pictures. For his part, Corman had never thought seriously about selling his company but, in 1979, he began to entertain offers to do exactly that.

US theatrical poster for *Humanoids from the Deep*

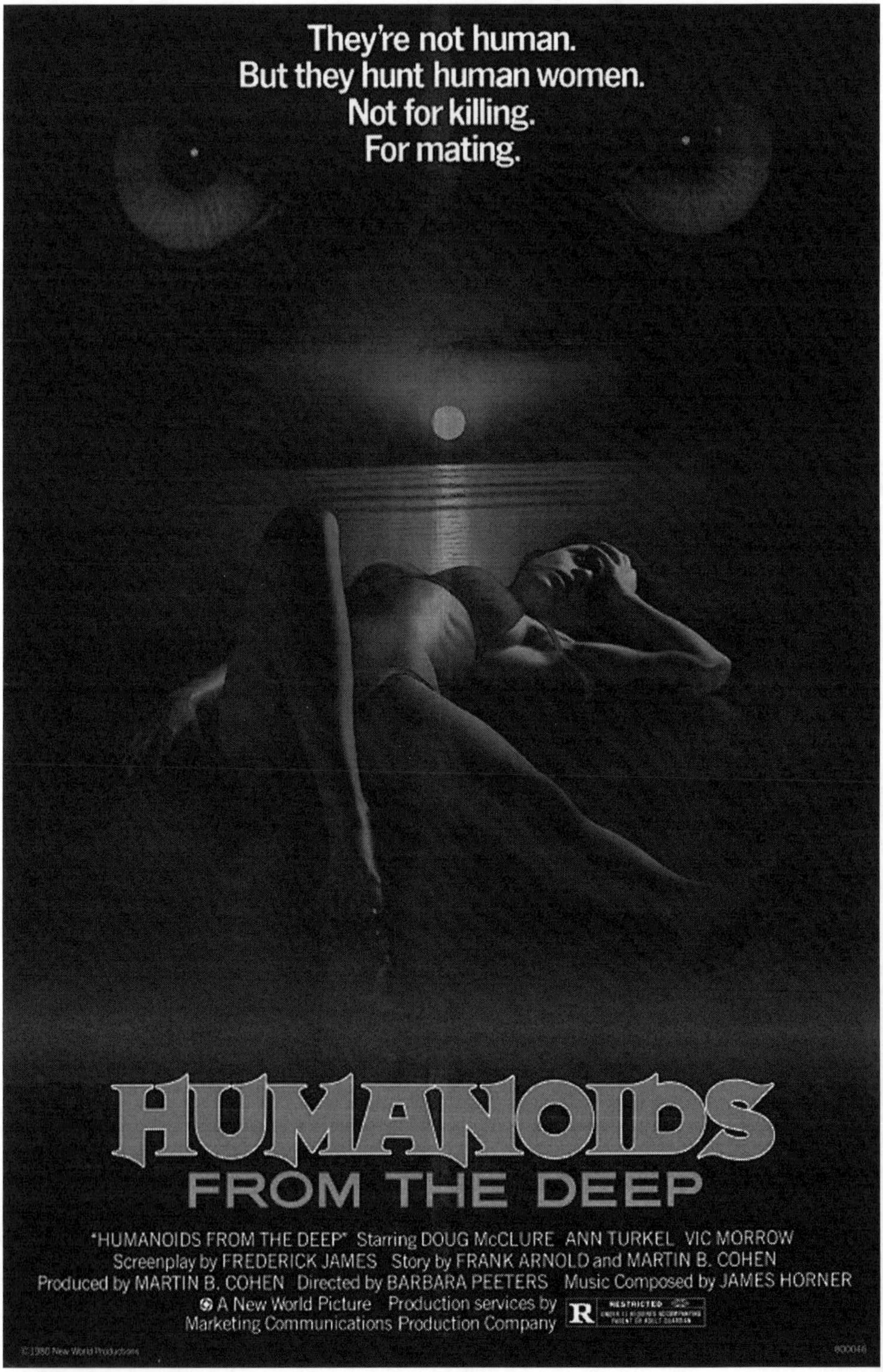

Chapter 5

SaiNTS, huManoids and galaxies

Deathsport (Claudia Jennings)

'This is a grind, to a certain extent. I'd never been in a position of coming to the office every morning, and I simply do not like it.'
—Roger Corman, 1979

'He's a very smart guy, Roger. I always thought, if he ever got off the idea that the main priority of a movie is that it dare not lose money, then he could've made some truly great pictures.'
—David Carradine, star of *Death Race 2000, Cannonball* and *Deathsport*

It was not only New World which found itself adjusting to a changing theatrical climate but independent film production in general. In 1974, indie companies had released 357 films; by 1979, that total was down to 189. In just two years (1977-79), the independents' share of the production pulse had dropped from 70% to 56%. The reasons for this were many but seemed primarily to be down to five key factors: increased production costs, increased printing and advertising costs, the emergence of so-called 'super-indies' like Orion Pictures and The Ladd Company producing A-list product and releasing it through the majors, restrictions on tax- shelter film financing, and recent blockbusters raising public expectations.

In the January 1979 issue of France's *Cahiers du Cinema*, Corman remarked, 'We're beginning to compete directly with the majors, which we didn't a few years ago. We thought they had a section of the market with a certain kind of film and we had a different market. So, while they are switching to what New World was doing, we're moving directly into their own area.'

'I don't live in the past. I just visit it once in a while.'
—Single mother Grace Wolf (Brenda Vaccaro) in *Fast Charlie, The Moonbeam Rider*

Though his relationship with Fox was over, Corman did produce one last film for a major studio—Universal's *Fast Charlie, The Moonbeam Rider*. It reunited him with director Steve Carver for the fourth and final time, as well as the actor who was fast becoming Corman's *numero uno* leading man: David Carradine. The title role of bike-racer Charlie Swattle had been written for Steve McQueen, but the superstar's battle with cancer turned terminal and prevented his involvement (he died in 1980). Carver had never worked with Carradine, and the former *Kung Fu* cowboy's erratic reputation had preceded him. 'I was a little worried,' Carver told *Shock Cinema*, 'because David had just come off this incident in Laurel Canyon with Barbara Hershey where he was out of his mind dancing on this piano and bleeding. I was really concerned I might be working with some dangerous actor. I remember first meeting him in Oklahoma only a week before shooting [in July 1978] and he walks in barefoot and sits in a chair and starts picking his toes and putting it in his mouth. I'm freaking out thinking I have a psycho on my hands.'

> *Charlie Swattle, war veteran and con-man, gathers his old Army buddies together and enters his 'Moonbeam Special' in the first-ever Transcontinental Motorcycle Race from St Louis to San Francisco. Along for the ride are waitress Grace and her son Wesley, to whom Charlie is a father figure. The first prize is $5,000, but rival biker Pop Bauer also needs the publicity that victory would bring to his ailing company and he offers Swattle $2,000 to throw the race. Swattle accepts the bribe, but a confrontation with his crew and new-found family persuade him to see things through to the end.*

Carver came to take Carradine's eccentricities in his stride, and he eventually developed a strong respect for the actor: 'To this day he's one of my good friends and I love him dearly. He's one of the best actors I've worked with.' *Fast Charlie, the Moonbeam Rider* was not the beginning of a beautiful friendship with Carver's equally unpredictable leading lady, Brenda Vaccaro—'She [got] married on set and then divorced a few days later and was hysterical'—who let it be known that she was making the movie under duress. Slumming through her contract with Universal, which had put her into disaster sequel *Airport '77* prior to *Fast Charlie*, Vaccaro later told the *Chicago Tribune*: 'I would never have done those movies if I hadn't been up against the wall.'

Universal evidently shared her lack of enthusiasm. *Fast Charlie* was released in March 1979 on the lower half of double bills for a quick playoff. The few critics who bothered to review it were unimpressed: 'Cynical Americana based on the rotten premise that a nifty con gets better results than boring bravery' (*Los Angeles Times*); 'There doesn't seem to be too much of a market for post-World War I motorcycle pictures, especially those that look like they're taking place somewhere on the wagon trails of the 1800s' (*Variety*). Carver must have taken this last critique to heart, as his next project with Carradine was the modern-day spaghetti western *Lone Wolf McQuade* (1983), co-starring Chuck Norris.

> *'We've been searching for you all* through *these damned haunted stars!'*
> —Stella Star (Caroline Munro) to Prince Simon (David Hasselhoff) in *Starcrash*

With its clichéd dialogue, poor acting, miniscule budgets, and over-ambitious miniature effects, 1960s' Italian sci-fi almost always looked as though it were made by fans, rather than professionals. But such naiveté also brought a refreshing lack of inhibition: the ideas were wilder, the set more colourful, the costumes flashier, as screens overflowed with the stuff of Tomorrowland. Ten years later, not much had changed, except that the fantasy fan as filmmaker was literalised in 30-year-old Luigi Cozzi, who had served as a foreign correspondent for *Famous Monsters of Filmland*, collaborated with Dario Argento on the *giallo* thrillers *The Cat O'Nine Tails* (1971) and *Four Flies on Grey Velvet* (1972), and self-distributed Douglas Trumbull's *Silent Running* (1972) in Rome. By 1976, Cozzi had directed six films—half of them for television—and his heart was set on an intergalactic disaster opus that he called *Starcrash*.

Starcrash (Luigi Cozzi [centre] on set)

'It was about a gigantic spaceship for passengers,' the director told Christophe Lemonnier. 'It's the first trip to Saturn, to see the shores of the rings. When crossing the rings, the ship [collides with] a space iceberg and then crashes on Titan, a moon of Saturn. So there's only a few survivors who try to wait for the rescue party.. When I proposed it to [producer] Nathan Wachsberger, he was not interested. He called me back after *Star Wars* opened in America. He tells me, "Luigi, I want—not your story—I want *Star Wars*!" I had a problem because it was the end of May 1977 and *Star Wars* would [not] open in Italy [till] November. I knew via the newspapers there was this science-fiction galactic adventure movie in America. But I didn't know how to see it. I didn't know what kind of movie it was. I was very, very lucky because.. I found in a bookstore a copy of *Star Wars* and I bought it.. I read the book and then I knew what *Star Wars* was about. When Nathan came to Italy to see what kind of *Star Wars* story I had to propose [to] him, I had already written the movie.'

> *Evil Count Zarth Arn of the League of the Dark Worlds wants to unseat the Emperor of the First Circle of the Universe and rule in his place. The Count has a weapon capable of projecting images which can drive men mad with fear. The Emperor dispatches ace*

157

star-pilot Stella Star and humanoid navigator Akton to locate the weapon and rescue the only survivor of an earlier expedition, the Emperor's son.

Being a sci-fi fan, Cozzi's inspiration for *Starcrash* derived from more sources than the films of George Lucas. Stella Star takes her cues from *Barbarella* (1968), while sundry creatures in Cozzi's galaxy have their origins in *Invaders from Mars* (1953), *Jason and the Argonauts* (1963), and *Zardoz* (1974). More direct allusions come in the form of the Emperor's probe ship (named after American sci-fi author Murray Leinster) and the summoning of 'Major (Ray?) Bradbury to the bridge.'

To fill Stella's leather bikinis, Cozzi had only one actress in mind—29-year-old British model Caroline Munro, who had started out in Hammer horror films and had graduated to playing the slave girl in *The Golden Voyage of Sinbad* (1974), as well as the villainous Stromberg's vixen in *The Spy Who Loved Me* (1977). Munro was not, however, Wachsberger's choice, and she landed the part only after the producer of *Starcrash* failed to persuade more iconic bikini-buster Raquel Welch to come aboard. Cozzi's script originally called for Stella's companion Akton to be half-man and half-crab ('I loved the image of Caroline in a bikini between a robot and an alien,' Cozzi said), but when Wachsberger arranged a distribution deal with AIP, Sam Arkoff insisted that the role be played by evangelist-turned-actor Marjoe Gortner.

The advertised budget for the film was $4 million, most of which went on sets at Cinecitta, location shooting in the Italian Alps, Sicily and Morocco, Christopher Plummer's cameo as the Emperor, and John Barry's musical score. Only a measly $30,000 was left for the various optical effects; as a result, many of Cozzi's ideas had to be drastically scaled back. His script describes the visions conjured by the Count's weapon as 'devilish, horrible creatures.. monsters which seem to come straight out of hell..' In the film, they are depicted by superimposing bubbles from a lava-lamp! The script describes the Count's ship as 'an enormous, mighty gothic cathedral with thousands of steel spires and hundreds of thousands of monstrous pinnacles.' In the film, it is a clumsy mechanical claw.

Some scenes were simply beyond the abilities of Cozzi's effects men, Armando Valcauda and Germano Natali. The script called for Stella's escape from a penal colony to initiate a sequence of events: while on the run, she falls into quicksand and the guards who pursue her are attacked by tentacled monsters called 'Vitons'; later on, she faces off against a gigantic, dragon-like creature before being rescued by a spaceship. Both of these scenes were shot—with a dead crab substituting for a model dragon!—but they were deemed too shoddy and were discarded.

The six-month shoot, which had begun in October 1977, became fraught with problems. Production was halted on several occasions when funds failed to come through and the crew went on strike as a result. Cozzi also had the misfortune to be at the helm of the only international production at Cinecitta when a communist workers' revolt broke out. Surrounding the studio offices, an irate mob confiscated the master print of *Starcrash* and held it for ransom. It was recovered intact only after six weeks of tense negotiations.

The film had originally been scheduled for an Easter 1978 release by AIP, but the dramas back-stage had caused that date to be pushed back to the fall, when it was set to premiere as *The Adventures of Stella Star*. But Arkoff might have been better prepared for what finally arrived in his projection-room had he paid more attention to Cozzi's comments to *Variety* when the film started shooting ('*Star Wars* is real science fiction; mine is science fantasy.. our galaxies have nothing in common with those in *Star Wars*').

The head of AIP was incensed by the overall shoddiness of the production and refused to release it. (The same thing happened in 1979 with another Italian *Star Wars* clone, *The Humanoid*). Roger Corman, desirous of testing the waters before jumping in with his own *Star Wars* imitation, promptly picked up Arkoff's option and released *Starcrash* in March 1979, just two months after its premiere in Italy.

The critical response was scathing. 'It's smudged badly by post synchronised dialogue of such surpassing corniness that it restricts its appeal to children and only the most undemanding of adults,' said Kevin Thomas. 'Everything about the plot is strictly kiddie-matinee,' declared *Cinefantastique*. 'This film is a big disappointment.' *Variety* was more specific: 'Photography almost never convinces that this is actually taking place anywhere but on the movie screen and special effects seem little more than poor imitations of what's been done before.' The *Washington Post* took exception to the film's lack of feminist sensitivity: 'Stella Star's hooker wardrobe seems to reveal more about the longings of producer Nat Wachsberger than one cares to know. The revelations get even more stark when Stella is briefly imprisoned on a planet of Amazons. For a while the screen teems with starlets striking threatening poses in flimsy costumes.'

The *Post*'s review only served to encourage the audience for *Starcrash*, which came out in force and gave New World its biggest opening week ever. Cozzi's film went on to earn over $2 million in rentals, making it one of the few successful films for New World in what would prove to be a very lean year. A sequel called *Star Riders* was announced at the Cannes Film Festival in 1979, to be produced on a $12 million budget for Cannon Films and feature a script by sci-fi writer A E Van Vogt. A year later, the project was relabelled *Star Patrol*, with no Cannon or Van Vogt and a budget slashed to $2 million. In the end, it never made it off the launch pad, and the statuesque Munro lost herself in a revolving door of cheap and nasty slasher films in the 1980s (*Don't Open 'Til Christmas, The Last Horror Film, Maniac et al*) before opting for motherhood in place of stardom.

> *'People make love for so many crazy reasons; why shouldn't money be one of them?'*
>
> —Singapore pimp Jack Flowers (Ben Gazzara) in *Saint Jack*

Peter Bogdanovich was out to prove that he could indeed 'go home' again. The 38-year-old had begun his directorial career under the auspices of Roger Corman, odd-jobbing on *The Wild Angels* and *Voyage to the Planet of Prehistoric Women* before being given his chance to fly solo with the excellent contemporary thriller *Targets*. From there, Bogdanovich became one of Hollywood's brightest lights, writing and directing three critical and commercial successes: *The Last Picture Show* (1971, for which he was nominated for two Oscars), *What's Up Doc?* (1972), and *Paper Moon* (1973). He then left his wife, production designer Polly Platt, set up house with model-turned-actress Cybill Shepherd, and started to live the life of Hollywood royalty—until the party came abruptly to an end. After three expensive flops in a row—*Daisy Miller* (1974), *At Long Last Love* (1975), and *Nickelodeon* (1976)—Bogdanovich went from being the toast of the town to the butt of many a cocktail-party joke.

Offers to direct were still coming in (he foolishly turned down *Heaven Can Wait* in 1978 but wisely steered clear of the disastrous Dino De Laurentiis remake of *Hurricane* in 1979), but battles with Columbia over *Nickelodeon* had taken their toll and Bogdanovich missed the creative freedom and lack of pressure that he had enjoyed when the budgets were modest. 'I'm tired, and I want a rest,' he told the *Los Angeles Times*. 'I've been going from picture to picture, and I need more time to prepare the next one, more time to figure out who I am and what I'm doing.'

One who knew only too well how fickle success could be was actor-director Orson Welles. In 1941, Welles had stunned the world with his debut tour-de-force, *Citizen Kane*, which he had followed in 1943 with *The Magnificent Ambersons*— another towering cinematic achievement, but one which fell victim to interference from makers RKO. This was the beginning of an unfortunate trend which would put Welles at loggerheads with his benefactors and eventually made him *persona non grata* as a director in Hollywood. Like many of his generation, Bogdanovich idolised both Welles and his films, and the young filmmaker had the good fortune to become biographer, friend and collaborator with the man himself. It was Welles who suggested the subject that was to be Bogdanovich's next film: a 1973 novel by Paul Theroux called *Saint Jack*.

Theroux's novel opens in Singapore in the 1950s, where ship's chandler Jack Fiori moonlights as a pimp for a variety of clients. Fiori makes a name for himself by trafficking prostitutes to cargo ships then by opening his own high-class brothel complete with bar and orchestra. The Chinese competition does not take kindly to the enterprise and Fiori is kidnapped and his brothel burnt to the ground. Some years later, he hooks up with a CIA agent to build a hotel/brothel for American GIs on leave from Vietnam. But when the army gets cold feet, Fiori finds himself out on his ear again. After a client dies of a heart attack in his bar, and the agent tries to persuade him to blackmail a US general, Fiori begins to suspect that he might be in the wrong line of work..

The original plan was for Bogdanovich to produce and Orson Welles to direct. For the opportunity to work with a legend, Jack Nicholson had agreed to play Jack Fiori for a fraction of his normal fee. Cybill Shepherd, who had won the film rights to *Saint Jack* in a legal settlement with *Playboy*, wrote the first draft of the script herself. Bogdanovich then came to realise why so many studios wanted no part of Welles: the portly *auteur* began to drag his feet, quixotically deciding against Jack Nicholson in favour of Dean Martin, and refused to work on the script. It became obvious that if *Saint Jack* were going to be made, Bogdanovich would have to take over the reins. Accordingly, he had Theroux try his hand at the screenplay, but the results were lacking, so he hired Pulitzer Prize-winning playwright Howard Sackler (*The Great White Hope*) to bring it up to scratch. Bogdanovich had wanted John Cassavetes to play 'Saint' Jack, but he took Cassavetes's advice and cast his buddy Ben Gazzara instead.

In order to do the film his way and keep Gazzara (who was not exactly box office) in the lead, Bogdanovich went to the one source of funding whom he knew he could convince—Roger Corman. New World's boss was known to tell his young directors, 'If the movie's a success, you'll never have to work for me again,' so he was no doubt flattered that one of his protégés who had made good was back on his doorstep. The nature of the material also attracted Corman, as he told author Ben Slater in the latter's excellent book, *Kinda Hot: The Making of Saint Jack*: 'It was unspoken and I never brought it up, but the scenes as written indicated that there was going to be nudity..'

Corman agreed to put up $1 million (the film ended up costing $1.5 million, though it was announced as $2.5 million) and shooting began in Singapore in April 1978. Because of the strict local censorship (the novel had been banned in Singapore), Bogdanovich and company called their film *Jack of Hearts* and submitted a *faux* screenplay to the authorities for their approval. But though it was able to keep the state at bay, *Saint Jack* encountered other problems during its 10-week shoot: the soundtrack was impounded until hotel bills were paid, the European crew filmed at the wrong camera speed (25 fps instead of 24), and the footage was processed in Hong Kong with markings that no one in America could understand.

Things were eventually sorted out, and *Saint Jack* premiered in New York in April 1979 to ecstatic reviews. 'A new kind of movie!' said Rex Reed. 'Tough, tight, two-fisted and uncompromising.' 'Bogdanovich's triumph!' raved Judith Crist. 'A rich and vibrant tapestry of truth.' 'A comeback victory for Peter Bogdanovich!' declared the *New York Post*. 'This is the real stuff—a stunning film!' 'A Saint in a Cathouse!' observed *Newsweek*. '*Saint Jack* returns Peter Bogdanovich to the sweetness and finely tuned sense of loss which are his true qualities.' One who did not appreciate the 'true qualities' of the film was Vincent Canby, who railed against its supposed colonialist mentality: 'I find it impossible to be moved or even much interested in this last vestige of a discredited colonialism. Jack.. is not only dead. He also represents a kind of fiction that wasn't all that great when he was alive.'

Saint Jack grossed a respectable $150,000 in a five-week, single-house run, but when the company tried to expand it westward, it ran smack into what was fast becoming New World's *bête noir*. 'All the quality theatres were already booked for the summer in January for pictures that exhibitors hadn't even seen,' Frank Moreno told *Variety*. 'Everything now is either being blind bid or there's product splitting and that's tying up all of the most important play time with major product. I don't have the wedge of an *Alien* or a film with Barbra Streisand to bargain with. And if [obtaining playdates] keeps being dependent on that, the visibility of independent companies is going to slowly disappear.' *Saint Jack* did not open in Los Angeles until late August; as a result, it was unable to capitalise on the momentum of its New York raves and ended up earning less than $1 million in rentals.

The film fared better in its overseas release in the fall. Moreno did a deal with the newly-formed Orion Pictures—headed by former United Artists executives who had walked out on parent company Transamerica—which saw *Saint Jack* achieve a $3 million foreign gross. It was small consolation to Bogdanovich, however, who made no secret of his feelings that New World had mishandled his film. 'It was not a big commercial success,' the director told Associated Press. '[New World] didn't even bother to distribute it properly.' He would run into the same problem with his next film, the ensemble comedy *They All Laughed* (1981), which was barely released by Time-Life Films and Bogdanovich had to buy it back and try to market it himself, to no greater effect.

> *'What's been happening to me is just too strange.. too strange for me to share with anyone from my old life.'*
> —Nola Carveth (Samantha Eggar), mother to killer dwarves in *The Brood*

David Cronenberg's fourth feature, *The Brood*, had begun to take shape in the immediate aftermath of *Rabid*—not because of that film's success, but because of failure in his private life. In 1977, Cronenberg divorced his wife of seven years and entered into a bitter custody battle over their young daughter. With art imitating life, Cronenberg wrote the film as the story of a father who is desperate to free his daughter from the physical and mental abuse of a psychotically deranged mother. 'It insisted on being made in a very personal way,' he confided to *Cinefantastique*. 'Almost *too* personal, as a matter of fact. It's as close to autobiography as I've ever come, and I hope I don't come that close again.' No doubt Cronenberg's ex-wife thought the same when she saw the climax in which the mother is strangled by the father. 'I can't tell you how satisfying that scene is,' said the director. 'I wanted to strangle my ex-wife..'

At the Somafree Institute of Psychoplasmics, Dr Hal Raglan, author of The Shape of Rage, *is conducting anger management courses by making his patients face up to their deep-rooted feelings of resentment and betrayal. In the case of Nola Carveth, victim of an abusive childhood and a broken marriage, violent impulse has literally taken on a life of its own: Nola's anger has manifested itself in a brood of deformed dwarves who act on her homicidal whims. 'The brood' kill Nola's parents and her daughter Candy's teacher, then they kidnap Candy and bring her to the Institute. Nola's husband Frank determines to rescue Candy, but to do so means facing up to his wife's other 'children'.*

US theatrical poster for The Brood

The Brood further develops what would become Cronenberg's trademark: the horror of 'the flesh'. As with his previous two horror films, terror is the internal made external—what threatens us actually has its metaphorical roots inside of us, whether it be parasitical, vampiric, or 'killer dwarves'. Cronenberg would continue this theme via telepathy (*Scanners*, 1981), precognition (*The Dead Zone*, 1983), self-mutilation (*Videodrome*, 1983), genetic mutation (*The Fly*, 1986), and even Siamese twins (*Dead Ringers*, 1988).

The catalyst for much of the mayhem is often the misappropriation of science and/or medicine. In a scene written but not shot for *The Brood*, Frank Carveth meets with a Dr Wessler to discuss Raglan's book and the dangers of his theories. 'He says that the body is the central fact of human existence,' Wessler explains, 'and that anxiety must be expressed through the body to be relieved. In other words, he *encourages* the psychosomatic symptoms to blossom. But *I* say, what happens once these physical symptoms have established themselves in the body? What happens if Dr Raskin [Raglan's original name] encourages you to express your anxiety through skin rashes—and the rash becomes infected or cancerous? How can you control it?'

In the case of Nola, Raglan's notion of 'psychoplasmics' spins completely out of control and materialises as described in the script: 'At random intervals over the entire surface of her skin, including her arms and legs, sprout translucent lumps of flesh ranging from walnut-size to—in two cases—the size of large watermelons. Through the backlit spheres of flesh, [Frank] can see clearly what appear to be human embryos and foetuses in varying stages of development.'

In this climactic scene, Nola reveals not only the source of the 'brood' but also the unintended consequences of self-serving science. Nola, played convincingly by British actress Samantha Eggar (*The Collector, Doctor Dolittle*), tears open one of the amniotic sacs, extracts the newborn, and begins to lick it clean. This act went unseen in America and Canada as it was excised to avoid an 'X' rating. 'The ironic thing is that when the censors, those animals, cut it out, the result was that a lot of people thought she was eating the baby,' said Cronenberg. 'That's much worse than what I was suggesting. What we're talking about here is an image that is not sexual, not violent, just gooey, gooey and disturbing. It's a bitch licking her pups.'

Despite this and other (minor) cuts, the critics were aghast at Cronenberg's bloody aesthetic. 'Now here's a particularly nasty little number,' wrote Roger Ebert. '*The Brood* is an el-sleazo exploitation film, camouflaged by the presence of several well-known stars but guaranteed to nauseate you all the same.' Kevin Thomas echoed that sentiment: '*The Brood* is so totally sickening it's an irresponsible work itself. You can't help but feel that the MPAA, in its lenient rating, hasn't been very responsible either.' 'Yet another horror entry which casts children in the role of malevolent little monsters,' observed *Variety*, '*The Brood* is an.. essentially unpleasant shocker which trades freely in elements found in other pics.' Only *Cinefantastique* took a different tack, declaring the film to be 'without a doubt Cronenberg's most accomplished work.'

Released by New World in June 1979, *The Brood* became the company's second biggest success of the year, earning nearly $3 million in rentals. Executive producers Pierre David and Victor Solnicki soon exchanged their distribution pact with New World for one with Avco Embassy Pictures, however, so Cronenberg's next film would be in the hands of Bob Rehme. *Scanners* was to be Cronenberg's biggest success to date, raking in some $6 million in rentals, and the sting of New World's former sales manager reaping the rewards was further compounded by the fact that Corman had been offered the script of the film years earlier (when it was titled *Telepathy 2000*) and had turned it down.

> '*People say that your music is loud and destructive and lethal to mice, but I think you're the Beethovens of our time!*'
> —Music teacher McGree (Paul Bartel) to The Ramones in *Rock 'n' Roll High School*

Partner Joe Dante had had his shot with *Piranha*—now Allan Arkush wanted *his* turn in the director's chair. 'When I was in high school,' he told Movieweb, 'I had these daydreams staring out the window, about putting on a rock 'n' roll concert in my high school and blowing up the school, and having motorcycle races in the hallways.' In 1977, Arkush turned his fantasy into a treatment that he called *Heavy Metal Kids*, which he and Dante fashioned into a screenplay that Corman rejected. The head of New World then had trade paper reporter Joseph McBride write five drafts in four months of a script entitled *Girl's Gym*, about a high school gymnastics team. When the project was abandoned, the decision was taken to mix elements from both into something that Corman wanted to call *Disco High*, given the popularity of *Saturday Night Fever* (1977) and disco music in general. For this task, he enlisted two more writers: National Lampoon's Richard Whitley and New World staffer Russ Dvonch.

Arkush was adamant that the movie be titled *Rock 'n' Roll High School*—'You can't blow up a high school to *disco* music,' he said in Corman's autobiography—and set out to find a group who could headline his self-confessed remake of AIP's *Shake, Rattle & Rock* (1956). First choice was Cheap Trick, but they wanted too much money, so the production went ahead instead with the world's first 'punk' band, The Ramones.

> At Vince Lombardi High School, the students are out of control. Strict disciplinarian Miss Togar becomes the new principal and, with her brown-shirted minions, she sets about laying down the law. This is all a drag for Riff Randell, who fancies herself as

an aspiring songwriter for her favourite group, The Ramones. When the band comes to town, Riff sends them her songs; impressed by her talent, they agree to a concert at Lombardi High. Miss Togar tries to sabotage Riff's dream gig, resulting in a standoff that ends with the school being blown sky-high.

Filmed at the abandoned El Segundo High School in Los Angeles, which had been the venue for *Rock Around the Clock* nearly 25 years earlier, the movie was a labour of love for Arkush that nearly finished him. The $200,000 budget was half what had been asked for and the gruelling, four-week shoot put him in the hospital with nervous exhaustion, leaving Dante (who received a 'special thanks' credit) to wrap the production. 'When you've busted your ass to make it work,' Arkush told *Penthouse*, 'Roger says, "See, I told you so." And mostly it *does* work. But it's always a fucking miracle. Corman teaches you how to do miracles by making sure a miracle is the only thing that'll save your ass!'

Released in June 1979, *Rock 'n' Roll High School* met with some enthusiastic reviews. 'The best non-documentary rock film in years,' declared *Rolling Stone*. 'It's rowdy, exuberant. Downright masterful in capturing the rebellious spirit of rock 'n' roll.' The *Detroit Free Press* called it 'A demented masterpiece. Hands down the best movie of 1979.' *Variety* was a little more subdued: 'New World has clearly filled the niche vacated by American International, when it moved up to bigger budgets, if not bigger returns. And as long as Roger Corman keeps finding young directors, writers and performers who have a clear grasp of what their peers want to see, it'll be a financially comfortable perch.'

As things turned out, Arkush and company did *not* have a clear grasp of what moviegoers wanted—the picture tanked. 'I was shocked when we did as badly as we did when it came out,' the director told Movieweb. 'I didn't think it was going to be a giant hit but.. I was surprised that we didn't do better when we played San Francisco and hipper places. There was kind of a schism within New World between who liked the picture and who didn't, because it was so different than your average exploitation movie of New World Pictures at the time.'

Fittingly, *Rock 'n' Roll High School* was the graduation for an entire class of New World filmmakers. Arkush initially went the studio route, but the failure of

Rock 'n' Roll High School (Paul Bartel)

165

his films *Heartbeeps* (1981) and *Get Crazy* (1983) caused a rethink and he settled instead into a highly profitable career in television. He directed episodes of 1980s' shows like *Fame* and *Moonlighting*, then he began both to produce and direct in the 1990s, with *Shannon's Deal* and *Parenthood*; he has spent most of the past decade as a producer/director on top-rated series *Crossing Jordan* and *Heroes*. In 1999, he received an Emmy award for his musical biopic *The Temptations*.

Joe Dante switched to Avco Embassy, where he directed cult werewolf picture *The Howling* in 1981 before really hitting the big time with the Steven Spielberg-produced blockbuster, *Gremlins* in 1984. He went on to direct several more films for Spielberg, such as *Twilight Zone: The Movie* (1983), *Innerspace* (1987), *Gremlins 2* (1990) and *Small Soldiers* (1998). He also co-produced the TV shows *Eerie, Indiana* (1991-92) and *Jeremiah* (2002-04). Second unit directors Jon Davison and Jerry Zucker teamed up to make the parody *Airplane* (1980) for Paramount, which became one of the most successful comedies of all time. Davison then went on to produce Paul Verhoeven's *Robocop* (1987) and *Starship Troopers* (1997), while Zucker co-produced the successful *Naked Gun* comedies (1988-94) and directed the hits *Ruthless People* (1986) and *Ghost* (1990).

In 1991, Roger Corman produced an ill-conceived sequel—*Rock 'n' Roll High School Forever*—in which the only returning cast member was Mary Woronov, the original's Miss Togar, though not in the same role. Four years later, Riff Randell herself—P J Soles of *Halloween* and *Stripes*—tried to interest Corman in making *Rock 'n' Roll High School Class Reunion*, but he passed. Radio shock jock Howard Stern is rumoured to be planning a remake for release in 2010.

> *'Revenge isn't the ticket. Try and get even.. you never get ahead.'*
> —Gangster John Dillinger (Robert Conrad) in *The Lady in Red*

In July 1979, while visiting New World's new distribution setup in London, Corman once again teased press and fans with the possibility that he might return to directing on an unnamed sci-fi film which was tentatively scheduled to start filming in England the following summer. Corman also let it be known that he was considering mounting additional productions in England, to take advantage of the country's Eady Fund for film production. He was not, however, about to open any more foreign offices.

That same month saw the premiere of Julie Corman's first production in three years, a period gangster piece not unlike her husband's Al Capone outings. 'I passionately believed in *The Lady in Red*,' she told Mollie Gregory, 'the [John] Dillinger story told through Polly Franklin [Hamilton in reality], the 'lady in red' character, and I believed in the political and moral issues of the story.. I hired John [Sayles] to develop the characters and explore social issues.. feminism, communism, racism, the haves versus the have-nots. There's that fine line between hitting the issues too hard and losing the audience, or just glancing over issues haphazardly. Sayles handled the balance brilliantly, and he really built people in the film.'

> *During the Great Depression, farm girl Polly Franklin runs away to Chicago, where she finds work in a sweatshop and as a dance-hall girl. Busted for prostitution, Polly is sent to prison but is freed when she agrees to work in a bordello run by a Romanian madam. When a prostitute is stabbed to death, the police close the cathouse, forcing Anna to waitress at a diner. There, Polly meets dapper movie-fan Jimmy, who claims to be a commodities broker; they fall in love, but Jimmy is gunned down by FBI agents who claim that he is notorious bank robber John Dillinger. Picking up where her lover left off, Polly forms her own gang and robs the mob before heading off to California.*

US theatrical posters for The Lady in Red/Up from the Depths

'What it tried to be about was *why* Dillinger and the FBI were shooting each other,' Sayles told the *Detroit Free Press*. 'Dillinger was just a PR job. J Edgar Hoover made stars out of the guys he knew he could catch. He never got anybody from the Mafia. He'd take smaller guys, bank robbers, and make them Public Enemy No 1. In other words, to me that movie was about *why* Dillinger became Public Enemy No 1 at a time when one-third of the women in Chicago between the ages of 15 and 35 were working as prostitutes.'

Beginning with *Dillinger* in 1945, nine films and TV shows had dramatised the life of the legendary bank robber, and Robert Conrad's characterisation of John Dillinger in *The Lady in Red* followed in the footsteps of Lawrence Tierney, Nick Adams and Warren Oates, among others. However, no previous film had featured Dillinger's last girlfriend, nicknamed 'The Lady in Red' by the press of the day because of the dress that she was reputed to have worn at Chicago's Biograph Theatre, scene of Dillinger's demise at the hands of FBI agents on July 22, 1934 (it was actually an orange skirt). Julie Corman cast television's former 'Nancy Drew', Pamela Sue Martin, in the title role, which led to her subsequent stint as Fallon Carrington on the '80s prime time soap *Dynasty*.

Having directed second unit on *Cockfighter, Death Race 2000, Thunder and Lightning* and *Avalanche*, *The Lady in Red* represented the full-fledged directorial debut of Lewis Teague. He would reunite with Sayles a year later for the surprise monster hit, *Alligator* (1980), featuring Robert Forster, who put in an unbilled cameo in *The Lady in Red* as a chivalrous hit man. Teague would go on to direct the Stephen King adaptations *Cujo* (1983) and *Cat's Eye* (1985), in addition to *The*

Jewel of the Nile (1985), the sequel to hit adventure *Romancing the Stone* (1984). Like many Corman alumni, Teague spent most of the '90s in television, directing for shows like *Shannon's Deal, Profiler* and *Nash Bridges*, as well as helming made-for-TV movies like *Tom Clancy's OP Center* (1995) and *Justice League of America* (1997). In 2001, he directed his last two made-for-TV movies—*Love and Treason* and *The Triangle*—and with the exception of the 2007 short film *Cante Jondo*, he has not graced the director's chair since.

Shot and released in a matter of just three months on a budget of $900,000, Teague's debut went totally unnoticed by the moviegoing public. Its cause was not helped by a particularly hostile review from Linda Gross in the *Los Angeles Times*: 'The film is corrupt and offensive because it sensationalises racism and sadism.. *The Lady in Red* is saying the criminals aren't sordid, the society they are defying is. Of course, the message is hollow. You can't indict society for its sins by wallowing in them.' This last comment evidently struck a chord in Roger Corman, who retitled the film *Guns, Sin, and Bathtub Gin*, gave it a new and more salacious ad campaign ('Her father said she was a tramp. Her customers said she was fantastic'), and watched as it fell flat on its face once again in the spring of 1980.

> '*We're not going to be intimidated by a* fish!'
> —Desperate hotel manager (Kedric Wolfe) in *Up from the Depths*

Since *Piranha* had been New World's biggest success so far, Corman decided to try another fish story, which he would have old friend Cirio Santiago produce on the cheap in the Philippines. This time, Corman reached into his own bag of tricks for inspiration—all the way back to *Monster from the Ocean Floor* and *Creature from the Haunted Sea* (1961), to be precise. He took the premise of the former (a pretty girl arrives in a Mexican village and falls in love with a local marine biologist while they hunt a sea monster), added the treasure-hunting of the latter, then mixed in the ending of *Jaws*, the flotilla from *Jaws 2*, and the diving scenes from *The Deep*. He took this grab-bag of ingredients to secretary Anne Dyer and asked her to cobble it together.

Creature from the Haunted Sea had been written by Chuck Griffith so, as with *Death Race 2000*, it fell to Corman's long-time associate to make something fresh out of what New World was now calling *Up from the Depths*. 'It was written.. with the intention that I would polish it up,' Griffith told Dennis Fischer. 'I was hired to direct, but Roger wouldn't pay Writers Guild prices.. so the idea was that I would use my director's prerogative to polish up an impossible script. So I wrote a zany version called *Something's Fishy* and the Filipinos were crazy about it. They made a funny-looking fish for it, and we were all set to go, but they sent the script to Roger, figuring he would love it, and of course, he hit his desk and told them to fire me and everybody else. They wouldn't fire me, so I still had to do the polish, but I did it just for action.'

> *An undersea earthquake unleashes a huge prehistoric fish that begins to prey on the guests at a Hawaiian resort. The hotel manager arranges a fishing expedition, with a prize of $1,000 and a free week in the presidential suite to anyone who can bring him the monster's head. An assortment of amateurs head out in search, but they are either eaten or blown up in their boats. A treasure hunter and the hotel's press officer finally booby-trap a corpse and see off the marauding mackerel.*

Unfortunately, Griffith was no more adept at making an action picture than he was a comedy. 'The action didn't work because the Filipinos didn't work. The fish [designed by future Oscar winners Chris Walas and Robert Short] never worked once. It was supposed to attack people, to chew them up, and thrash all sorts of things, but it didn't do anything.. The speedboats never worked because the propellers were beaten up by the coral reefs. The underwater shots didn't work, because there were no lead weights to get people down. They were bobbing to the surface. And nobody would show up. You would get ballroom extras on the beach and beach extras in the ballroom. There weren't any American cars available because all American cars belonged to rich people who wouldn't rent them. It was great being there for six months.'

Apparently so: Griffith sent back an unbelievably-long 106-minute work print, which Corman chopped down to 75 minutes for the film's August 1979 release. At any length, the movie is boring and inept, as the *Los Angeles Times* was quick to point out: 'The screenplay.. neither sustains interest nor creates suspense.. Director Charles B Griffith allows the confusion to prevail.' *Variety* warned about the film's 'flipped-out sense of humour and dubbing that must have been done blindfolded.. preview audience came expecting one thing and stayed to laugh their heads off, which is the only response this Filipino-made programmer will ever elicit.' 'The image is grainy, the sound is muddled, the actors mug uncontrollably, and nothing happens after the first two minutes' was *Cinefantastique*'s verdict.

The only creativity in evidence on *Up from the Depths* came—as was often the case—from New World's publicity department, which produced the following suggestions to exhibitors:

- 'Have the local dental clinic sponsor an *Up from the Depths* look-alike smile contest with the winner getting a custom made pair of shark skin shoes and a free teeth filing'
- 'Sneak into your local yacht club and cut giant teeth marks into the boats using a sabre saw. Leave some blood in the area and some shark teeth stuck into the boats.. the following day go to the club with some friends and begin screaming and pointing at the bites.. watch your grosses soar.. (Sell your boat dealership before you do this one!)'
- 'Scatter ripped and bloody bathing suits around the lakefront after kidnapping a few of the local children.. watch your grosses soar and perhaps get a book and maybe a movie deal out of it when you are released from the federal penitentiary.'
- 'Invite the local YMCA to stage a charity 'Swim For Your Life' contest at the shark tank of the local aquarium. Coat the little boys and girls with bacon grease and throw them into the tank. For every minute that the little buggers survive get sponsors to donate money to the cause. Just in case none of the kiddies swim more than a minute, film the event and sell it to the local television station billed as 'The Making of *Up from the Depths*'. Don't forget to consult the local SPCA for approval before you do this one!'

In the interest of furthering détente between the superpowers, Corman had proposed a joint Soviet-American co-production in remaking Sergei Eisenstein's two-part epic, *Ivan the Terrible* (1944, 1958). Supposedly, the king of the multi-million-dollar cameo, Marlon Brando, had expressed interest in essaying the title role, but the return of Soviet troops to Cuba in the fall of 1979 put Russo-American relations back in the deep freeze, which effectively ruined this cinematic attempt at fence-mending.

Never one to let world affairs slow him down, Corman next set New World's sights on mounting a belated answer to *Star Wars*. He began by taking bids from the various Hollywood effects shops, including John Dykstra's Apogee, which had worked on *Star Wars* and *Battlestar Galactica*. True to form, when he received the $2 million budget estimate, he decided to go the do-it-yourself route; if it was going to cost him that much, then he would build his own studio, do all the work in-house, and then rent the facilities to other productions. In scouting properties, New World's business affairs manager Paul Almond came across the Hammond

Lumber Yard on Main Street in LA's Venice district, four miles from the company's Brentwood offices. Corman put down $1.5 million for the half-block property and its buildings, which were then converted into three makeshift soundstages and one post-production facility. Lee Grant, a writer for the *Los Angeles Times*, was given a tour of the complex, and she described the main building as follows:

> '..It is a faded structure built more than a half-century ago. The words 'hardware,' 'electrical' and 'plumbing' from the previous tenant are barely painted over. On hand running the place is a group of young people, another contingent of those who over the years have passed under Corman's aegis. A sleeping dog lies like a bulky throw rug in the foyer, clips from Corman movie reviews are stuck on the wall, a schedule from the neighbouring Fox Venice revival theatre is pinned near a desk. There also are posters from early Corman endeavours like Monster from the Ocean Floor..'

When Grant pointed out to Corman that the Hammond Lumber sign was still hanging at the entrance, he told her matter-of-factly, 'I found out it would cost $200 to take the sign down. I couldn't see a profit in that so I left it up.' In charge of the studio and its 20 staffers was 25-year-old Mary Ann Fisher, a Stanford University graduate with a degree in child development, which doubtless came in handy in dealing with some of Corman's underlings. In addition to buying the lot, Corman also stumped up $200,000 to a company called Elicon for the development of a computer-controlled motion repeat camera for SFX shots.

In the fall of 1979, preliminary effects work began on what was to be Corman's most expensive film ever—*Battle Beyond the Stars*, a sci-fi take on *The Seven Samurai* (1954) and its retread, *The Magnificent Seven* (1960). The budget of $5 million was split between New World and Orion Pictures (which picked up foreign distribution rights) and included the almost $2 million Corman had already spent in acquiring and developing his Venice studios. The effects work would take eight months, while the actual film would be shot in five weeks between February and March 1980 for a projected mid-summer release.

Why was the notoriously-cautious Corman taking such an ambitious gamble? 'I just thought the budget was a necessary step,' he told the *Times*. 'The market is turning away from smaller films. Movies-of-the-week and specials for TV are costing millions. It's difficult now to convince an audience to spend $5 a ticket on something less than what they can see for free at home.' Not all of his associates felt that it was a wise move, however: 'The second he moved into that studio,' Allan Arkush told *Los Angeles Weekly*, 'everything had to fit within four walls and you lost all the freedom of location shooting.'

'Women can make a difference.'
—Crusading schoolteacher April Thomas (Jacqulin Cole) in *Angel's Brigade*

Perhaps as a dry run for the *Battle* to come, New World acquired another riff on *The Magnificent Seven*, this time in an unlikely blend of *Charlie's Angels* and *Gilligan's Island*. Shot as *Seven Angels* and released in Canada as *Seven from Heaven*, the film was retitled *Angel's Brigade* for its October 1979 release in the southeastern US. The movie was the production of Greydon Clark, the '70s answer to low-budget fifties' schlockmeister Ed Wood, who had such trash classics as *Black Shampoo* (1976), *Nigger Lover*, and *Satan's Cheerleaders* (1977) to his, er, credit.

When her brother is hospitalised by pushers, Vegas nightclub singer Michelle Wilson is recruited by schoolteacher April Thomas to join her crusade against the drug barons.

They enlist five others—a karate instructor, a stuntwoman, a model, a policewoman and a student—and these 'Seven Angels' attack a drug factory using a souped-up van and attack a drug processing plant. This does not play well with the local drug kingpin, who has April kidnapped and tortured. The remaining 'angels' have now to discover her whereabouts before it is too late..

Clark came to specialise in casting has-beens in his films, and *Angel's Brigade* is the *Cannonball Run* of the seen-better-days crowd. Lucky Jack Palance was given above-title billing as the enforcer of former Rat Pack-er Peter Lawford, who has two scenes by the pool as a drug lord. *Gilligan's Island* veterans Alan Hale and Jim Backus show up briefly as, respectively, Michelle's manager and a right-wing extremist, while 'Ol' Redhead' Arthur Godfrey is also on hand to give his blessing to former *Playboy* Playmate Susan Kiger's lip-synching. Neville Brand, of *Eaten Alive!* and TV's *The Untouchables* (in which he guest-spotted as Al Capone), gives out with his usual inebriate tongue-lashing as a dishevelled police captain.

'It's not how good you are.. it's how good you want to be.'
—Boxing manager Shake (Don Knotts) in *The Prize Fighter*

After producing two successful comedies—*The Billion Dollar Hobo* (1977) and *They Went That-A-Way & That-A-Way* (1978)—for International Picture Show, an Atlanta-based company which he had co-founded, indie producer Lang Elliott left IPS in August of 1978 and established TriStar Pictures with fellow producers Eric Weston and Wanda Dell. *Hobo* and *That-A-Way* had both been co-written by star Tim Conway, a comedy actor from the TV series *McHale's Navy* (1962-66) and a regular guest on *The Carol Burnett Show* (1967-78). Conway had also starred with fellow comedian Don Knotts (best known for his role as Barney Fife on *The Andy Griffith Show*, 1960-1968) in the Disney hits *The Apple Dumpling Gang* and *Gus* (1975 and '76 respectively), and TriStar's first production would reunite the two in another Conway script entitled *The Prize Fighter*.

During the Depression, Bags, a fighter with a perfect record—20 fights, 20 losses—and his manager are on the skids. Their luck changes when Bags accidentally knocks out a

The Prizefighter (Tim Conway)

fighter at a carnival, which brings him to the notice of syndicate boss Mike. Mike and his partners plan to build a convention hall, but a gym run by Pop Morgan stands in their way. Mike rigs Bags's fights to make him look like a winner, and Morgan takes him under his wing, betting his gym that Bags will win a championship fight against 'The Butcher'. Morgan's downfall seems like a sure bet, but Mike has underestimated Bags's new-found confidence and will to succeed.

Shot in Atlanta in early 1979 on a budget of $2 million, *The Prize Fighter* is a combination of *The Sting* (1973) and *Rocky* that actually predates the similar plot of *The Sting II* (1983), some four years off. Its release via New World during Thanksgiving of '79 was a stroke of good fortune, as some major studio flops like *Avalanche Express, Meteor*, and *Skatetown USA* left a hole in exhibitors' booking patterns that needed to be filled. Also, for the first time in years, Disney did not have a traditional family comedy readied for the holiday season, opting instead for big-budget sci-fi extravaganza *The Black Hole*. New World opened *Prize Fighter* in 234 theatres in Atlanta, New Orleans, Dallas, Charlotte, and Indianapolis, and watched as the comedy gave the company its first-ever million-dollar week.

'Had we not broken the picture the week of Thanksgiving and proven it could do well we'd have nothing for Christmas,' Frank Moreno told *Variety*. 'Exhibitors double-booked us with something else and when they saw *The Prize Fighter* would do okay they decided to go with us rather than risking it with something else.' A spokesman for United Artists Theatres told *Variety*: 'We got some Christmas pictures but we need product for our multiplex theatres. We're happy to have a picture like this at this time of the year that has performed elsewhere.'

The Prize Fighter played through the holidays and well into the New Year, not reaching Los Angeles until Easter 1980. Initial critical response was negative, with *Variety* lambasting, 'What [Knotts and Conway] need here is a script and the lame, predictable, hackneyed mess cooked up by Conway and John Myhers leaves them with nothing but shtick and aged sight gags.' The *Chicago Daily Herald* thought likewise: '*The Prize Fighter* is only a few humorous sketches by screenwriter/star Tim Conway stretched far beyond an audience's interest.' However, the film found a better reception for itself when it reached Los Angeles, with Charles Champlin considering it 'as good a Disney film as Disney ever made, a silly, enjoyable family entertainment.'

Audiences agreed: with $6.5 million in rentals, *The Prize Fighter* edged out *Piranha* to become New World's highest-grossing film. Both Corman and Elliott were delighted and declared that this was only the first of many projected TriStar-New World ventures. In May 1980, production began on another Knotts-Conway comedy for the holidays, *The Private Eyes*, filmed at the famous Biltmore Estate in Asheville, North Carolina, on a $2.3 million budget.

In taking stock of 1979, Corman told *Variety*, '[It] was the first [year] in our 10-year history where our profits have not risen over the previous year. But with.. the release of *The Prize Fighter* we'll make a slight profit.' But the head of New World had other problems beside the balance sheet. In December, the Director's Guild of America newsletter blasted Corman for his 'steadfast' refusal to sign the DGA's basic motion picture agreement, in which film companies agreed to employ only DGA members. In his defence, Corman told *Variety*, 'I offered almost one year ago to sign with the DGA, but asked that my assistant directors also be permitted to join the Guild. They refused to sign with me on that basis.' He then demanded that the Guild retract the accusations and apologise, something it had no intention of doing.

It also seemed that Corman was losing his touch in the speciality market. *Saint*

Jack had been a failure, and two Francois Truffaut films—*Love on the Run* and *The Green Room*—had not found the usual art house audience in respective April and September releases. In fact, Truffaut was so dismayed by the films' poor reception that he signed with United Artists Classics for the American release of his next film, *The Last Metro* (1980), which went on to earn rentals of $1.5 million in 1981. The only specialty success that New World could point to in 1979 was *The Kids Are Alright*, a documentary on the rock group The Who, released that June to $1.5 million in rentals.

In announcing his plans for the coming year, Corman told *Variety* that New World would be concentrating on the type of films the company 'has always made money on. I still maintain a $3,000,000 film of mine is equal to any $9,000,000 major production.' Once again, his answer to the increasing incursions into his cinematic territory was to aim high: 'My answer to competing with the majors is upping the budgets on my films. They took away what was traditionally our playing time, and, in a sense, I have to play more in their ball-game if I'm going to compete. Compared to other films we've done, we really have no low budget projects in 1980.' With that, he unveiled New World's 1980 production/release slate, minus the already-in-production *Battle Beyond the Stars* and *The Private Eyes*:

- *Humanoids from the Deep*, a $1.5 million co-production with United Artists, scheduled for March release.
- *Galaxy Express*, a $5 million animated feature from Japan's Toei Films, which had broken box office records in Tokyo on its September 1979 release; its US premiere was scheduled for Easter.
- *Don't Open the Door*, a $1.5 million thriller for July, written by feminist novelist Rita Mae Brown.
- *Kung Fu 2000*, a $3 million martial arts picture scheduled for August release.
- *The Disk Jockey*, a $2.5 million comedy for October, written by *Thunder and Lightning*'s William Hjortsberg.
- *Hawk the Slayer*, a $4 million sword-and-sorcery co-production with New England's Monument Films, scheduled for October.
- *Journey Beyond This Galaxy*, scheduled for late 1980 production on a $5 million budget. The screenplay by sci-fi writer Alfred Bester was described by *Variety* as 'dealing with an epic voyage of the first ship from a mechanistic civilisation making contact beyond its home galaxy with an alien civilisation functioning on non-materialistic, mystical principles.'
- *The Last World War*, also set to go in late 1980 on an $8.5 million budget and concerning an atomic war that takes place 100 years in the future.

Of these, only *Humanoids from the Deep* was delivered as promised (albeit a month late). *Galaxy Express* was shelved, then sold to cable TV, *Don't Open the Door* was postponed for two years before being morphed into *The Slumber Party Massacre*, *Hawk the Slayer* slipped away to Lew Grade's ITC Entertainment when it agreed to bankroll the entire project, and the rest were never made at all. This was becoming a familiar refrain, which made it increasingly difficult to take New World's announcements seriously.

Corman also revealed to *Variety* that he had received a sizeable offer from a Japanese company early in 1979 to purchase New World, which he had considered seriously. 'I had five films in production simultaneously and I could not control them,' he said. 'Frankly I had done so well for so long that I got over-confident.' But he had a change of heart when he saw that the deal called for him to stay and run the company, meaning that he would effectively work for his Japanese buyer—a prospect that was anathema to the fiercely-independent filmmaker. Two other offers were received subsequently, but both were summarily rejected.

Humanoids from the Deep (Ann Turkel)

After a mere 18 months, New World decided in March 1980 to close its British distribution set-up. The firm had released eight films in England, but it had been able to get only half of them—*Deathsport, Dynamite Women, I Never Promised You a Rose Garden*, and *Saint Jack*—into the main cinema hub in London's West End, while *Avalanche, Grand Theft Auto*, and *Starcrash* had to settle for Birmingham or the outskirts of East Anglia. In the event, it mattered little where they played—none of them took any money. Managing director Bev Pearman was sacked, and the distribution chores for New World product were passed to the Barber-Rose organisation.

> 'These creatures are driven to mate with man.. to further develop their incredible evolution.'
> —Marine biologist Susan Drake (Ann Turkel) in *Humanoids from the Deep*

'As a producer,' Corman told the *Bright Lights Film Journal*, 'I probably am a little stronger than most, since I was a director originally. So I exercise quite a bit of control over the story, the preparation and some of the cutting. I generally leave the directors to themselves during the actual shooting. I don't go on the location or on the set more than a few times. I'll do it at the beginning to see that it's all rolling well and if it is going well during production and the rushes seem good to me, I try to stay away from the set.'

While he was usually absent from the set, Corman nevertheless exercised his power of veto in the editing suite; on occasion, he might also arrange for additional footage to be shot, to spice things up if the product did not meet his expectations. Such would be the case with New World's first release of 1980, *Humanoids from the Deep*.

> *In the coastal town of Noyo, the Canco company is about to open a cannery to process salmon—but in an attempt to increase yield, Canco has accidentally released a batch*

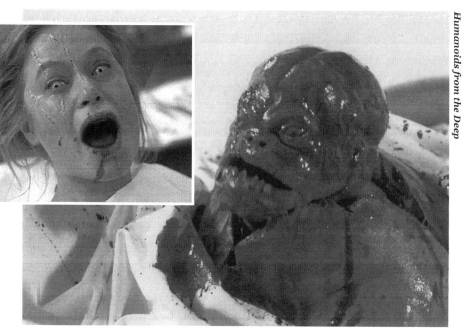

of DNA-enhanced fish into the ocean; prehistoric coelocanths have fed on the salmon, and the DNA has accelerated their evolution into humanoid monsters. The humanoids launch night-time attacks on the town and abduct women for mating. All hell breaks loose at the annual Salmon Festival, when the monsters stage a mass attack and local fisherman Jim Hill, marine biologist Susan Drake, and Indian activist Johnny Eagle have to fight to drive them back into the sea.

The project was originally offered to Joe Dante, but he opted to hitch himself instead to two films which ultimately were never made: Dino De Laurentiis's *Orca II* and National Lampoon's *Jaws 3, People 0*. Corman's second choice for director was Barbara Peeters, returning to New World for the first time since serving as the location manager on *Rose Garden*. Peeters had actually been ill for much of 1979 and her inability to find work through the Director's Guild had led her to accept Corman's offer, even though she was fined by the Guild for taking on a non-union picture. As things turned out, that was to be the least of her worries.

Shot under the title of *Beneath the Darkness* in October 1979 in California's Mendocino County, the picture was the first film in a decade for producer Martin B Cohen, whose last had been the Jack Nicholson biker opus *Rebel Rousers* in 1970. Cohen had also co-written the story for *Humanoids*, as he told the *Los Angeles Times*: 'I felt it was time for a modern-day monster picture, based on the old ones like *The Creature from the Black Lagoon* [1954], and do one that would tie in with a modern problem. I look at the movie from a point of ecology and pollution of the world with chemicals—in this case, the ocean—and to me that's an important problem.' On the strength of such exemplary aspirations, Cohen was able to sign up Doug McClure, Vic Morrow and ex-model Ann Turkel (then Mrs Richard Harris).

The 'hook' in the story that undoubtedly sold Corman had nothing to do with ecology, however. It was the fact that these monsters do not just attack people, but rape unsuspecting females. In the original script by William Martin (who adopted the pseudonym 'Frederick James'), these heinous acts are only implied—they are never actually shown. Such was also the way that Peeters shot the film, but neither Cohen nor Corman felt that was good enough.

The film's second unit, under the direction of James Sbardellati, was sent back to rectify the situation. Peeters was informed that additional shooting was being undertaken, but told that it was simply 'filler' material. In reality, it was to make the picture a great deal more explicit. Peeters had filmed actress Lynn Theel being dragged off by the humanoids and then being discovered by Turkel and McClure, covered in seaweed. Sbardelatti added shots of her being stripped and violated by her captors. He also filmed a whole new sequence of a couple on a beach, whose foreplay is interrupted by attacking humanoids who then rape the girl. During the climactic attack on the Salmon Festival, a scene was added involving 'Miss Salmon' —Linda Shayne—battling with a humanoid before having her bikini-top ripped off and running towards camera. Additional gore shots were also added, including a particularly gruesome decapitation that was cut for an 'R' rating but reinstated for the film's overseas release.

Before its premiere in April 1980, *Los Angeles Times* writer Joyce Sunila, the author of a series of articles entitled 'Women and Power and Hollywood', was invited to a private screening of *Humanoids from the Deep* by Peeters and Turkel. Along with its director and star, Sunila sat in stunned silence as she watched the abundant scenes of rape and gore. She later described the atmosphere as she left the theatre: 'I looked at the faces of the women crew-members. They'd been elated and warm before the screening, but now they were mostly staring at the floor. Some had angry, disgusted looks on their faces. That's a look I see more and more on women these days. I call it the desperado look. More than anger, more than bitterness, more than the fight-back warning of people beyond being charmed or cajoled, it's a look of betrayal. All these women looked, one way or another, as though they could write the book on betrayal.'

Needless to say, Turkel and Peeters were incensed. Turkel immediately filed a petition with the Screen Actors Guild to either have her name taken off the film or to halt its release, but she was unsuccessful on both counts. 'What it is,' the actress told columnist Marilyn Beck, 'is degrading, disgusting soft-core pornography. I'm still stunned.. it was supposed to be just a straight science-fiction story—with no sex. And everything seemed great while we filmed it. But after principle photography was completed.. Peeters was taken off the picture, and they added some awful nude scenes with other performers, edited out a lot of the work we had done—and put in this terrible, disgusting garbage.'

Peeters likewise asked for her name removed from the film but was informed by New World's boss that she would have to pay for the credits to be redone. She chose instead to take her case to the press, telling Sunila, 'I never made a picture about women being sexually ravished by monsters.. *Humanoids* is offensive to me and all of the women who worked on it. And now everyone is saying that with credit on it I'll be doing all the B pictures in Hollywood for years to come. That idea makes me sick.' In a separate interview, she told the *Los Angeles Times*, 'I may sound lame standing around with my hands in my pockets saying, "I didn't shoot it." And it may sound like sour grapes now, but I'm really goddamned mad.. I'm worried that feminists will see this movie and say "How can she do this? How can she justify it?"'

Suddenly put onto the defensive, Cohen, Corman, and Barbara Boyle offered up lame apologies for the situation in both interviews and letters to the *Times*: 'What's too much T&A? How do you argue that? You and I are men and we look at women differently; we look at sex differently. A woman director just has a different point of view toward sexuality' (Cohen); 'I find a majority of critics who discuss such things in their reviews felt *Humanoids* was a strong feminist statement in the guise of a horror film' (Corman); 'I think it would be awful if women weren't allowed to direct pictures like [*Humanoids*]. People have got this idea that women are only interested in small pictures about human relationships. But women ought to be able to direct *The Dirty Dozen* if they want to, or *Apocalypse Now*. They should be able to do the whole range' (Boyle).

Despite Corman's statement to the contrary, the reviews of *Humanoids from the Deep* were almost universally dismissive. 'Irony of the entire production,' said *Variety,* 'which will confound feminist-minded critics, is that a female helmer was behind one of the more woman-degrading pix to come down the pike in some seasons.' The *Los Angeles Times* called it 'a mangled, monster horror movie.. the screenplay.. is a muddled mess which includes a murky ecological message.' For a change, Gene Siskel was unusually astute: 'These scenes [of rape] look as though they have been edited in from another movie. Take them out and *Humanoids* could have been laughable filler for a drive-in theatre. Include them, and the resulting film is nothing to be laughed at.' Across town, the *Chicago Sun-Times* observed, 'It is a brutal movie. The final scene, in which a human woman gives birth to a humanoid child, is one of the most disgusting ever filmed.' *Cinefantastique* summed up *Humanoids* as 'A schizoid mixture of 50s sf, soft-core porn and mad rape fantasy.'

Only the *Washington Post* was in Corman's camp, commenting, 'Perhaps because a woman directed it, the women in *Humanoids*, especially heroine Ann Turkel.. are not, refreshingly enough, just screaming, helpless bimbos. In fact, McClure's wife fends off two libidinous fiends by herself after they come crashing into the house where she and her child are trapped alone.'

The humanoid creatures themselves were impressive, designed and built (and worn) by 20-year-old effects whiz Rob Bottin, who had also worked on *Piranha* and *Rock 'n' Roll High School*. Labouring on a criminally low $40,000 budget, Bottin found the rape scenes ludicrous, as he told the *Chicago Daily Herald*: 'So there I am in this rubber fish suit, and the director tells me to get down and rape this woman on the beach. This is not a serious way to make a living, my friend.' Bottin was in fact very serious about his work, and went on to such films as *The Howling, The Thing* (1982), *Legend* (for which he received an Oscar nomination), *Robocop, Total Recall* (1990), *Se7en* (1995) and *Mission: Impossible* (1996).

Controversy creates cash, they say, and such was the case with *Humanoids*. After a month in release in 400 theatres, the film had earned itself $1.3 million in rentals; it eventually went on to earn $2.5 million more as it traversed the country that summer. 'I give [Turkel] credit for 3% of the box office,' Frank Moreno told the *Los Angeles Times*. 'Hey, if she comes in here I've got a box for her to stand on and complain some more.' Allotted the more generic title of *Monster*, *Humanoids* was equally successful for United Artists overseas from July.

Buoyed by the success, Martin Cohen announced that he was reactivating his old company, Baruch Productions, and embarking on a $36 million production slate, to include sequels to *Piranha* and *Humanoids*, as well as *Sherlock Holmes vs Dracula* and *The House Where Evil Dwells*. Only the latter came to pass (he made it for MGM in 1982), though Cohen resurfaced briefly in 1991 as one of the names (along with *Eaten Alive*'s Mardi Rustam and *Raptor Island*'s Stanley Isaacs) who were to be involved in 21st Century Film Corporation's proposed *Humanoids from the Deep Part 2* (aka *Humanoids from the Deep: The Next Generation*), to star Malcolm McDowell and be directed by first-timer Kevin Pine.

This incarnation never made it off the drawing board either, but *Humanoids* was too good a property to lie idle forever. As with *Piranha*, Corman remade the film in 1996 for Showtime. Written and directed by Jeff Yonis, the remake starred Robert Carradine and *Dynasty*'s Emma Samms in the McClure and Turkel roles;

this time, the humanoids were the product of injecting fish DNA into death row inmates in order to create amphibious super-soldiers. The monsters (a mixture of footage from the original and poor modern imitations) still kidnapped women, but the rape scenes were kept off-screen.

Humanoids from the Deep turned out to be the last feature that Barbara Peeters would make for Roger Corman, as well as the last film that she would ever direct. She subsequently moved into television, where she helmed numerous episodes of series like *Matt Houston, Berrenger's, Falcon Crest,* and *Misfits of Science* between 1982 and 1986. She then left the industry, and she has not been heard from since.

Press advertisement for Battle Beyond the Stars

From the horror of rape to the horrors of fascism: New World's second release of the year was a West German import, Volker Schlöndorff's *The Tin Drum*. Based on Gunter Grass's Nobel Prize-winning novel of 1959, it tells the story of a child genius in Weimar Germany who steadfastly refuses to grow up, then relentlessly beats his toy drum in protest at the rise of Nazism. Schlöndorff's film had opened in Wiesbaden in May 1979, and then, in a controversial split decision, it went on to share the *Palme d'Or* Award at the Cannes Film Festival with *Apocalypse Now*. It became one of the most successful German films in history, and it was hailed in Europe as a masterpiece.

In an effort to restore some of New World's lost prestige as a purveyor of fine foreign films, Roger Corman upped the ante to $400,000 (the most that he had ever paid for distribution rights) to release *The Tin Drum* in the US. The film's international sales representative, Gabriel Desdoits, told *Variety*, 'Three or four large exhibition contracts were possible, which would have given us $1 million quickly, and several tax shelter-style proposals were also received. But New World was the winner due to its track record and very favourable terms.'

New World timed the film's release in April 1980 to take full advantage of the fact that it had won the Oscar for Best Foreign Film and almost unanimous critical acclaim. The ploy worked a treat, bringing over $2 million in rentals to Corman's company.

'To fight creatures of violence, you must use creatures of violence!'
—Akiran elder Zed (Jeff Corey) in *Battle Beyond the Stars*

Battle Beyond the Stars (Richard Thomas/Darlanne Fleugel)

'I had always wanted to make *The Magnificent Seven* in space,' Corman told the UK's *Starbust* magazine, 'but I really didn't feel that the timing was right until *Star Wars* came out and was so enthusiastically received. Now my idea doesn't seem quite so bizarre.' It had never seemed so to the Japanese, who had not only made the film on which *The Magnificent Seven* was based (*The Seven Samurai*), but their own interstellar derivative as well. In late 1977, anticipating the Japanese release of *Star Wars* in the summer of 1978, Toei Films and Tohokushinsha joined forces to

179

produce the $6 million *Message from Space* (*Uchu kara no messeji*)—the most expensive Japanese film ever made. In *Message from Space*, the planet Jillucia is under attack from the ruthless forces of Rockseia XII. In response, the Jillucian ruler summons the planet's saviours, who include a gang of space hot-rodders called The Rough Riders, alcoholic General Garuda and his robot Beba 2, Prince Hans, and Jillucian warrior Urocco, the traitor in their midst.

Message from Space premiered in Japan in April 1978, taking a disappointing $4 million at the box office. Its release in the States came seven months later via United Artists, for whom the picture earned a mere $1.1 million in rentals—but this might have come as a relief to Corman, who did not want anyone else to steal the thunder from his own *Battle Beyond the Stars*.

> *The planet Akir is under attack from ruthless conqueror Sador; Shad takes the planet's only space-worthy vessel to find mercenaries to help in the struggle. He enlists the aid of a motley crew, including a computer technician, a gun-runner, a lizard-man, albino clones, an interplanetary hit-man, and a Valkyrie warrior. With a variety of motives to spur them on, the space-saviours ride to Akir's rescue.*

For his third and final screenplay for New World script, John Sayles was given a treatment by Anne Dyer and told to expand upon it. 'That was fun,' he told *Ain't It Cool News*. 'I basically was able to give it a kind of theme, which was all these different versions of death because I could go into other species and they could have different kinds of death. A lot of *The Magnificent Seven* is this Samurai thing about having an honourable death even though you've kinda been thrown away by society already. That's one of my favourite movies, the original *Seven Samurai* and then *The Magnificent Seven* was a great use of it in another context.'

As with *Death Race 2000*, an urban legend has grown up accusing Corman of cutting out much of the humour in *Battle Beyond the Stars*. Again, a study of the script shows this to be untrue. Most of the humour in Sayles's script is in the film, whereas some of the film's gags (including Space Cowboy's wearable bar) were not in the script. In fact, it was Cowboy—who, amazingly, was nearly played by John

Wayne—who was altered the most, ostensibly because George Peppard did not like the 'redneck trucker' character that Sayles had written; as such, Peppard virtually ad-libbed the entire role. Sayles had included more material relating to Cowboy's training of the Akiran forces and his romance with Lux which did not make it into the final cut. As he told *Twilight Zone* magazine, 'At the end of the day, they say, "We didn't get to this page, so there it goes!"'

Another discarded item was the original ending. In the script, the climax had Sador's cruiser chasing Shad's ship through an asteroid field before being sucked into Akir's sun. As written by Sayles, it is an exciting sequence which prefigures a similar one in *The Empire Strikes Back* (1980), which had not yet been released. 'They wanted to end *Battle* five minutes early,' said Sayles, 'because.. their process shots of spaceships.. didn't work. They said, "Can you write a scene that has Richard Thomas and Darlanne Fleugel in a space capsule? We don't have many sets left. And do it without a close-up. Richard Thomas has grown a moustache since we last shot." I wrote the scene on the phone.' (In it, Shad and Nanelia take an escape pod back to Akir while Shad's ship, caught in Sador's tractor beam, self-destructs, creating a chain reaction that destroys Sador's cruiser.)

Given that *Battle* was New World's biggest production to date, there was some talk of Corman himself directing it (there was even a rumour that Ingmar Bergman had been offered the job), but the director's chair went instead to old friend Jimmy Murakami. 'It's not typical science-fiction,' the former animator told *Starlog*. 'It's got a lot of serious stuff in there—a lot of drama and a lot of conflict between characters. If you can imagine all these mercenaries, each with their own identity, spaceship, problems—they are very complex. It's sort of a heavy adventure film with a lot of characters. It's not just a special effects film.'

That must have come as news to the crew who were labouring at New World's Venice effects studio. Supervisor Chuck Comisky told *Starburst*, 'It was a difficult job, especially considering the time we had to do it in! But we came up with some innovative, fantasy-like solutions, with Shad's spaceship being very organic, somewhat antiquated and passive looking, while Sador's craft is definitely sinister and lethal looking. It was a very unconventional approach because we worked without plans or designs.'

And without a net, apparently. Corman told interviewer Andrew Rausch, 'We were having trouble with the special effects and I sent my ace assistant Gale Anne Hurd down to the set to find out what was going wrong. She came back after a couple of days and said the staff is not as competent as they should be, but there's a young model maker at the bottom of the list who knows more than anyone else.'

The young man in question was 25-year-old James Cameron, whose only real experience in filmmaking had been a 12-minute demo that he had shot for a group of Mormon investors who were interested in making a *Star Wars*-type film. While that project may have failed to materialise, it gave Cameron something to present when he showed up at the Venice facility. 'That was the best possible place for me,' he told *Omni* magazine. 'I can't imagine moving up as quickly as I did if I hadn't gone directly into that kind of environment.' Literally overnight, Cameron went from being low man on the totem pole to the film's official art director—though he had to wear many hats: 'I did matte paintings, was a visual effects cameraman, ran my own visual effects motion control unit, designed and built three-quarters of the sets.. I was a model builder and designed and built a front projection system.'

Released in July 1980, *Battle Beyond the Stars* suffered the disadvantage of following in the two-month wake of *The Empire Strikes Back*, which set the visual effects bar that much higher. The Venice crew had acquitted itself admirably on its inaugural outing—20 different models and 350 effects shots—but the critics were unimpressed by its efforts. 'Special effects are all important in outer space movies,' said Gene Siskel, 'but not once does *Battle* dazzle us. Instead we get laser beams shaped like pink hot dogs that shoot across the screen regardless of the position of the actors shooting at each other. And the film's spacecraft are all sloppy pieces of plastic photographed against muddy backgrounds.' 'Unfortunately for *Battle*, at least one area theatre at which it's now showing precedes it with the trailer for *The Empire Strikes Back*, one of the most sensational and inviting pieces of 'coming attraction' art ever. *Battle* is bound to look seedy and tatty after that, and does,' remarked the *Washington Post*. Kevin Thomas agreed: '*Battle Beyond the Stars* is yet another *Star Wars* carbon, a bit smudged here and there by cut-rate special effects but blessed with a sense of humour. Its lack of originality, however, limits it to that portion of the audience so turned on by *Star Wars*-type fare that it can't get enough of it, even if it's inferior to the original.'

Battle did have its share of admirers. *The Hollywood Reporter* declared that 'For sheer entertainment, *Battle Beyond the Stars* may well eclipse *Star Wars*.' The *Chicago Sun-Times* gave the film three stars, commenting, 'This light-hearted and unpretentious romp through outer space reminds us that movies are meant to be entertaining.' *The New York Times* called *Battle* 'science-fiction inspired by Kurosawa.. and visited by the spirit of a wiseacre Lewis Carroll.' *Variety* summed things up thus: '*Battle*, other than in its genre, doesn't resemble *Empire* much and occasionally the difference is refreshing. An obviously lavish outing by New World standards, pic boasts of credible special effects.. and a pleasant sort of brashness resulting from its blending of several pic styles.'

Corman's brainchild immediately broke the New World record which had been set by *The Prize Fighter*, taking $1.7 million in its first week. It would go on to earn nearly $7.5 million in rentals (also besting *Prize Fighter* in the number one spot) and was sold to NBC-TV for an additional $2 million. This was peanuts in comparison to the rental haul of $120 million for *The Empire Strikes Back*, but *Battle Beyond the Stars* had cost only a quarter as much to make. The picture also did good business for Orion overseas, when it was released in the spring of 1981.

What to do for an encore? For Cameron and company at New World Venice, the answer was not soon enough in coming. 'A week or so before *Battle* ended,' he told *Omni*, 'it occurred to me that we were all going to be out of a job. But there was this opportunity. At a party, I met Joe Alves, Spielberg's production designer on *Jaws*. Joe was working with John Carpenter [on *Escape from New York*]; they were looking for a visual effects facility. I said come on down to the facility. I'll bet we can underbid everybody. We're hungry, we've got nothing else to do, the place will be empty in a week. I was selling Roger's place, and Roger didn't even know about it.' Cameron continued: 'Joe brought Carpenter and [producer] Debra Hill. They had 25 shots that needed to be done.. so we just smoothed right in. Suddenly Roger had a viable enterprise on the side that he could keep alive using other people's money until he needed it again.' The fact that the money, in this instance, was from Bob Rehme and Avco Embassy must have been doubly satisfying.

Given the success of *Battle Beyond the Stars* and the lucrative possibilities that Cameron had demonstrated for the Venice studio, Corman proclaimed to the *Los Angeles Times* that August, 'We're planning to become a very heavy science-fiction company.' He then went on to list three projects set to roll before the end of the year: *Planet of Horrors*, a $5 million co-production with United Artists, the previously-announced *Journey Beyond This Galaxy*, now budgeted at $7 million and arranged as a co-production with Orion, and a $6 million adaptation of Isaac Asimov's 1941 short story *Nightfall*, to be produced by Julie Corman as a German co-production. Two other big-budget sci-fi films were in the planning stages for 1981—*Millennium*, and the also-announced *Last World War*—and Roger Corman was 'considering' directing one of them.

Thanks to *The Prize Fighter, Humanoids from the Deep* and *Battle Beyond the Stars,* New World's 10th anniversary year was shaping up to be the company's most profitable ever, with a combined gross of nearly $20 million in rentals being reported in September. At the same time, Corman announced that he was going to restructure the company, largely to provide himself with some breathing space. 'I would like to slow down,' he told *Variety.* 'That's part of the concept of re-staffing the company, to put me in a position where I would have a number of associate producers so that I could still be a producer but entrust several jobs to others.' Corman also indicated that, once freed from administrative duties, he wanted to get back to directing one or two pictures a year.

A quartet of new pictures was trumpeted for 1981, including a Filipino martial arts film called *Firecracker*, a second attempt at a sword-and-sorcery adventure called *Alaric the Avenger* (and made in the UK), a musical called *Shopping Center* featuring rock group The Doobie Brothers, and a car-chase comedy called *Follow that Car*. Also planned for production was New World's second movie for CBS-TV, *The Georgia Peaches*, featuring *Battlestar Galactica*'s Dirk Benedict and country singer Tanya Tucker. And New World was in negotiations with the cable network Home Box Office (which had just bought *Battle* for $800,000) to produce movies directly for HBO, with Corman retaining overseas rights.

> '*Here in this island,* I *am absolute master.*'
> —English potentate Edmond Rackham (Richard Johnson) in *Island of the Fish Men*

When the previously announced *Don't Open the Door* was still at the scripting stage, Corman had considered re-titling it *Friday the 13th.* But he was too late off the mark; Paramount Pictures had beaten him to the punch by picking up an independent quickie which had been shot by *Last House on the Left* producer Sean Cunningham. It was filmed in the fall of 1979 as *A Long Night at Camp Blood* on a $700,000 budget. When Paramount released it as *Friday the 13th* in the summer of 1980, it took in an astounding $16.5 million in rentals and spawned a franchise which ultimately would encompass a total of ten sequels, as well as a remake of the original in 2009.

Having missed out on the title, Corman was determined not to miss out on the craze. He already had a name for his entry—*Something Waits in the Dark*. Now what he needed was a movie to go along with it. Coincidentally, Dick Kaye and Harry Rybnick's United Producers Organisation had one that needed a distributor. What they brought to New World was the imported *Island of the Fish Men*, which had been shot on the island of Sardinia in October 1978 and subsequently released in Italy the following February. Featuring Barbara Bach, Richard Johnson and Joseph Cotten, *Island* was based on a short story by H P Lovecraft ('The Shadow over Innsmouth') but was actually a hodge-podge of Jules Verne (*Mysterious Island*), H G Wells (*The Island of Dr Moreau*), the 1965 AIP undersea fantasy *City Under the Sea* (aka *War Gods of the Deep*), and 1978's *Warlords of Atlantis*.

> *In 1891, a doctor and a group of prisoners are shipwrecked on a volcanic island in the Caribbean. They discover that it is the private domain of Lord Edmond Rackham, his consort Amanda, and a tribe of voodoo-practicing natives. It is also home to a race of amphibious monsters, who kill the castaways one by one until only the doctor is left. He learns that the creatures are the original inhabitants of the island, who have been*

transformed by into amphibians by Amanda's father so that they can find the treasure of the lost city of Atlantis for Rackham.

This was about as far from a backwoods 'slasher' as one could get, so Corman decided to adopt the same tactic that he had employed on *Humanoids from the Deep*. He cut over 20 minutes of footage, including much of Beryl Cunningham's part as a voodoo priestess. He then sent a crew, including writer/director Miller Drake, cameraman Gary Graver, and effects maven Chris Walas, to Maui to film a 12-minute prologue where a slimy monster guts and/or decapitates Mel Ferrer, Cameron Mitchell, Eunice Bolt, and Tom Delaney when they land on the island as part of an expedition. A 90-second insert was also shot, with one of the prisoners discovering Bolt's corpse on the beach and then being attacked himself. Back at New World Venice, another scene was shot which substituted a Walas fish-man in a tank for the less-than-convincing one in the Italian version (as well as providing it with a bloodier end).

Something Waits in the Dark played a few engagements in the fall of 1980 and did poorly. Frustrated, Corman resigned himself to consigning the film to the dustbin when, early in 1981, newly-installed publicity director Jim Wynorski asked if he might take a crack at putting the Italian gill-men back into action. He started by changing the title to *Screamers* (a riff on the then-current *Scanners*), came up with a totally bogus ad campaign ('Be Warned! You will actually see a man turned inside-out!'), and shot a *faux* trailer that had nothing to do with the actual film. 'I went to the studio, where they were currently

European/US posters

184

Something Waits in the Dark (Richard Johnson/Barbara Bach)

shooting [*Planet of Horrors*], hired a hottie, put her in black bra and panties and shot her being chased around the big, futuristic sets by a slimy creature,' Wynorski told the Retromedia Forum. 'Rob Bottin.. came in to create and play the monster. We shot all afternoon and came up with some pretty exciting stuff. Once the new TV spot and trailer were edited, there really wasn't a frame of footage left from the original Italian picture.'

Screamers premiered that May in Atlanta, and drive-in patrons were not best pleased when they neither saw a man 'turned inside out' nor a half-naked lady being chased by same; something had to be done quickly to appease them. 'Roger looked at all the footage I'd shot,' continued Wynorski, 'and then had main editor Clark Henderson cobble together a 90 second 'scene' out of the material. The piece was then negative cut, scored and mixed in the record time of about 48 hours. All 26 prints of *Screamers* were recalled and the new section was hand spliced into each reel 3.'

Wynorski had feared for his job as a result of the debacle, but he had shown a resourcefulness that Corman admired in his underlings. It was to be the beginning of a creative relationship which would continue for many years.

> *'They will pay.. in rivers of blood!'*
> —Renegade samurai Lone Wolf (Tomisaburo Wakayama) in *Shogun Assassin*

In September 1970, Japanese comic magazine *Weekly Manga Action* began to serialise the violent exploits of 'Lone Wolf and Cub'—a shogunate executioner and his three-year-old son, out to seek revenge for Lone Wolf's dishonour. Written by Kazuo Koike and illustrated by Goseki Kojima, the story was an instant hit and ran for nearly six years, spanning 28 volumes. In 1972, *Lone Wolf and Cub* became a film series from Toho, which started out with *Sword of Vengeance* and continued through four more of the same before ending with *White Heaven in Hell* in 1974. Between 1973 and 1976, a TV series based on *Lone Wolf* was also produced, which eventually totalled 78 episodes.

While *Lone Wolf* was immensely popular in Japan, it was virtually unknown in America. Taking their cue from Woody Allen's *What's Up Tiger Lily*, which was a comedy reworking of the Japanese spy film *Key of Keys*), actor Robert Houston and producer David Weisman (*Ciao! Manhattan*) decided to change that. They set about condensing the first two *Lone Wolf* films into a single feature, utilising 12 minutes from the first instalment and 68 from the second. They commissioned a new electronic score from Mark Lindsay, former lead singer of Paul Revere and

Shogun Assassin

Shogun Assassin (Tomisaburo Wakayama)

the Raiders, and then painstakingly constructed a script from words that synchronised exactly with the mouth-movements of the Japanese actors. 'Japanese movies can't be dubbed in English because of the linguistic realities,' Houston told *Variety*. 'So we had to write our own script that played into the mouths of the characters. We'd look at a woman's mouth forming a 'w' and then an 'o' and try to come up with a word that began with 'wo'. Looking back, it's hard to believe we finally finished.'

Houston, Weisman and Lindsay all lent their voice talents to the 27-page script, along with comedians Marshall Efron and Sandra Bernhard, and director Lamont Johnson (*The McKenzie Break, The Groundstar Conspiracy*). This new *Lone Wolf* incarnation was titled *Shogun Assassin*, and the entire enterprise had cost $350,000, including the $50,000 that Weisman had paid Toho for the rights. Houston received directorial credit, Weisman producer credit, and the two shared the writing credits.

> *In feudal Japan, a demented shogun sends a ninja to kill his executioner, Ogami Itto. The ninja kills Itto's wife instead, and the shogun's son challenges Itto to a duel for his freedom. Itto wins but when the shogun demands the life of Itto's baby son, the former samurai escapes and embarks upon a life of wandering. Now known as Lone Wolf, he earns a living as an assassin for hire while fending off attacks by the shogun's soldiers. Hired by persecuted villagers to kill the shogun's brother, Lone Wolf must first face the brother's three invincible guards, known as the Masters of Death..*

In October 1980, New World acquired distribution rights to *Shogun Assassin*. 'I decided rather whimsically to acquire and release it,' Corman explained in his autobiography. 'It just pushed everything to the absolute limit and beyond.' The film was released the following month and it grossed $1.6 million in its first four weeks. Critical response was sharply divided, with Vincent Canby dismissing it as 'an unimportant joke', Gene Siskel walking out of the press screening after the first few bouts of bloodshed, and the *Chicago Daily Herald*'s Dann Gire declaring that '*Shogun Assassin* is a horrible movie, the worst I've seen in 1980. It either bores you to death (between killings) or grosses you out (during killings).' Finding more to appreciate in the Houston-Weisman opus were *Variety* ('a real curiosity item. A fast-paced, almost absurdly bloody actioner.. very slick and very playable on the exploitation circuit') and Kevin Thomas ('the high quality of Weisman's enterprise places it far above the laughably dubbed routine kung foolishness from Hong Kong').

In mid-December, it was brought to the MPAA's attention that the version of *Shogun Assassin* being screened in theatres was more violent than the one which had been submitted to the board and received an 'R' rating. Despite an additional warning on the film's advertising that the film 'contains scenes depicting graphic violence which may be considered shocking,' the MPAA rescinded its rating and demanded that it be stricken from all prints and advertising. Corman decided that as *Shogun Assassin* had already played all of the major markets, it was not worth the trouble of trying to book an unrated film (which many theatre chains would decline to show) and withdrew it from circulation.

Shogun Assassin virtually disappeared after that, but its influence can be seen in everything from John Carpenter's *Big Trouble in Little China* (1986) to Quentin Tarantino's *Kill Bill* duo (2003-04). In 2002, a revival took place in Japan when a new *Lone Wolf* TV series premiered and ran for two years.

> '*Mother always said that if you had another brain you'd be lonesome.*'
> —Dr Tart (Tim Conway) to Inspector Winship (Don Knotts) in *The Private Eyes*

Whereas *The Prize Fighter* had been a lucky strike, New World's strategy in marketing its second Conway-Knotts vehicle was much more deliberate. Instead of filling in at the last minute, *The Private Eyes* was booked into theatres months in advance. As a result, the company was able to upgrade the quality of its venues for an expanded audience. New World was also spending more on promotion—$2 million over $1.4 million—and asking for four-week guaranteed playing schedules. New World followed the same booking pattern that it had instituted for *The Prize Fighter*—*The Private Eyes* opened regionally at Thanksgiving, then it widened its release, playing through Christmas and into the new year.

> *Exiled from the US for their bumbling, Inspector Winship and Dr Tart wind up in the employ of Scotland Yard. They are sent to investigate the murder of Lord and Lady Morley by a hooded assassin. At the Morley estate, they meet the staff—who include a samurai chef, a homicidal butler, a German governess, a buxom maid, a hunchbacked stable-hand, and a grave-robbing handyman. One by one, these weirdoes meet their demise, a note attached to each corpse, until Winship and Tart come face-to-face with the killer.. and the hooded assassin.*

While Knotts and Conway represent an idiot version of Holmes and Watson, *The Private Eyes* is actually another variation on the old Agatha Christie chestnut, *And Then There Were None*, a fact which failed to endear it to the critics. 'I wish someone would put Conway and Knotts through their dopey paces at a dramatically accelerated tempo,' said *The Washington Post*'s Gary Arnold. 'At the leisurely tempo imposed by director Lang Elliott, this less than dynamic duo becomes perilously draggy.' Sheila Benson of the *Los Angeles Times* was more negative still, finding the film's sight-gags offensive: '*Private Eyes* comes off as small-minded, mean-spirited and nasty. Almost the only thing worse than being a pigeon in *Private Eyes* would be being the pigeon who buys a ticket to it, or takes a child to be exposed to its vulgar cruelties.' Dann Gire warned potential patrons: 'If your tastes are like mine, you'll walk out of the theatre right after Conway puts his calling card in the maid's cleavage.' The film's sole defender was none other than Gene Siskel, who gave *Private Eyes* three stars and commended it as 'a perfectly delightful movie made for Saturday matinees.'

As with *The Prize Fighter*, audiences ignored the critical bashing and flocked to *The Private Eyes* in droves. Its first week earned it nearly $400,000 in just 74 theatres; when it expanded to 625 theatres the next week, it grossed $3.3 million. The film went on to earn a staggering $12 million in rentals, making it the biggest hit New World would ever have under Roger Corman's aegis (though as it was not

The Private Eyes (Tim Conway/Don Knotts)

an in-house production, the company had to split the take with TriStar Pictures). Surprisingly, TriStar folded after this huge success (the name was resurrected in 1984 by Coke, Columbia Pictures, and HBO for a new distributorship) and Conway and Knotts were accorded only one more big screen pairing—a cameo as highway patrol officers in *The Cannonball Run II* (1984).

At New World's fifth annual sales convention that December, Corman and Moreno decided to take advantage of the company's most profitable year ever and lay down the law to their sub-distributors regarding a problem that was a thorn in the side of independents everywhere—delayed payment of rentals from exhibitors. 'We want exhibitors to stop building theatres with our money,' Moreno told *Variety*. 'They're paid right away by the public, and that's what we want.. If [the exhibitors] don't like it, they won't be serviced by us. It's that simple.'

With New World controlling some 60% of the indie market, Moreno felt that the company now had enough clout to demand equal treatment with the majors. 'I mean who else is there?' he asked. 'We've taken our shot..' New World meant to keep taking its shots in 1981, with *Planet of Horrors* and *Nightfall* on the schedule for release—though *Journey Beyond This Galaxy* had been pushed back to 1982. Taking its place on the sci-fi slate for '81 was *Kain of Dark Planet,* to be produced by Corman and written/directed by John Broderick; Corman announced that he was in negotiations with Chuck Norris to play the title role.

New World would also be continuing its art house comeback in earnest, with Alain Resnais's *Mon Oncle d'Amerique*—winner of the Grand Jury Prize at Cannes 1980—and Bruce Beresford's *Breaker Morant*—winner of 10 Australian Academy Awards—both set for December premieres in New York, to be followed in early 1981 by the independent UK production *Richard's Things*, starring Liv Ullmann. Corman's company was additionally taking a one-third stake in Werner Herzog's $6 million *Fitzcarraldo*, with Jason Robards, Mick Jagger, and Claudia Cardinale, which after three years in preparation, was now scheduled to begin shooting in the Peruvian jungle in January 1981.

> *'You're the most excitement to hit this county since the hurricane of '68.'*
> —Jenny (Linda Blair) to drifter Kyle (Dirk Benedict) in *Ruckus in Madoc County*

New World Pictures' first release of 1981 was a pick-up from indie producer Paul Maslansky (who would earn a fortune out of the *Police Academy* comedies) which starred Dirk Benedict, in his second feature under Roger Corman's banner in as many months—*The Georgia Peaches* had debuted the previous November. Originally titled *Ruckus*, New World changed the title to *Ruckus in Madoc County* and marketed the film as another in its series of car-chase comedies, which it most definitely was not.

> *After escaping from a psycho ward, disturbed Vietnam vet Kyle Hanson runs into a posse of rednecks in Madoc County. He takes refuge at the farm of Sam Bellows and his daughter-in-law Jenny. While Bellows is away on business, Kyle begins to fill the vacuum in Jenny's life, and that of her young son. But when her husband is declared dead by the military, she is seen as available by a cadre of potential suitors, including the deputy sheriff. Hanson is kidnapped, but the former POW escapes and engages his tormentors in a war of attrition.*

An uneasy blend of redneck humour, social drama, and shoot-'em-up action, *Ruckus in Madoc County* plays like a combination of *Smokey and the Bandit* and *The Deer Hunter* (1978). That would be curious enough, but the film also makes

190

an interesting companion-piece to Sylvester Stallone's *First Blood*, which came out the following year. The Stallone film would also feature a wandering Vietnam vet, who ends up in a war with the locals in a small town, as well as a motorcycle chase almost identical to one featured in *Ruckus*. *First Blood* was based on a 1972 novel by David Morrell, so it is possible that *Ruckus* writer/director Max Kleven read the book as well.

Where *Ruckus* differs from *First Blood* is in its inclusion of a love interest for its protagonist, in the form of 21-year-old Linda Blair, immediately prior to her career-reviving stint as an exploitation movie queen. The former equestrian had shot to fame at the age of 14 as the demon-possessed Regan in horror-blockbuster *The Exorcist* (1973), for which she received an Oscar nomination and a Golden Globe Award. She then appeared in a number of controversial TV movies (*Born Innocent, Sarah T: Portrait of a Teenage Alcoholic, Sweet Hostage*) before her career nose-dived in 1977 after the disastrous reception afforded *Exorcist II: The Heretic* and her subsequent arrest for drug possession.

'I want people to know what is really me,' the actress told the *Los Angeles Times*. 'I'm a nice person, I swear. I want to do right and I think people have a different image of me.' That image—of an obscenity-spouting fiend—became one of a grind-house headliner in the 1980s with such movies as *Hell Night* (1981), *Chained Heat* (1983), *Savage Streets* (1984), *Red Heat*, *Savage Island* (both 1985), and *Night Force* (1987). 'I'm hanging in there, and things are looking up,' Blair said. 'Maybe they're not big-budget [movies] but at least I'm working.' She would subsequently spoof her most famous role in *Repossessed* (1990), make numerous guest appearances in TV series, star in several direct-to-video movies, and play an uncredited cameo as an obnoxious reporter in Wes Craven's horror hit *Scream* (1996). In recent years, Blair has become a tireless crusader for animal rights causes, while making regular appearances on TV shows such as *The Scariest Places on Earth* (2001-06).

'I don't know me at all today.. I'm breaking rules that I really believed in!'
—Homecoming queen Peggy Sue Turner (Janet Julian) in *Smokey Bites the Dust*

Previously announced as *Follow that Car* (a title that ended up being given to *The Georgia Peaches* for ancillary screenings), New World's second release of 1981 had actually started its engines some four years earlier: 'It all started with a news broadcast [in 1977],' director Charles Griffith told Dennis Fischer. 'The police were complaining that *Eat My Dust* and other pictures like it inspired kids to chase down the freeways and challenge the cops and run other cars off the road. There were lots of people blamed for this, and [the police] called this 'Car Wars'. As soon as the newscast was over, the phone rang, and it was Roger. 'I want you to do a picture called *Car Wars*,' he said, 'using the stunts from five old New World pictures.'

'I wrote a script which wound up being called *Wham Bam, Merci, Madame*. It was insane and used all the stunts in different ways. But Roger hated the script and never did the picture. In [1980], however, he called again and offered me a lot more money than he ever had before. I guess I got flattered, and I went ahead and did it. He had [novelist] Max Apple in Texas go ahead and write a script around all the wrecks and chases. But Max wasn't allowed to see the footage. It was too expensive to rent a Movieola and send Max prints or anything else, so he had only vague descriptions written down on what the stunts were—and nothing worked. So I made a lot of changes in it, and that made Roger angry. He tried to cut it just to the action of the old pictures, but he couldn't.. Then he cut all the motivations and all the character development. It was a mess, a jumbled mess!'

Local hot-rodder Roscoe Wilton kidnaps homecoming queen Peggy Sue Turner, who just happens to be the daughter of Wilton's nemesis, Sheriff Turner. Freed from her father's heavy hand, Peggy Sue is more than willing to join Wilton on his multi-county joyride, with most of the townsfolk in hot pursuit.

With a plot which was an amalgam of *Eat My Dust* and *Grand Theft Auto*, as well as a good deal of footage 'borrowed' from both those films, what was released as *Smokey Bites the Dust* that April met with complete indifference, from both critics and audiences alike. '*Smokey Bites the Dust* is the kind of movie that defies reviewing,' said the *Los Angeles Times*. 'It's simple-minded, silly and boring, but innocuous and not mean-minded. The youngsters are attractive and the adults are dullards. If you like car chases and cornpone humour, this could be right up your alley. Otherwise leave it alone.' *Variety* was much less charitable: '*Smokey* offers nothing but bits of dumb dialogue randomly uttered by equally dumb people in between the roaring of engines and the crashing of car metal.'

Smokey was the last New World outing for Charles Griffith, who did not make another movie until Corman's *Wizards of the Lost Kingdom II* in 1989: '*Smokey* and *Up from the Depths..* were both so butchered that it made it impossible for me to get work,' Griffith told Fischer. He subsequently retired from the industry and died of a heart attack in September 2007 at the age of 77.

'*A woman who walks into my place like she's looking for something is* not *just another dame.*'
—Martial arts club owner Erik Stollard (Ken Metcalfe) in *Firecracker*

Smokey Bites the Dust was the fourth New World film shot by Gary Graver, a cinematographer who had started out in the '60s on no-budget wonders like *The Girls from Thunder Strip* (1966), *Wanda the Sadistic Hypnotist*, and *Satan's Sadists* (both 1969). During the 1970s, Graver worked both ends of the spectrum, shooting Al Adamson 'Z' movies like *Dracula vs Frankenstein* and collaborating with Orson Welles on TV specials and his final, unfinished film, *The Other Side of the Wind*. Covering all the bases, Graver also began a profitable sideline as a porn director under the *nom-de-plume* of Robert McCallum; he directed his last adult film, *Veronica 2030*, in 1999. He shot low-budget and direct-to-video movies throughout the '80s, '90s and into the new millennium, and he died of cancer in 2006.

Graver's widow was actress Jillian Kesner; the two had met on the set of *The Student Body* in 1976. Kesner was primarily a TV performer—appearing in such '70s series as *SWAT, The Blue Knight, Happy Days*, and *The Rockford Files*—but she branched out into films in the '80s, co-starring in *Raw Force, Trick or Treats* (both 1982), *Evil Town* (1987), and *Beverly Hills Vamp* (1989). In the 1990s, she became a production co-ordinator on Graver's films, a role that she occupied until his death. In December 2007, a little over a year after Graver's passing, Kesner died of leukaemia at the age of 58. Her last film as an actress was a 1998 Roger Corman kung fu opus with Don 'The Dragon' Wilson called *Operation Cobra* (aka *Inferno*), which brought things full circle from when Kesner had played sixth-degree black belt Susanne Carter in Corman's *Firecracker*.

When her journalist sister goes missing in the Philippines, karate instructor Susanne Carter travels to Olongapo to search for her. Carter traces her sister's movements to a martial arts nightclub that features deathsport combat and is a front for a trafficking ring. There she becomes romantically involved with the club's star attraction—only to discover that he was the one behind her sister's death; in response, she challenges him to a stick-fighting duel to the death..

Firecracker marked the return to New World of Filipino producer/director Cirio Santiago, who fashioned the film as a straight remake of his *TNT Jackson*. While *Firecracker* benefits from better choreographed kung fu action and a more convincing female lead, Corman still felt the need to pad Kesner's credentials, and christened her the winner of the fictitious 'North American Black Belt Olympics'. Corman also felt that the film did not show enough of Kesner's busty form, and he had Allan Holzman (second unit director on *Smokey*) shoot her in a topless kung fu fight (*a la* Jeannie Bell) and a rather ridiculous love scene with Darby Hinton, in which the two shred each other's clothes with pocket knives before having sex.

'*Firecracker* is just another martial arts movie but the catch is that the kung fu addict is an attractive woman.. Is this progress?' asked the *Los Angeles Times*, while *Variety* felt that its commercial attraction was limited 'to those who are intellectually stimulated by the sight of a kicky young blonde without underwear.' Corman himself seemed to be one of those individuals, as he had Santiago remake *Firecracker* in 1993 as *Angel Fist*, with Vidal Sassoon's daughter Catya in the lead; following the New World tradition for fictitious gongs, she was awarded the title of 'World Karate Association North American Champion'. Maria Ford took the call for Corman's next remake, *Angel of Destruction* (1994), when original lead Charlie Spradling refused to participate in the requisite topless rumble.

'*There's no horror here we don't make ourselves.*'
—Space ranger Cabren (Edward Albert) on the apparitions in *Planet of Horrors*

In October 1979, Corman informed *Penthouse*: 'When I did *Monster from the Ocean Floor*, people came because they wanted to see that *kind* of film. If *Jaws* had been there, people wouldn't have come to see *Monster*. Same thing with *War of the Satellites* [1958] if *Star Wars* had been out. The exploitation business has become respectable because now there's more money. You buy respect.'

If ever there was a 'respectable' exploitation film, Ridley Scott's *Alien* was it.

Planet of Horrors

Written by Dan O'Bannon—who had worked on John Carpenter's debut *Dark Star* (1974) and Alejandro Jodorowski's abandoned *Dune* project—and Ronald Shusett, the project had been around for several years in the '70s under the title *Starbeast*, and was basically a reworking of the 1958 United Artists shocker, *It! The Terror from Beyond Space*, coupled with elements from Mario Bava's phantasmagorical *Planet of the Vampires* (*Terrore nello spazio*, 1965).

The script passed through the hands of producer Arnold Orgolini (*Embryo, Meteor*) and was also rejected by 20th Century-Fox and Sam Arkoff's son Louis at AIP (he told O'Bannon and Shusett that 'the market for science fiction had dried up') before landing on the desk of Roger Corman. Corman saw the potential in the script and agreed to produce *Starbeast* and let O'Bannon direct, provided that he and Shusett could come up with a share of the proposed $700,000 budget. It was deal-killing condition that cost New World what could well have been their biggest hit ever.

The script finally arrived at the offices of Brandywine Productions, headed by producers David Giler and Gordon Carroll, and director Walter Hill. It was greatly reworked by Giler and Hill (although O'Bannon was awarded sole credit after the case went to arbitration) before Brandywine put what had become retitled as *Alien* before the cameras in the summer of 1978 for the same 20th Century-Fox that had rejected the idea just a few years earlier. The difference now was the cash bonanza that Fox was enjoying with *Star Wars* and was eager to duplicate with other space adventures—albeit horrific ones. But Fox's delay had proved costly: what was once budgeted at under $1 million now cost over $10 million.

Released in the summer of 1979, *Alien* did not hit the box office stratosphere, but its $40 million in rentals made it the top-grossing 'R'-rated picture of the year. The film won an Oscar for Best Visual Effects and launched the careers of director Scott and star Sigourney Weaver.

Just as he had waited two years to capitalise on *Star Wars*, so Corman would wait two years to mount his own version of *Alien: Planet of Horrors*. And just as he had hedged his bets on *Battle Beyond the Stars* by co-financing it with Orion, so he would split the difference on *Planet* with United Artists (despite announcing it as a $5 million dollar film, *Planet* would actually cost only $1.8 million).

> *When all contact is lost with the starship Remus after it crash-lands on Morganthus, a rescue ship is sent to investigate. On Morganthus, the ship's crew find no survivors of the Remus but come upon a large pyramid jutting from the barren landscape. Once inside the vast structure, they are plagued by horrific apparitions; eight of the ten are either disembowelled, raped by space-worms, assaulted by 'doppelgangers', or ripped apart by monsters. Only two crew remain—Cabren the space ranger, who has figured out that the planet's horrors are the manifestations of individual fears—and Kore the cook, who is more than he seems..*

The whole 'Monsters from the Id' concept, and the discovery of remnants of an advanced race, comes from MGM's *Forbidden Planet* (1956), while the idea of a sentient force that is capable of altering perceptions of reality can also be found in Ray Bradbury's *The Martian Chronicles* (1950) and Arthur C Clarke's short story of 1951, 'The Sentinel'—which formed the basis for Stanley Kubrick's *2001* (1968). And these are without mentioning a host of AIP sci-fi movies like *The Angry Red Planet* (1959) and *Journey to the Seventh Planet* (1962), along with any number of episodes of *The Twilight Zone, The Outer Limits*, or *Star Trek*.

However, in not only addressing the physical manifestations of subconscious fears but the metaphysical and psychological undertones, *Planet of Horrors* is in truth an

exploitation version of Andrei Tarkovsky's 1971 Soviet sci-fi masterpiece *Solaris*, which was based on Stanislaw Lem's 1961 novel. When contact is lost with the inhabitants of a space station orbiting the planet of Solaris, cosmonaut Kris is sent to investigate. What he finds is a derelict, where all but two of the crew have fallen victim to visions engineered by the omnipotent planet below and committed suicide. Kris is subject to a visitation by his dead wife, who poisoned herself after the break-up of their marriage, and he gradually succumbs to her presence; in the end, he 'goes home' to an island in the vast Solaris ocean, where he will relive his nightmares forever.

Lest this be considered an analogy too far, it should remembered that Corman had been exploring the 'Monsters from the Id' theme for years in his Poe films, and he even subjected himself to Freudian psychoanalysis to get in touch with his own suppressed emotions and fears. 'Whether you call it science fiction, whether you call it horror, whether you call it fantasy, I think that all of these sorts of films represent extrapolations from the workings of the conscious and the unconscious mind,' Corman told *Fangoria*. 'In science fiction, you're working more with the conscious mind.. in fantasy and horror you begin to move more toward the unconscious. On [*Planet of Horrors*], it's a matter of blending those two different elements.. I wanted a story set on a distant planet, involving characters from a culture similar to our own; a story that would deal in some way with the unconscious mind, and would lead into a metaphysical, philosophical realm.'

Planet of Horrors was written by producer Marc Siegler and director Bruce Clark, whose connection to Corman went back to 1970, when he acquired the duo's first film, biker picture *Naked Angels* (1969), as a co-feature for *Angels Die Hard*. Siegler and Clark moved on to adapt the 1965 Romain Gary novel *The Ski Bum* for Joseph E Levine in 1971, and then they split up. *Planet of Horrors* was their first project together in a decade. In reference to working at New World's Venice studio, Siegler told *Fangoria*: 'It's really strange, almost like working at the turn of the century, at the dawn of the motion picture era, 'cause you've got people's kids and mothers and buses parked here, people who're working on the picture sleeping in worksheds; we shot the film on two stages, one at a former lumber yard that still has the sign up—we now use the saws to build the sets, but it still looks like a lumber yard if you squint your eyes.. So, even though the budgets are a little bigger, we're still flying by the seat of our pants; it's delightful—you might call it Felliniesque if you didn't know it was Cormanesque!'

Gigeresque would be a good description of the bio-mechanical production designs of James Cameron (who was also second unit director) and Robert Skotak (Swiss artist H R Giger had been responsible for much of the conceptual work on *Alien*). Their otherworldly creatures, however, were definitely Lovecraftian. Effects supervisor Tom Campbell and his team utilised every trick in the book to bring Cameron and Skotak's designs to life: stop-motion, full-size mock-ups, hand puppets, men in suits, beam-splitters, motion-control, blue screen, you name it. Given the budget and time constraints, the film's look and effects are very impressive.

Over the course of its production and release, the movie would come to give new meaning to the term 'working title'. 'Originally, the script was called *Planet of Horrors*,' Cameron told *Omni*. 'Roger knew he'd never be able to cast it with that name, so he put it out under a cover called *The Quest*, then changed it later to whatever title tested the best as being the most horrific. He had a couple of titles: *Mindwarp* and *Infinity of Terror*. The film actually went out as *Mindwarp: An Infinity of Terror* for test screenings or a limited release in the Seattle area. It didn't do too well. Roger always attributes that to the poster being wrong or the title being wrong. He knows that his films aren't in the market long enough for word-of-mouth to be a factor. If the title and poster are working, he's selling tickets.' People were beginning to wise up to such strategies, though, as Richard Harrington of the *Washington Post* noted in his piece: 'Beware of films that sneak into town on multiple screens and past review deadlines; they generally intend to benefit before word of mouth catches up with them.'

After its Seattle test run in July 1981, the film reverted back to its original title of *Planet of Horrors* for its engagements in August. When they too were lacking, Corman changed the title one last time to *Galaxy of Terror* for the film's national release in September. It was under that moniker that it was finally reviewed, and critics grudgingly had to admit that this latest effort was quite a showcase for New World Venice: 'New World has produced a glossy new movie with a look similar to the high-budget space films *Outland* [1981] and *Alien*' (*Chicago Daily Herald*); 'Production designers Jim Cameron and Bob Skotak.. are the film's real stars. Other technical credits are pretty impressive, too' (*Los Angeles Times*); 'Visual qualities, including the spaceships, overall production design and monster mock-ups, are excellent across the board. While not as frightening or graphic as *Alien*, the major scare scenes are well handled and never unconvincing, and Jacques Haitkin's moody lensing is a major plus' (*Variety*); 'There are several good kicks in the eyeball.. the breakneck editing pace.. turns the movie into an hallucination of science fiction movie style, gesture and cliché' (*Cinefantastique*).

However, all four publications respectively felt the need to qualify their praise: '*Galaxy of Terror* is 50 percent *Alien* and 50 per cent recycled *Star Trek* episodes aided and abetted by a generous supply of overacting and horrendous dialogue'; 'If only the dialogue and characterisations were half as imaginative as the production design of *Galaxy of Terror*, it might have been fun. As it is, however, it's no more than routine exploitation fare for the undemanding'; 'As long as *Galaxy of Terror* sticks to stuff like rocket ships making rough landings on hostile terrain or monsters devouring space explorers, it nicely passes muster. But when all the exposition about cosmic mind games is laid out toward the end, pic comes crashing down like an early Vanguard missile'; 'It would seem like a commentary on the genre if it weren't so goofy and fast paced.'

Goofy and fast-paced it may have been, but it was also a money-maker, which brought in $4 million in rentals. Corman subsequently recommended Cameron to Chako van Leeuwen for his first full-fledged directorial assignment, *Piranha II: The Spawning*, a disastrous experience which saw him fired by executive producer Ovidio Assonitis after the completion of principal photography. But Assonitis was unaware of the 'can do' spirit that Cameron had demonstrated at New World—he flew to Rome on his own, broke into the editing room after hours, and re-cut the film the way he wanted it ('It was probably the best movie about flying piranha in the history of the cinema,' Cameron joked to *Variety*). It was in his Rome hotel that Cameron dreamed up an idea about a robot killer from the future that became the basis of his script, *The Terminator*. In 1984, after two years of false starts, *The Terminator* went into production for Hemdale, HBO, and Orion Pictures as a $6 million feature starring Arnold Schwarzenegger. It earned $17 million in rentals and made its writer/director a hot property.

Cameron's name subsequently became synonymous with action blockbusters—*Aliens* (1986), *The Abyss* (1989), *Terminator 2: Judgment Day* (1991), *True Lies* (1994)—before becoming the skipper of a teen-romance *Titanic* (1997) that earned almost $1 billion worldwide to become the most successful film of all time. (He also received the Academy Award for Best Director and famously proclaimed, 'I'm the king of the world!').

The Terminator was also the launch-pad for another Hollywood heavyweight who was herself a Corman protégé: producer Gale Anne Hurd. She had worked on *Humanoids, Battle Beyond the Stars, Screamers* and co-produced *Smokey Bites the Dust* before forming Pacific Western Productions with James Cameron for the production of *Terminator*. The two were married in 1985 and divorced four years later, but Hurd produced all of Cameron's movies through to *Terminator 2* while also producing films such as *Alien Nation* (1988), *Tremors* (1990), *Armageddon*

(1998), *The Hulk*, and *Terminator 3: Rise of the Machines* (both 2003) in her own right. '[Corman] is the only person I've known in the industry who wanted his protégés to succeed and perhaps have even more impressive credentials than his own,' Hurd told Beverly Gray.

> '*It gets bad on Friday the 13th.. But it gets worse on Saturday the 14th.*'
> —From 'The Book of Evil' in *Saturday the 14th*

In October of 1978, a film that was originally titled *The Babysitter Murders* was released as *Halloween*. Co-written and directed by John Carpenter, it told the story of a seemingly-unstoppable masked maniac who escapes from an asylum and terrorises babysitters on Halloween night. A real cinematic blending of visual style and unbearable tension, it became the most successful independent production of its time, costing just $360,000 and earning $55 million at the box office. It made a star out of its leading lady, 19 year-old Jamie Lee Curtis (daughter of Janet Leigh and Tony Curtis), it set Carpenter and producer Debra Hill firmly on the road to their respective Hollywood careers, and it initiated a series of seven sequels (one in name only) and two remakes. It also inspired an onslaught of similar so-called 'slasher' films between 1979-1981, which included *Don't Answer the Phone, Don't Go in the House, Dressed to Kill, Fade to Black, The Fan, Final Exam, Friday the 13th, Friday the 13th Part 2, Happy Birthday to Me, Hell Night, He Knows You're Alone, Maniac, My Bloody Valentine, Prom Night, The Prowler, Terror Train,* and *When a Stranger Calls.*

In 1981, three comedies employed the *Airplane* formula to spoof the 'slasher' trend as it started to wear thin. The first was Paramount's *Student Bodies*, which was ritten and directed by Woody Allen collaborator Mickey Rose and featured comedian Richard Belzer as 'The Breather', who makes obscene phone calls and kills sexually-active high school students. The film was so bad that Belzer used a pseudonym ('Richard Brando') and producer Michael Ritchie hid behind the 'Alan Smithee' credit more usually employed by disgruntled directors. The next attempt, UA's *Thursday the 12th*, held more promise—it was directed by Alfred Sole, who had made the critically acclaimed, pre-*Halloween* psycho movie *Alice, Sweet Alice* (1976), and it featured comedians like Eve Arden, Eileen Brennan, Phil Hartman, Carol Kane, Judge Reinhold, Paul Reubens and Tom Smothers, who starred as the Canadian Mountie trying to apprehend a killer of cheerleaders at a summer camp. Originally scheduled for an October '81 release, *Thursday the 12th* sat on the shelf until April '82, when it was retitled *Pandemonium* and given a quick play-off.

The reason for *Thursday the 12th*'s delay and name-change had to do with the third comedy-horror of 1981, New World's *Saturday the 14th*, which came out in August—the same month as *Student Bodies*. Despite its title, Julie Corman's latest production was not in fact a slasher spoof but a monsters-on-the-loose, *Old Dark House*–style send-up.

> Dim-witted John and Mary Hyatt, with their children Debbie and Billy, inherit the old family estate in Erie, Pennsylvania, which just happens to be cursed. After moving in, the Hyatts have encounters with monsters, a vampire puts the bite on Mary, and Billy discovers 'The Book of Evil'. They call on Van Helsing the Exterminator for help, but he is only interested in finding The Book. On Saturday the 14th, the whole of the Hyatt clan arrives for a housewarming, but monsters crash the party and Van Helsing and Waldemar the vampire face off over who is to have The Book—and control the world!

In 1980, Jeff Begun, producer of *Jackson County Jail* and *Outside Chance*, had approached writer Howard Cohen (*Unholy Rollers, The Young Nurses, Cover Girl*

Models) with the title and opening scene for *Saturday the 14th*. Cohen typed up a three-page synopsis for the film on the strength of those and it was submitted to Roger Corman.

'He called me on Christmas Eve and said he had a present for me,' Cohen told the *Chicago Daily Herald*. 'He asked if I would like to write the film. I said, "On one condition—that I direct it." He said, "All right." It was that simple. It took me by surprise.' Julie Corman supplied the cold bath, however, as Cohen told Beverly Gray: 'She said, "I know it's going to go to your head, now that Roger's going to let you be a big director. Here's the truth. Directing is very easy for Roger. He thinks anybody can do it. And if he likes you he'll let you do it."'

Nevertheless, Cohen relished the opportunity to make his directorial debut, as he told the *Daily Herald*: 'I'm amazed. All I set out to do was to learn to direct by making a little picture. All of a sudden I had Richard Benjamin and [wife] Paula Prentiss in the leads. The budget went up. Everything started growing. For the first time, I had complete control over the work. Best of all, nobody changed a single line of my dialogue without permission.'

As far as the critics were concerned, someone should have changed more than just dialogue. 'This is simply a feeble comedy with a husband-and-wife star acting team mugging for the camera,' said Gene Siskel. The *Los Angeles Times* called *Saturday the 14th* 'a silly spoof of horror movies whose appeal probably will be limited to younger people who haven't been exposed to making fun of Dracula for as long as the rest of us.' *Variety* described it as 'a pathetic farce which will seem frail even on TV, for which it should probably have been made in the first place.' *Cinefantastique* rendered similar judgment: 'It's silly rather than funny, and probably an ideal movie for cable-TV, the new final resting place for low-grade filler like this.' Last but not least was Vincent Canby, whose opinion of Cohen was that he 'shouldn't be trusted to park the cars of [his stars], much less make a movie with them.'

Despite such dismal notices, the film earned $4 million in rentals, which was enough to keep Cohen in the director's chair. He would go on to helm five more films, four of them for Corman, including the 1988 sequel/remake *Saturday the 14th Strikes Back*. He died of a heart attack in April 1999, at the age of 56.

Thanks to the efforts of Frank Moreno, 1981 would be a sterling year for New World's art-house product. The Australian *Breaker Morant*, a drama of the Boer War, became New World's most successful foreign film ever, earning $5 million in rentals and receiving an Oscar nomination for Best Screenplay and a Golden Globe nomination for Best Foreign Film. *Mon oncle d'Amerique* also received an Oscar nomination for Best Screenplay and brought in $2 million in rentals. New World's acquisition of the Merchant-Ivory production *Quartet*, which was based on Jean Rhys's 1928 novel and starred Alan Bates, Maggie Smith and Isabelle Adjani, was less successful, but it was another prestige production which could only reflect well on Corman's company.

Moreno had three other films lined up to continue this success into 1982—two German (*Christiane F, Fitzcarraldo*) and one Italian (*Three Brothers*). But these were to be his parting gift to New World, as he left the company for the second and final time in October 1981, though he would be retained as a 'consultant' for six more months, mainly to oversee the release of the films that he had shepherded.

Moreno's departure came at a time when New World was on the threshold of major expansion. Future plans called for the company to diversify its film line-up, capitalise on the burgeoning pay-TV market via its own library and acquisitions (including *Hollywood's Wild Angel* and a documentary on the band Spyro Gyra), enter into more co-financing deals, and sell shares to the public in upcoming films. Corman had dabbled in the latter in the '70s with a Chicago real-estate syndicate called Balcor, which had put money into *Jackson County Jail* and *Grand Theft Auto*. Now, he was having Barbara Boyle put together a prospectus seeking $15-20 million in a proposed public share offer.

New World was also enjoying the benefits of having the largest independent distribution network in North America, with offices in twelve US cities, plus the New World-Mutual distributorship in Canada. Irwin Yablans, head of Compass International Pictures and executive producer of *Halloween*, called New World 'the major alternative' and was one of several producers using Corman's network for the release of his films. To consolidate its position, New World dropped its five remaining sub-distributors in November and shifted their responsibilities to its own offices, to which it planned to add three more—in San Francisco, Boston, and Detroit—by the end of 1982.

A highly-ambitious slate of films was now announced for the coming year, to include already-pitched projects like *Alaric the Avenger, The Disc Jockey, Journey Beyond This Galaxy*, and *Shopping Center*, as well as several new titles:

- *101 Uses for a Dead Cat*, based on Simon Bond's novelty bestseller.
- *The Barbarian*, a sword-and-sorcery picture based on a story by publicity director Jim Wynorski, which he described as 'Frank Frazetta meets Sam Peckinpah meets Russ Meyer meets Sergio Leone.'
- A sequel to *Battle Beyond the Stars*.
- *Battletruck*, a post-apocalyptic opus shooting in New Zealand.
- *Grand Prix 2000*, a futuristic racing picture to be produced by Corman.
- *Guardian Angels*, recounting the true story of Curtis Sliwa and his red-bereted, citizen crime patrol unit.
- *Labyrinth*, a sci-fi film to be produced by Corman and Gale Anne Hurd and directed by Miller Drake.
- *Mausoleum*, a horror film written by Katherine Rosenwink.
- *Mutant*, an *Alien*-type thriller written by Wynorski and effects technician R J Robertson.
- Remakes of old Corman movies *The Last Woman on Earth* and *Tales of Terror*.
- *Sector 13*, to be shot on video tape, and described in *Variety* as 'an action-adventure film set about 15 years from now in which mass communications go haywire and start to bring individuals into the action of the screen.'
- *TAG: The Assassination Game*, a campus thriller written and directed by former John Carpenter associate Nick Castle.
- *The Territory*, a survival thriller produced by Pierre Cottrell and directed by Raoul Ruiz.

As ever, the final score-card featured a lot of no-shows in the New World column. Those which *were* produced all ended up changing titles: *The Barbarian* became *Sorceress*, *Battletruck* became *Warlords of the 21st Century*, *Mutant* became *Forbidden World*, and *TAG* became first *Kiss Me, Kill Me* then *Everyone Gets It in the End*. *Guardian Angels*, *Mausoleum* and *The Territory* went to other companies, and the rest never made it off the ground, though *Sector 13* seemed to be similar in tone to Disney's in-production, $17 million proto-CGI feature *Tron*, which was released in the summer of 1982.

Corman continued to be approached with offers to buy New World, including one that was upwards of $15 million. 'I can't conceive of anyone dumb enough to offer that amount,' he remarked to *Variety*. 'The company is simply not for sale.' But by the end of 1982, he had changed his tune, when he found himself with not one but three buyers 'dumb enough' to offer even more than what he had already considered to be 'an outrageous figure.'

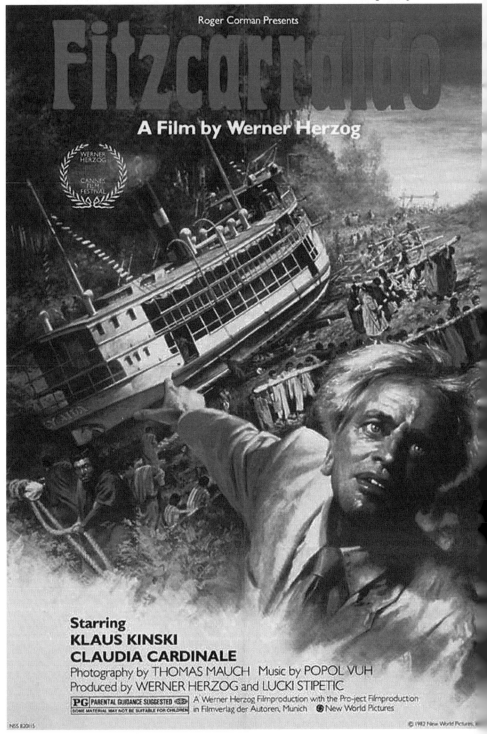

Chapter 6

haRRy, laRRy and laRRy

Galaxy Express

'I'm finally going to be able to do the type of picture I've wanted to do all along. We'll have bigger budgets, a bigger look.. bigger movies.'
—Roger Corman, 1982

'Don't bother interviewing Roger. He's slick, he tells the same stories, he denies everything.. Hang around a New World shoot—that's where you'll get the real Corman story. See what it's like shooting a movie on an imaginary budget.'
—New World staffer to *Penthouse* magazine

In outward appearance, at least, it seemed that New World was poised to become a major-league player, but those on the inside knew better. Although he continued to make grandiose announcements about public offerings, increased budgets, and high-profile films, the truth was that Roger Corman was perfectly content to carry on churning out schlock like *Firecracker*, *Saturday the 14th*, and *Smokey Bites the Dust*, where the risk was low and the profit margin high.

After nearly eight years as New World's legal adviser, Barbara Boyle followed Frank Moreno's lead and left the company in April 1982. She had tried in vain to persuade Corman to take New World public and raise the capital that it needed to make the big-budget movies which it was constantly announcing. 'I told Roger, 'You only want to move and grow so much,' she said in his autobiography. 'We talked about this endlessly and I grew discontent. I just wanted to lock in Roger's wealth and never have it at risk again. Going public could do this and put us in a more important part of the business, but Roger would always back away. Disclosure, scrutiny—he didn't want it. He couldn't give up any control and control meant manipulation of revenue in a completely personal way.. There's never been a Standard & Poor's, no credit rating on Roger, you can't look him up. Which he likes. There's nothing.'

Corman's reasoning for keeping New World private was two-fold. As he said himself, 'I knew Sam Arkoff cursed the day he and Nicholson went public because suddenly they had to deal with scrutiny and accountability and run a company with the public's money. You hire someone who accounts to the Securities and Exchange Commission and to stockholders for your expenditures. And besides, bigger budgets meant further risk. By not going public, I could keep budgets down and take the company in any direction I wanted with utter autonomy. As long as it was my money at stake.. I was there to instill the virtues and tactics of quick, efficient low-budget filmmaking.'

Mind Warp

The irony is that Boyle had come to Corman in 1974 after having worked for Arkoff; now she was to become senior vice president of production at Filmways Pictures—the inheritors of AIP: 'I've come full circle,' she told *Variety*. Boyle's exit was soon replicated by that of sales manager Roger Lewin, who had just arrived to replace Moreno. Clearly, the writing was on the wall.

Not that this made any difference to the New World publicity machine. More new films were announced in early 1982, including an underwater sci-fi story from Howard Cohen called *Lords of the Deep*, a new script by Robert Freedman for the previously announced *Disc Jockey*, and an $8 million remake of the 1952 Doris Day-starrer *The Winning Team*, which was set to feature Houston Astros pitcher Don Sutton as Hall of Famer Grover Cleveland Alexander, a role played originally by Ronald Reagan. Julie Corman was to produce the film, which was scheduled to begin shooting in November, after the baseball season. Of these three prospects, only *Lords of the Deep* made it out of the batter's box—and that, seven years after the fact.

US theatrical poster for The Slumber Party Massacre

'It takes a lot of love for a person to.. do this.'

—Driller killer Russ Thorn (Michael Villella) in *The Slumber Party Massacre*

In 1979, New World had hired lesbian feminist writer Rita Mae Brown—whose debut novel *Rubyfruit Jungle* had become something of a *cause célèbre* in 1973—to script a contemporary drama called *Room to Move*, about a truck driver who wants to be Fred Astaire. That idea went nowhere, so Brown wrote another script, *Sleepless Nights*, as a spoof of the slasher movie craze. Frances Doel changed the title to *Don't Open the Door*, but the script sat on the shelf for two years.

Enter American Film Institute alumnus Amy Jones, who had started out as an assistant director on *Taxi Driver* and an editor on *Hollywood Boulevard*, *Corvette Summer* (1978) and *Second-Hand Hearts* (1981) before being hired by Steven Spielberg to cut his *ET—The Extra-Terrestrial*.

But what Jones really wanted to do was direct, as she told author John Gaspard in his book *Fast, Cheap and Written That Way*:

> I thought, 'I'll be a film editor unless I make a movie,' so I went back to Roger Corman.. and said, "What would I have to do to be a director?".. He said, "You have to show me that you can do what I do." I had never written anything, so I was looking for an existing script. I went into his library of scripts.. that he hadn't made, and I took several of them. I read one called

Don't Open the Door.. it had a prologue that was about eight pages long. It
had a dialogue scene, a suspense scene and an action scene. I rewrote the
scenes somewhat to make it better, and then I got short ends [leftover film
stock] from shooting projects—my husband was a cinematographer. My
neighbour was a soundman. We borrowed some lights, used our own house.
I did the special effects, and I got UCLA theatre students to act in it. We spent
three days and shot those first eight pages. Then I put them together at night
on Joe Dante's system—he was doing *The Howling.* I would work at night,
after hours, on his Movieola and he gave me some temp music cues. Then
I dropped off this nine-minute reel for Roger.. He called me up and had me
come in and asked me how much it had cost me to do it. And I said it cost
about $2,000.. He said, "You have a future in the business," and asked me
how much I would need to direct the rest of the script. The truth was, I had
never read the rest of the script, all I had read was the first eight pages. So I
just, out of the air, said '$200,000.' And he said, "Let's do it, you're directing
this movie."'

Murderer Russ Thorn escapes from an institution and makes his way to the local high
school; there he begins to stalk the co-eds, four of whom are planning a slumber party.
That night, he kills the girls' boyfriends, their neighbour, a pizza delivery boy and, one
by one, the girls themselves—until only one is left to fight back..

Directing the movie meant that Jones would no longer be available to edit *ET.*
(Carol Littleton took over and received an Oscar nomination.) It also meant that
Brown's script required an overhaul. 'It was a complete mess,' Jones told Gaspard.
'I rewrote [it] in about four weeks as I cast it.' Brown had seen the film differently:
'[It was] made as a straight slasher movie, with no humour, called *Slumber Party*
Massacre,' she wrote in her 1997 autobiography, *Rita Will.* 'I wish they'd had the
guts to do the send-up version because it was pretty funny, on the page anyway.'

Despite Jones's later admission to *Cinefantastique* that her film 'doesn't really
appeal to a feminist impulse in the audience,' *Variety* was still appreciative of her
efforts: 'Convincing lingo, good ensemble performances and funny exaggeration of
the genre's clichés make this a better-than-average teen market entry.' The female
critics of the *LA Times* and the *New York Times* were not so gracious: 'Yet another
reprehensible and gory exploitation movie about a crazed killer who goes around
butchering innocent victims' (Linda Gross); 'The fact that Miss Brown and Miss
Jones have obviously tried to inject a little satire and innovation into the genre just
makes the ultimate vulgarity of their film all the more disappointing' (Janet Maslin).
Cinefantastique's Charlotte Wolter also found the experience off-putting: 'Brown
and.. Jones victimise women on screen as well as any male chauvinist.'

Curiously, *The Slumber Party Massacre* was not advertised as a New World
picture; Corman put it out under the banner of Pacific Films instead. It turned out
to be lightweight at the box office but found an audience on cable and video, which
was enough for Corman to commission not one but three sequels/remakes in 1987,
1990, and 2003.

'It's a new world, with new rules.. learn them.'
—Megalomaniac Colonel Straker (James Wainwright) in *Battletruck*

Futuristic high-speed car chases and crashes had been a New World *forte* with
Death Race 2000 and *Deathsport,* but the venue for such movie mayhem switched
continents in 1979 when Australians George Miller and Byron Kennedy took an
unknown actor named Mel Gibson and put him into the title role of *Mad Max.* Set
in an apocalyptic near future, where law and order have broken down in the wake

of massive oil shortages, *Mad Max* had the highways taken over by roving bands of ruthless thugs. When they murder the family of cop Max Rockatansky, he decides to seek revenge and relentlessly pursues the villains to extinction. The movie was a huge hit in its country of origin and it became a cult film in the US, where it was released in 1980 by AIP/Filmways.

In December 1981, *Mad Max 2* premiered in Australia. Costing $2 million—more than five times the original film—it again featured Gibson as Max, this time wandering the wastelands in search of gasoline when he stumbles across a fortified community built around an old refinery; in exchange for fuel, he agrees to help the inhabitants when they are targeted by another band of motorised renegades. The sequel—released in the US and some other territories as *The Road Warrior*—was a worldwide smash and led to a third outing for Gibson's character in 1985: *Mad Max—Beyond Thunderdome*.

At the same time that *Mad Max 2* was filming in Australia, another post-apocalyptic demolition-derby was being shot to the west in New Zealand. This was not a quickie knock-off, however, but a project which had been percolating in the mind of its creator since 1976, when it was announced to the trades by producer Mark Forstater (*Monty Python and the Holy Grail*) as *Battletruck*.

> *In the not-too-distant future, after the Oil Wars have turned America into a lawless wasteland, Colonel Straker and his crew roam the countryside in an armoured truck in search of plunder. Straker's daughter Corlie runs away; she is pursued by Straker's men but rescued by a lone biker named Hunter, who takes her to the safety of a local commune. Straker's battletruck shows up, and Hunter and Corlie have to convince the inhabitants to fight back against imminent enslavement.*

The original idea for *Battletruck* had come from Harley Cokliss, an expatriate American who had directed children's films (*The Battle of Billy's Pond, Glitterball*) and documentaries for the BBC—one of which happened to be on Roger Corman. After their filming session at Corman's home, Cokliss had mentioned *Battletruck* and Corman had agreed to finance half the project, provided that he and Forstater could come up with the other half.

Fast-forward five years: Forstater had dropped out of *Battletruck* (producing *Xtro* instead), Cokliss had made a name for himself by directing second unit on *Empire Strikes Back*, and *Mad Max 2* was now in production. It was undoubtedly this last item that piqued the interest of New Zealand producers Rob Whitehouse and Lloyd Phillips, who agreed to join Corman in funding the project provided that it was shot on New Zealand's South Island. Cokliss would spend eleven months in production before *Battletruck* was finally ready for release in April 1982.

Unfortunately, *Battletruck*'s opening coincided with Warner's release of *The Road Warrior*, which completely overwhelmed New World's meagre publicity for the film. *Battletruck* found no audience, in the event, but it did find some positive reviews: 'Cokliss.. creates a credible and grim frontier reality. He displays a sure hand in conveying the new-old material' (*Los Angeles Times*); 'A well-made and engaging action picture which should pick up speed in its intended marketplace' (*Variety*); 'Cokliss.. shows real promise in directing his first feature film' (*Cinefantastique*). When the film broke box office records in New Zealand in May, Corman decided to try it again with a new title—*Warlords of the 21st Century*, and the film racked up $3 million in rentals.

Cokliss would go on to direct three more films (*Black Moon Rising, Malone, Dream Demon*) before returning to the TV arena, where he has helmed episodes of series such as *Hercules: The Legendary Journeys, Xena: Warrior Princess, The New Adventures of Robin Hood, Dark Knight*, and *The Immortal*.

'May the best killer win!'
—Nick Carpenter (Frazer Smith), MC for *TAG: The Assassination Game*

The namesake son of a well-known choreographer, Nick Castle had been with John Carpenter since the beginning of his career in films. In 1970, the two had co-written James Rooks's Oscar-winning short *The Resurrection of Bronco Billy*; Castle was also cinematographer, while Carpenter handled editing and composing chores. He had then played an alien and was assistant cameraman on Carpenter's feature debut, *Dark Star*, and Carpenter later recruited him to play the homicidal maniac Michael Myers (aka 'The Shape') in *Halloween*. The two friends went on to write *Escape from New York*.

Castle had written two films on his own—*Skatetown USA* (1979) and *Pray TV* (1980)—and he was looking for a chance to direct. His third solo script was based on a real-life campus phenomenon called TAG—an acronym for 'The Assassination Game'. This time Castle attached himself to the project as its director, and he was given the opportunity to call the shots.

> *Loren Gersh is the five-times undefeated champion of TAG, a game in which college students are given profiles on other players whom they then attempt to 'kill' with dart guns before being tagged themselves. When Gersh is accidentally tagged by another player, he goes berserk and begins to murder the competition for real. The finals come down to Loren and newcomer Susan, and the psychopathic champion is determined to retain his crown at all cost.*

TAG was shot independently in the spring of 1981; New World picked it up that December and announced that it was planning a summer 1982 release with 500 prints, one of the largest openings ever for the company. The print order was subsequently cut back and release brought forward to April, and *TAG* was greeted coldly by both audiences and critics: 'A rather odd thriller with some admirable ambitions never fully realised.. the confusion is bound to create problems of unfulfilled expectations at the box office' (*Variety*); 'Castle.. hasn't come up with enough characterisation or story. Once we're introduced to the game of TAG.. the entire film becomes predictable.. Castle's future films could be interesting—provided they're more personal than *TAG*' (Kevin Thomas). Corman tried out two more titles on *TAG* (*Kiss Me, Kill Me* and *Everybody Gets It in the End*), but he failed to hit the target with either version.

The movie features a fun credits sequence courtesy of New World Venice that spoofs Maurice Binder's classic James Bond titles, and Castle loads his debut with jokey references to *film noir* (a journalist is a Dashiell Hammett fan; Susan repeats Lauren Bacall's famous 'press your lips together and blow' line from *To Have and Have Not*). *TAG* is also good for playing the 'spot-them-before-they-were-famous' game: it was the feature debut for future Oscar-winner Forest Whitaker (*Bird, The Last King of Scotland*), as well as future couple Linda Hamilton—who went on to find fame as Sarah Connor in the *Terminator* movies—and Bruce Abbott (Cain in the *Re-Animator* movies). *TAG* also features a turn by Michael Winslow before he became better known as Sergeant Jones in the *Police Academy* franchise.

Nick Castle went on to direct several films in the '80s and '90s—*The Boy Who Could Fly, Tap, Dennis the Menace, Major Payne*—as well as co-writing two Robin Williams vehicles, *Hook* (1991), and *August Rush* (2007). In recent years, he has directed black-oriented films like *The Seat Filler* (2004) and *Connors' War* (2006) and has been planning a remake of his 1984 hit, *The Last Starfighter*.

> '*I've got a motto: if it moves and it's not one of us, shoot it.*'
> —Federation troubleshooter Mike Colby (Jesse Vint) in *Forbidden World*

Having directed second unit on *Firecracker* and *Smokey Bites the Dust*, and edited *Battle Beyond the Stars*, Allan Holzman wanted his turn in the line for New World's revolving door of directors. Corman pointed out that the sets from *Planet of Horrors* were still standing at the Venice studio and that the rented equipment was not due back until the end of the week. 'Show me what you can do in one day,' he told the 25-year-old AFI graduate.

Holzman grabbed the ball and ran with it: he hired actor Jesse Vint, typed out a makeshift script, and shot 94 set-ups in a single day (breaking Ron Howard's record). He then edited his footage with space battle scenes from *Battle Beyond the Stars* and presented the seven-minute masterpiece to Corman. The president of New World was so impressed by what he saw that he not only gave Holzman a script to shoot—*Mutant*—but asked him to incorporate his test footage into it as a prologue to the film.

> *On the planet Xarbia, an experimental life-form known as Subject 20 has been created by a research group in the hope of staving off a galactic food crisis. But the resultant mutation kills its human host and begins to grow larger and more deadly. Federation trouble-shooter Mike Colby is called in to deal with the threat, but the monster proves invulnerable. As it murders the researchers one by one, it turns their bodies into solid masses of protein that enable it to exist indefinitely. Only one thing can stop the beast: the cancerous liver of an ailing scientist..*

US theatrical poster for Forbidden World

Shot almost entirely at the New World studio in just 20 days for less than $1 million, *Mutant* was an object lesson in improvised filmmaking. Everything from offices to hallways to the studio's exterior was used, and the sets themselves were constructed from egg cartons, milk crates, McDonald's food trays, and PVC piping. To keep his crew focussed on the job in hand, Holzman hired British actress June Chadwick and Pia Zadora-lookalike Dawn Dunlap and undressed them as often as possible (jointly and separately). He also called on future Mechanical and Makeup Imageries head John Carl Buechler (*Re-Animator, From Beyond*) to provide the buckets of blood, including that for the climactic scene where Colby operates on Dr Timbergen (Fox Harris) without the aid of morphine, removes his liver, feeds it to the mutant, and stands back while the monster throws its guts up.

Retitled *Forbidden World* for its release in May 1982, the film earned $4 million in rentals and gained some kind critical words. 'Quite well crafted

under the circumstances,' said *Variety*. 'Pic possesses a fine technical sheen for the budget, with particular kudos going to Tim Suhrstedt's darkly effective lensing. Susan Justin's Giorgio Moroder-like electronic score also helps.' Kevin Thomas called *Forbidden World* 'a lively, amusingly gruesome space-horror show that gives the drive-in trade its money's worth in thrills, chills and laughs while showing off lots of young talent.' The *Chicago Tribune* declared, 'At last, a science fiction film that has it all: sadism, masochism, voyeurism and even a touch of lesbianism.'

Holzman went on from this to exploitation films like *Out of Control, Grunt! The Wrestling Movie* (both 1985), *Programmed to Kill* (1987), and *Critters 2* (1988), before becoming an Emmy Award-winning documentarian with films like *Survivors of the Holocaust* (1996), *Old Man River* (1998), *Sounds of Memphis* (2002), and *A Tribute to Disney's Nine Old Men* (2005).

In 1990, Corman had *Forbidden World* remade as *Dead Space*, with Marc Singer (of *The Beastmaster*) in the Colby role. The plot was essentially the same— although this time the scientists were trying to find a cure for an AIDS-type virus— but the sex and gore quotient was substantially reduced, and the monster was even less convincing than the one that was fabricated by Steve Neill in 1982.

New World was honoured by UCLA that July with a month-long tribute which featured 27 films, beginning with *The Student Nurses* and ending with *Battle Beyond the Stars* (a similar season had been hosted a year earlier at London's National Film Theatre). Corman took advantage of the opportunity to make his now-annual announcement about returning to directing, this time on yet another Al Capone film, featuring small-screen stars Ed Marinaro (*Hill Street Blues*) and Morgan Fairchild (*Flamingo Road*). Like all similar announcements before it, this Corman comeback never happened either—but there was always next year..

'The train runs through this endless flow. It carries on its infinite tracks the hopes, the ambitions and youth of all humanity. And for one youth, the train runs again today.'

—Opening narration to *Galaxy Express 999*

By 1980, Japanese animation—*anime*—was a $500 million business, and the undisputed market-leader was the Toei Company, which had produced the first colour *anime* feature in 1958 (*The Tale of the White Serpent*). Between 1977 and 1980, Toei released three highly successful films based on their *Space Cruiser Yamato* TV series and, in 1979, the company actually had the highest-grossing domestic film of the year with *Galaxy Express 999*, which took in $8 million in Japanese rentals. (Only *Superman*, *Grease*, and *Death on the Nile* earned more.) Created by Leiji Matsumoto, who also authored *Yamato*, *Galaxy Express* began life as a *manga* comic-book in 1977, then it became a TV series the following year, eventually running to 113 episodes before ending in 1981.

Anime had first begun to make in-roads into the US in the 1960s, with the *Astro Boy* and *Speed Racer* series. But it was the success of *Star Wars* and the resultant sci-fi boom that gave *anime* its biggest push in the American market. In the spring of 1978, the Japanese animated teleseries *Gatchaman* (1972-74) was dubbed, rescored, and re-edited into *Battle of the Planets*. Over 85 episodes, the series pitted the G-Force—a team of five orphans headquartered at a secret base beneath the Pacific Ocean—and their robot commander 7-Zark-7 against the evil alien forces of Spectra. *Battle of the Planets* was so successful that the TV serial from which Toei's *Yamato* films had been culled was also Americanised and shown as *Star Blazers* in 1979-81; its 78 episodes told of a derelict Japanese battleship that is retrofitted for space combat against the evil Gamilan Empire.

Recognising *anime*'s new-found American appeal, New World had acquired the American distribution rights to the *Galaxy Express* feature in December 1979 and announced the film for release the following May. Corman then had a change of heart and shelved the picture, eventually selling it to cable television where it premiered in March 1981. However, future video deals were dependent on films having theatrical releases. Not wishing to leave anything to chance, he arranged to give *Galaxy Express* a token outing in New York theatres in July 1982.

> *When his mother is killed by robot hunter Count Mecha, young Tetsuro vows revenge. Accompanied by the mysterious Maetel, Tetsuro boards the Galaxy Express in pursuit of Mecha's Time Castle. Along the way, the rocket-train encounters the pirate ships of Captain Harlock and Queen Emeraldas. Tetsuro kills Mecha and vows to destroy the Mechanised Homeworld of Queen Promethium, where men are turned into machines; what he does not realise, however, is that his companion on the journey is actually the queen's daughter—Princess Maetel.*

As with all of New World's other Asian films, *Galaxy Express* was cut by over 40 minutes: out went the developing romance between Tetsuro and Maetel (which had an incestuous overtone, given that she reminded him of his mother) as well as his involvement with a train stewardess; Queen Emeraldas pining for her own lost love was also all-but eliminated. What remained was then dubbed and the names were changed—Tetsuro became 'Joey Smith', Harlock became 'Warlock', Techiro became 'Sundown', and so on.

When the *Galaxy Express* TV show came off-air in Japan, another feature— *Adieu Galaxy Express 999*—was released, which closed the book on the concept until 1998, when Toei made a new film: *Galaxy Express 999—Eternal Fantasy*. Its success paved the way for a direct-to-video miniseries in 2000 (*Maetel Legend*) and a short-lived TV serial in 2004-05 (*Space Symphony Maetel*). While other *animes* has achieved mainstream success in the US through mass-marketed shows like *Robotech*, *Dragon Ball Z*, *Pokemon*, and *Yu-Gi-Oh!*, *Galaxy Express* remains largely unknown outside of its native country.

'I don't know about any [lethal] telephones.. and what you know gets you less than bus fare.'
—Phone company exec (Alan Scarfe) to Nat Bridger (Richard Chamberlain) in *The Calling*

The summer of 1982 saw another belated New World release with the August premiere of *The Calling*, which had been shot in Toronto two years earlier under the title of *Bells*. After the huge success of the TV miniseries *Shogun* in September 1980, TV's former *Dr Kildare*, Richard Chamberlain, was again hot stuff. He took the lead in *Bells* solely because he wanted to remodel his house, but his presence made the piece attractive to Roger Corman, who promptly snapped up the rights and announced it for release towards the end of the year.

Bells did not ring, however, and it was put on hold until Chamberlain's early 1982 landing of the male lead in the highly-anticipated *The Thorn Birds* miniseries put him back in the press. Renewed interest in Chamberlain gave Corman impetus to dust off *Bells* and rechristen it *The Calling* for an initial engagement in Atlanta.

riginal poster for Bells (The Calling)

Heading to Toronto for a symposium, ecology professor Nat Bridger offers to collect the belongings of a student who is alleged to have died of a heart attack in the subway. Bridger discovers that the girl was a victim of a vindictive phone company employee, out to revenge himself on those who have stolen from him; he has engineered a device that can send electromagnetic pulses down phone lines, incinerating those on the other end. The phone company is aware of the threat but has been trying to cover it up so as not to spread panic. Bridger soon finds himself targeted not only by the company, but by the killer whose identity he is beginning to suspect.

In fashioning *The Calling*, Corman had cut 10 minutes from *Bells*, including much of co-star John Houseman's role as Bridger's former mentor, who is secretly in league with the phone company's cover-up. The courtship between Bridger and artist Ridley Taylor (Sara Botsford) was also abridged. *The Calling* played through the fall in places like Denver and Indianapolis, but it never picked up an audience. In December, Corman changed the title again to *Murder by Phone* for its Chicago and New York releases, but the movie was itself murdered by the critics: 'Exhibits a penchant for robbing the most trite and contrived elements from third-rate late shows' (*Chicago Daily Herald*); 'The lighting is poor; the acting is pure ham; the overall product takes itself surprisingly seriously' (*Chicago Tribune*); 'A sorry excuse for a horror/ sci-fi programmer.. it's due for a quick playoff' (*Variety*). Only *Cinefantastique* saw a bright side: 'Thoroughly absurd but consistently engaging; one of [director Michael] Anderson's few satisfying films.'

In looking at New World's fall release schedule, Corman told *Variety*, 'I really do believe we'll have more releases than any other company.' Once again, New

World was betting heavily on a Thanksgiving family picture—*Jimmy the Kid*, in this instance, featuring pint-sized Gary Coleman, star of TV's hit sitcom *Diff'rent Strokes*. Unlike the Don Knotts-Tim Conway comedies, *Jimmy* was slated to open nationwide and Corman was anticipating between $4 and $5 million in advances and guarantees on the back of it.

The rest of New World's fall slate was a mixture of in-house genre pictures (*Android, Sorceress*), foreign films (*Fitzcarraldo, Next Year If All Goes Well*), and independent pick-ups (*The Funny Farm, The Personals, Time Walker, Utilities*). Newly-appointed general sales manager (the company's third in a year) Elliot Slutzky told *Variety* that New World's strategy was to focus on 'more mainstream, wider appeal-type movies. It gives us a chance to make our pictures more successful.'

> *'I shall move a mountain.'*
> —Entrepreneurial opera fan Brian Sweeney Fitzgerald (Klaus Kinski) in *Fitzcarraldo*

Having already notched up two notable foreign releases for 1982 (*Christiane F* and *Three Brothers* had each brought $2 million in rentals), New World's German co-venture, *Fitzcarraldo*, had its American premiere in October. That the film was finished at all was a testament to the determination of its writer-producer-director Werner Herzog who, along with Rainer Werner Fassbinder and Wim Wenders, was at the forefront of the New German Cinema which had emerged in the '70s. In Les Blank's 1982 documentary on the making of *Fitzcarraldo*, *Burden of Dreams*, Herzog gave his reason for what drove him to spend four years on the production: 'If I abandon this project, I would be a man without dreams, and I don't want to live like that.'

The planning of the film had begun in 1978 and pre-production on the Peru-Ecuadorian border had started the following year, but trouble with the locals and a simmering border war had forced Herzog to pull his crew out of the jungle. A new Peruvian location was found and shooting started in January 1981, but it was suspended five weeks later when star Jason Robards contracted amoebic dysentery and had to return to America for treatment. On the orders of his doctor, Robards refused to return to Peru (he and Herzog subsequently sued each other for breach of contract). While Herzog cast about for a replacement for Robards, co-star Mick Jagger also exited the production due to his commitment to the upcoming Rolling Stones album *Tattoo You*. Rather than try to replace both leading actors, Herzog chose instead to scrap Jagger's role as Robards's right-hand man.

In desperation, Herzog turned to the actor with whom he had worked three times previously—Klaus Kinski. The two had collaborated on *Aguirre, The Wrath of God* (1972), *Nosferatu the Vampyre*, and *Woyzeck* (both 1979). Shooting on *Fitzcarraldo* resumed in April, with Claudia Cardinale (who was playing Molly, a brothel-keeper, and the title character's love interest) having to re-shoot all of the scenes that she had already filmed with Robards.

> *After seeing his idol, opera-singer Enrico Caruso, in Lima, Brian Sweeney Fitzgerald—known as 'Fitzcarraldo'—determines to build an opera house in Iquitos on the Amazon River. Fitzgerald realises that the only way to raise enough money in Peru is through the rubber trade; he sets out to claim the rubber trees that lie deep in the jungle region of the Campas Indians. Fitzgerald heads south by steamship but finds his path blocked by an isthmus between two rivers. The indians see Fitzgerald as the god of an ancient prophecy and agree to help him haul the boat overland. After a huge effort, they make it to the other side but as Fitzgerald nears his goal, the indians conspire to use his ship to appease the demons of the Pongo Das Mortes—the Rapids of Death.*

In many ways, *Fitzcarraldo* is Herzog's *Apocalypse Now*. Both films share a tropical river odyssey, were years in the making, had to replace their leading actors (on *Apocalypse*, Captain Willard was originally played by Harvey Keitel before he was fired and replaced by Martin Sheen), dealt with numerous logistical problems on location, and were chronicled in on-set documentaries (*Apocalypse* was the subject of 1991's *Hearts of Darkness: A Filmmaker's Apocalypse*). They are both also magnificent cinematic experiences.

Released to wide acclaim in Germany in March 1982, the film was nominated for the *Palme d'Or* at the Cannes Film Festival and won it for Best Director. In anticipation of *Fitzcarraldo*'s US release, Roger Corman told Marilyn Beck, 'It's turned out great, a really big motion picture. It's ended up costing $8 million—more than Herzog has ever spent making a movie.'

As far as American critics were concerned, it was money well spent. Vincent Canby called *Fitzcarraldo* 'A stunning spectacle, an adventure-comedy not quite like any other, and the most benign movie ever made about 19th-century capitalism running amok.' Roger Ebert declared it to be a film that he would 'not have missed for the world.' Gene Siskel found it 'a primordial experience.' Kevin Thomas judged it to be 'a fabulous one-of-a-kind movie, the logical, inevitable film from.. Herzog in his quest to express the extremes of human experience.' *Variety* called the German director's labour of love 'an adult daydream. A magnificent one at that.' *Fitzcarraldo* was nominated for Best Foreign Film at both the British BAFTA awards and the Golden Globes, and its rental take of $2 million was far and away the most that a Herzog movie had ever made in the States.

Herzog and Kinski followed up *Fitzcarraldo* with *Cobra Verde* in 1987. Based on Bruce Chatwin's 1980 novel *The Viceroy of Ouidah*, it told of a larger-than-life African slave trader not unlike the previous film's Fitzgerald. *Cobra Verde* ended the temperamental relationship between Herzog and an increasingly paranoid and misanthropic Kinski, who used his 1988 autobiography *All I Need is Love* to rant against the director. Kinski died of a heart attack in November 1991, at the age of 65, which gave Herzog the last word with the release of the documentary *My Best Fiend* (1999), a personal chronicle of his collaborations with the actor.

> *'We're not made to be governed by the whims of men.'*
> —Android Cassandra (Kendra Kirchner) in *Android*

Aaron Lipstadt first set foot in the offices of New World in 1980, ostensibly to interview Roger Corman for a dissertation at Chicago's Northwestern University. His PhD plans were put on hold, however, when Corman hired the 27-year-old on the spot to be assistant production manager on *Battle Beyond the Stars*. Lipstadt

Android (Don Opper)

met fellow Chicagoan Don Opper at the Venice studio, where Opper was working as a carpenter; the two hit it off, and what had started with stick-ball in the hallway soon turned into a more creative association.

Two years later, the pair grabbed an opportunity to put their ideas into action. 'Roger.. intimated that he wanted to make another movie on the sets of *Forbidden World*,' Lipstadt told the *Chicago Tribune*. 'So Don and another staff carpenter [Jim Reigle] wrote the *Android* script. Don and I came up with half the financing, and asked for Roger's approval. It was practically a risk-free venture for him, so he couldn't bring himself to say no.'

Since he had directed second unit on *Forbidden World*, Lipstadt knew his way around the sets fairly well, but Corman remained determined that the new kids on the block should not over-extend themselves. 'Roger made us re-write that script over and over,' Opper told the *Tribune*, 'telling us to drop characters, delete special effects, cut any outdoor location scenes. On our budget, he said, we'd better skip the *Flash Gordon* approach. He suggested we shoot from as far back as possible to make the sets look bigger than they are. And he always advised diagonal angles to give the illusion of depth and spaciousness.'

> In 2036, the only inhabitants of space station UL-C53 are Dr Daniel and android Max 404. But Daniel is intent on creating a female android named Cassandra; once she is operational, he will have no more need for Max. Three fugitives arrive at the station; when two of them are murdered by the third, Daniel programs Max to exact revenge. Cassandra is brought to life, but she soon makes it clear that she has no intention of taking orders from Daniel..

The major coup that Lipstadt and Opper were able to pull off in relation to *Android* was in getting a copy of the script to Klaus Kinski, via Les Blank. After his seven-month *Fitzcarraldo* shoot, Kinski was no doubt eager to do something quick and easy, and he had found *Android*'s Dr Daniel just the ticket. 'He's famous for turning down fantastic directors if the pay isn't right,' said Lipstadt, 'but he'll work with a nobody if it is.'

'The idea was to make a science-fiction picture unlike *Star Wars* or anything of that ilk,' the young director continued. 'My idea of a science-fiction film is one that tells us something about the present, from the vantage point of the future. I prefer a science-fiction film for the mind.' Given an advance screening in October 1982, *Variety* felt Lipstadt and company had achieved that goal: '*Android* is both one of the best low budget sci-fiers and the most interesting in-house New World production to come down the pike in some time. Making the most of its severe monetary limitations and consistently applying wit and intelligence to formulaic genre requirements, pic will particularly delight cognoscenti of futurism, ensuring cult status.'

Unfortunately for the film's makers, Roger Corman was not quite sure what to do with *Android*. It showcased some good model and make-up effects work from the Venice Studio (James Cameron had been design consultant), but with no blood or sex and comparatively little action, it presented a marketing challenge. 'Roger was planning to market the picture as a space exploitation film, which we knew wouldn't work,' said Lipstadt. 'If people went into that film expecting sex and special effects, they were going to be sorely disappointed.'

Rather than sit by and let that happen, Lipstadt and Opper (along with Rupert Harvey and Opper's brother Barry) formed their own company, SHO Films, and bought *Android* from New World. After some play-dates in Europe, Android had its first US screening at the Chicago International Film Festival in November 1983. It was there that it acquired a distributor in Island Alive Films, which opened the film in Chicago and New York in February 1984, and in Los Angeles two months later. The movie garnered good notices in all three cities, including from Vincent Canby ('an essentially cheerful, knowing little science-fiction film that positively celebrates the shoestring on which it was made'), Judith Crist ('a jim-dandy science-fiction movie with a brain, a sense of humour and an offbeat plot to please non-sci-fiers as well'), Gene Siskel ('A clever, funny sci-fi adventure that is a more auspicious filmmaking debut than was George Lucas' heavy, similarly themed *THX 1138*') and Kevin Thomas ('the kind of low-budget, high-imagination science-fiction film that acquires a cult').

Lipstadt and Opper were able to capitalise on their *Android* reviews to mount another sci-fi project, the poorly received *City Limits* (1985). From there, the two split up, with Lipstadt becoming both a producer/director on TV shows like *The Marshal, The Division* and *Medium*, while Don Opper pursued an acting career in addition to writing and producing Wayne Wang's *Slam Dance* (1987).

> '*Is it unrealistic to think that a relationship can last?*'
> —Single White Male Bill Henrikson (Bill Schoppert) in *The Personals*

Based in Minneapolis, Minnesota, 30-year-old Peter Markle had been making documentaries, industrial films and commercials. None of his output had caught the attention of Hollywood, so he teamed up with real estate investor Patrick Wells to make a short about the dating scene. 'About $40,000 in, we realised we didn't have a prayer of getting the money back from a short film,' Markle told the *Los Angeles Times*—so the two instead created a limited partnership with shares going for $15,000 apiece and raised a total of $375,000. With that budget, Markle wrote and directed, and Wells produced, their debut feature: *The Personals*.

Recently divorced, publisher Bill Henrikson places an ad in the personal column of his local paper. He is shocked by the number of replies he receives but manages to find a partner in a psychologist named Adrienne. However, it turns out that she is married and that her husband is unwilling to let go easily—a point driven home forcibly when he disrupts their rendezvous at an art museum. Rather than be one side of a triangle, Henrikson heads back to the 'personals' to try again.

Filmed entirely in Minneapolis using local talent, *The Personals* rode the film festival circuit, where its good word-of-mouth eventually reached the ear of Roger Corman. Markle's opus was an economical way to add some diversity to the New World line-up, so Corman bought the film and set out a six-month release pattern. 'With a neutral title and a cast of unknowns, *The Personals* has little going for it other than that it's a terrific little picture,' observed *Variety*, but Kevin Thomas begged to differ: '*The Personals* has everything going for it: a fresh premise, fresh faces and even a fresh setting.' Vincent Canby did not sense freshness, but he did admit that Markle 'appeared to be a funny man, and though the butts of his jokes aren't entirely new, his manner is pleasingly light.' *The Washington Post* was similarly impressed, finding *The Personals* an 'admirably polished and attractive low-budget gem.'

The Personals' rental tally of $2 million was solid enough for Markle to be handed the same amount to make another film, MGM/UA's ski comedy *Hot Dog: The Movie* (1984). Thereafter he made a hockey film (*Youngblood*) and a Vietnam War movie (*Bat*21) before settling into television, where has directed numerous episodes of hit shows like *The X Files, CSI* and *Without a Trace*, as well as topical TV movies like *Saving Jessica Lynch* (2003), the John McCain biopic *Faith of My Fathers* (2005) and the 9/11 drama *Flight 93* (2006), which earned him an Emmy Award nomination for Best Director.

> '*Even the gods will do as I command!*'
> —Evil sorcerer Traigon (Robert Ballesteros) in *Sorceress*

In December 1932, Texan writer Robert E Howard published 'The Phoenix on the Sword,' the first of what would be a long-running series of stories in *Weird Tales* magazine featuring Conan the Barbarian. By the time of his suicide in June 1936, Howard had written twenty-one Conan stories, seventeen of which had been published. In 1955, L Sprague de Camp began to adapt Howard's non-Conan tales into Conan adventures also; this cross-fertilisation of the two strands of Howard's work laid the foundation for a whole new series of Conan epics that began in 1966, were mostly written by Camp and Lin Carter, and featured evocative (and erotic) cover art by Frank Frazetta. In 1970, Marvel Comics published a comic book based on the character of Conan; in 1974, the series expanded to two separate titles.

Plans for a film based on Conan were first announced by producer Edward R Pressman in 1975, based on a script by Edward Summer (who was also slated to direct) and Roy Thomas. But by the time the film went into production in January 1981, that script had been completely overhauled by Oliver Stone and new director John Milius. The final $20 million Dino De Laurentiis production of *Conan the Barbarian* earned $23 million in rentals during its 1982 release and represented a breakthrough role for beefcake action-hero and future California governor Arnold Schwarzenegger (who reprised the role two years later in the less-successful *Conan the Destroyer*). The film was also the centrepiece of a sword-and-sorcery craze in the early '80s, which was heavily influenced by the runaway success of role-playing board game *Dungeons and Dragons*. Between 1981 and 1984, films such as *Ator, The Beastmaster, Dragonslayer, Excalibur, Hercules, Krull*, and *The Sword and the Sorcerer* all featured some Howardesque combination of muscles, monsters, magic, mirth, and mammaries.

Though he stumbled at first with the non-starters *Hawk the Slayer* and *Alaric the Avenger*, Roger Corman nevertheless took to the sword-and-sorcery genre like a duck to water. In anticipation of *Conan*, he had had Jim Wynorski write a script called *The Barbarian*, which was then handed over to be reworked, produced, and directed by Jack Hill. After being ejected from *The Bees*, Hill had paid the rent by writing Canadian tax-shelter movies for one-time Fox producer Sandy Howard, including *City on Fire* (1979) and *Death Ship* (1980), and he had been looking for something splashier to get him back into the thick of things. '[Roger] had this special effects house.. that was doing really good work, and he wanted to do a really big-looking movie, so I went for it,' Hill revealed to website CineSchlock-O-Rama. 'That's what I needed. A movie that looked big and flashy to get me out of the category of shoestring budget movies.'

> *Evil sorcerer Traigon tries to sacrifice his children to the god Kalgara but their mother refuses; for this, she is hunted down and killed. When the first of Traigon's three lives is taken by the wizard Krona, Traigon's twins are put into his care and bestowed with magical powers. Twenty years later, their father is resurrected and renews his search for the twins. Helped by a Nordic warrior, a goat-man, and an amorous thief, Mira and Mara seek to end Traigon's reign of terror. A climactic confrontation takes place on the celestial plain, where the gods themselves join in the battle.*

Shot in Mexico as a co-production of New World and CONACINE (producers of *Foxtrot*), *The Barbarian* was the screen debut of the 27-year-old Harris twins, Leigh Ann and Lynette, who had been featured in a *Playboy* spread in March 1981. The two subsequently became the in-house playmates of octogenarian Milwaukee millionaire David Kritzik, who spent half-a-million dollars on each of them before his death in 1989. The following year, they were convicted of income tax evasion for never having declared their honorariums, but the conviction was overturned in 1991 when they successfully convinced the court that the monies were a gift and therefore non-taxable.

Roger Corman was no David Kritzik, and despite his promises to Hill, he was determined not to lavish any extra attention on *The Barbarian*. 'He simply tried to get out of it [as] cheaply as he could,' Hill told *Fangoria*, 'because he'd lost $2 million in that year on other pictures. He was desperate. He didn't do sound effects, he didn't do special effects, he dubbed in all the actors' voices with secretaries from the office and students. He used music just patched in hastily from other pictures [*Battle Beyond the Stars, Humanoids from the Deep, Piranha*], which didn't fit at all, and it was just totally a mess.' Intent on limiting the damage to his reputation, Hill gave the screenplay credit solely to Wynorski and directorial credit to the fictional 'Brian Stuart'.

Critics tended to agree with Hill's assessment when the finished result, cut by twenty minutes and retitled *Sorceress,* was released in October 1982. 'The film.. is so poorly lit that we miss much of its murky plot and the rinky-dink special effects,' said the *Los Angeles Times*. 'The phoney beards, tacky sets and silly jokes make *Sorceress* resemble the quaint soft-core porn pageants (eg *The Lustful Turk*) of the 1960s,' observed *Variety*. 'If you have trouble getting sword and sorcery adventures out of your system, this film might make a good laxative,' advised *Cinefantastique*.

Two rather astounding things happened to *Sorceress*, however. The first was a relatively glowing review from the usually glum Dann Gire of the *Chicago Daily Herald*: 'Despite gaping flaws, *Sorceress* keeps things moving with a sense of high camp throughout, making it the best film New World Pictures has produced in years.' The second was the fact that it made $4 million in rentals. 'The distribution department was quite astonished,' said Hill, 'because they had not planned on it being held over anywhere. They figured a weekend and out, but it was getting holdovers and they weren't ready for it. It messed up their whole schedule, and they had to make new prints.'

Sorceress meant the end of the line for Jack Hill and Roger Corman—the two never worked together again. Neither did Hill ever direct another feature, though he has enjoyed a revival of interest in his work recently, thanks mainly to his chief advocate, Quentin Tarantino. 'In spite of all his craziness, Roger gave me my first break,' Hill later acknowledged. 'He gave Francis his first break; so many people.. He would trust us to do things that nobody else would've done. And we could get going that way, get a start. And I think we all feel to a certain extent grateful for Roger.'

'You look for your mummy, doctor. I'm looking for a murderer.'
—No-nonsense cop Lt Plummer (Darwin Joston) in *Time Walker*

The discovery in 1922 by archaeologist Howard Carter of Tutankhamen's tomb received worldwide press coverage and sparked a renewed public interest in all things ancient Egyptian, but it was not until the treasures of the tomb were put on display at the British Museum in 1972 that the boy-pharaoh became a full-fledged phenomenon. The exhibits travelled the world, and 'King Tut'

US theatrical poster for *Sorceress*

mania swept America during the 'Treasures of Tutankhamen' tour between 1976 and '79, which was patronised by over eight million people.

Comedian Steve Martin enjoyed a Top 20 hit with his 1978 novelty song 'King Tut', and several movies exploited the craze, including *Cruise into Terror* (1978), *The Awakening, The Curse of King Tut's Tomb* (both 1980), *Dawn of the Mummy*, and *Sphinx* (both 1981). In March 1982, production began at the California State University's Northridge campus on *Pharaoh*, a different kind of mummy movie— one that would combine the myth of revivified Egyptian corpses with the science fiction of Steven Spielberg's *Close Encounters of the Third Kind* (1977) and yet-to-be-released *ET*.

> While exploring Tutankhamen's tomb, archaeologist Doug McCadden comes across a hidden chamber containing a sarcophagus. Back in the States, he opens it and finds a mummy inside covered in a toxic mold; a dose of x-rays reanimates the mummy, and it sets out to recover crystals that were stolen by a radiologist. Deciphering an ancient scroll, McCadden discovers that the mummy is actually an alien! The being needs the crystals for a device which will allow it to transport itself back to its home planet—and it will kill anyone who stands in its way.

Produced independently on a budget of $750,000, *Pharaoh* was a veritable who's-who of B movie and TV talent, with a cast that included Nina Axelrod (*Motel Hell*), Antoinette Bower (*Prom Night*), Darwin Joston (*Eraserhead*), James Karen (*Frankenstein Meets the Space Monster*), Ben Murphy (*Alias Smith and Jones*), Melissa Prophet (*Van Nuys Blvd*) and Austin Stoker (*Assault on Precinct 13*). The

film was co-written and co-produced by Jason Williams, star of 1972's X-rated *Flesh Gordon*, and directed by Tom Kennedy, editor of *Joe* and the X-rated version of *Uncle Tom's Cabin* (also 1972).

Pharaoh was pre-sold to New World and retitled *Time Walker* for its October release. It left critics unimpressed—'The sight of a bandaged actor or mannequin obviously being wheeled along through billowing fog elicits more laughs than gasps' (*Chicago Daily Herald*); '*Time Walker*.. has been cut and conceived like those old-fashioned serials or daily soap operas. That means there has been no attempt made to develop a straightforward plot line' (*LA Times*)—but its $2 million in rentals made a nice return on a relatively modest investment.

'I read a lot, think a lot.. go the psychiatrist a lot.'
—Adolescent abductee Jimmy Lovejoy (Gary Coleman) in *Jimmy the Kid*

In 1976, show-biz lawyers Harry Evans Sloan and Lawrence Kuppin set up shop in Hollywood and quickly built up a client list that included TV stars Gary Coleman, Erik Estrada, Ron Howard and Henry Winkler. The pair became known for negotiating lucrative deals on behalf of their clients, as well as helping them to form their own production companies, such as the 13-year-old Coleman's Zephyr Productions.

Coleman's deal with NBC-TV called for Zephyr to produce one two-hour film for every year that the hit show *Diff'rent Strokes* was on the air (it ran from 1978 to

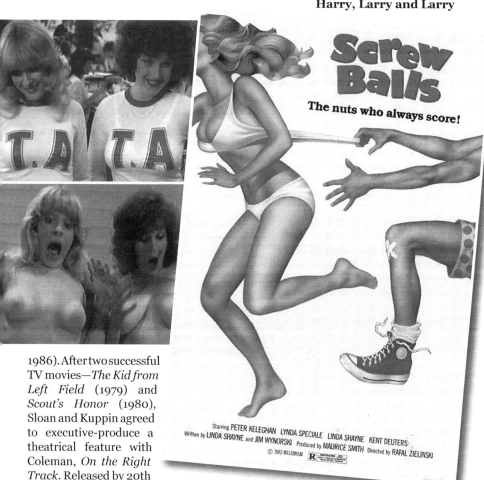

Screw Balls
The nuts who always score!

Starring PETER KELEGHAN LYNDA SPECIALE LINDA SHAYNE KENT DEUTERS
Written by LINDA SHAYNE and JIM WYNORSKI Produced by MAURICE SMITH Directed by RAFAL ZIELINSKI
© 1983 MILLENIUM R

1986). After two successful TV movies—*The Kid from Left Field* (1979) and *Scout's Honor* (1980), Sloan and Kuppin agreed to executive-produce a theatrical feature with Coleman, *On the Right Track*. Released by 20th Century-Fox in 1981, the film earned $5.5 million in rentals—a decent return given the movie's $2.5 million budget. That same summer, Sloan/Kuppin/Zephyr began production of another Coleman theatrical feature, *Jimmy the Kid*.

The film was based on a 1974 novel by crime writer Donald E Westlake, which concerned a quintet of small-time New York crooks who read a book called *Child Heist* and use it as a blueprint to kidnap a youth and hold him for ransom. Their target is a 12-year-old genius and aspiring film director named Jimmy Harrington, and they abduct him and take him to an abandoned farmhouse, from where they demand $150,000 for his release. The money is delivered—but with a transmitter that lets the FBI know the gang's location; Jimmy helps the gang to escape through the woods but on reaching a subway station, they realise that they have been had— Jimmy has stolen the money! Some time later, a movie about the kidnapping of a child genius opens in New York, directed by Jimmy Harrington..

While the basic plot of the book was retained, several changes were made in its transition to the screen. The setting was switched to Los Angeles, but the film-making angle was jettisoned (though it turns out that Jimmy himself wrote *Child Heist*). In the novel, Jimmy is the son of a high-powered corporate attorney; the film has Jimmy's parents performing an Ike and Tina Turner-type soul act known

221

as Herb and Nina. Herb owns his own detective agency, fronted by a lame-brain named Walker, which substitutes for the book's FBI investigation.

With Coleman backed up by a cast that included Don Adams (*Get Smart*), Ruth Gordon (*Every Which Way But Loose*), Paul LeMat (*American Graffiti*), Cleavon Little (*Blazing Saddles*), Pat Morita (*Happy Days*), and Dee Wallace (*ET*), Sloan and Kuppin were confident that Fox would be eager to release *Jimmy the Kid*; they were surprised to discover otherwise. 'They told us that they weren't that excited unless the movie could generate huge grosses,' Sloan told the *Los Angeles Times*. 'We got an equally lukewarm reception from the other majors.'

The film remained unsold for nearly a year, until Sloan and Kuppin took it to Roger Corman, who agreed to make it New World's Christmas holiday release for 1982. Premiering in November, *Jimmy the Kid* received mixed reviews, with Gene Siskel calling it 'precisely the kind of passé kiddie film that even Walt Disney Productions stopped making last year.' *Variety* felt differently—'There's enough going on to intrigue and tickle the younger viewing segment'—as did the *LA Times*: 'The film is amusing, lightweight, television-sitcom fare that probably works fairly well as fantasy entertainment for young children.'

Coleman was undeniably a draw with youngsters, and *Jimmy the Kid* pulled in $5 million in rentals, making it New World's most successful film in nearly two years. Sloan and Kuppin were delighted—and then intrigued.. 'Roger pointed out something to me that I hadn't thought about,' Sloan told the *Times*. 'There were four [main] companies [AIP, Allied Artists, Avco Embassy, New World] distributing lower-budget films—or so-called 'B' movies in the '70s. As we sat with him in 1982, [three] had all but disappeared.. What Roger was questioning was whether or not he wanted to invest the kind of money necessary to take advantage of that situation and fill the vacuum now left by the others.' He did not—but Sloan and Kuppin *did*.

In his autobiography, Corman wrote, 'I had a reputation, I had offers to make bigger films. But once New World built up momentum, there was no getting out.' Sloan and Kuppin—who were soon joined by a third partner, producer/manager Larry Thompson (the trio became known as Harry, Larry and Larry)—were to be a get-out clause from what Corman termed 'the albatross of distribution.' And the timing could not have been better: 'Growth was slowing,' he wrote. 'The New World formulas.. weren't working as well in the changing theatrical and pay markets.. we were making fewer movies. The market for low-budget exploitation films was shrinking because the majors were making the same kind of films.. at an average cost of $15 to $20 million and getting much bigger production value on the screen.'

After almost three months of intense negotiations, Roger Corman agreed to sell New World Pictures to Harry, Larry and Larry for $16.5 million. Corman's original asking price had been $22 million; the three suitors had originally offered between $12 and $15 million. The sale would become official in February 1983, and Corman agreed to remain with the company as a consultant for two years. During the first year he would produce exclusively for New World; after that, New World would have first-look privileges on his projects for another year. In a non-competition clause which would come back to haunt the deal, Corman also agreed not to form a new distribution company.

For their millions, according to *Variety*, Harry, Larry and Larry got 'the film library, which includes both domestic exploitationers and foreign art-house items; the New World distribution organisation, which consists of 11 domestic distribution branches and a joint venture for distribution in Canada; an ongoing company with a name recognised by exhibitors and industryites; filmmaking equipment, and assorted 'financial assets' which were not otherwise identified or detailed.' As

Corman wrote, 'It was a good deal for them: they got a turnkey operation. They were overnight operators of a going and internationally respected concern. They wouldn't have to start from scratch and spend five years building.' The only things the deal did not cover were New World's Brentwood offices and the Venice Studio, both of which were to remain in Corman's hands (though Harry, Larry and Larry rented New World's office space for six months before moving to more high-end digs in Century City).

The policy of New World's new owners was outlined to *Variety* accordingly: 'We believe the domestic market for commercial and exploitable theatrical films is stronger than ever. One of our major objectives will be to attract major theatrical motion picture talent who will make a broad spectrum of motion pictures with proper financial responsibility.' Their stated aim was to distribute eighteen to twenty pictures a year and to produce films in the $5 million category. Before that could happen, however, the new ownership was contractually bound to distribute what was left over from Corman's watch—two Canadian comedies (*Funny Farm* and *Utilities*), a French comedy (*Next Year If All Goes Well*), a horror film made by porn producers (*The Prey*), and the last two films to enter production under Corman's aegis, the teen comedy *Crazy Times* and the drama *My Love Letters*. All but the latter two were pick-ups that had been sitting on the shelf for as long as three years; not surprisingly, they were given only the token releases necessary to fulfil their video distribution contracts.

'I'm not about to have a few bad seeds take root, contaminating my divine garden of higher education!'
—Principal Stuckoff (Donnie Bowes) in *Screwballs*

While Corman took most of the staff from the Brentwood office across the street and set up shop as Millennium Films, the new management at New World took advantage of the 1983 Cannes Film Festival to announce a production slate of five multi-million dollar features. They included the $3 million prostitution drama *Angel*, the $3.5 million horror spoof *Mark of the Devil* (aka *Oh Hell*), the $4 million Vietnam actioner *The Eleventh Parallel*, and two $9 million features from director Ron Howard—time-travel sci-fier *The Philadelphia Experiment* (executive produced by John Carpenter) and Greenpeace flag-waver *Rainbow Warrior*. The catch was that the first film off the assembly line, *Angel*, would not be ready for release until January 1984.

For the time being, New World had to make do with what they had, which was a gross-out comedy that had been shot in Canada in October 1982 under a title of *Crazy Times*. The previous March, another juvenile Canadian smut-fest, *Porky's*, had been released by 20th Century-Fox and become a runaway smash, earning $55.5 million in rentals. *Porky's II: The Next Day* was already in production for a June 1983 release, but New World was able to get its *Porky's* clone—now retitled *Screwballs*—into theatres a full month before.

At Taft & Adams ('T&A') High School, Peter, Brent, Howie, Melvin and Tim are put in detention thanks to the school's one remaining virgin, Purity Busch; they make a pact to catch Purity naked, but all their efforts are thwarted. Finally they sabotage Purity's Homecoming Queen dress so that it can be ripped off by a giant magnet, exposing her assets for all to see.

The film had been written by the suddenly prolific Jim Wynorski, along with actress Linda Shayne, who had appeared as Miss Salmon in *Humanoids from the*

Deep and featured in *Screwballs* as the buxom Bootsie Goodhead. Wynorski and Shayne also served as 'creative consultants' on the $800,000 film, which Corman told *Variety* 'might herald a step back to reality,' given the rising costs of Canadian production. *Variety* offered the closest thing to a good review that something like *Screwballs* could hope for: 'This compendium of horny high school jokes is full of youthful exuberance and proves utterly painless to watch,' its critic opined, but the *New York Times* was not so charitable, judging *Screwballs* to be 'afflicted with an intermittent greenish tint, bereft of adequate acting, starved for wit and originality, generally miscast and directed with a palpable lack of grace.' The *Chicago Daily Herald* was slightly more succinct: '*Screwballs* is so low class, it gives teenybopper sexploitation a bad name.'

Although the film only managed $1.4 million in rentals, it did well on video, prompting producer Maurice Smith and director Rafal Zielinski to make a follow-up for Corman in 1985 called *Loose Screws*. A third entry—*Screwball Hotel*—was produced for Universal in 1988.

> '*Sometimes it's right to do the wrong thing.. isn't it?*'
> —Lovesick disc jockey Anna Winter (Jamie Lee Curtis) in *Love Letters*

While the finishing touches were being put to the deal with Harry, Larry and Larry, Corman green-lit *My Love Letters*, which made it noteworthy as both the last feature of the old New World and the first for Millennium Films. In producing the 30-day, $600,000 feature, Corman was making good on a promise that he had made to himself some years before. After *I Never Promised You a Rose Garden*, Corman had told *Variety* that he 'intended to put an increasing emphasis on art films, while moving into big-budget films, still making the occasional low-budget picture.' The failure of *Saint Jack* and the success of *Battle Beyond the Stars* had led him to alter those plans; now, on the verge of a new beginning, he was looking forward to indulging his artistic tastes again.

Not surprisingly, Corman's choice for this endeavour was a woman; what *was* a surprise was that she would be Amy Jones, whose only directorial experience had been as helmer of *The Slumber Party Massacre*. With Corman's encouragement, however, Jones had written an intimate drama which she had constructed in part from personal correspondence, as she told John Gaspard:

> **My husband and I had written each other love letters. We had been apart when we first met.. I moved to the west coast and he was on the east coast. So we wrote letters.. I was casting around for an idea for an art film and I came upon those letters. And I thought, well this is really interesting. What would happen if our daughter someday read all of our love letters? How would that affect her? At the same time, I saw a movie called *Shoot the Moon* [1982], which was about an extramarital affair and the traumas of the married man dealing with his wife and the girlfriend. I thought at the time, man, have I seen this a zillion times. Forever I've seen the point of view of the man, torn between his wife and the girlfriend.. But I had never seen the story of the girlfriend and what it was like for her. I put that together with the love letters and thought it would be interesting.. Basically, it was designed to be a movie about what happens to the woman outside of the marriage, who in fiction is usually painted as a terrible villain [but] often is a victim who gets left in the end.**

After her mother's death, Anna finds a box of love letters detailing her mother's affair with another man. Spurred by the letters to follow her heart, Anna embarks upon an affair with Oliver, who is married with two children. As Anna falls deeper in love with

*Oliver, she begins to realise that he will never leave his family for her. Determined not
to play second fiddle, she decides to have it out with Oliver and his wife.*

My Love Letters was a distinct change-of-pace for star Jamie Lee Curtis, and
she was in sorely in need of one. Beginning with *Halloween*, Curtis had cultivated a
'Scream Queen' image by starring in a rapid succession of low-budget horror movies,
including *Terror Train, The Fog, Prom Night, Halloween II*, and *Road Games*.
This had led to typecasting that the actress was eager to shake off, even if it meant
accepting a $25,000 pay-cheque and agreeing to several nude scenes. 'I auditioned
[for *My Love Letters*] over and over and over again,' she told *Variety*. 'When I read
it I really wanted to do it very badly.. It's hard to find a screenplay with any depth.'
Meg Tilly had been Jones's first choice to play Anna, but when Tilly's agent balked
at the salary, Curtis won the part. Along with the role of kind-hearted prostitute
Ophelia in the Dan Aykroyd-Eddie Murphy comedy vehicle *Trading Places* (1983),
My Love Letters helped to change the direction of Curtis's career in Hollywood.

The film was given an advance screening at the Filmex festival in Los Angeles
in April 1983, where it received a rave review in *Variety*: '*My Love Letters* is a fine
intimate drama.. and constitutes a most welcome surprise from producer Roger
Corman.. In a decided change of pace from her horror roles, Curtis is onscreen
constantly and holds her own impressively, never flinching from the bare emotional
and physical demands of the part.' New World had originally planned to release the
film in September, but ended up pushing it back to January 1984, when it premiered
in New York with the shortened title of *Love Letters*.

The New York critics were suitably impressed: 'Curtis is an arresting screen
presence. Her direct, no-nonsense manner and style give the film a sense of urgency'
(Vincent Canby); 'A rollercoaster ride of graphically depicted sexual highs and
dramatically portrayed emotional lows' (*Newsday*); 'One of those rare little films
where honesty permeates each scene's intention' (Rex Reed). In April, *Love Letters*
opened in Chicago and Los Angeles, where it won more critical kudos: 'I've been

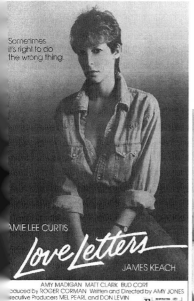

starved for serious human movies like this' (Roger
Ebert); 'To watch *Love Letters* is to wish that more
American movies covered the same small-scale,
personal territory with a full range of emotion'
(Gene Siskel); 'Curtis is extraordinary, a direct,
challenging, passionate screen presence whose
conviction lifts the film to very nearly her level'
(*Los Angeles Times*).

Mind Warp

'If *Love Letters* is successful I'd like to do more of this type of film,' Corman told *American Cinematographer*. 'I'm not planning to give up on the low-budget action films, but I'd like to be able to produce more serious projects as well.' Unfortunately, *Love Letters* did not light too many commercial fires and Jones has directed only two other films—the comedy *Maid to Order* (1987) and the domestic abuse thriller *The Rich Man's Wife* (1996). She has, however, managed to carve out a successful screenwriting career, penning the scripts to such films as *Mystic Pizza* (1988), *Beethoven* (1992), *Indecent Proposal* (1993), the remake of *The Getaway* (1994), and *The Relic* (1997).

> *'My old man's coming back later.. if we're still here, he's gonna shit twinkies!'*
> --Jack Diddley (Chris Pedersen), leader of The Rejected in *Suburbia*

It did not take very long for Corman to grow uncomfortable paying rent for the new offices of Millennium Films in Brentwood, so he packed up again and took everyone downtown to the Venice studio. While he was organising office space in a converted warehouse, Corman was also producing a film about kids who lived in abandoned 'tract' houses.

Suburbia would be the first feature film for 37-year-old director Penelope Spheeris. Born in New Orleans, she had moved to California in the '60s, studied film at UCLA, and paid the bills by working as a cocktail waitress at a strip club. In 1968, while still a student, Spheeris directed Richard Pryor in his film debut, the unfinished rape drama *Uncle Tom's Fairy Tales*. She then teamed with comedian and filmmaker Albert Brooks and produced his vignettes for the *Saturday Night Live* TV show between 1975 and 1976, as well as his feature debut, *Real Life* (1979).

In 1981, Penny Spheeris wrote, produced and directed *The Decline of Western Civilization*, a documentary about the Los Angeles punk music scene. This milieu would figure heavily in *Suburbia* as well; Spheeris told the *Los Angeles Times* that her background made her uniquely qualified to make films about society's fringe: 'My father was a Greek immigrant carny and I grew up travelling with the carnival, so I was around freaks, junkies and weirdos all my life. My father was murdered in Alabama and my mother was married nine times. She was an alcoholic then, and I'd always water down her vodka bottle because when she'd get drunk she'd beat me. But when she found out I'd thrown out her vodka, she'd beat me anyway.'

> *Tired of his alcoholic mother's tirades, Evan runs away and meets Jack Diddley, punk leader of 'The Rejected', a group of dropout kids who live in condemned housing. Evan joins the group and finds himself by participating in garage raids and punk concerts, but 'Citizens Against Crime' see The Rejected and their ilk as a menace to society. CAC forms a posse to evict the kids from their squat, and Jack's stepfather tries to warn the group to pack up and leave. They decide to stand their ground—with tragic results.*

'This isn't something I made up,' Spheeris said. 'Almost everything in the film came from watching the news. I've spent lots of time with kids who live like squatters in these abandoned crash pads.' To heighten the sense of realism, she deliberately cast the film with youngsters whom she knew from punk concerts and hangouts: 'We lost a lot of kids who walked out of auditions because they couldn't read enough to get through a script. But they helped me improve the script a lot through their own ideas.'

Suburbia was retitled *The Wild Side* for its premiere at the Montreal World Film Festival in August 1983; it went on to win Best First Feature at the Chicago International Film Festival that November. Despite its festival success, the subject

226

matter of the film made New World wary, forcing Spheeris to handle much of the film's promotion herself. 'It's been an uphill battle,' she confessed. 'We can't even get the trailer shown in a lot of art houses because they're afraid of offending their audiences.'

The Wild Side did not receive a general release until April 1984, when it was once again known as *Suburbia*. The film elicited a mixed reaction from the critics, with *Variety* raving, 'Spheeris works wonders with a low budget, non pro cast in a film of commercial appeal with exploitable elements for both art and mainstream audiences,' and Vincent Canby declaring it to be 'the best teenagers-in-revolt movie since Jonathan Kaplan's *Over the Edge*.' However, the *Chicago Tribune* felt that it descended 'into a rather trite sentimentality about these poor mixed-up kids from bad homes as it races toward its predictably tragic conclusion,' and Kevin Thomas likewise took Spheeris to task: 'In slamming across her warning to irresponsible parents on the one hand and in supplying the hard action required by the exploitation genre on the other, she fails to work up enough sympathy for her kids.'

Like *Western Civilization*, *Suburbia* became a cult hit, which led to Spheeris being hired by producer Sandy Howard to direct *The Boys Next Door* (1985) and *Hollywood Vice Squad* (1986). In 1988, she made her second documentary, *The Decline of Western Civilization Part II: The Metal Years*, while her break into the big time came in 1992 with the smash *Saturday Night Live* spin-off *Wayne's World*. More studio comedies followed: *The Beverly Hillbillies* (1993), *The Little Rascals* (1994) and *Black Sheep* (1996). In the past decade, Penelope Spheeris has continued to divide her time between comedies (*Senseless, The Kid and I*) and documentaries (*The Decline of Western Civilization III, We Sold Our Souls for Rock 'n' Roll, The Crooked E*).

> 'The kid thinks I'm a hero. I'm just another loser trying to stay alive.'
> —Space pirate Hawkins (Vince Edwards) in *Space Raiders*

Just before the sale of New World, Roger Corman had been guest of honour at the First World Drive-In Movie Festival, held in Dallas, Texas, in December 1982. Standing atop a concession stand and flanked by the finalists in the 'Miss Custom Body' contest, he was presented with an engraved hub-cap by self-styled 'gonzo' movie critic Joe Bob Briggs. In an interview earlier in the day with the Associated Press, Corman admitted, 'There is no question.. we have hyped the ad campaign at times.. just as automobiles are very often sold by advertising certain aspects of performance that it's difficult to find once you get behind the wheel.' With that, he made an announcement that New World was to produce a $5 million adaptation of Marvel Comics' most popular character, *Spider-Man*. (When the film was actually made 20 years later by Columbia Pictures, it ended up costing $139 million.)

Corman also confessed to used the same shots repeatedly in his Poe films for AIP, especially 'that damn house burning time after time.' Corman fans could take heart that even after twenty years, Millennium's third film, *Space Raiders*, would show that nothing had changed.

> *A crew of pirates led by Colonel Hawkins steals a spaceship from 'The Company' and finds young Peter Trackton stowed away on board. After landing on a space station, Peter is kidnapped by ruthless overlord Zariatin and held for ransom—Hawkins must capture four fuel ships and bring them to the station. The Company has dispatched its new Robot Death Ship, however, and it destroys the station as Hawkins, Peter, and the crew narrowly escape with their lives.*

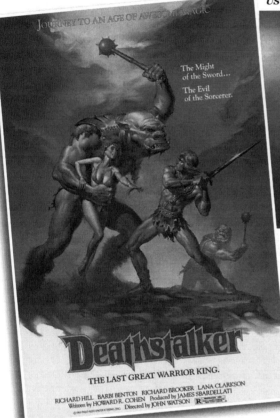

With a plot stolen from *Treasure Island*, alien cantina scenes ripped off from *Star Wars*, and most of its effects and music carried over from *Battle Beyond the Stars*, *Space Raiders* was, in the bemused view of *Cinefantastique*, an 'Extremely inauspicious debut film for Roger Corman's new Millennium Pictures [though not the first film produced, it was the first one released].'

Having ripped off everybody else in sight, Corman is now ripping off himself.' What new effects the Venice studio *did* create for the film utilised models from *Battle* and *Android*, along with additional footage from the latter as well.

While the *Los Angeles Times* described *Space Raiders* as 'a diverting, low-budget Saturday matinee-type science-fiction yarn,' *Variety* was having none of it: 'With *Space Raiders*, producer Roger Corman hits the lowest ebb of his career, fashioning a nonsensical, uninteresting Outer Space picture out of leftovers from an earlier film.' With a release through New World which began in May 1983, the same month as *Return of the Jedi*, and limped along through the summer, *Space Raiders* made an amusing counterpoint to yet more Corman hype: he was now to produce a 15-hour *Iwo Jima* TV miniseries with Burt Lancaster, Jane Seymour, and Morgan Fairchild.

'When Norman Lear and Jerry Perenchio bought [Avco] Embassy [in 1982],' Corman told the *New York Times*, 'they paid something like $24 million for it, and then had no pictures. They took a loss of over $10 million in the first 18 months, because they had a giant overhead, and no pictures to feed it.' Harry, Larry and Larry were now facing the same problem.

The future was not looking too bright: Millennium's product had only limited appeal and New World's own vaunted production programme was already in flux. *Angel* did, in fact, make it before the cameras, but *The Philadelphia Experiment* was on hold until November (Ron Howard had opted instead to direct *Splash* for Disney and was replaced on *Philadelphia* by Stewart Raffill), and everything else had been dropped. The only replacement item was Fritz Kiersch's *Children of the Corn*, based on Stephen King's 1977 short story and starring Peter Horton and Linda Hamilton.

New World's new management had to act fast to assure exhibitors that it was serious about the company remaining a reliable distributor. Accordingly, it went on a buying spree, acquiring a dozen films in the summer of 1983, including *Cross Country, Dreamworld* (released as *Covergirl*), *Far East, The Highest Honour, Highpoint, Hostage* (released as *Savage Attraction*), *Last Plane Out, The Pit, A Rare Breed, Stryker, Turkey Shoot* (released as *Escape 2000*), and *Wavelength*. Releases for the films began that August and continued well into 1984. 'I can't tell you there were any hits,' New World's new president Roger Burlage told *Variety*. 'But they softened the blow of getting the company on its feet.'

> *'Heroes and fools are the same thing.'*
> —Rogue he-man Deathstalker (Rick Hill) in *Deathstalker*

In Corman's words to the *New York Times*, 'Nobody could spell it, nobody knew what it meant,' so Millennium Films was history. His next two productions were sword-and-sorcery co-ventures with Argentina's Aries Cinematografica and were shot back-to-back in that country. The first, *Deathstalker*, was produced and directed by James Sbardellati, who had handled the controversial insert footage on *Humanoids from the Deep*. Working from a script by Howard Cohen, Sbardellati gave himself the directorial pseudonym of 'John Watson', while Corman chose to revive his old Palo Alto Productions as the movie's copyright holder.

> *When elderly King Tulak is robbed of his kingdom, and his daughter Princess Codille, he asks a warrior named Deathstalker to come to his aid—but is refused. Deathstalker has a change of heart after an old witch tasks him with reuniting a sword, amulet, and chalice in the possession of evil sorcerer Munkar; these three 'Powers of Creation' will give him the edge that he needs to win the warrior tournament underway at Munkar's castle, rescue Princess Codille, and restore Tulak to his throne.*

As Princess Codille, 33-year-old country singer Barbi Benton (former *Playboy* cover-girl and Hugh Hefner's longtime lover) was supposed to be the film's centre of attraction but she was upstaged by 21-year-old Lana Clarkson, a nearly-six-foot-tall blonde bombshell who had made her debut in *Fast Times at Ridgemont High* (1982). In *Deathstalker*, Clarkson played the scantily-clad swordfighter Kaira, and made such an impression on Corman that he gave her a film series of her own as Amethea, the Barbarian Queen. She also appeared on numerous TV shows in the '80s, and featured in bit-parts in *Brainstorm, Scarface* (both 1983), and *Amazon Women on the Moon* (1987).

Clarkson's career slowed considerably in the '90s, so much so that by 2003, she was working as a hostess in the House of Blues nightclub in West Hollywood. It was there, on February 3rd, that she met legendary record producer Phil Spector and accepted an invitate to his home. The next morning, she was found dead from a gunshot wound to the mouth. Spector claimed that it was an 'accidental suicide,' but he was arrested for murder and went to trial in April 2007. A hung jury forced the judge to declare a mistrial, however, and new hearings began in October 2008. On April 13th, 2009, Spector was found guilty of second-degree murder by a jury of six men and six women, after nine days of deliberation. The man who produced for The Ronettes, the Righteous Brothers, and Beatles John Lennon and George Harrison,

was sentenced to 19 years behind bars in a federal penitentiary.

Deathstalker opened in September 1983 to more mixed reviews, with Kevin Thomas calling it 'a sword-and-sorcery epic with a difference.. as fast and action-filled as it is amusing.' *Variety* felt differently: 'With bountiful action and acres of naked flesh, both male and female, film pretty accurately captures the intended heavy-metal look, but limp script and threadbare production values relegate this to quick-as-possible playoff status,' while the *Chicago Daily Herald* also objected to the extent of the female exploitation on display: '*Deathstalker* isn't a sword and sorcery tale for actresses who want meaty roles, unless it's only as meat.'

With over $5 million in rentals, *Deathstalker* was certainly meaty at the box office, and its subsequent success on video and cable led Corman to commission three sequels between 1987 and 1990—only the last one of which, *Deathstalker IV: Match of Titans*, returned former college football star Rick Hill (*The Devastator*, *Warrior Queen*) to the title role.

'The world we knew is dead.'
—The Dark One (David Carradine) in *The Warrior and the Sorceress*

The second half of the double feature was *Kain of Dark Planet*, which was first announced in 1980 as a possible vehicle for Chuck Norris. When it finally came time to raise Kain, it was instead in the guise of Corman stalwart David Carradine. This might be seen as fitting, given the fact that Carradine had played Kwai Chang Caine for three years in his TV series *Kung Fu*.

A warrior known as the Dark One comes to the village of Yamatar, where warlords Zeg and Bal Caz are locked in a struggle over who will control the well. The Dark One plays one off against the other, while ascertaining a way to drain the well. He rescues Princess Naja from the clutches of Zeg, and she uses her powers to forge the Sword of Ura. Armed with the sword, the Dark One leads the villagers in a revolt against those who have oppressed them.

A film that was said to have cost $4.5 million exhibited almost none of that on the screen, but *Kain* did end up being a groundbreaker in four respects: it was the first non-porn movie to feature its lead actress topless throughout the entire film, the first movie to feature the lead character's name in the title but nowhere in the

US theatrical poster for The Warrior and the Sorceress

film itself, the first to feature a four-breasted belly-dancer, and the first production to be credited to Corman's latest company, New Horizons Picture Corporation. On the other side of the coin, it was also the last Roger Corman film to be released by New World Pictures.

Just as *Battle Beyond the Stars* was Corman's version of Kurosawa's *Seven Samurai* by way of *The Magnificent Seven*, so *Kain* was his version of Kurosawa's *Yojimbo* (1961) by way of Sergio Leone's *A Fistful of Dollars* (1964). Even the score is ersatz Ennio Morricone—what little there is of it that was not an out-take from *Battle Beyond the Stars* or *Humanoids from the Deep*.

When the picture took its bow as *The Warrior and the Sorceress* in April 1984, it saw just $1.4 million in rentals and a good deal of hostility from the critics: 'The writing is laughable, the make-up terrible and the acting atrocious' (*Chicago Daily Herald*); 'The movie has awkward action, a general air of determined viciousness and.. so much ludicrous overacting that it sometimes seems that a new dramatic style is being forged' (*Los Angeles Times*); 'Late-in-the-cycle sword and sorcery item is a lowercase effort in all departments and has minimal potential even in quick playoff release' (*Variety*).

The year 1984 was to prove that what was new was old at the new New World Pictures. Larry Thompson sold his interest in the company to Harry Sloan and Larry Kuppin, preferring instead to become an independent producer of New World product such as Ken Russell's *Crimes of Passion* (1984) and *Fraternity Vacation* (1985). In Thompson's place came Robert Rehme, fresh from his short-lived tenure as president of Universal's Theatrical Motion Picture Group, to take on the post of co-owner and CEO. It was a homecoming for Rehme, who had been New World's general sales manager from 1975 to 1978: 'We're gonna make hit pictures,' he told the *Los Angeles Times*, 'high-concept pictures.'

'High-concept' is Hollywood-speak for projects that can be described in ten words or less and require no name star—the *idea* is the attraction. A good example was New World's first in-house production, *Angel*, released in January with the tag line: 'High School Honour Student by Day; Hollywood Hooker by Night.' The film was a success, earning $7 million in rentals, but *Variety* noted that 'the difference between the old New World and the new New World is the difference between good sleaze and dull sleaze. To put the bottom line up front, Roger Corman would never have made a picture about a Hollywood Boulevard hooker who never takes her clothes off and never turns a trick, but that's exactly what *Angel* is.' New World's second in-house production, *Children of the Corn*, was released in March and also earned $7 million in rentals.

In May, New World launched a $50 million production line-up of 'reasonably priced, high concept pictures,' which, Rehme told *Variety*, 'is only the beginning.' Titles included a sequel to *Angel*, the John Carpenter thriller *Black Moon Rising*, an adaptation of V C Andrews's best-selling 1979 horror novel *Flowers in the Attic*, a campy prison drama called *Reform School Girls* ('We will not abandon our roots,' said Rehme), and a new horror film from Larry Cohen, *The Stuff*. But, as *Variety* noted, missing was any entry from Corman—'who under terms of the sale agreement has been using the company as his distribution outlet.'

As if to account for his absence, Corman announced a five-picture slate for New Horizons the following month, which included two carry-overs from the New World days—*Iwo Jima* (now written by Richard Adams) and *World War III* (now written by Lawrence Hanson and projected as a $12 million project). The other three were *The Bloodshot Private Eyes*, *King's Ransom*, and *The Movie Star,* from a script by *Inside the Actors Studio* host James Lipton. In addition, Julie Corman had formed her own company, Trinity Productions, and was planning to make the comedy *Crazy Wheels* in Canada with *Screwballs* producer Maurice Smith. Not a single one of these films made it past the press release, though the Cormans were blessed with their fourth and last child, Mary Tessa, late in 1984.

Things were a little brighter over at New World, where June brought an announcement that agreement had been reached with Balcor/American Express for an investment of $160 million in New World's film production over a period of three years. This was widely seen as the first step towards Harry, Larry and Bob's ultimate goal of taking the company public by offering Balcor investors the chance to put money into films and allow for an equity interest in New World, as well. As 1984 played out, it was becoming clear that New World was going to have to find its revenue streams from some place other than the box office—its 'event' picture *The Philadelphia Experiment* made just $3.8 million in rentals, and only three other films (*Body Rock, C.H.U.D., Crimes of Passion*) rang up $1 million or more.

Undeterred, Harry, Larry and Bob saw in 1985 with yet another $50 million production announcement, including the aforementioned *Black Moon Rising* and *Flowers in the Attic* (now to be written and directed by Wes Craven). New projects included the horror comedies *Monster Night* and *Transylvania 6-5000,* as well as films from producers Pierre David (*Defenders*), Arnold Kopelson (*Totally Gross*), and Raymond Wagner (*Trax*). Films further down the development pipe included *Chickenhawk*, a John Carpenter project based on the 1983 novel by Robert Mason about Vietnam helicopter pilots, *Monopoly,* based on the popular board game, *The Tomb*, an adaptation of F Paul Wilson's 1984 best-seller to be produced by Tamara Asseyev, *The Tourist*, to star and be directed by Jerry Lewis, and two thrillers from John Boorman associate Rospo Pallenberg—*Last Man on Earth* and *Robot*. In the final analysis, only *Black Moon Rising, Flowers in the Attic* (*sans* Wes Craven), and *Transylvania 6-5000* were actually made.

New World had not released a New Horizons feature in nearly a year, and things finally came to a head when it flatly refused to distribute two new Corman offerings—the comedy *School Spirit* and the post-apocalyptic action movie *Wheels of Fire*—and Corman responded by announcing his intention to release the films himself. In March 1985, New World sued Corman, both to prevent him from going back into distribution and to claim for $40 million in defamation damages. In his defence, Corman wrote, 'They never gave my pictures a full release, and they never paid me the money the pictures earned.. It was obviously a waste of time for them to distribute these films. For me, it was an absolute necessity, backed up by an iron-clad contract.. The last thing I wanted to do was get back into distribution, but I had no choice. My pictures needed distribution and I needed the revenues.'

Corman counter-sued New World to the tune of $400 million, claiming fraud and conspiracy and demanding the return of New World to his ownership. As far as New World was concerned, the timing of Corman's actions was highly suspect: '[He] threatened on numerous occasions to institute legal proceedings seeking rescission of the agreements in order to destroy or substantially disrupt the success of the proposed public offering of limited partnership interests in New World,' *Variety* was informed. 'Corman and Brad Krevoy, general counsel of New Horizons, have made numerous statements to Sloan, Kuppin and Robert Rehme.. of Horizons' intention to sabotage the public offering.'

Two weeks later, Corman and New World reached an out-of-court settlement and dropped their respective lawsuits. New World was freed from its contractual obligation to distribute New Horizons films and could pursue its public offering without being hampered by a suit. But in the long run, it was Corman who was the real winner—he regained the rights to the entire pre-1983 New World Pictures film library and was free to distribute those films and other new product by himself.

At the end of March, Roger and Julie Corman announced the formation of their new distribution company: Concorde Pictures. Originally planned as a co-operative venture with other financiers, it ended up as a solo project when every one of its prospective partners backed out at the last minute. Concorde would not lack for product, however—it had eight New Horizons features in the pipeline, including action films (*The Devastator, Naked Vengeance, Wheels of Fire*), comedies (*Loose Screws, School Spirit*), sword and sorcery pictures (*Barbarian Queen, Wizards of the Lost Kingdom*), and its own version of New World's *Angel* (*Streetwalkin'*).

Roger Corman *(photo by Joseph Henry Ritter)*

Epilogue

liFe aFTeR New woRLd

'Traditionally, every film went in the theatres before it went into video, but starting about five, maybe six, years ago we started sending some films to video without a theatrical release because frankly theatrical releases for low-budget films were becoming more difficult and more expensive.'

--Roger Corman, 1995

'[Concorde-New Horizons was] an insane place where no one paid attention to you.. Everybody did their own thing and it was a creative hot-bed, but no one took it very seriously.'

—Robert King, writer of *The Nest*, *Bloodfist* and *Silk 2*

In September 1985, New World Pictures became a publicly-held company. It also became a diversified one, as New World International, New World Television and New World Video. In 1986, it acquired Learning Corporation of America and Marvel

Comics; the following year, it tried unsuccessfully to buy toy manufacturers Kenner and Mattel, when it changed its name to New World Entertainment. The other thing that Roger Corman's former film production and distribution company somehow failed to buy was successful movies.

Between 1985 and 1989, New World released nearly 100 films, but only six of them made more than $10 million at the box office—*Creepshow 2, Flowers in the Attic, Hellraiser* and *Hellraiser 2, House, Soul Man*—and none made more than $30 million. While New World managed to avoid the megaflops that had sunk the other 'mini majors' of the time, like the Cannon Group (*Over the Top, Superman IV*) and De Laurentiis Entertainment Group (*King Kong Lives, Tai Pan*), it could not produce a consistent revenue stream from its filmmaking endeavours, nor did it have a substantial enough library of titles to see it through the lean times.

In 1989, faced with mounting debt, Harry, Larry and Bob Rehme sold Marvel Comics to financier Ronald Perelman for $82.5 million. Ironically, New World had just produced its first feature based on a Marvel character—*The Punisher* with Dolph Lundgren—and it was planning another (*She Hulk* with Brigitte Nielsen). While *The Punisher* was released overseas, it sat on the shelf in America before being sent directly to video in 1991.

In 1990, Perelman bought New World Entertainment for $300 million. The theatrical and video divisions were shut down, putting several completed films in limbo, including *Brenda Starr* with Brooke Shields, *Felix the Cat: The Movie* and *Warlock*, which eventually did well enough on video to warrant two sequels. Perelman's interest was driven solely by New World's television division, which produced the soap opera *Santa Barbara* (1984-93) and shows like Michael Mann's *Crime Story* (1986-88), the Vietnam War series *Tour of Duty* (1987-90), and the '60s slice-of-life comedy-drama *The Wonder Years* (1988-93).

In 1993, New World Communications was born with the acquisition of seven television stations; eight more would be added before NWC was bought by Rupert Murdoch's News Corporation in 1996 for $3 billion. All of NWC's holdings were subsequently merged into the Fox network and New World ceased to exist.

After the sale of New World in 1990, Harry Sloan went to Europe and founded the Scandinavia Broadcasting System, which he eventually sold in 2005 for $2.6 billion. He then returned to Hollywood and joined the board of MGM, where he is now the chairman and CEO of the perpetually-ailing studio. Lawrence Kuppin became an overseer of various entertainment and real estate holdings. Robert Rehme formed a production company with Mace Neufeld and made blockbusters such as *Patriot Games* (1992), *Clear and Present Danger* (1994), and *Lost in Space* (1998). He has also served two terms (1992-93 and 1997-2001) as president of AMPAS (Academy of Motion Picture Arts and Sciences).

In a radical departure from his strategy at New World, Roger Corman decided early on largely to forego the theatrical market and instead concentrate his new company's energies on the burgeoning video arena. While New World was falling heavily into debt as the 1980s wore on, Concorde-New Horizons had doubled its production between 1986-89 and was seeing grosses of upwards of $100 million each year, thanks to video deals with Columbia Pictures, Embassy Pictures, Media Home Entertainment, MGM/UA, Vestron Video, and Warner Brothers—all of which it was supplying with product *concurrently*. Much of that product ended up being sequels/remakes of earlier Corman films, including *Big Bad Mama II* (featuring a returning Angie Dickinson), *Demon of Paradise* (a reworking of *Up from the Depths*), *Hollywood Boulevard II, Masque of the Red Death*, and *Not of This Earth*, but it was product nonetheless.

In terms of theatrical releases, Concorde-New Horizons' all-time champion was the erotic thriller *Body Chemistry* (1990), which took in just $2.4 million at the box office but was followed by three direct-to-video sequels between 1992-95, though the company's most profitable franchise proved to be the *Bloodfist* series of martial arts films starring kick-boxing champion Don 'The Dragon' Wilson, which began in 1989 and continued through to 1996, totalling eight movies and selling hundreds of thousands of cassettes. Concorde-New Horizons' biggest single video release was *Carnosaur* (1993), a *Jurassic Park* knock-off ostensibly based on the 1984 Harry Adam Knight (née John Brosnan) novel, which sold 85,000 units and spawned two sequels in 1995-96.

In May 1989, Corman's almost 20-year absence from directing finally came to an end when production began on *Frankenstein Unbound*, based on Brian Aldiss's 1973 revisionist take on the Mary Shelley novel. Corman had a standing offer from Thom Mount, president of Universal Pictures from 1979 to 1983, to make a version of *Frankenstein* for the studio, and when Mount went into independent production (*Bull Durham, Frantic, Tequila Sunrise,* etc), the offer went with him. The sci-fi horror film was more lavish than anything that Corman had ever made before—a budget of $11.5 million (of which $1 million was Corman's salary), major stars (Bridget Fonda, John Hurt, Raul Julia), Italian locations, and a 10-week shooting schedule. Corman also co-produced the film and shared writing chores with film critic F X Feeney (previous drafts from Wes Craven and Floyd Mutrux were discarded). The notion that the film was something of an 'event' was compounded when two major studios—20th Century-Fox and Warner Brothers—respectively acquired domestic and foreign rights.

Frankenstein Unbound tells the story of 21st century scientist Joe Buchanan, who, in working on the ultimate weapon, accidentally transports himself and his talking car back to 19th-century Switzerland, where he meets Byron, and Percy and Mary Shelley, who is basing her novel *Frankenstein* on a real scientist who lives nearby and has created a 'monster'. The film surfaced as a kind of a cross between *Back to the Future* (1985) and Ken Russell's *Gothic* (1986), although Aldiss's novel itself bears more than a passing resemblance to Anne Edwards's *Haunted Summer* (1972), which was also turned into a film in 1988.

Corman's comeback premiered in New York and Los Angeles in November 1990, and critical response was lukewarm at best. 'The movie.. looks fine, and the performers are mostly good,' said Vincent Canby, while Kevin Thomas wrote, 'The film emerges as a cautionary tale about the dangers of tampering with nature and of playing God, which becomes tedious in its familiarity for all of Hurt and Julia's welcome theatricality.' *Variety* judged *Frankenstein Unbound* to be 'a competent but uninspired riff on the venerable legend.' When it grossed a paltry $37,000 in its two-city engagement, Fox pulled it from release and sent it straight to video. It fared little better overseas, and Warners even passed its British release over to a small independent distributor, Blue Dolphin.

Despite the abject failure of *Frankenstein Unbound*, Corman was riding high in 1990-91, with the release of eight of Concorde-New Horizons' Top 10-grossing movies, the publication of his autobiography, a feature article in *GQ* magazine, and his being honoured with a star on Hollywood's Walk of Fame. He could also take great comfort in the fact that he was one of only a handful of survivors amid the wreckage of numerous independents who had over-extended themselves in the 1980s and paid for it at decade's end, including New World Pictures.

Roger Corman had been one of the first to be in on the home video revolution, and he was equally interested in the surge in entertainment programming which had been brought about by the advent of satellite TV and the imminent start of two new networks in the US by Paramount and Warner Brothers in 1995. There was talk that a 500-channel cable/satellite universe was on the way, and Corman knew that such a beast would eat up a lot of product; to that end, he proposed to sell his 250-picture library for between $20 and $30 million. It was not just revenue that he was seeking, however, but another chance to start over.

Concorde-New Horizons was averaging twenty productions a year, and it was becoming too much for Corman to handle, as he told the *Los Angeles Times*: 'We are doing too many pictures for a little company.. I want to do fewer films and I want to concentrate more on them.' While he could find no takers for the library, even after lowering the price to $18 million, he soon found himself being courted as grist for the cable mill.

In the fall of 1994, the Showtime network contracted Concorde-New Horizons to produce thirteen films for a series called *Roger Corman Presents*. Shooting on the movies began in January 1995 and continued to June, with the first film, the thriller *Suspect Device*, premiering that July. In addition to remakes of *Piranha* and *Humanoids from the Deep*, *Roger Corman Presents* also featured modern versions of Corman classics such as *Bucket of Blood, Not of This Earth* (which had been remade once already with ex-porn star Traci Lords), and *Wasp Woman*.

The series lasted for two years and produced a total of 32 films, including such titles as *Alien Avengers, Bram Stoker's Burial of the Rats* (shot in Moscow on huge sets left over from a local epic), *Club Vampire, Inhumanoid, Last Exit to Earth* (yet another vehicle for stock *Battle Beyond the Stars* footage), *Marquis de Sade, Sawbones, Spacejacked, Subliminal Seduction, Vampirella* (a cheap version of the cult comic book), and *Virtual Seduction*. All of the films were subsequently released to video by the newly-created New Horizons label, though many of the titles were inexplicably changed.

Despite Corman's desire to rein in production at Concorde-New Horizons, the series did not supplant the company's product, merely increased it. The company was still producing direct-to-video features and the Venice studio simply could not handle the production overload. As a result, Corman established Concorde Anois and built a new studio in Galway, Ireland in late 1995 for $3.4 million, half of which was paid for by subsidies from the Irish Ministry of Culture.

In February 1997, just before his 71st birthday, Roger Corman announced that he was selling Concorde-New Horizons to producer Elliott Kastner (*Rancho De Luxe, Equus, et al*) for $100 million. The sale would include the distributorship, the film library (now numbering some 378 titles), the Venice studio, the company's

Brentwood headquarters, and other assorted holdings. Excluded from the deal was the Galway studio, where it was expected that Corman would continue to produce films under a new banner. A closing date was set for May 1st, but that came and went without things being finalised. Negotiations dragged on for more than a year but, in the end, Concorde-New Horizons remained with Corman.

As if to compensate for his failure to sell the company, Corman decided to enter the risky world of TV series production on his own. In the spring of 1998, Concorde-New Horizons began production of what would be 22 hours of a female superhero show called *Black Scorpion*. Atypical of Corman, it was financed totally out-of-pocket at $400,000 per episode and produced completely on spec, without a network sale.

Black Scorpion was not an unknown commodity, however. She had made her debut in 1995 as part of *Roger Corman Presents*, before returning for a second outing in 1996. The character was the brainchild of writer-producer Craig Nevius, who had written a version of Marvel Comics' *The Fantastic Four* for Corman that was produced in 1993 but never officially released (it was made so that German producer Bernd Eichinger could corner the rights and hold out for a big-budgeted studio version, which finally happened at Fox in 2005). *Black Scorpion* herself was cop Darcy Walker (played by softcore porn star Joan Severance), who by night dons a skimpy outfit and drives a souped-up Corvette Stingray in vigilante pursuit of the justice that she sees villains elude by day.

For the *Black Scorpion* series, Walker was played by former Miss Kansas Michelle Lintel, and Nevius set out to make the show all things to all people, as he told the *Chicago Daily Herald*: 'I believe it will play to everyone, from boys who read comic books to their fathers who read *Playboy*. Mothers and daughters will even want to watch because our superhero is a superheroine. She doesn't wait for a man to save her—she saves the men.'

The series was a throwback to the campy humour of '60s *Batman*, a fact that it acknowledged by having Adam West and 'Riddler' Frank Gorshin make guest appearances as villains, along with others like Lana Clarkson, Lou Ferrigno, Sam J Jones, and Martin Kove. *Black Scorpion* also showcased numerous softcore stars and *Playboy* Playmates, including Lisa Boyle, Ava Fabian, Shae Marks, Victoria Silvstedt, Kimber West and Shannon Whirry.

'I have plans for a second season, a cartoon, a comic book*, even a toy line,' said Nevius. But his plans were put on indefinite hold when *Black Scorpion* spent two years shopping for a network. It ended up on the Sci-Fi Channel, which aired the series between January and June of 2001. Initial ratings were encouraging, but the network changed *Black Scorpion*'s time-slot after the first five weeks and it began a rapid downhill descent. Despite Corman announcing that he was going to produce another 44 episodes at $1 million each, *Black*

239

Scorpion's crime-fighting was at an end (a third film, *Sting of the Black Scorpion*, was produced in 2002 by combining three episodes of the series).

By the late 1990s, Roger Corman was receiving a wide range of accolades, with lifetime and professional achievement awards from American Cinema Editors, the Cannes Film Festival, Casting Society of America, Florida Film Festival, Los Angeles Film Critics Association, Malibu Film Festival, Raindance UK Film Festival, and the Sitges Fantasy Film Festival. He was host of the American Movie Classics cable channel's Monsterfest in October 1999, and he was even asked to play the sinister Professor Gorman in the AMC mini-serial *The Phantom Eye*.

Something which portrayed Roger Corman and Concorde-New Horizons in a less-than-positive light, however, was musician and opera singer Odette Springer's documentary, *Some Nudity Required*. Springer had been the music supervisor at Concorde for four years, and while her movie was an indictment of the exploitation film business in general, it naturally focused on her former place of employment (Corman was one of several interviewees in the picture, along with Sam Arkoff, Maria Ford, Fred Olen Ray, Andy Sidaris, Julie Strain, Jim Wynorski, and others). *Some Nudity Required* caused quite a stir at the 1998 Sundance Film Festival and supposedly enraged Corman so much that he attempted to block its release.

Springer's film thrust into the spotlight one of the most glaring contradictions about Roger Corman. On the one hand, he was one of the most progressive people in Hollywood when it came to employing women as producers, directors and corporate executives ('I never even realised sexism *existed* in Hollywood until I got outside New World,' Gale Anne Hurd wrote in Corman's autobiography). But at the same time, his films relentlessly exploited women in front of the camera with an endless procession of nudity, sex, brutality, and rape ('As I was watching these clips,' Springer told the *Los Angeles Times*, 'I found myself getting turned on, and it horrified me').

To some, the former compensated for the latter, and the exploitation quotient in Corman's films was an acceptable trade-off for the chance to make movies. 'He wants sex, violence, or humour,' Amy Jones told John Gaspard. 'He actually told me [on *Love Letters*] that lovemaking wasn't so much required as nudity. And he didn't mind if she could just be lounging around the house nude, but there had to be nudity. He had to have some way to sell the thing.. I find some of the nudity really gratuitous. But it was the price we paid to get it made.'

Others, including ex-Concorde-New Horizons development executive Beverly Gray, questioned whether such trade-offs of dignity for experience were necessary. As she wrote in *Roger Corman: An Unauthorised Biography of the Godfather of Indie Filmmaking*, 'To what extent is Corman going beyond the demands of the marketplace and tapping into his own preoccupation with the undraped female form?.. [Concorde sales executive Pamm Vlastas] is convinced that 'Roger would make those films with the strippers in them just so he could watch them.' Some alumni even argue that, for the ageing filmmaker, getting young women to remove their clothes on cue became a kind of power issue..'

As the new millennium dawned, major changes were in the works. Corman shortened his company's name to the more user-friendly New Concorde and cut down on its output, while simultaneously striking a deal with Disney (!) to release his library on DVD. He sold the Venice studio for $4.3 million to a developer who planned to build shops and apartments; in typical fashion, Corman took advantage of the sale to make the burning down of the studio the centrepiece in a horror film that he called *Slaughter Studios*. Roger and Julie Corman also became bi-coastal commuters when the latter served as chair of New York University's graduate film and TV department from 2000-02.

While his wife involved herself in academic politics, Roger Corman continued to be showered with awards. During the past decade, he has been lionised by the American Cinémathèque, American Film Market, Empire UK Awards, Moscow International Film Festival, New York City Horror Film Festival, and Universal's Eyegore Awards, as well as receiving tributes from the Producer's Guild of America and the Society of Camera Operators.

Corman's post-New World companies have yet to produce a Ron Howard or a Martin Scorsese (most of the hot young talent these days seems to come from the film festival circuit), but they nevertheless have upheld the Corman tradition of turning out recognised names in the industry, including director Carl Franklin (*One True Thing, Out of Time*), cinematographer Janusz Kaminski (Oscar-winner for *Schindler's List* and *Saving Private Ryan*), writer Robert King (*Speechless, Cutthroat Island*), and producer Brad Krevoy (*Dumb & Dumber, Kingpin*).

Since selling New World Pictures, Corman has produced some 250 films, but the lion's share came before the year 2000; the past decade has seen him produce only forty, with names like *Avalanche Alley, Dinocroc, Escape from Afghanistan, The Hunt for Eagle One, Nightfall* (first announced in 1980 and previously filmed in 1988), *Raptor, Scorpius Gigantus*, and *Supergator*. In 2008, Corman was one of seven producers on Paul W S Anderson's remake *Death Race*, which featured *The Transporter*'s Jason Statham in the David Carradine role. (Carradine lent his voice to the film before being found hanged the following year in a Bangkok hotel, during the shooting of *Stretch*.) That year also saw the end of one of his longest-term professional relationships when Cirio Santiago died of lung cancer at the age of 72, but not before leaving Corman one last film: *Road Raiders*.

In 1996, when scientists mistakenly believed that they had discovered 'life' on Mars, Roger Corman declared he would make a $20 million movie called *Mars Lives*. More recently, he has stated his intention to make a $20 million biography of the late Vietnamese revolutionary, Ho Chi Minh.

The truth is that Roger Corman has not—and most likely will not now—ever make these films. He is not a big-league player; he is a big fish in a small pond, and that suits him just fine. As he passes his 83rd year in 2009, he can take comfort in the fact that his legacy is secure: he has survived, thrived even, in an industry known more for the fast fade than the slow burn. Of all the independents of the '70s and '80s, he is the only one who has not sold out or shut down. And countless people in Hollywood have him to thank for their careers. A stern taskmaster, a genuine *cinéaste*, an unabashed exploiter, and one of American cinema's elder statesmen—Roger Corman is all of these, and much more besides. As Howard Cohen told Beverly Gray, 'There are two of him. There's the one you talk to and the one you do business with. The one you talk to I still like a lot.'

---

*The Black Scorpion comic book, one of a series entitled 'Roger Corman Presents', finally came to fruition in November 2009 through a tie-in with Washington-based Bluewater Comics.

Mind Warp

ROGER CORMAN/NEW WORLD PICTURES

1970-1984

ANGELS DIE HARD

Cast

Tom Baker	Blair
William Smith	Tim
Carl Steppling	Sheriff
Frank Leo	Martin
Alan DeWitt	Undertaker
Gary Littlejohn	Piston
Beach Dickerson	Shank
Rita Murray	Naomi
William Bonner	Houston
Mike Angel	Dirty
R G Armstrong	Mel
Connie Nelson	Nancy
Les Otis	Tommy
Dianne Turley	Patsy
Michael Donovan	O'Donnell
Dan Haggerty	Monk
Michael Stringer	Seed
Bambi Allen	Restaurant owner's wife

Selected credits

Directed/Written by Richard Compton
Produced by Charles Beach Dickerson
Executive Producers Jane Schaffer/James Tanenbaum
Music by Richard Hieronymus
Cinematographer Arch Archambault
Edited by Tony de Zarraga
Released June 1970
86 mins

THE STUDENT NURSES

Cast

Elaine Giftos	Sharon
Karen Carlson	Phred
Brioni Farrell	Lynn
Barbara Leigh	Priscilla
Reni Santoni	Victor Charlie
Richard Rust	Les
Lawrence Casey	Jim Caspar
Darrell Larson	Greg
Paul Camen	Mark
Richard Stahl	Dr Warshaw
Scottie MacGregor	Miss Boswell
Pepe Serna	Luis
John Pearce	Patient
Mario Aniouv	Ralpho
Ronald Gans	Psychiatrist

Selected credits

Directed by Stephanie Rothman
Written by Don Spencer
Story/Produced by Stephanie Rothman/Charles S Swartz
Associate Producer Paul Rapp
Music by Clancy B Grass III
Cinematographer Stevan Larner
Edited by Stephen Judson
Art Director David Nichols
Released August 1970
89 mins

GAS-S-S-S-S

Cast

Robert Corff	Coel
Elaine Giftos	Cilla
Bud Cort	Hooper
Tally Coppola	Coralee
Ben Vereen	Carlos
Cindy Williams	Marissa
Alex Wilson	Jason
Lou Procopio	Marshal McLuhan
Phil Borneo	Quant
Alan Braunstein	Dr Drake
Jackie Farley	Ginny
David Osterhout	Texas Ranger
Juretta Taylor	Zoe
Michael D Castle	Burroughs
Alan DeWitt	Dr Murder
Bruce Karcher	Edgar Allen
Stephen White	Sergeant Sentry Collar
Ray Birk	Mort Catafalque
George Armitage	Billy the Kid
Abe Santillanes	Na Wanka
Pat Patterson	Demeter

Selected credits

Directed/Produced by Roger Corman

Written by George Armitage
Associate Producers George Armitage/Frances Doel
Music by Barry Melton
Cinematographer Ron Dexter
Edited by George Van Noy
Art Director David Nichols
Produced November 1969/Released October 1970
79 mins

BURY ME AN ANGEL

Cast
Dixie Peabody...Dag
Terry Mace..Jonsie
Clyde Ventura..Bernie
Joanne Jordan...Annie
Marie Denn..Bernice
Dennis Peabody...Dennis
Stephen Wittaker..The Killer
Gary Littlejohn....................................Bike shop proprietor
David Atkins..Preacher
Janelle Pransky................................Dag as a little girl
Wayne Everett Chesnut.....................Dennis as a little boy
Corky Williams...Sheriff
Beach Dickerson...Harry
Dan Haggerty..Ken
Maureen Math..School girl
Dianne Turley..Secretary
Alan DeWitt..Principal
Richard Compton..Pool player
Dan Knapp...Pool player

Selected credits
Directed/Written by Barbara Peeters
Produced by Paul Nobert
Executive Producers Rita Murray/John Meier
Associate Producer Charles Beach Dickerson
Music by Richard Hieronymus/East-West Pipeline
Cinematographer Sven Walnum
Edited by Tony de Zarraga
Art Director Lawrence Paull
Released March 1971
89 mins

THE BEAST OF THE YELLOW NIGHT

Cast
John Ashley.........................Joseph Langdon/Philip Rogers
Mary Wilcox...Julia Rogers
Leopoldo Salcedo...Insp Santos
Eddie Garcia...Det Lt Campo
Ken Metcalfe..Earl Rogers
Vic Diaz...Satan
Andres Centenera...Blind man
Ruben Hastia/Don Lieman/Jose Garcia/James Spencer/
Carol Asturias/Jose Roy Jr/Criselda/Joonee Gamboa/Peter
Magurean/Nora Nunez/Johnny Long

Selected credits
Directed/Written by Eddie Romero
Produced by John Ashley/Eddie Romero
Executive Producers Beverly Miller/David J Cohen
Music by Nestor Robles
Cinematographer Justo Paulino
Edited by Ben Barcelon
Produced September 1970/Released April 1971
87 mins

THE BIG DOLL HOUSE

Cast
Judy Brown...Collier
Roberta Collins...Alcott
Pam Grier...Grear
Brooke Mills..Harrad
Pat Woodell..Bodine
Sid Haig...Harry
Christiane Schmidtmer....................................Miss Dietrich

Kathryn Loder...Lucian
Jerry Franks..Fred
Gina Stuart...Ferina
Jack Davis...Dr Phillips
Letty Mirasol...Leyte
Shirley de las Alas..Guard

Selected credits
Directed by Jack Hill
Written by Don Spencer
Produced by Jane Schaffer
Executive Producers John Ashley/Eddie Romero
Music by Hall Daniels
Cinematographer Fred Conde
Edited by Cliff Fenneman
Production Designer Ben Otico
Produced November 1970/Released April 1971
95 mins

THE CREATURE WITH THE BLUE HAND

Cast
Harald Leipnitz..Inspector Craig
Klaus Kinski.....................Dave Emerson/Richard Emerson
Carl Lange..Dr Albert Mangrove
Ilse Steppat..Lady Emerson
Hermann Lenschau..........................Rechtsanwalt Douglas
Diana Körner...Myrna Emerson
Gudrun Genest....................................Schwester Harris
Albert Bessler...Butler Anthony
Richard Haller......................................Edward Appleton
Ilse Pagé..Miss Mabel Finley
Siegfried Schürenberg...Sir John
Fred Haltiner...Wärter Reynolds
Peter Parten...Robert Emerson
Thomas Danneberg.....................................Charles Emerson
Heinz Spitzner..Richter

Selected credits
Directed by Alfred Vohrer
Written by Herbert Reinecker (as Alex Berg)
Based on the novel 'Blue Hand' by Edgar Wallace
Produced by Horst Wendlandt
Music by Martin Böttcher
Cinematographer Ernst W Kalinke
Edited by Jutta Hering
Art Directors Wilhelm Vorwerg/Walter Kutz
Released April 1971
72 mins

VON RICHTHOFEN AND BROWN/THE RED BARON

Cast
John Phillip Law....................Baron Manfred von Richthofen
Don Stroud...Roy Brown
Barry Primus...Hermann Goering
Corin Redgrave............................Major Lanoe Hawker VC
Karen Huston..Ilse
Hurd Hatfield..Anthony Fokker
Stephen McHattie...Werner Voss
Brian Foley.............................Lothar von Richthofen
Robert La Tourneaux..Ernest Udet
Peter Masterson...............................Major Oswald Boelke
Clint Kimbrough.............................Major von Höppner
Tom Adams...Owen
Ferdy Mayne.................................Father Richthofen
David Weston...Murphy
John Flanagan...Thompson
Lorraine Rainer...Girl in woods
Brian Sturdivant..May
Maureen Cusack..................................Mother Richthofen
George Armitage..Wolff
Gordon Phillips..Cargonico

Selected credits
Directed by Roger Corman

Written by John William Corrington/Joyce Hooper
Corrington
Produced by Gene Corman
Associate Producer Jimmy T Murakami
Music by Hugo Friedhofer
Cinematographer Michael Reed
Edited by Alan Collins
Art Director Jimmy T Murakami
Produced August 1970/Released May 1971
96 mins

On April 21, 1918, the Red Baron of Germany and the Black Sheep of the R.A.F. met in the skies of France. One came for a gentlemen's duel, the other—to kill!

THE VELVET VAMPIRE
Cast
Michael Blodgett..Lee Ritter
Sherry Miles...Susan Ritter
Celeste Yarnall..Diane LeFanu
Gene Shane...Carl Stoker
Jerry Daniels..Juan
Sandy Ward..Amos
Paul Prokop...Cliff
Chris Woodley...Cliff's girl
Robert Tessier...Biker
Selected credits
Directed by Stephanie Rothman
Written by Maurice Jules/Charles S Swartz/Stephanie
Rothman
Produced by Charles S Swartz
Music by Clancy B Grass III/Roger Dollarhide
Cinematographer Daniel Lacambre
Edited by Stephen Judson/Barry Simon
Art Director Teddi Peterson
Produced February 1971/Released June 1971
80 mins

SCREAM OF THE DEMON LOVER
Cast
Carlos Quiney (as Jeffrey Chase)....................Janos Dalmar
Erna Schurer (as Jennifer Hartley)..........Ivanna Rakowsky
Agostina Belli...Cristiana
Cristiana Galloni..Olga
Antonio Gimenez Escribano/Mariano Vidal Molina/
Enzo Fisichella/Ezio Sancrotti/Giancarlo Fantini/Franco

Moraldi/Paracchi Renato
Selected credits
Directed by José Luis Merino
Written by Enrico Colombo/José Luis Merino
Produced by Sergio Newman
Music by Luigi Malatesta
Cinematographer Emanuele Di Cola
Edited by Alessandro Lena
Art Director Francesco Di Stefano
Produced July 1970/Released June 1971
94 mins

ANGELS HARD AS THEY COME
Cast
Scott Glenn..Long John
Charles Dierkop...General
James Inglehart..Monk
Gilda Texter..Astrid
Gary Littlejohn..Axe
Gary Busey...Henry
Don Carerra...Juicer
Brendan Kelly..Brain
Janet Wood...Vicki
Dennis Art...Rings
Neva Davis...Clean Shiela
Cherie Latimer.................................Lucifer's girl Cheri
Marc Seaton..Louie
Steve Slauson..Magic
John Taylor...Crab
Larry Tucker..Lucifer
William Carter..Charlie
Ron Starr...Ron
Frank Charolla...Frank
Evelyn Littlejohn..Eve
Selected credits
Directed by Joe Viola
Written by Jonathan Demme/Joe Viola
Produced by Jonathan Demme
Music by Richard Hieronymus
Cinematographer Stephen Katz
Edited by Joe Ravetz
Art Director Jack Fisk
Released July 1971
85 mins

PRIVATE DUTY NURSES
Cast
Kathy Cannon...Spring
Joyce Williams..Lola
Pegi Boucher...Lynn
Joseph Kaufmann...Dr Doug Selden
Dennis Redfield...Domino
Robert F Simon...Dr Sutton
Morris Buchanan..Kirby
Herb Jefferson Jr..Dr Elton Sanders
Paul Hampton...Dewey
Paul Gleason..Dr McClintock
George Sawaya...Ahmed
Cliff Carnell..Bartender
Selected credits
Directed/Written/Produced by George Armitage
Music by Sky
Cinematographer John McNichol
Edited by Alan Collins
Released July 1971
80 mins

WOMEN IN CAGES
Cast
Judy Brown..Sandy
Roberta Collins..Stoke
Jennifer Gan..Jeff

Pam Grier...Alabama
Bernard Bodine..Acosta
Charles Davis..Rudy
Johnny Long/Holly Anders/Dwight Howard/Roberta Swift/
Paul Sawyer/Jeffrey Taylor

Selected credits
Directed by Gerardo de Leon
Written by James H Watkins
David Osterhout
Produced by Ben Balatbat
Music by Tito Arevalo
Cinematographer Felipe Sacdalan
Edited by Ben Barcelon
Art Director Ben Otico
Released July 1971
78 mins

LADY FRANKENSTEIN
Cast
Joseph Cotten..Baron Frankenstein
Rosalba Neri (as Sara Bay).......................Tania Frankenstein
Mickey Hargitay...Captain Harris
Paul Muller..Dr Charles Marshall
Paul Whiteman...Thomas Stack
Herbert Fux..Tom Lynch
Renate Kasché (as Renata Cash)............................Julia Stack
Lorenzo Terzon (as Lawrence Tilden).........Harris' assistant
Ada Pometti (as Ada Pomeroy)........................Farmer's wife
Andrea Aureli (as Andrew Ray)............................Jim Turner
Johnny Loffrey...John
Richard Beardley...Simon Burke
Petar Martinovitch (as Peter Martinov)............Jack Morgan
Adam Welles..Child
Selected credits
Directed/Produced by Mel Welles
Written by Edward Di Lorenzo
Story by Edward Di Lorenzo/Dick Randall
Executive Producers Harry Cushing/Hurbert Case/Jules
Kenton

Music by Alessandro Alessandroni
Cinematographer Riccardo Pallottini (as Richard Pallotin)
Edited by Cleofe Conversi (as Cleo Converse)
Production Designer Francis Mellon
Produced March 1971/Released March 1972
85 mins

SWEET KILL
Cast
Tab Hunter..Eddie Collins
Cherie Latimer...Lauren
Nadyne Turney...Barbara
Isabel Jewell..Mrs Cole
Linda Leider...Vickie
Roberta Collins...Call girl
John Aprea..Richard
Kate McKeown...Sherry
Rory Guy...Henry
Frank Whiteman...Willard
Harv Selsby...Davidson
Josh Green..Danny
John Pearce...Mr Howard
Sandy Kenyon..Newscaster
Selected credits
Directed/Written by Curtis Hanson
Produced by Tamara Asseyev
Music by Charles Bernstein
Cinematographers Daniel Lacambre/Edmund Anderson
Edited by Gretel Ehrlich
Art Director James Kenney
Produced November 1970/Released March 1972
85 mins

THE FINAL COMEDOWN

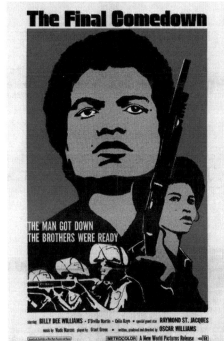

Cast
Billy Dee Williams...Johnny Johnson
D'Urville Martin..Billy Joe Ashley
Celia Kaye..Rene Freeman

Raymond St Jacques...Jimi
R G Armstrong..Mr Freeman
Maidie Norman...Mrs Johnson
Ed Cambridge..Dr Smalls
Billy Durkin...Michael Freeman
Morris D Erby...Mr Johnson
Pamela Jones...Luanna

Selected credits
Directed/Written by Oscar Wllliams
Produced by Oscar Williams/Edgar Charles/Mel Taylor
Associate Producer D'Urville Martin
Music by Wade Marcus/George Butler
Cinematographer William B Kaplan
Edited by Dick Van Enger Jr
Released April 1972
83 mins

THE HOT BOX
Cast
Carmen Argenziano...Flavio
Andrea Cagan...Bunny Kincaid
Margaret Markov...Lynn Forrest
Rickey Richardson..Ellie St George
Laurie Rose...Sue Pennwright
Zaldy Zshornack...Ronaldo
Jose Romulo...Chao
Rocco Montalban..Carragiero
Charles Dierkop.....................Journalist Garcia/Major Dubay
Gina Laforteza...Florida
Ruben Ramos..Mimmo
Carmen Baredo...Tomara
Roy Alvarez..Leyo
Robert Rivera...Pedro
Greg Luzano...Perde
Lazaro Calvag...Carragiero's boys
Ernesto Montaya...Carragiero's boys
Mardo Dilansig...Carragiero's boys
Arturo Blanco...Carragiero's boys
Benny Pebtano...Benny

Selected credits
Directed by Joe Viola
Written by Joe Viola/Jonathan Demme
Produced by Jonathan Demme
Associate Producer Evelyn Purcell
Music by Restie Umali
Cinematographer Felipe Sacdalan
Edited by Ben Barcelon/Nonoy Santillan/Richard S
Brummer/Barbara Pokras
Art Director Ben Otico
Second Unit Director Jonathan Demme
Produced January 1972/Released May 1972
85 mins

THE BIG BIRD CAGE
Cast
Pam Grier...Blossom
Anitra Ford...Terry
Candice Roman...Carla
Teda Bracci...Bull Jones
Carol Speed...Mickie
Karen McKevic...Karen
Sid Haig...Django
Marissa Delgado...Rina
Vic Diaz...Rocco
Andy Centenera...Warden Zappa
Rizza Fabian...Lin Tsiang
Subas Herrero...Moreno
Wendy Green...Gertie

Selected credits
Directed/Written by Jack Hill
Produced by Jane Schaffer
Music by William Loose/William Castleman
Cinematographer Felipe Sacdalan

Edited by James Mitchell/Jere Huggins
Art Director Ben Otico
Produced March 1972/Released June 1972
88 mins

BOXCAR BERTHA
Cast
Barbara Hershey...Boxcar Bertha
David Carradine...Big Bill Shelly
Barry Primus...Rake Brown
Bernie Casey...Von Morton
John Carradine...Sartoris
Victor Argo ....McIver #1
David Osterhout...McIver #2
Grahame Pratt...Emeric Pressburger
'Chicken' Holleman...M Powell
Harry Northrup...Harvey Hall
Ann Morell...Tillie Parr
Marianne Dole...Mrs Mailler
Joe Reynolds...Joe Cox

Selected credits
Directed by Martin Scorsese
Written by John William Corrington/Joyce Hooper
Corrington
Based on the book 'Sister of the Road' by Ben L Reitman
Produced by Roger Corman
Executive Producers James H Nicholson/Samuel Z Arkoff
Associate Producer Julie Corman
Music by Gib Guilbeau/Thad Maxwell
Cinematographer John Stephens
Edited by Buzz Feitshans
Produced October 1971/Released June 1972
92 mins

NIGHT CALL NURSES
Cast
Patti T Byrne...Barbara
Alana Collins...Janis

Mittie Lawrence...Sandra
Clint Kimbrough.....................................Dr Bramlett
Felton Perry...Jude
Richard Young...Kyle
Dennis Dugan...Kit
Christopher Law...Zach
Stack Pierce...Jon Sampson
Bobby Hall...................................Warden Kelley
Martin Ashe.............................Bathrobe Benny
Robert Staats............................E Eddie Edwards
Kate Monahan...............................Nurse Mamall
Dick Miller.................................Mr Jensen
James Millhollin.........................Dr Rolland
Dixie Peabody..Robin
Tris Coffin.......................................Miles Bailey
Carlos Varzeas...Carlos
Barbara Keene..Chloe
Bob Brogan..George

Selected credits
Directed by Jonathan Kaplan
Written by George Armitage
Produced by Julie Corman
Music by Clancy B Grass III
Cinematographer Michael Stringer
Edited by Alan Collins
Second Unit Director George Van Noy
Released June 1972
74 mins

THE CREMATORS
Cast
Maria De Aragon...Jeanne
Marvin Howard..............................Dr Ian Thorne
Eric Allison.................................Dr Willy Seppel
Mason Caulfield..Mason
R N Bullard/Cecil Redick/Tim Frawley/Jax Jason Carroll/
Ola Kauffman/Barney Bossick/Al Ward/Chuck Hillig/Jim
Ragan
Selected credits
Directed/Written by Harry Essex
Based on the story 'Dune Roller' by Julian May (as Judy
Dikty)
Produced by Harry Essex
Associate Producer Jax Jason Carroll
Music by Albert Glasser
Cinematographer Robert Caramico

Edited by Robert Freeman
Released October 1972
75 mins

NIGHT OF THE COBRA WOMAN
Cast
Joy Bang...Joanna
Marlene Clark.......................................Lena Aruza
Roger Garrett...Duff
Vic Diaz...Lope
Rosemarie Gil.......................................Francisca
Slash Marks.............................Sergeant Markle
Vic Silayan...Dr Tezon
Bert Rivera...Ramon
Jimmy Milianios..Benito
Logan Clarke..Collins
Andrew Meyer..Weston
Selected credits
Directed/Written by Andrew Meyer
Story by Andrew Meyer/Kerry Magness
Produced by Kerry Magness/Harvey Marks
Music by Restie Umali
Cinematographer Nonong Rasca
Edited by Gervacio Santos/Barbara Pokras
Art Director Ben Otico
Produced October 1971/Released October 1972
85 mins

UNHOLY ROLLERS
Cast
Claudia Jennings.............................Karen Walker
Louis Quinn...Mr Stern
Betty Anne Rees...Mickey
Roberta Collins...Jennifer
Alan Vint...Greg
Candice Roman..Donna
Jay Varela...Nick
Charlene Jones.............................Beverly Brayton
Joe E Tata..Marshall

Maxine Gates..Angie Striker
Kathleen Freeman..Karen's mother
John Harmon...Doctor
Karl Rizzo..Referee
Mike Miller..Referee
John Steadman..Guard
John Mitchell..Horace McKay
Roxanna Bonilla...Consuela
Dan Seymour...Used car dealer
Eve Bruce...Woman in bar
Alvin Hammer...Man in bar

Selected credits
Directed by Vernon Zimmerman
Written by Howard R Cohen
Story by Vernon Zimmerman/Howard R Cohen
Produced by John Prizer/Jack Bohrer
Executive Producer Roger Corman
Music by Bobby Hart
Cinematographer Mike Shea
Edited by Martin Scorsese/George Trirogoff/Yeu-Bun Yee
Art Director Spencer Quinn
Produced August 1972/Released November 1972
88 mins

THE WOMAN HUNT
Cast
John Ashley...Tony
Pat Woodell..Wanda
Sid Haig..Silas
Laurie Rose...Laurie
Charlene Jones...Billie
Lisa Todd...McGee
Alona Alegre...Sam
Eddie Garcia..Spiros
Ken Metcalfe..Carp
Liza Belmonte..Rita
Lotis Key/Alfonso Carvajal/Ruben Rustia/Don Lipman/
Tony Gosalvez/Paquito Salcedo
Selected credits
Directed by Eddie Romero
Written by David Hoover
Story by Jack Hill/David Hoover
Produced by Eddie Romero/John Ashley
Executive Producer David J Cohen
Music by Jerry Dadap
Cinematographer Justo Paulino
Edited by Ben Barcelon Joseph Zucchero
Production Designer Roberto Formoso
Produced April 1972/Released November 1972
81 mins

CRIES AND WHISPERS
Cast
Liv Ullmann...Maria
Harriet Andersson..Agnes

Kari Sylwan...Anna
Ingrid Thulin..Karin
Selected credits
Directed/Written/Produced by Ingmar Bergman
Released December 1972
91 mins

THE HARDER THEY COME
Cast
Jimmy Cliff...Ivanhoe 'Ivan' Martin
Janet Bartley...Elsa
Carl Bradshaw..Jose
Ras Daniel Hartman...Pedro
Selected credits
Directed/Produced by Perry Henzell
Written by Perry Henzell/Trevor D Rhone
Released February 1973
120 mins

SAVAGE!
Cast
James Iglehart...Jim Heygood
Lada Edmund Jr...Vicki
Carol Speed..Amanda
Sally Jordan...Sylvia
Rossana Ortiz...Julia
Ken Metcalfe..Melton
Vic Diaz...Minister
Aura Aurea..China
Eddie Gutierrez..Flores
Selected credits
Directed/Produced by Cirio H Santiago
Written by Ed Medard
Music by Don Julian
Cinematographer Felipe Sacdalan
Edited by Richard Patterson
Released March 1973
81 mins

THE BIG BUST OUT
Cast
Vonetta McGee/Monica Taylor/Linda Fox/Karen Carter/
Gordon Mitchell/Christin Thorn/Tony Kendall/Mara
Krup/Giorgio Dolphin/Herb Andress/Margaret Rose Keil/
Rebecca Mead
Selected credits
Directed by Ernst R von Theumer (as Richard Jackson)
Written/Produced by Sergio Garrone
Music by Berto Pisano (as Burt Rexon)/Elsio Mancuso
Cinematographer Umberto Galeassi (as Robert Galeasi)
Edited by Cesare Bianchini/Barbara Pokras
Released April 1973
75 mins

FLY ME
Cast
Pat Anderson...Toby
Lenore Kasdorf..Andrea
Lyllah Torena...Sherry
Richard Young..David
Naomi Stevens..Mother
Dick Miller..Taxi driver
Ken Metcalfe...Donald
Vic Diaz...Enriquez
Richard Roake..Co-Pilot
Carmen Barredo..Receptionist
Cole Mallard..Bill
Leo Martinez..Tourist guide
Pat Munzon..Chiang
Roger Lee..Customer on airplane
Daniel Fauré..Young man at airport
Curtis Wong...Thug

Mind Warp

Larry Wikel..2nd thug
Eileen Koch..Female attacker
Sharon Wikel..2nd attacker
Rebecca Aston Smith..Tourist
Selected credits
Directed/Produced by Cirio H Santiago
Written by Miller Drake
Cinematographer Felipe Sacdalan
Edited by Barbara Pokras/George Santos
Art Director Ben Otico
Kung fu sequences directed by Jonathan Demme
Fight Choreographer David Chow
Cinematographers Stephen Katz/Sean Doyle
Released June 1973
72 mins

THIS AIRLINE SERVES THREE WILD DISHES
TAKE YOUR CHOICE

"I'm Toby,
fly me as far
as you want."

"I'm Sherry,
buy a ticket
and I come free!"

"I'm Andrea,
my foreign lay-overs
are very stimulating."

METROCOLOR

SEE STEWARDESSES
BATTLE
KUNG FU
KILLERS!

Fly Me

starring PAT ANDERSON • LENORE KASDORF • LYLLAH TORENA • NAOMI STEVENS
KUNG FU sequences by DAVID CHOW produced by CIRIO SANTIAGO   A NEW WORLD PICTURES RELEASE

STACEY

Cast
Anne Randall..Stacey Hanson
Alan Landers..Bob Eastwood
James Westmoreland..Rodney
Marjorie Bennett..Florence Chambers
Anitra Ford..Tish Chambers
Cristina Raines..Pamela Chambers
Nicholas Georgiade..Matthew
Richard LePore..Luke
John Alderman..John Chambers
Eddie Ryder..Frank
Michael Keep..Lt Brodsky
Lothar Motschenbacher..Himself
Mikki Garcia..Marian
Madelaine Peterson
Selected credits
Directed by Andy Sidaris
Written by William Edgar
Story by Leon Mirell/Andy Sidaris
Produced by Leon Mirell
Executive Producer Michael Trikilis
Associate Producer Beverly McAfee

Music by Don Randi
Cinematographer Mark Zavad
Edited by Craig Stewart
Produced February 1973/Released June 1973
81 mins

THE STUDENT TEACHERS

Cast
Susan Damante..Rachel Burton
Brooke Mills..Tracy Davis
Brenda Sutton..Jody Hawkins
Johnny Ray McGhee..Carnell Smith
Bob Harris..Dinwiddie
John Kramer..Alex Boslick
Dick Miller..Coach Harris
Richard Doran..Mickey J Noonan
James Millhollin..Principal Peters
Douglas Anderson..Buffalo
Tom Mohler..Luis
Rose Cyprus..Melissa Manoogian
Nora Heflin..Sally Updegrove
Jac Emil..Big Red
Ernest Garner..Fat Ike
Frances Heflin..Mrs Updegrove
Ruth Warshawsky..Miss Hamilton
Leslie Oliver..Marge Fielding
Susan Madigan..Cindy Shine
Gary Morgan..Joe Dante
Selected credits
Directed by Jonathan Kaplan
Written by Danny Opatoshu
Produced by Julie Corman
Music by David Nichtern
Cinematographer Stephen Katz
Edited by George Van Noy
Art Director James William Newport
Second Unit Director Barbara Peeters
Released June 1973
79 mins

THE YOUNG NURSES

Cast
Jean Manson..Kitty
Ashley Porter..Joanne
Angela Gibbs..Michelle
Zack Taylor..Donahue
Jack La Rue Jr..Ken
William Joyce..Fairbanks
Allan Arbus..Krebs
Mary Doyle..Nurse Dockett
Don Keefer..Chemist
Linda Towne..Chris Whiting
Jay Burton..Chicken's manager
John Thompson..Chicken
Kimberly Hyde..Peppermint
Nan Martin..Woman reporter
Sally Kirkland..Woman at clinic
Terrill Maguire..Girl at clinic
Dick Miller..Cop
Sam Fuller..Doc Haskell
James Anthony..Male nurse
Jeff Young..Anesthetist
Selected credits
Directed by Clint Kimbrough (as Clinton Kimbro)
Written by Howard R Cohen
Produced by Julie Corman
Music by Gregory Prestopino
Cinematographer Sam Clement
Edited by Karen Johnson
Production Designer Tim Kincaid
Art Director Barbara Peeters
Second Unit Director Pancho Kohner

Released July 1973
77 mins

I ESCAPED FROM DEVIL'S ISLAND
Cast
Jim Brown..Lebras
Christopher George..Devert
Rick Ely...Jo-Jo
James Luisi..Dazzas
Paul Richards...Maj Marteau
Richard Rust...Sgt Zamorra
Roland 'Bob' Harris..The Barber
Jan Merlin...Rosenquist
Robert Phillips...Blassier
Stephen Whittaker...Leper Count
Eduardo Rosas López.....................................Sgt Brescano
Jonathan Dodge...Lt Duplis
Quintín Bulnes..Sgt Grizzoni
Gabriella Rios...Indian girl
Ana De Sade...Bedalia
Max Kerlow..Pollizerro
Aubert Knight..The Dealer
Enrique Lucero..Esteban
Aurora Núñez..Whore
Gastón Melo..Police captain

Selected credits
Directed by William Witney
Written by Richard L Adams
Produced by Roger Corman/Gene Corman/Jack Bohrer/
Miguel Zacarías
Music by Les Baxter
Cinematographer Rosalío Solano
Edited by Alan Collins/Barbara Pokras/Tom Walls
Art Director Roberto Silva
Produced April 1973/Released September 1973
89 mins

SEVEN BLOWS OF THE DRAGON
Cast
David Chiang...Yen Ching
Ti Lung..Wu Sung
Lily Ho...Lu San Niang
Ku Feng...Sung Chiang
Chin Feng...Wu Yung
Yueh Hua...Lin Chung
Tetsuro Tamba...Lu Chun Yi
Toshio Kurosawa...Shih Wen Kung
Fan Mei Sheng..Li Kwei
Cheng Lei..Wang Ying
Liu Tan..Lei Heng
Wu Ma..Shih Chien
Wang Chung..Shi Hsiu
Wu Chih Ching..Yang Hsung
Chin Pei..Hua Yung
Liang Shang Yun..Liu Tang
Peng Peng..Lu Chin Sheng
Lo Wei...Chu Tung
Li Hsiu Hsien...Chang Shun
Ho Han Chow..Chang Meng
Chen Kuan Tai...Shin Chin
Li Heng...Tai Chung

Selected credits
Directed by Chang Cheh
Written by Ni Kuang/Chang Cheh
Based on the novel 'The Water Margin' by Luo Guanzhong
Produced by Run Run Shaw
Music by Chen Yang-Yu
Cinematographer Kung Mu-To
Edited by Hung Kuo Ting
Art Director Johnson Tsao
Released September 1973
80 mins

FANTASTIC PLANET
Voices
Jennifer Drake..Tiwa
Eric Baugin..Terr
Jean Topart..Grand Master
Jean Valmont..Narrator
Max Amyl/Yves Barsacq/Eric Baugin/Denis Boileau/Andre
Lambert/Michele Chahan/Madeleine Clervannes/William
Coryn/Hubert de Lapparent/Poupy de Monneron/Christian
de Tiliere/Christian Echelard/Jeanine Forney/Gerard
Hernandez/Claude Joseph/Pascal Kominakis

Selected credits
Directed by René Laloux
Written by Roland Topor/René Laloux
Based on the novel 'Oms en serie/Oms by the Dozen' by
Pierre Pairault (as Stefan Wul)
Produced by Simon Damiani/André Valio-Cavaglione
Music by Alain Goraguer
Cinematographers Lubomir Rejthar/Boris Baromykin
Edited by Hélène Arnal/Marta Látalová
Production Designer Roland Topor
Released December 1973
72 mins

THE ARENA
Cast
Margaret Markov..Bodicia
Pam Grier...Mamawi
Lucretia Love...Deidre
Paul Muller..Lucilius
Daniel Vargas..Timarchus
Marie Louise...Livia
Maria Pia Conte (as Mary Count)............................Lucinia
Rosalba Neri (as Sara Bay).......................................Cornelia
Vassili Karis (as Vic Karis)...Marcus
Silvio Laurenzi (as Sid Lawrence)..........................Priscium
Mimmo Palmara (as Dick Palmer)..........................Rufinius
Antonio Casale (as Anthony Vernon)...........................Lucan
Franco Garofalo (as Christopher Oakes)..................Aemilius
Pietro Ceccarelli (as Peter Cester)..........................Septimus
Jho Jhenkins..Quintus
Ivan Gasper..Wulfstan
Pietro Torrisi..Gladiator
Salvatore Baccaro..Winekeeper
Anna Melita...Gladiator girl

Selected credits
Directed by Steve Carver
Written by John William Corrington/Joyce Hooper
Corrington
Produced by Mark Damon
Music by Francesco De Masi
Cinematographer Aristide Massaccesi
Edited by Joe Dante
Produced May 1973/Released January 1974
83 mins

CAGED HEAT
Cast
Juanita Brown...Maggie
Roberta Collins..Belle Tyson
Erica Gavin..Jacqueline Wilson
Ella Reid...Pandora
Cheryl 'Rainbeaux' Smith..Lavelle
Barbara Steele..Supt McQueen
Warren Miller..Dr Randolph
Crystin Sinclaire (as Lynda Gold)........................Crazy Alice
Toby Carr Rafelson...Pinter
Irene Stokes..Hazel
Cynthia Songey...Rosemary
Ann Stockdale..Bonnie
Dorothy Love...Kitchen matron
Carol Terry...Kitchen guard

Layla Gallaway..Shower guard
Essie Hayes..Essie
John Aprea...Dream man
Carmen Argenziano.........................Undercover wrestler
Gene Borkan/Mikki Fox

Selected credits
Directed/Written by Jonathan Demme
Produced by Evelyn Purcell
Executive Producer Samuel W Gelfman
Music by John Cale
Cinematographer Tak Fujimoto
Edited by Johanna Demetrakas/Carolyn Hicks/Michal Goldman
Art Director Eric Thiermann
Produced January 1974/Released April 1974
83 mins

CANDY STRIPE NURSES

Cast
Candice Rialson...Sandy
Robin Mattson..Dianne
María Rojo...Marisa
Roger Cruz...Carlos
Rod Haase...Cliff
Rick Gates...Wally
Don Keefer...Dr Wilson
Kendrew Lascelles.....................................Owen Boles
Michael Ross Verona....................................Freddie
Kimberly Hyde..April
Elana Casey...Zouzou
John Hudson...Dr Krause
Ruth Warshawsky.......................................Head nurse
June Christopher...........................Emergency room nurse
James Espinoza..The witness
Al Alu...The hood
Frank Lugo...The fat hood
Ray Galvin...........................Gas station attendant
Tom Baker....................................First mechanic
Rick Garcia...............................Second mechanic
Selected credits
Directed/Written by Alan Holleb
Produced by Julie Corman
Associate Producer Nicole Scott
Music by Thompson & Tabor
Cinematographer Colin Campbell
Edited by Allan Holzman
Second Unit Director Barbara Peeters
Produced January 1974/Released May 1974
80 mins

BIG BAD MAMA

Cast
Angie Dickinson.......................................Wilma McClatchie
William Shatner.................................William J Baxter
Tom Skerritt...Fred Diller
Susan Sennett...Billy Jean

Robbie Lee..Polly
Noble Willingham.......................................Uncle Barney
Dick Miller...Bonney
Tom Signorelli...Dodds
Joan Prather..Jane Kingston
Royal Dano...................................Reverend Johnson
William O'Connell....................................Crusade preacher
John Wheeler..Lawyer
Ralph James..Sheriff
Sally Kirkland....................................Barney's woman
Wally Berns..Legionnaire
Shannon Christie...Stripper
Michael Talbott...............................Sheriff's son
Charles Pinney..Mr Kingston
Rob Berger.....................................Charlie Johnson
Jay Brooks...Wesley
Selected credits
Directed by Steve Carver
Written by William Norton/Frances Doel
Produced by Roger Corman
Associate Producer Jon Davison
Music by David Grisman
Cinematographer Bruce Logan
Edited by Tina Hirsch
Art Director Peter Jamison
Second Unit Director Paul Bartel
Produced April 1974/Released July 1974
83 mins

COCKFIGHTER

Cast
Warren Oates.................................Frank Mansfield
Richard B Shull........................Omar Baradansky
Harry Dean Stanton.............................Jack Burke
Ed Begley Jr.....................................Tom Peeples
Laurie Bird.................................Dody White Burke
Troy Donahue..........................Randall Mansfield
Warren Finnerty.................................Sanders
Robert Earl Jones....................................Buford
Patricia Pearcy.............................Mary Elizabeth
Millie Perkins.......................Frances Mansfield
Steve Railsback..Junior
Tom Spratley............................Mister Peeples
Charles Willeford.......................Ed Middleton
Pete Munro..Packard
Kermit Echols...................................Fred Reed
Ed Smith...Whipple
Jimmy Williams...........................Buddy Waggoner
John Trotter.......................................Hansen
Lois Zeitlin...Lucille
Joe Bentley...................................Peach Owen
Selected credits
Directed by Monte Hellman
Written by Charles Willeford, based on his novel/Earl MacRauch
Produced by Roger Corman/Samuel W Gelfman
Music by Michael Franks
Cinematographer Néstor Almendros
Edited by Lewis Teague/Monte Hellman
Art Directors Charlie Hughes/Pat Mann
Produced May 1974/Released August 1974
83 mins

THE LAST DAYS OF MAN ON EARTH

Cast
Jon Finch.....................................Jerry Cornelius
Jenny Runacre..............................Miss Brunner
Sterling Hayden...................Maj Wrongway Lindbergh
Harry Andrews...John
Hugh Griffith....................................Professor Hira
Julie Ege...Miss Dazzle
Patrick Magee.....................................Dr Baxter

Graham Crowden...Dr Smiles
George Coulouris...Dr Powys
Basil Henson...Dr Lucas
Derrick O'Connor...Frank
Gilles Millinaire...Dimitri
Ronald Lacey...Shades
Sandy Ratcliffe..Jenny
Mary Macleod..Nurse
Sarah Douglas..Catherine
Delores Delmar...Fortune teller
Sandra Dickinson..Waitress

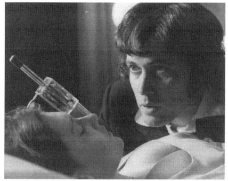

Selected credits
Directed/Written by/Production Designer Robert Fuest
Based on the novel 'The Final Programme' by Michael Moorcock
Produced by John Goldstone/Sanford Lieberson
Executive Producers Roy Baird/David Puttnam
Music by Paul Beaver/Bernard Krause
Cinematographer Norman Warwick
Edited by Barrie Vince
Art Director Philip Harrison
Produced January 1973/Released August 1974
76 mins

AMARCORD
Cast
Bruno Zanin...Titta Biondi
Pupella Maggio..Miranda Biondi
Armando Brancia...Aurelio Biondi
Magali Noël..Gradisca
Ciccio Ingrassia...Teo
Nando Orfei..Patacca
Luigi Rossi..Lawyer
Selected credits
Directed by Federico Fellini
Written by Federico Fellini/Tonino Guerra
Produced by Franco Cristaldi
Released September 1974
123 mins

TENDER LOVING CARE
Cast
Donna Young (as Dona Desmond)................................Karen
Marilyn Joi (as Ineda King)..Lynn
Lauren Simon (as Leah Simon).....................................Tracy
Tony Victor..Jackie
Michael Asher..David
John Daniels..Ed
Josh Taylor (as Tim Taylor)..Reno
Martin Miles...Bad News
George 'Buck' Flower (as CD Lafleur).......................Simpson
Laurence Cohen/John Joseph/Brad Peterson/Ellen Prince/
Carona Faoro/Kathy Hilton/Roger Panca/Tim Paola/Dean
Russo/Eric Watts/Maxayn

Selected credits
Directed/Written by Don Edmonds
Produced by Don Edmonds/Chako van Leeuwen
Executive Producer David Holliday
Associate Producer Bethel Buckalew
Music by Steve Michaels
Cinematographer William B Kaplan
Edited by Robert Freeman
Art Director Ellen Prince
Produced March 1973/Released October 1974
72 mins

TNT JACKSON
Cast
Jeanne Bell...Diana 'TNT' Jackson
Stan Shaw...Charlie
Pat Anderson..Elaine
Ken Metcalfe...Sid
Chiquito...Joe
Imelda Ilanan..Joe's Assistant
Leo Martin/Max Alvarado/Percy Gordon/Chris Cruz/John
Gamble
Selected credits
Directed by Cirio H Santiago
Written by Dick Miller/Ken Metcalfe
Produced by Cirio H Santiago
Cinematographer Felipe Sacdalan
Edited by Gervacio Santos/Barbara Pokras
Art Director Ben Otico
Released January 1975
72 mins

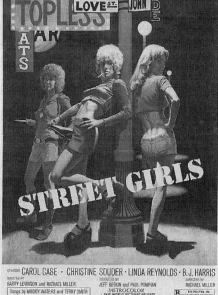

STREET GIRLS
Cast
Carol Case..Sally
Paul Pompian...Irv
Art Burke...Sven
Christine Souder...Angel
Jimmy Smith..Jimmy
Michael Weber...Michael Albert

253

Jay Deringer	Mario
Fred Garra	Roy
John Freeman	Les
BJ Harris	Mitzi
Linda Reynolds	Adelle
Jeannie Mitchell	Girl with banana
Saul B Vincent	Bob
Levi Fergus	Ed

Selected credits
Directed by Michael Miller
Written by Michael Miller/Barry Levinson
Produced by Paul Pompian/Jeff Begun
Executive Producer David B Dahl
Music by Terry Smith
Cinematographer Bob Wilson
Second Unit Director Lou Melson
Produced January 1974/Released February 1975
77 mins

CAPONE

Cast

Ben Gazzara	Al Capone
Harry Guardino	Johnny Torrio
Susan Blakely	Iris Crawford
Sylvester Stallone	Frank Nitti
John Cassavetes	Frankie Yale
Frank Campanella	Big Jim Colosimo
John Orchard	Dion O'Banion
Carmen Argenziano	Jack McGurn
George Chandler	Robert E Crowe
John D Chandler	Hymie Weiss
Royal Dano	Anton J Cermak
Joe De Nicola	Charles Fischetti
Angelo Grisanti	Angelo Genna
Peter Maloney	Jake Guzik
Dick Miller	Joe Pryor
Robert Phillips	Bugs Moran
Martin Kove	Pete Gusenberg
Mario Gallo	Giuseppe Aiello
George Milan	William H Thompson
Russ Marin	Joseph Stenson

Selected credits
Directed by Steve Carver
Written by Howard Browne
Produced by Roger Corman
Associate Producer John C Broderick
Music by David Grisman
Cinematographer Vilis Lapenieks
Edited by Richard C Meyer
Art Director Ward Preston
Produced November 1974/Released April 1975
101 mins

DEATH RACE 2000

Cast

David Carradine	Frankenstein
Simone Griffeth	Annie Smith
Sylvester Stallone	Machine Gun Joe Viterbo
Mary Woronov	Calamity Jane
Roberta Collins	Matilda the Hun
Martin Kove	Nero the Hero
Louisa Moritz	Myra
Don Steele	Junior Bruce
Joyce Jameson	Grace Pander
Carle Bensen	Harold
Sandy McCallum	Mr President
Paul Laurence	Special agent
Harriet Medin	Thomasina Paine
Vince Trankina	Lt Fury
Bill Morey	Deacon
Fred Grandy	Herman the German
William Shephard	Pete

Leslie McRay	Cleopatra
Wendy Bartel	Laurie
Jack Favorite	Henry

Selected credits
Directed by Paul Bartel
Written by Robert Thom/Charles B Griffith
Based on the story 'The Racer' by Ib Melchior
Produced by Roger Corman
Associate Producer Jim Weatherill
Music by Paul Chihara
Cinematographer Tak Fujimoto
Edited by Tina Hirsch
Art Directors Robinson Royce/B B Neel
Second Unit Directors Lewis Teague/Charles B Griffith
Produced October 1974/Released April 1975
84 mins

TIDAL WAVE

Cast

Tetsuro Tamba	Prime Minister Yamamoto
John Fujioka	Narita
Keiju Kobayashi	Dr Tadokoro
Ayumi Ishida	Abe Reiko
Shogo Shimada	Watari
Hiroshi Fujioka	Toshio Onodera
Tadao Nakamaru	Kuni-eda
Yusuke Takita	Assistant Professor Yukinaga
Hideaki Nitani	Dr Nakata
Nobuo Nakamura	Japanese Ambassador to Australia
Isao Natsuyagi	Yuuki
Lorne Greene	Ambassador Warren Richards
Rhonda Leigh Hopkins	Fran

Selected credits
Directed by Shirô Moritani/Andrew Meyer
Written by Shinobu Hashimoto/Andrew Meyer
Based on the novel 'Japan Sinks' by Sakyo Komatsu
Executive Producer Tomoyuki Tanaka
Associate Producer Osamu Tanaka
Music by Masaru Satô
Cinematographers Hiroshi Murai/Daisaku Kimura
Edited by Michiko Ikeda
Art Director Yoshirô Muraki
Released May 1975
82 mins

SUMMER SCHOOL TEACHERS

Cast

Candice Rialson	Conklin T
Pat Anderson	Sally
Rhonda Leigh Hopkins	Denise
Will Carney	Jeremy
Grainger Hines	Bob
Christopher Barrett	Jeff
Dick Miller	Sam
Vince Barnett	Principal Adams
Norman Bartold	Agwin

Michael Greer	John John Lacey
Barbara Deil	Janice
Ka-Ron Sowell Brown	Jessie
Merie Earle	Ethel
Cecil Elliott	Frieda
John Kerry	Hiram
CD Smith	Cy
Brian Enright	Slick
Walter O Miles	Mr Carter
Beach Dickerson	Apartment manager
Gary Morgan	Doger

Selected credits
Directed/Written by Barbara Peeters
Produced by Julie Corman
Associate Producer Nicole Scott
Music by JJ Jackson
Cinematographer Eric Saarinen
Edited by Barbara Pokras
Art Director Marty Bercaw
Second Unit Director Mel Damski
Released June 1975
85 mins

CRAZY MAMA

IN 1957
CHERYL DROVE
MOM'S CHEVY
ON A HEAVY DATE:
GOT KNOCKED UP,
KNOCKED OVER A BANK,
SMASHED
FOUR POLICE CARS
AND KIDNAPPED
HER STEPFATHER

IT WAS A CRAZY YEAR!

CLORIS LEACHMAN IN CRAZY MAMA

STARRING STUART WHITMAN ANN SOTHERN · LINDA PURL
JIM BACKUS · TISHA STERLING · DONN MOST   AND 10 GOLDEN OLDIES!
Screenplay by ROBERT THOM   Directed by JONATHAN DEMME · Produced by JULIE CORMAN
A NEW WORLD PICTURE   **PG** PARENTAL GUIDANCE SUGGESTED   METROCOLOR

Cast

Cloris Leachman	Melba
Stuart Whitman	Jim Bob
Ann Sothern	Sheba
Jim Backus	Mr Albertson
Donn Most	Shawn
Linda Purl	Cheryl
Bryan Englund	Snake
Merie Earle	Bertha
Sally Kirkland	Ella Mae
Clint Kimbrough	Daniel
Dick Miller	Wilbur Janeway

Carmen Argenziano	Supermarket manager
Harry Northup	FBI agent
Ralph James	Sheriff - 1932
Dinah Englund	Melba - 1932
Robert Reece	Mover
John Aprea	Marvin
Mickey Fox	Mrs Morgan
Hal Marshall	Bartender
Cynthia Songey	Lucinda

Selected credits
Directed by Jonathan Demme
Written by Robert Thom
Story by Frances Thom
Produced by Julie Corman
Associate Producer Peter Cornberg
Music by Snotty Scotty and The Hankies
Cinematographer Bruce Logan
Edited by Allan Holzman/Lewis Teague
Art Director Peter Jamison
Second Unit Director Evelyn Purcell
Produced April 1975/Released July 1975
83 mins

COVER GIRL MODELS

Cast

Pat Anderson	Barbara
Lindsay Bloom	Claire
Tara Strohmeier	Mandy
John Kramer	Mark
Rhonda Leigh Hopkins	Pamela
Mary Woronov	Diane
Vic Diaz	Kulik
Tony Ferrer	Ray Chua
AC Castro	Rebel leader
Nory Wright	Tracy Marks
Mark LeBuse	Sam Melson
Ken Metcalfe	Tom Mahoney
Joseph Zucchero	The ambassador
Zenaida Amador	Juanita
Jordan Rosengarten	The sailor
Joonee Gamboa	Chen
Leo Martin	Wong
Bernard Beam	Ric
Howard Shaw	The publisher
Barbara Perez	The model

Selected credits
Directed/Produced by Cirio H Santiago
Written by Howard R Cohen
Associate Producer Robert E Waters
Music by D'Amarillo
Cinematographer Felipe Sacdalan
Edited by Gervacio Santos/Richard Anderson
Second Unit Director Mel Damski
Released August 1975
73 mins

DARKTOWN STRUTTERS

Cast

Trina Parks	Syreena
Edna Richardson	Carmen
Bettye Sweet	Miranda
Shirley Washington	Theda
Roger E Mosley	Mellow
Christopher Joy	Wired
Stan Shaw	Raunchy
DeWayne Jessie	VD
Norman Bartold	Commander Cross
Charles Knapp	Officer Tubbins
Edward Marshall	Officer Emmo
Dick Miller	Officer Hugo
Milt Kogan	Officer Babel
Gene Simms	Flash

Sam Laws..Philo Raspberry
Frankie Crocker..Stuff
Della Thomas..Lixie
Ed Bakey...Rev Tilly
Fuddle Bagley...Casabah
Frances Nealy..Cinderella
Selected credits
Directed by William Witney
Written by George Armitage
Produced by Gene Corman
Cinematographer João Fernandes
Edited by Morton Tubor
Production Designer Jack Fisk
Art Director Peter Jamison
Released August 1975
90 mins

THE ROMANTIC ENGLISHWOMAN
Cast
Glenda Jackson..Elizabeth Fielding
Michael Caine..Lewis Fielding
Helmut Berger...Thomas
Michael Lonsdale...Swan
Selected credits
Directed by Joseph Losey
Written by Tom Stoppard/Thomas Wiseman, from his novel
Produced by Daniel M Angel
Released November 1975
115 mins

THE LOST HONOR OF KATHARINA BLUM
Cast
Angela Winkler...Katharina Blum
Mario Adorf......................................Kommissar Beizmenne
Dieter Laser...Werner Tötges
Jürgen Prochnow...Ludwig Götten
Selected credits
Directed/Written by Volker Schlöndorff/Margarethe von
Trotta, from the novel by Heinrich Böll
Produced by Willi Benninger/Eberhard Junkersdorf/
Gunther Witte
Released December 1975
106 mins

THE STORY OF ADELE H
Cast
Isabelle Adjani...Adèle Hugo
Bruce Robinson..Lt Albert Pinson
Sylvia Marriott...Mrs Saunders
Joseph Blatchley...The bookseller
Selected credits
Directed by François Truffaut
Written by Jean Gruault/Suzanne Schiffman/François
Truffaut/Jan Dawson
Story by Frances V Guille
Produced by Marcel Berbert/Claude Miller/François
Truffaut
Released December 1975
96 mins

HOLLYWOOD BOULEVARD
Cast
Candice Rialson..Candy Wednesday
Mary Woronov..Mary McQueen
Rita George...Bobbi Quackenbush
Jeffrey Kramer...Patrick Hobby
Dick Miller..Walter Paisley
Richard Doran..PG
Tara Strohmeier...Jill McBain
Paul Bartel..Erich Von Leppe
John Kramer..Duke Mantee
Jonathan Kaplan...Scotty

George Wagner..Cameraman
W L Luckey...Rico Bandello
David Boyle...Obnoxious kid
Glenn K Shimada.................................Ubiqutious Filipino
Joseph McBride..Drive-in rapist
Barbara Pieters...Drive-in mother
Shawn Pieters..Drive-in kid
Sue Veneer...Drive-in dyke
Charles B Griffith...Mark Dentine
Todd McCarthy...Author
Selected credits
Directed by Joe Dante/Allan Arkush
Written by Danny Opatoshu (as Patrick Hobby)
Produced by Jon Davison
Associate Producer Teri Schwartz
Music by Andrew E Stein
Cinematographer Jamie Anderson
Edited by Amy Jones/Allan Arkush/Joe Dante
Art Director Jack DeWolfe
Produced October 1975/Released February 1976
83 mins

NASHVILLE GIRL/NEW GIRL IN TOWN
Cast
Monica Gayle..Jamie
Glenn Corbett..Jeb
Roger Davis...Kelly
Johnny Rodriguez...Himself
Jesse White...CY Ordell
Marcie Barkin...Alice
Shirley Jo Finney...Frisky
Judith Roberts..Fran
Leo Gordon...Burt
Byron Warner...Jerry
Diana Murrell...Kathy
Adrian Marshall...Carl
Jonathan Leitz...Mishmash
Barbara Moore...Matron
Jack Irvin..Ben Sr
Jane J Jones...Mother
Phillip R Jones...Jeremy
Martin L Clayton III..Ben Jr
Donald W McCormick III..Clay
Michael Wise..Guitar salesman

Selected credits
Directed by Gus Trikonis
Written/Produced by Peer J Oppenheimer
Associate Producer Lamar Card
Music by Kim Richmond
Cinematographer Irving Goodnoff
Edited by Jerry Cohen
Art Director Russell Schwartz
Produced September 1975/Released February 1976
90 mins

FOXTROT
Cast
Peter O'Toole..Liviu

Charlotte Rampling...Julia
Max von Sydow..Larsen
Jorge Luke..Eusebio
Helena Rojo..Alexandra
Claudio Brook..Paul
Max Kerlow...Captain
Christa Walter...Gertrude
Mario Castillon...Bracho sailor
Anne Porterfield..Marianna

Selected credits
Directed by Arturo Ripstein
Written by Arturo Ripstein/José Emilio Pacheco/HAL Craig
Produced by Gerald Green
Executive Producers Maximiliano Vega Tato/Anuar Badin
Music by Pete Rugolo
Cinematographer Peter Zinner
Art Director Lucero Isaac
Produced June 1975/Released March 1976
91 mins

EAT MY DUST!
Cast
Ron Howard..Hoover Niebold
Christopher Norris...Darlene Kurtz
Brad David..Billy B Westerby
Kathy O'Dare...Miranda Smith
Clint Howard..George Poole Jr
Pete Isacksen...Junior Hale
Jessica Potter...Lallie Chandler
Warren Kemmerling......................................Sheriff Niebold
Charles Howerton..Dep Jay Beah
Kedric Wolfe...Dep Brookside
John Kramer..Dep Sebastiani
WL Luckey...Dep Gallo
Rance Howard..Clark
Dave Madden...Big Bubba Jones
Robert Broyles..Bud
John Thompson..Oly
Ronald C Ross..Driver
Speed Stearns..Driver
Von Deming..Driver
Rick Deming..Driver

Selected credits
Directed/Written by Charles B Griffith
Produced by Roger Corman
Music by David Grisman
Cinematographer Eric Saarinen
Edited by Tina Hirsch
Art Director Peter Jamison
Second Unit Director Barbara Peeters
Produced December 1975/Released April 1976
89 mins

FIGHTING MAD
Cast
Peter Fonda...Tom Hunter
Gino Franco...Dylan Hunter
Harry Northup...Sheriff Len Skerritt
Philip Carey..Pierce Crabtree
Noble Willingham.......................................Senator Hingle
John Doucette...Jeff Hunter
Scott Glenn..Charlie Hunter
Lynn Lowry...Lorene Maddox
Kathleen Miller...Carolee Hunter
Ted Markland...Hal Fraser
Laura Weatherford..Fraser child
Gerry Wetherford..Fraser child
Peter Fain...Gillette
Allan Wyatt...Judge O'Connor

Selected credits
Directed/Written by Jonathan Demme
Produced by Roger Corman/Evelyn Purcell

Music by Bruce Langhorne
Cinematographer Michael Watkins
Edited by Anthony Magro
Second Unit Director Evelyn Purcell
Produced October 1975/Released April 1976
90 mins

JACKSON COUNTY JAIL
Cast
Yvette Mimieux...Dinah Hunter
Tommy Lee Jones...Coley Blake
Robert Carradine..Bobby Ray
Frederic Cook..Hobie
Severn Darden...Sheriff Dempsey
Howard Hesseman...David
John Lawlor..Deputy Burt
Mary Woronov..Pearl
Britt Leach..Dan Oldum
Betty Thomas...Waitress
Patrice Rohmer...Cassie Anne
Lisa Copeland......................................Girl in commercial
Clifford Emmich..Mr Bigelow
Michael Ashe..Mr Cooper
Edward Marshall..Mr Blight
Marciee Drake..Candy
Nan Martin...Allison
Ken Lawrence..Paulie
Arthur Wong...Cook
Marci Barkin..Girl in restaurant

Selected credits
Directed by Michael Miller
Written by Donald Stewart
Produced by Jeff Begun
Executive Producer Roger Corman
Associate Producer Paul Gonsky
Music by Loren Newkirk
Cinematographer Bruce Logan
Edited by Caroline Ferriol
Art Director Michael McCloskey
Second Unit Director Jan Kiesser
Released April 1976
89 mins

CANNONBALL
Cast
David Carradine..........................Coy 'Cannonball' Buckman
Bill McKinney..Cade Redman
Veronica Hamel...Linda Maxwell
Gerrit Graham...Perman Waters
Robert Carradine..Jim Crandell
Belinda Balaski..Maryann
Judy Canova...Sharma Capri
Archie Hahn...Zippo Friedman
Carl Gottlieb...Terry McMillan
Mary Woronov..Sandy Harris
Diane Lee Hart...Wendy
Glynn Rubin..Ginny

James Keach...Wolf Messer
Dick Miller..Bennie Buckman
Stanley Clay...Beutell
David Arkin.....................................TV producer anchorman
John Herzfeld..Sharpe
Louisa Moritz..Louisa
Patrick Wright...Brad Phillips
John Alderman...Ken Hooper

Selected credits
Directed by Paul Bartel
Written by Paul Bartel/Donald C Simpson
Produced by Samuel W Gelfman
Executive Producers Gustave Berne/Run Run Shaw
Associate Producer Peter Cornberg
Music by David A Axelrod
Cinematographer Tak Fujimoto
Edited by Morton Tubor
Art Director Michel Levesque
Second Unit Director Alan Gibbs
Released July 1976
93 mins

THE GREAT TEXAS DYNAMITE CHASE
Cast
Claudia Jennings...Candy Morgan
Jocelyn Jones..Ellie-Jo Turner
Johnny Crawford...Slim
Chris Pennock..Jake
Tara Strohmeier...Pam Morgan
Miles Watkins...Boyfriend
Bart Braverman...Freddie
Nancy Bleier..Carol
Buddy Kling..Mr Sherman
Oliver Clark...Officer Andy
Tom Rosqui..Jason Morgan
Ed Steef...Todd
Danny Sullivan..Young Texan
Peggy Brenner...Bank teller
Jim Boles...Mr Ralston
Priscilla Pointer...Miss Harris
Jock Livingston...Mr Scott
Gary Kaskell...Man in crowd #1
Jay Hamburger..Man in crowd #2
Lawrie Driscoll...Officer Carl

Selected credits
Directed by Michael Pressman
Written by David Kirkpatrick
Story by Mark Rosin
Produced by David Irving
Executive Producers Marshall Backlar/Karen Whitfield/
Marshall Whitfield
Associate Producer Peter MacGregor Scott
Music by Craig Safan
Cinematographer Jamie Anderson
Edited by Millie Moore
Production Designer Russell J Smith

Released August 1976
90 mins

MOVING VIOLATION
Cast
Stephen McHattie.......................................Eddie Moore
Kay Lenz...Cam Johnson
Eddie Albert..Alex Warren
Lonny Chapman...Sheriff Rankin
Will Geer..Rockfield
Jack Murdock...Bubba
John S Ragin...Agent Shank
Dennis Redfield...Tylor
Michael Ross Verona...Harvey
Francis de Sales..Lawyer
Dick Miller..Mack
Richard O'Brien..Police Chief
Paul Linke...Frank
Jason Wingreen...Psychiatrist
George Ball ....George the cop
Norman Bartold...Attorney general
Ted Hartley...District attorney
Brooks Almy...Secretary
Michael Quinn...Police official
David R Osterhout..............................Gas station attendant

Selected credits
Directed by Charles S Dubin
Written by David R Osterhout/William Norton
Produced by Julie Corman
Executive Producer Roger Corman
Music by Don Peake
Cinematographer Charles Correll
Edited by Richard Sprague/Howard Terrill
Art Director Sherman Loudermilk
Produced April 1976/Released August 1976
91 mins

GOD TOLD ME TO
Cast
Tony Lo Bianco....................................Det Lt Peter J Nicholas
Deborah Raffin...Casey Forster
Sandy Dennis...Martha Nicholas
Sylvia Sidney...Elizabeth Mullin
Sam Levene...Everett Lukas
Robert Drivas..David Morten
Mike Kellin ....Deputy commissioner
Richard Lynch..Bernard Phillips
Sammy Williams...Harold Gorman
Jo Flores Chase...Mrs Gorman
William Roerick..Richards
Lester Rawlins...Board chairman
Harry Bellaver...Cookie
George Patterson..Zero
Walter Steele...Junkie
John Heffernan..Bramwell
Alan Cauldwell.......................................Bramwell as a youth
Robert Nichols...Fletcher
Andy Kaufman..Police assassin
Sherry Steiner..Mrs Phillips

Selected credits
Directed/Written/Produced by Larry Cohen
Music by Frank Cordell
Cinematographer Paul Glickman
Edited byArthur Mandelberg/William J Waters/
Christopher Lebenzon/Mike Corey
Produced October 1975/Released October 1976
91 mins

SMALL CHANGE
Cast
Nicole Félix...Grégory's mother
Chantal Mercier...Chantal Petit

Jean-François Stévenin.........................Jean-François Richet
Virginie Thévenet.................................Lydie Richet
Selected credits
Directed/Produced by François Truffaut
Written by François Truffaut/Suzanne Schiffman
Released October 1976
104 mins

LUMIÈRE

Cast
Jeanne Moreau..Sarah
Francine Racette.......................................Julienne
Lucia Bosé...Laura
Caroline Cartier...Caroline
Selected credits
Directed/Written by Jeanne Moreau
Produced by Claire Duval
Released November 1976
95 mins

BLONDE IN BLACK LEATHER

Cast
Monica Vitti/Claudia Cardinale/Ninetto Davoli/Guido
Leontini/Fernando Camerini/Mario Danieli/Salvatore
Baccaro/Santo Triolo/Franco Vienna/Alfredo D'Ippolito/
Viviana Pezzani/Gennaro Ombra/Marcello Fiocchetti/
Luciano Fiocchetti/Paolo Zilli/Enzo Guarini
Selected credits
Directed by Carlo Di Palma
Written by Barbara Alberti/Amedeo Pagani/Carlo Di Palma
Produced by Franco Cristaldi
Music by Riz Ortolani
Cinematographer Dario Di Palma
Edited by Ruggero Mastroianni
Production Designer Luciano Ricceri
Art Director Ezio Di Monte
Released March 1977
100 mins

TOO HOT TO HANDLE

Cast
Cheri Caffaro.....................................Samantha Fox
Aharon Ipalé..Domingo De La Torres
Vic Diaz..Sanchez
Corinne Calvet....................................Madame Ruanda
John Van Dreelen................................MacKenzie Portman
Jordan Rosengarten............................Justin Stockwell
Butz Aquino...Carlos Rossimo
Subas Herrero......................................Octavio Calderone
Grace Lee...Miss Chow
Paquito Salcedo...................................Lu Chang
Vic Silayan..District attorney
June Gamboa..Mr Bulacon
Selected credits
Directed by Don Schain
Written by Jan Michael Sherman/Don Buday
Story by Don Schain/Jan Michael Sherman/Don Buday
Produced by Ralph T Desiderio
Music by Hugo Montenegro
Cinematographer Fredy Conde
Edited by Barbara Pokras
Produced January 1976/Released March 1977
85 mins

ANDY WARHOL'S BAD

Cast
Carroll Baker.......................................Hazel Aiken
Perry King..LT
Susan Tyrrell.......................................Mary Aiken
Stefania Casini.....................................PG
Cyrinda Foxe..RC
Mary Boylan..Grandmother
Charles McGregor.................................Detective Hughes
Tere Tereba..Ingrid Joyner
Brigid Polk...Estelle
Susan Blond..Young mother
Gordon Oas-Heim..................................Mr Aiken
Maria Smith..Marsha Montemorano
Geraldine Smith....................................Glenda Montemorano
Lawrence Tierney...................................O'Reilly
Joe Lamba..Russell Joyner
John Starke..Joe Leachman
Renee Paris...Sara Leachman
Barbara Allen..SF
Matthew Anton......................................Drugstore boy
Cathy Roskam..Drugstore mother
Selected credits
Directed by Jed Johnson
Written by Pat Hackett/George Abagnalo
Produced by Jeff Tornberg
Executive Producers Andy Warhol/Fred Hughes
Associate Producer Fred Caruso
Music by Mike Bloomfield
Cinematographer Alan Metzger
Edited by Franca Silvi
Art Director Eugene Rudolf
Produced May 1976/Released April 1977
105 mins

BLACK OAK CONSPIRACY

Cast
Jesse Vint...Jingo Johnson
Karen Carlson.......................................Lucy Metcalf
Albert Salmi...Sheriff Grimes
Seymour Cassel....................................Homer Metcalf
Douglas Fowley.....................................Bryan Hancock
Robert F Lyons......................................Harrison Hancock
Mary Wilcox..Beulah Barnes
James Gammon......................................Deputy Bullard
Janus Blythe...Melba Barnes
Will Hare...Doc Rhodes
Jeremy Foster.......................................Billie Bob
Peggy Stewart.......................................Virginia Metcalf
Jo Anne Strauss....................................Sadie Grimes
Vic Perrin..Mr Finch
Darby Hinton..Miner at cafe
Dana Derfus..Miner
Bill Cross..Stunt gaffer
Rock Walker..Policeman
Buff Brady...Policeman
Stephanie Pineo....................................Kazoo band leader
Selected credits
Directed by Bob Kelljan
Written by Hugh Smith/Jesse Vint
Produced by Jesse Vint/Tom Clark
Executive Producer Gail Clark
Associate Producer Richard Franchot
Music by Don Peake
Cinematographer Chris Ludwig
Edited by Jerry Garcia
Released April 1977
92 mins

CATASTROPHE

Cast
William Conrad...Narrator
Selected credits
Directed/Written/Produced by Larry Savadove
Released April 1977
91 mins

MOONSHINE COUNTY EXPRESS

Cast
John Saxon...J B Johnson

Susan Howard..Dot Hammer
William Conrad..Jack Starkey
Morgan Woodward...Sweetwater
Claudia Jennings..Betty Hammer
Jeff Corey...Hagen
Dub Taylor..Uncle Bill
Maureen McCormick...Sissy Hammer
Albert Salmi...Sheriff Larkin
Len Lesser..Scoggins
Bruce Kimball...Harley
Candice Rialson...Mayella
E J André...Lawyer Green
Fred Foresman..Pap Hammer
Dick Esterly...Hackberry
Tom Heaton..Tiny
Rick Langston...Gabe
Bill Luckey..Hood
Lenka Novak..Manicurist
Dean Christianson...Leroy

Selected credits
Directed by Gus Trikonis
Written by Hubert Smith/Daniel Ansley
Produced by Ed Carlin
Executive Producers Paul Joseph/Doro Hreljanovic
Music by Fred Werner
Cinematographer Gary Graver
Edited by Gene Ruggiero
Art Director Peter Jamison
Produced April 1976/Released April 1977
95 mins

ASSAULT ON PARADISE/ THE TOWN THAT CRIED TERROR

Cast
Oliver Reed..Nick McCormick
Deborah Raffin...Cindy Simmons
James Mitchum..Tracker
Stuart Whitman...William Whitaker
John Ireland...Chief Haliburton
Paul Koslo..Victor
Arch Archambault..Inspector Davey
Robert Lussier..Wolf
Dennis Redfield...Jackson
Kipp Whitman...Officer Steiner
Bill Allen...Carson
Daniel Knapp..T J Caulfield
Richard Michael Alexander...............................Larry Owens
Richard Ellman Kennedy....................................Texan
Julian Wells..Floozy
Thomas J Conlan...................................Mayor of Paradise
Paul Roland..Barney
Wendy Donohue..Miss Davis
John Hirohata..Tommy
Judith Nugent-Hart..Miss Paradise

Selected credits
Directed by Richard Compton
Written by John C Broderick/Ron Silkosky
Produced by James V Hart/Peter MacGregor Scott
Associate Producers John M Hawn/Bond Denson Ferrell
Music by Don Ellis
Cinematographer Charles Correll
Edited by Tina Hirsch
Executive Producer Patrick S Ferrell
Released May 1977
90 minutes

DIRTY DUCK

Voices
Howard Kaylan/Mark Volman/Robert Ridgely/Cynthia Adler/Walker Edmiston/Janet Lee/Lurene Tuttle/Jerry Good

Selected credits
Directed/Written/Animated by Charles Swenson
Produced by Jerry Good
Music by Mark Volman/Howard Kaylan
Released May 1977
75 mins

EATEN ALIVE!/DEATH TRAP

Cast
Neville Brand...Judd
Mel Ferrer..Harvey Wood
Carolyn Jones...Miss Hattie
Marilyn Burns...Faye
William Finley..Roy
Stuart Whitman..Sheriff Martin
Roberta Collins...Clara
Kyle Richards..Angie
Robert Englund..Buck
Crystin Sinclaire.......................................Libby Wood
Janus Blyth...Lynette
Betty Cole..Ruby
Sig Sakowicz...Deputy Girth
Ronald W Davis...Country boy
Christine Schneider...Waitress
David Hayward...The cowboy
David Carson...Marlo
Lincoln Kibbee......................................First guy in bar
James Galanis...Second guy in bar

Selected credits
Directed by Tobe Hooper
Written by Alvin L Fast/Mardi Rustam/Kim Henkel
Produced by Mardi Rustam/Alvin L Fast
Executive Producer Mohammed Rustam
Associate Producers Samir Rustam/Larry Huly/Robert Kantor
Music by Tobe Hooper/Wayne Bell
Cinematographer Robert Caramico
Edited by Michael Brown
Art Director Marshall Reed
Produced March 1976/Released May 1977
91 mins

GRAND THEFT AUTO

Cast
Ron Howard...Sam Freeman
Nancy Morgan...Paula Powers
Elizabeth Rogers..Priscilla Powers
Barry Cahill..Bigby Powers
Rance Howard..Ned Slinker
Paul Linke..Collins Hedgeworth
Marion Ross..Vivian Hedgeworth
Don Steele...Curly Q Brown
Peter Isacksen...Sparky
Clint Howard..Ace
James Ritz..Officer Tad
Hoke Howell..Preacher
Lew Brown..Jack Klapper
Ken Lerner...Eagle I
Jack Perkins..Shadley
Paul Bartel..Groom
Bill Conklin...Eagle Hingleman
Robby Weaver...Harold Hingleman
Garry Marshall..Underworld boss
Leo Rossi.......................................Vegas muscle chief
Bobs Watson...Minister

Selected credits
Directed by Ron Howard
Written by Rance Howard/Ron Howard
Produced by Jon Davison
Executive Producer Roger Corman
Associate Producer Rance Howard
Music by Peter Ivers

Cinematographer Gary Graver
Edited by Joe Dante
Art Director Keith Michl
Second Unit Director Allan Arkush
Produced March 1977/Released June 1977
84 mins

RABID

Cast
Marilyn Chambers..Rose
Frank Moore...Hart Read
Joe Silver...Murray Cypher
Howard Ryshpan.................................Dr Dan Keloid
Patricia Gage...................................Dr Roxanne Keloid
Susan Roman...Mindy Kent
Roger Periard..Lloyd Walsh
Lynne Deragon...................................Nurse Louise
Terry Schonblum...............................Judy Glasberg
Victor Désy..Claude LaPointe
Julie Anna...Nurse Rita
Gary McKeehan.......................................Smooth Eddy
Terence G. Ross...Farmer
Miguel Fernandes.....................................Man in cinema
Robert O'Ree..................................Police sergeant
Greg Van Riel.............................Young man in plaza
Jérôme Tiberghien.....................................Dr Karl
Allan Moyle..................................Young man in lobby
Richard W Farrell...................................Camper man
Jeannette Casenave.........................Camper lady

Selected credits
Directed/Written by David Cronenberg
Produced by John Dunning
Executive Producers Ivan Reitman/André Link
Associate Producer Danny Goldberg
Cinematographer René Verzier
Edited by/Second Unit Director Jean LaFleur
Art Director Claude Marchand
Produced November 1976/Released June 1977
91 mins

THUNDER AND LIGHTNING

Cast
David Carradine..Harley Thomas
Kate Jackson........................Nancy Sue Hunnicutt
Roger C Carmel..............................Ralph Junior Hunnicutt
Sterling Holloway...Hobe Carpenter
Ed Barth...Rudi Volpone
Ron Feinberg...Bubba
George Murdock...Jake Summers
Pat Cranshaw...Taylor
Charles Napier...Jim Bob
Hope Pomerance...Mrs Hunnicutt
Malcolm Jones...Rainey
Charles Willeford..Bartender
Christopher Raynolds...Scooter
Claude Jones..Carl
Emilio Rivera...Honeydew driver

Selected credits
Directed by Corey Allen
Written by William Hjortsberg
Produced by Roger Corman
Associate Producer Teri Schwartz
Music by Andy Stein
Cinematographer James Pergola
Edited by Anthony Redman
Second Unit Director Lewis Teague
Released June 1977
95 mins

I NEVER PROMISED YOU A ROSE GARDEN

Cast
Bibi Andersson..Dr Fried
Kathleen Quinlan...Deborah Blake
Sylvia Sidney...Miss Coral
Ben Piazza...Jay Blake
Lorraine Gary..Ester Blake
Darlene Craviotto...Carla
Reni Santoni..Hobbs
Susan Tyrrell..Lee
Signe Hasso...Helene
Norman Alden...McPherson
Martine Bartlett..Secret wife
Robert Viharo..Anterrabae
Jeff Conaway...Lactamaeon
Richard Herd...Dr Halle
Sarah Cunningham...Mrs Forbes
June C Ellis...The Spy
Diane Varsi..Sylvia
Patricia Singer...Kathryn
Mary Carver...Eugenia
Barbara Steele...Idat

Selected credits
Directed by Anthony Page
Written by Gavin Lambert/Lewis John Carlino
Based on the novel by Joanne Greenberg (as Hannah Green)
Produced by Edgar J Scherick/Terence F Deane
Executive Producers Roger Corman/Daniel H Blatt
Associate Producer Teri Schwartz
Music by Paul Chihara
Cinematographer Bruce Logan
Edited by Garth Craven
Art Director William Sandell
Produced February 1977/Released August 1977
96 mins

DERSU UZALA

Cast
Maksim Munzuk...Dersu Uzala
Yuri Solomin...........................Captain Vladimir Arseniev
Svetlana Danilchenko......................................Mrs Arseniev
Dmitri Korshikov................................Wowa son of Arsenjev

Selected credits
Directed by Akira Kurosawa
Written by Akira Kurosawa/Yuri Nagibin
Based on the book 'Dersu, okhotnik' by Vladimir Arsenyev
Produced by Yoichi Matsue/Nikolai Sizov
Released November 1977
141 mins

A HERO AIN'T NOTHIN' BUT A SANDWICH

Cast
Cicely Tyson...Sweets
Paul Winfield..Butler
Larry B Scott..Benjie
Helen Martin...Mrs Bell
Glynn Turman..Nigeria
David Groh...Cohen
Kevin Hooks..Tiger
Kenneth Green...Jimmy Lee
Harold Sylvester..Doctor
Erin Blunt..Carwell
Claire Brenner.......................................Social worker
Arthur French.......................................Security guard
Bill Cobbs..Bartender
Sheila Wills.....................................Admissions clerk
Arnold Johnson...Patient
Barbara Alston...Girl friend
Keny Long...Male nurse
Hartwell Sims..Minister
Claire Brennen......................................Social worker

Selected credits
Directed by Ralph Nelson
Written by Alice Childress, based on her Novel
Produced by Robert B Radnitz
Associate Producers Terry Nelson/Hal De Windt
Music by Tom McIntosh
Cinematographer Frank Stanley
Edited by Fred A Chulack
Production Designer Walter Scott Herndon
Produced September 1976/Released December 1977
107 mins

A LITTLE NIGHT MUSIC

Cast
Elizabeth Taylor..........................Desiree Armfeldt
Diana Rigg..........................Charlotte Mittelheim
Len Cariou...............................Frederick Egerman
Lesley-Anne Down..........................Anne Egerman
Hermione Gingold..........................Mme Armfeldt
Laurence Guittard.............Carl-Magnum Mittelheim
Christopher Guard..............................Erich Egerman
Lesley Dunlop...Petra
Chloe Franks.........................Fredericka Armfeldt
Heinz Marecek...Frid
Jonathan Tunick......................................Conductor
Hubert Tscheppe..Franz
Rudolph Schrympf.........................Band conductor
Franz Schussler....................................The mayor
Johanna Schussler..............................The mayoress
Jean Sincere................................Lady in theatre
Dagmar Koller.....................................First lady
Ruth Brinkman...................................Second lady
Anna Veigl...Concierge
Stephan Paryle..........................Uniformed sergeant

Selected credits
Directed by Harold Prince
Written by Hugh Wheeler
Suggested by the film 'Smiles of a Summer Night' by Ingmar Bergman
Produced by Elliott Kastner
Associate Producer Denis Holt
Music and Lyrics by Stephen Sondheim
Choreographer Patricia Birch

Cinematographer Arthur Ibbetson
Edited by John Jympson
Art Director Herta Pischinger
Produced August 1976/Released December 1977
124 mins

THE EVIL

Cast
Richard Crenna...CJ
Joanna Pettet..Caroline
Andrew Prine..Raymond
Cassie Yates..Mary
George O'Hanlon Jr.......................................Pete
Lynne Moody...Felicia
Mary Louise Weller......................................Laurie
Georget Viharo...Dwight
Victor Buono..Devil
Milton Selzer...Realtor
Ed Bakey..Sam
Galen Thompson..Vargas
Emory Souza...Demon

Selected credits
Directed by Gus Trikonis
Written by Donald G Thompson
Produced by Ed Carlin
Executive Producers Paul Joseph/Malcolm Levinthal
Music by Johnny Harris
Cinematographer Mario Di Leo
Edited by Jack Kirschner
Production Designer Peter Jamison
Produced May 1977/Released March 1978
89 mins

LEOPARD IN THE SNOW

Cast
Susan Penhaligon..............................Helen James
Keir Dullea.......................................Dominic Lyall
Jeremy Kemp..Bolt
Billie Whitelaw..................................Isabel James
Kenneth More...........................Sir Philip James
Yvonne Masters...Bessie
Gordon Thomson.......................Michael Framley
Peter Burton...................................Mr Framley
Tessa Dahl.....................................Miss Framley
Terence Durrant...........................Man in barn

Selected credits
Directed by Gerry O'Hara
Written by Anne Mather, based on her novel/Jill Hyem
Produced by John Quested/Chris Harrop
Music by Kenneth V Jones
Cinematographer Michael Reed
Edited by Eddy Joseph
Art Director Anthony Pratt
Produced January 1977/Released March 1978
89 mins

DEATH SPORT

Cast
David Carradine.......................................Kaz Oshay
Claudia Jennings.....................................Deneer
Richard Lynch...Ankar Moor
William Smithers..................................Doctor Karl
Will Walker...Marcus Karl
David McLean....................................Lord Zirpola
Jesse Vint...Polna
H B Haggerty...Jailer
John Himes............................Tritan president
Jim Galante...Tritan guard
Peter Hooper..Mr Bakkar
Brenda Venus...Adriann
Gene Hartline.......................Enforcer sergeant
Chris Howell...........................Stateman officer

Valerie Rae Clark..Dancer
Archie Freeman...Mutant

Selected credits
Directed by Nicholas Niciphor (as Henry Suso)/Allan
Arkush
Written by Nicholas Niciphor/Donald Stewart
Story by Frances Doel
Produced by Roger Corman
Music by Andrew Stein
Cinematographer Gary Graver
Edited by Larry Bock
Art Director Sharon Compton
Produced October 1977/Released May 1978
82 mins

THE TIGRESS

Cast
Dyanne Thorne...Michel-René Labelle
Gilbert Beaumont...Jean-Guy Latour
Ray Landry..Terry Haig
Jacques Morin..Henry Gamer
Jorma Lindqvist..Gil Viviano
Anne Marie Guenette..Nicole Fortin
Bertha Pierre...Carole Péloquin
Carol Down..Kirk McColl
Judy Galt...Lucie Hutchins
Michel Mathiot..Tony Angelo

Selected credits
Directed by Jean LaFleur
Written by Marven McGara
Produced by Ivan Reitman/John Dunning/Andre Link (all
as Julian Parnell)
Cinematographer Richard Ciupka
Edited by Debra Karjala
Art Director Claude Marchand
Produced February 1977/Released May 1978
85 mins

AVALANCHE

Cast
Rock Hudson...David Shelby
Mia Farrow..Caroline Brace
Robert Forster...Nick Thorne
Jeanette Nolan...Florence Shelby
Rick Moses..Bruce Scott
Steve Franken...Henry McDade
Barry Primus..Mark Elliott
Cathey Paine...Tina Elliott
Jerry Douglas..Phil Prentiss
Antony Carbone...Leo the coach
Peggy Browne...Annette River
Pat Egan...Cathy Jordan
Joby Baker...TV director
X Brands...Marty Brenner
Cindy Luedke...Susan Maxwell
John Cathey...Ed the pilot
Angelo Lamonea...Bruce's coach

Selected credits
Directed by Corey Allen
Written by Gavin Lambert (as Claude Pola)/Corey Allen
Story by Frances Doel
Produced by Roger Corman
Executive Producer Paul Rapp
Associate Producer Michael Finnell
Music by William Kraft
Cinematographer Pierre-William Glenn
Edited by Skip Schoolnik/Larry Bock
Production Designer Sharon Compton
Art Director Philip Thomas
Second Unit Director Lewis Teague
Produced February 1978/Released August 1978
91 mins

JOKES MY FOLKS NEVER TOLD ME

Cast
Dixie Edgar/Daniel Fee/Sandy Johnson/Hal Landon/Lisa
Marlowe/Andras Maros/Bob Molinari/Bunny Summers/
Mariwin Roberts/Joe Warfield/Wally Berns/Raven De La
Croix/Mark Montgomery/Dave Shelly

Selected credits
Directed by Gerry Woolery
Written by Steven Vail
John G Thompson
Produced by Steven Vail/Ted Woolery
Executive Producer Andras Maros
Associate Producer Hana Cannon
Music by Ralph Kessler
Cinematographer Tom Denove
Edited by Jay Wertz
Production Designer John G Thompson
Released August 1978
82 mins

PIRANHA

Cast
Bradford Dillman..Paul Grogan
Heather Menzies...Maggie McKeown
Kevin McCarthy...Dr Robert Hoak
Keenan Wynn...Jack
Dick Miller...Buck Gardner
Barbara Steele..Dr Mengers
Belinda Balaski...Betsy
Melody Thomas...Laura
Bruce Gordon...Colonel Waxman
Barry Brown...Trooper
Paul Bartel..Dumont
Shannon Collins..Suzie Grogan
Shawn Nelson...Whitney
Richard Deacon..Earl Lyon
Janie Squire...Barbara
Roger Richman...David
Bill Smillie..Jailer
Guich Koock..TV pitchman
Jack Pauleson..Boy in canoe
Eric Henshaw..Father in canoe

Selected credits
Directed by Joe Dante
Written by John Sayles
Story by Richard Robinson/John Sayles
Produced by Jon Davison/Chako van Leeuwen
Executive Producers Roger Corman/Jeff Schechtman
Music by Pino Donaggio
Cinematographer Jamie Anderson
Edited by Mark Goldblatt/Joe Dante
Art Directors Bill Mellin/Kerry Mellin
Second Unit Director Dick Lowry
Produced March 1978/Released August 1978
94 mins

BLACKOUT

NEW YORK CITY:
When the lights go out ...
The *terror* begins!

JIM MITCHUM · ROBERT CARRADINE · BELINDA J. MONTGOMERY
"BLACKOUT"
with
JUNE ALLYSON · JEAN PIERRE AUMONT · RAY MILLAND as "STAFFORD"
A NEW WORLD PICTURE **R** RESTRICTED

Cast
Jim Mitchum...Dan Evans
Robert Carradine.......................................Christie
Belinda J Montgomery.........................Annie Gallo
June Allyson...Mrs Grant
Jean-Pierre Aumont....................................Henri
Ray Milland.......................................Richard Stafford
Don Granberry...Chico
Terry Haig...Eddy
Victor B Tyler...Marcus
Fred Doederlein......................................Mr Grant
Selected credits
Directed by Eddy Matalon
Written by John C W Saxton
Story by John Dunning/Eddy Matalon
Produced by Nicole M Boisvert/Eddy Matalon/John
Dunning
Executive Producers André Link/Ivan Reitman/John
Vidette
Music by Didier Vasseur
Cinematographer Jean-Jacques Tarbès
Edited by Debra Karen
Art Director Jocelyn Joly
Produced November 1977/Released September 1978
92 mins

AUTUMN SONATA

Cast
Ingrid Bergman.....................................Charlotte Andergast
Liv Ullmann...Eva
Lena Nyman...Helena
Halvar Björk..Viktor
Selected credits
Directed/Written by Ingmar Bergman
Produced by Richard Brick/Katinka Faragó/Lew Grade/
Martin Starger

Released October 1978
99 mins

THE BEES

Cast
John Saxon...John Norman
Angel Tompkins..Sandra Miller
John Carradine....................................Dr Sigmund Hummel
Claudio Brook...Dr Miller
Alicia Encinas..Alicia
Júlio César...Julio
Armand Martin..Arthur
José Chávez Trowe...Father
George Bellanger...........................Undersecretary/Brennan
Deloy White...Winkler
Roger Cudney...Blankeley
Julia Yallop..Model
Chad Hastings...Gray
Elizabeth Wallace..Secretary
Al Jones...Mugger 1
Gray Johnson...Mugger 2
Whitey Hughes..Gentleman in park
Selected credits
Directed/Story/Produced by Alfredo Zacharias
Written by Jack Hill
Executive Producer Michel Zacharias
Associate Producer Teri Schwartz
Music by Richard Gillis
Cinematographer León Sánchez
Edited by Sandy Nervig
Art Director Jose Rodriguez Granada
Produced January 1978/Released November 1978
86 mins

OUTSIDE CHANCE

Cast
Yvette Mimieux...Dinah Hunter
Royce D Applegate...Larry O'Brien
Beverly Hope Atkinson...Clair
Susan Batson...Mavis
Babbett Bram...Miss Hopkins
Fredric Cook..Deputy Hobie
Severn Darden...Sheriff Dempsey
Howard Hesseman...David
Britt Leach..Alfred
John Lawlor..Bill Hill
Nan Martin..Allison
Ira Miller..Dale
Robin Sherwood..Tootie
Nancy Noble...Lola
Betty Thomas..Katherine
Lee Fergus...Doctor
Charles Young...Luther
Kimo Owens..Mirror glasses
Dick Armstrong..Arnold Bradfield
Janina T White..Matron
Selected credits
Directed by Michael Miller
Written by Ralph Gaby Wilson/Michael Miller
Produced by Jeff Begun
Executive Producer Roger Corman
Associate Producer Richard Schor
Music by Michael Dunne/Lou Levy
Cinematographer Willy Kurant
Edited by Bruce Logan
Art Director John Carter
Produced April 1978/Released December 2, 1978
92 mins

FAST CHARLIE THE MOONBEAM RIDER

Cast
David Carradine...Charlie Swattle

Brenda Vaccaro..Grace Wolf
L Q Jones..Floyd
R G Armstrong...Al Barber
Terry Kiser...Lester Neal
Jesse Vint...Calvin Hawk
Noble Willingham...Pop Bauer
Ralph James...Bill Bartman
Bill Bartman...Young man
David Hayward.....................................Cannonball McCall
Stephen Ferry...Official
Tracy Harris...Black man
Robert Plumb..Drummer
Jack Brennan..Howard Johnson
Lynda Abbott..Waitress
Hal Earley..Owen Hazlitt
William S Bartman...Second farmer
Whit Clay...Wesley Wolf III
Joe Unger...Bank teller

Selected credits
Directed by Steve Carver
Written by Michael Gleason
Story by Ed Spielman/Howard Friedlander
Produced by Roger Corman/Saul Krugman
Music by Stu Phillips
Cinematographer William Birch
Edited by Tony Redman/Eric Orner
Art Directors Bill Sandell/J Michael Riva
Produced July 1978/Released March 1979
98 mins

STARCRASH
Cast
Marjoe Gortner...Akton
Caroline Munro..Stella Star
Christopher Plummer.......................................The Emperor
David Hasselhoff...Simon
Robert Tessier..Thor
Joe Spinell...Count Zarth Arn
Nadia Cassini.....................................Queen of the Amazons
Judd Hamilton..Elle
Hamilton Camp...Voice of Elle

Selected credits
Directed by Luigi Cozzi (as Lewis Coates)
Written by Luigi Cozzi (as Lewis Coates)/Nat Wachsberger
Produced by Nat and Patrick Wachsberger
Music by John Barry
Cinematographers Paul Beeson/Roberto D'Ettorre Piazzoli
Edited by Sergio Montanari
Production Designer Aurelio Crugnolla
Produced October 1977/Released March 1979
92 mins

LOVE ON THE RUN
Cast
Jean-Pierre Léaud...Antoine Doinel
Marie-France Pisier...Colette Tazzi
Claude Jade..Christine Doinel
Dani...Liliane

Selected credits
Directed/Produced by François Truffaut
Written by François Truffaut/Marie-France Pisier/Jean
Aurel/Suzanne Schiffman
Released April 1979
94 mins

SAINT JACK
Cast
Ben Gazzara...Jack Flowers
Denholm Elliott...William Leigh
James Villiers...Frogget
Joss Ackland..Yardley
Rodney Bewes...Smale

Mark Kingston...Yates
Lisa Lu..Mrs Yates
Monika Subramaniam...Monika
Judy Lim...Judy
George Lazenby...Senator
Peter Bogdanovich.......................................Eddie Schuman

Selected credits
Directed by Peter Bogdanovich
Written by Howard Sackler/Paul Theroux, based on his
novel/Peter Bogdanovich
Produced by Roger Corman
Executive Producers Hugh M Hefner/Edward L Rissien
Associate Producer/George Morfogen
Cinematographer Robby Müller
Edited by William Carruth
Art Director David Ng
Produced April 1978/Released April 1979
112 mins

THE BROOD
Cast
Oliver Reed...Dr Hal Raglan
Samantha Eggar..Nola Carveth
Art Hindle...Frank Carveth
Henry Beckman...Barton Kelly
Nuala Fitzgerald...Juliana Kelly
Cindy Hinds..Candice Carveth
Susan Hogan...Ruth Mayer
Gary McKeehan..Mike Trellan
Michael Magee...Inspector
Robert Silverman..Jan Hartog
Joseph Shaw..Coroner
Larry Solway...Lawyer
Reiner Schwartz...Dr Birkin
Felix Silla...Creature
John Ferguson...Creature
Nicholas Campbell...Chris
Mary Swinton...Wendy
Jerry Kostur...Construction worker
Christopher Britton...................................Man in auditorium

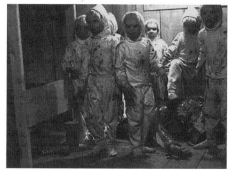

Selected credits
Directed/Written by David Cronenberg
Produced by Claude Héroux
Executive Producers Victor Solnicki/Pierre David
Music by Howard Shore
Cinematographer Mark Irwin
Edited by Alan Collins
Art Director Carol Spier
Produced November 1978/Released June 1979
92 mins

THE KIDS ARE ALRIGHT
Cast
Roger Daltrey...Himself (The Who)
John Entwistle...Himself (The Who)

Keith Moon..Himself (The Who)
Pete Townshend.....................................Himself (The Who)
Selected credits
Directed/Written by Jeff Stein
Produced by Bill Curbishley/Tony Klinger
Released June 1979
101 mins

ROCK 'N' ROLL HIGH SCHOOL

Cast
PJ Soles...Riff Randell
Vincent Van Patten...Tom Roberts
Clint Howard...Eaglebauer
Dey Young ....Kate Rambeau
Mary Woronov..Miss Evelyn Togar
Paul Bartel...Mr McGree
Dick Miller..Police Chief
Don Steele............................Screamin' Steve Stevens
Alix Elias...Coach Steroid
Loren Lester...Fritz Hansel
Daniel Davies...Fritz Gretel
Lynn Farrell...Angel Dust
Herbie Braha..Manager
Grady Sutton....................................School board president
Chris Somma...Shawn
Marla Rosenfield..Cheryl
Barbara Ann Walters...................................Cafeteria lady
Terry Soda..Norma
Joe Van Sickle..Cop
The Ramones..Themselves
Selected credits
Directed/Story by Allan Arkush/Joe Dante (uncredited)
Written by Richard Whitley/Russ Dvonch/Joseph McBride
Produced by Michael Finnell
Executive Producer Roger Corman
Cinematographer Dean Cundey
Edited by Larry Bock/Gail Werbin
Art Director Marie Kordus
Second Unit Directors Jon Davison/Jerry Zucker
Produced January 1979/Released June 1979
93 mins

THE LADY IN RED

Cast
Pamela Sue Martin..Polly Franklin
Robert Conrad..John Dillinger
Louise Fletcher...Anna Sage
Robert Hogan...Jake Lingle
Laurie Heineman...Rose Shimkus
Glenn Withrow..Eddie
Rod Gist...Pinetop
Peter Hobbs..Pops Geissler
Christopher Lloyd..Frognose
Dick Miller...Patek
Nancy Parsons...Tiny Alice
Alan Vint...Melvin Purvis
Milt Kogan...Preacher
Chip Fields..Satin
Buck Young...Hennessey
Phillip R Allen...Elliot Ness
Ilene Kristen...Wynona
Joe Flaherty...Frank
Terri Taylor..Mae
Peter Miller...Fritz
Selected credits
Directed by Lewis Teague
Written by John Sayles
Produced by Julie Corman/Steven Kovacs
Music by James Horner
Cinematographer Daniel Lacambre
Edited by Larry Bock/Ron Medico/Lewis Teague
Production Designer Jac McAnelly

Art Director Philip Thomas
Second Unit Director Pat Crowley
Produced April 1979/Released July 1979
93 mins

UP FROM THE DEPTHS

Cast
Sam Bottoms...Greg Oliver
Susanne Reed...Rachel McNamara
Virgil Frye...Earl Sheridan
Kedric Wolfe...Oscar Forbes
Charles Howerton.............................Dr David Whiting
Denise Hayes..Iris Lee
Chuck Doherty...Ed Bennett
Helen McNeely.....................................Louellen Bennett
Ken Metcalfe...Mr Holland
Randy Taylor..Jimmy
Dave D'Martyn...Tourist #1
Clem Persons..Maintenance man
Peter Cooper...Nieberg
Katherine Scholy..Darleen
Ken Petruic..Harry
Bobby Greenwood......................................Tourist #2
Selected credits
Directed by Charles B Griffith
Written by Anne Dyer/Charles B Griffith (both as Alfred M Sweeney)
Produced by Cirio H Santiago
Executive Producer Jack Atienza
Associate Producers Jill Griffith/Manny Norman
Music by Russell O'Malley
Cinematographer Ricardo Remias (as Rick Remington)
Edited by G V Bass
Art Director Ben Otico
Second Unit Director Pete Gallagher
Released August 1979
75 mins

THE GREEN ROOM

Cast
François Truffaut..Julien Davenne
Nathalie Baye...Cecilia Mandel
Jean Dasté...Bernard Humbert
Patrick Maléon...Georges
Selected credits
Directed/Produced by François Truffaut
Written by Jean Gruault/François Truffaut
Based on novellas by Henry James
Released September 1979
94 mins

ANGEL'S BRIGADE

Cast
Sylvia Anderson...Terry Grant
Lieu Chinh...Kako Umaro
Jacqulin Cole..April Thomas
Liza Greer...Trish
Robin Greer..Elaine Brenner
Susan Kiger..Michelle Wilson
Noela Velasco...Maria
Jack Palance..Farrell
Peter Lawford...Burke
Jim Backus..Commander
Neville Brand..Miller
Pat Buttram...Van salesman
Arthur Godfrey..Himself
Alan Hale..Manny
Darby Hinton..Sticks
Ken Minyard..Joe
Ralph Harris...Billy
Howard Ray Huff..Compound thug
Dee Cooper...Compound thug

Norma Fernandez...Housekeeper

Selected credits
Directed/Produced by Greydon Clark
Written by Greydon Clark/Alvin L Fast
Executive Producer Louis George
Associate Producer Donn Greer
Music by Gerald Lee
Cinematographer Dean Cundey
Edited by Earl Watson
Production Designer Jack DeWolf
Released October 1979
97 mins

THE PRIZE FIGHTER
Cast
Tim Conway...Bags
Don Knotts..Shake
David Wayne...Pop Morgan
Robin Clarke..Mike
Cisse Cameron...Polly
Mary Ellen O'Neill..Mama
Michael LaGuardia..The Butcher
George Nutting..Timmy
Irwin Keyes...Flower
John Myhers...Doyle
Alfred E Covington.....................................Ring announcer
Dan Fitzgerald..Big John
Holly Conover...Judy
Bill Crabb..Turk
Kenneth Daniel..Stubby
Joe Dorsey..Stranger
J Don Ferguson...Referee #1
Mike DeFabis...Referee #2
Charles Franzen..Reporter #1
Bill Ash..Towel man

Selected credits
Directed by Michael Preece
Written by Tim Conway/John Myhers
Produced by Wanda Dell/Lang Elliott
Executive Producer Lang Elliott
Music by Peter Matz
Cinematographer Jacques Haitkin
Edited by Fabien Tordjmann
Art Director Vincent Peranio
Produced February 1979/Released November 1979
99 mins

HUMANOIDS FROM THE DEEP

Cast
Doug McClure..Jim Hill
Ann Turkel..Susan Drake
Vic Morrow..Hank Slattery
Cindy Weintraub...Carol Hill
Anthony Penya...Johnny Eagle
Denise Galik..Linda Beale

Lynn Theel..Peggy Larson
Meegan King...Jerry Potter
Breck Costin..Tommy Hill
Hoke Howell...Deke Jensen
Don Maxwell...Dickie Moore
David Strassman...Billy
Greg Travis..Radio announcer
Linda Shayne..Miss Salmon
Lisa Glaser...Becky
Bruce Monette...Jake Potter
Shawn Erler...Hill baby
Frank Arnold..Old man
Amy Barrett...Amy

Selected credits
Directed by Barbara Peeters
Written by William Martin (as Frederick James)
Story by Frank Arnold/Martin B Cohen
Produced by Martin B Cohen/Hunt Lowry
Music by James Horner
Cinematographer Daniel Lacambre
Edited by Mark Goldblatt
Art Director Michael Erler
Second Unit Director James Sbardellati
Produced October 1979/Released April 1980
82 mins

THE TIN DRUM
Cast
Mario Adorf...Alfred Matzerath
Angela Winkler..Agnes Matzerath
Katharina Thalbach...Maria Matzerath
David Bennent...Oskar Matzerath

Selected credits
Directed by Volker Schlöndorff
Written by Jean-Claude Carrière/Volker Schlöndorff/Franz
Seitz/Günter Grass, based on his novel
Produced by Franz Seitz/Volker Schlöndorff/Anatole
Dauman
Released April 1980
142 mins

BATTLE BEYOND THE STARS
Cast
Richard Thomas..Shad
Robert Vaughn...Gelt
John Saxon..Sador
George Peppard..Cowboy
Darlanne Fluegel..Nanelia
Sybil Danning...St Exmin
Sam Jaffe...Dr Hephaestus
Morgan Woodward...Cayman
Earl Boen...Nestor 1
John Gowan..Nestor 2
Steve Davis...Quepeg
Lawrence Steven Meyers...Kelvin 1
Lara Cody...Kelvin 2
Lynn Carlin...Nell
Jeff Corey..Zed
Marta Kristen...Lux
Julia Duffy...Mol
Eric Morris...Feh
Doug Carlsson...Pez
Ron Ross..Dab

Selected credits
Directed by Jimmy T Murakami
Written by John Sayles
Story by John Sayles/Anne Dyer
Produced by Ed Carlin
Executive Producer Roger Corman
Associate Producer Mary Ann Fisher
Music by James Horner
Cinematographer Daniel Lacambre

Edited by Allan Holzman/RJ Kizer
Art Directors James Cameron/Charles Breen
Produced February 1980/Released July 1980
104 mins

SOMETHING WAITS IN THE DARK

Cast

Barbara Bach..Amanda Marvin
Claudio Cassinelli.......................................Lt Claude de Ross
Richard Johnson......................................Edmond Rackham
Beryl Cunningham...Shakira
Joseph Cotten.......................................Prof Ernest Marvin
Franco Iavarone..José
Roberto Posse...Peter
Giuseppe Castellano...Skip
Francesco Mazzieri......................................François
Mel Ferrer...Radcliffe
Cameron Mitchell...Decker
Eunice Bolt...Samantha
Tom J Delaney...Patterson
James Alquist...Jim

Selected credits

Directed by Sergio Martino
Written by Sergio Donati/Cesare Frugoni/Sergio Martino
Story by Cesare Frugoni/Luciano Martino
Produced/Music by Luciano Michelini
Cinematographer Giancarlo Ferrando
Edited by Eugenio Alabiso
Production Designer Massimo Antonello Geleng
Produced October 1978
81 mins

THE GEORGIA PEACHES

Cast

Dirk Benedict.......................................Dusty Tyree
Tanya Tucker.......................................Lorette Peach
Terri Nunn...Sue Lynn
Lane Smith.......................................Randolph Dukane
Sally Kirkland.......................................Vivian Stark
Dennis Patrick.......................................Wade Holt
David Hayward...Marco
Burton Gilliam...............................Delbart Huggins
Noble Willingham..........................Jarvis Wheeler

Selected credits

Directed by Daniel Haller
Written by Mick Benderoth/Monte Stettin/William
Hjortsberg
Story by Mick Benderoth/Monte Stettin/Lois Luger
Produced by James Sbardellati/Thomas M Hammel
Executive Producer Roger Corman
Music by R Donovan Fox
Cinematographer David Sanderson
Edited by Sandy Nervig
Art Director Michael Erler
Produced August 1980/Released November 1980
96 mins

THE PRIVATE EYES

Cast

Tim Conway..Dr Tart
Don Knotts...............................Inspector Winship
Trisha Noble..Phyllis
Bernard Fox..Justin
Grace Zabriskie..Nanny
John Fujioka...Mr Uwatsum
Stan Ross...Tibet
Irwin Keyes..Jock
Suzy Mandel...Hilda
Fred Stuthman...Lord Morley
Mary Nell Santacroce.............................Lady Morley
Robert V Barron..................Gas station attendant
Patrick Cranshaw...Roy

Selected credits

Directed by/Executive Producer Lang Elliott
Written by Tim Conway/John Myhers
Produced by Lang Elliott/Wanda Dell
Music by Peter Matz
Cinematographer Jacques Haitkin
Edited by Fabien Tordjmann/Patrick M Crawford
Art Director Vincent Peranio
Produced May 1980/Released November 1980
91 mins

SHOGUN ASSASSIN

Cast

Tomisaburo Wakayama.........................Lone Wolf
Masahiro Tomikawa...................................Daigoro
Kayo Matsuo......................................Supreme Ninja
Minoru Ohki..................................Master of Death
Shoji Kobayashi............................Master of Death
Shin Kishida..................................Master of Death

Selected credits

Directed by Kenji Misumi/Robert Houston
Written by Kazuo Koike/Robert Houston/David Weisman
Story by Kazuo Koike/Goseki Kojima
Produced by Shintarô Katsu/Hisaharu Matsubara/David
Weisman
Executive Producer Peter Shanaberg
Associate Producers Larry Francoise/Michael Maiello/
Albert Ellis Jr/Joseph Ellis
Music by W Michael Lewis/Mark Lindsay/Robert Houston
Cinematographer Chishi Makiura
Edited by Lee Percy/Toshio Taniguchi
Art Director Akira Naito
Released November 1980
86 mins

'BREAKER' MORANT

Cast

Edward Woodward....................Lt Harry 'Breaker' Morant
Jack Thompson...............................Maj JF Thomas
John Waters...........................Capt Alfred Taylor
Bryan Brown..........................Lt Peter Handcock

Selected credits

Directed by Bruce Beresford
Written by Jonathan Hardy/David Stevens/Bruce Beresford
Based on the play by Kenneth G Ross
Produced by Matthew Carroll
Released December 1980
107 mins

MON ONCLE D'AMERIQUE

Cast

Gérard Depardieu....................René Ragueneau
Nicole Garcia.....................................Janine Garnier
Roger Pierre..Jean Le Gall
Nelly Borgeaud..................................Arlette Le Gall

Selected credits

Directed by Alain Resnais

Written by Jean Gruault/Henri Laborit/Nelly Borgeaud/
Pierre Arditi/Philippe Laudenbach/Gerard Darrieu/Marie
Dubois
Produced by Philippe Dussart
Released December 1980
125 mins

RUCKUS IN MADOC COUNTY

Cast

Dirk Benedict..Kyle Hanson
Linda Blair..Jenny Bellows
Richard Farnsworth.............................Sheriff Jethro Pough
Ben Johnson...Sam Bellows
Matt Clark...Cece
Jon Van Ness..Deputy Dave
Taylor Lacher..Sarge
Clifford A Pellow...Homer
Ben Bates..Big Ben
Jerry Gatlin...Bubba
Bennie E Dobbins...Joe
Bobby Hughes..Bobby Bellows
A J Blake...Sally the barmaid
Melanie Weeks..Counter girl
Patrick Connolly.................................Gas station attendant
Bob Peeler...Farmer at fair
Ken DeGusta...................................Shooting gallery man
Sam Johnson...Kind man at fair
Jeannie Medina...Bus driver

Selected credits

Directed/Written by Max Kleven
Produced by Paul Maslansky
Associate Producer Timothy Rabbitt
Executive Producer Richard P LaCivita
Music by Tommy Vig/Corelli Jacobs
Cinematographer Don Michael Burgess
Edited by Angelo Bernarducci
Art Director Vincent Peranio
Second Unit Director Walter Scott
Released March 1981
93 mins

SMOKEY BITES THE DUST

Cast

Jimmy McNichol..Roscoe Wilton
Janet Julian..Peggy Sue Turner
Walter Barnes...Sheriff Turner
Patrick Campbell..Lester
Kari Lizer..Cindy
John Blyth Barrymore..Harold
Kedric Wolfe...Bentley
Bill Forsythe...Kenny
Charles Howerton...Sheriff Lamar
Mel Welles...Abu Habib
Michael Green..Tall arab
Don Corey...Short arab
Dick Miller...Otis Wilson
Linda Gary...Woman sheriff
Adriana Shaw..Woman deputy
Rance Howard...Coach
Robert Beecher..Principal
Nancy Parsons..Harold's mother
Dan Sturkie..Bell hop
Angelo Rossitto...Desk clerk

Selected credits

Directed by Charles B Griffith
Written by Max Apple
Story by Brian Williams
Produced by Roger Corman/Gale Anne Hurd
Music by Bent Myggen
Cinematographer Gary Graver
Edited by Larry Bock
Art Directors Francesca Bartoccini/J Rae Fox

Second Unit Director Allan Holzman
Produced December 1980/Released April 1981
87 mins

FIRECRACKER

Cast

Jillian Kesner...Susanne Carter
Darby Hinton..Chuck Donner
Reymond King...Rey
Ken Metcalfe...Erik
Peter Cooper...Pete
Carolyn Smith...Bonnie Carter
Chanda Romero..Alice
Tony Ferrer..Tony
Vic Diaz...Grip
Don Bell/Omar Camar/Rubiah Suparman/Yasmin Yusuff/
Malik Salamat

Selected credits

Directed by/Executive Producer Cirio H Santiago
Written by Ken Metcalfe/Cirio H Santiago
Produced by Syed Kechik
Associate Producer Ernie Rojas
Music by Nonong Buencamino
Cinematographer Ricardo Remias
Edited by Gervacio Santos
Art Director Ben Otico
Produced December 1980/Released May 1981
77 mins

RICHARD'S THINGS

Cast

Liv Ullmann...Kate Morris
Amanda Redman..Josie
Tim Pigott-Smith...Peter
Peter Burton...Colonel

Selected credits

Directed by Anthony Harvey
Written by Frederic Raphael, from his novel

Produced by Mark Shivas
Released June 1981
104 mins

MINDWARP: AN INFINITY OF TERROR
Cast
Edward Albert..Cabren
Erin Moran...Alluma
Ray Walston..Kore
Bernard Behrens..Ilvar
Zalman King...Baelon
Robert Englund...Ranger
Taaffe O'Connell...Dameia
Sid Haig...Quuhod
Grace Zabriskie...Trantor
Jack Blessing...Cos
Mary Ellen O'Neill...Mitri
Selected credits
Directed by Bruce D Clark
Written by Marc Siegler/Bruce D Clark
Produced by Roger Corman/Marc Siegler
Music by Barry Schrader
Cinematographer Jacques Haitkin
Edited by R J Kizer/Larry Bock/Barry Zetlin
Production Designers James Cameron/Robert Skotak
Art Directors Alex Hajdu/Steve Graziani
Second Unit Director James Cameron
Produced May 1981/Released July 1981
81 mins

SATURDAY THE 14th
Cast
Richard Benjamin..John
Paula Prentiss...Mary
Jeffrey Tambor...Waldemar
Severn Darden...Van Helsing
Kari Michaelson...Debbie
Kevin Brando..Billy
Rosemary DeCamp...Aunt Lucille
Stacy Keach Sr..Attorney
Nancy Lee Andrews..Yolanda
Carole Androsky..Real estate lady
Roberta Collins..Cousin Rhonda
Paul Garner...The Major
Annie O'Donnell..................................Annette Muldowney
Thomas Newman...Cousin Phil
Allen Joseph...Uncle Bert
Craig Coulter...Delivery boy
Renee Braswell..Stuntperson
Elizabeth Charlton Davey................................French maid
Irwin Russo...Truck driver
Selected credits
Directed/Written by Howard R Cohen
Story by Jeff Begun
Produced by Julie Corman/Jeff Begun
Music by Parmer Fuller
Cinematographer Daniel Lacambre
Edited by Joanne D'Antonio/Kent Beyda
Art Director Arlene Alen
Second Unit Director Aaron Lipstadt
Produced June 1981/Released August 1981
75 mins

QUARTET
Cast
Alan Bates...HJ Heidler
Maggie Smith...Lois Heidler
Isabelle Adjani...Marya Zelli
Anthony Higgins..Stephan Zelli
Selected credits
Directed by James Ivory
Written by Ruth Prawer Jhabvala/Michel Maingois/James

Ivory.
Based on the novel by Jean Rhys
Produced by Jean-Pierre Mahot de la Querantonnais/Ismail
Merchant
Released October 1981
101 mins

THREE BROTHERS
Cast
Philippe Noiret..Raffaele Giuranna
Michele Placido...Nicola Giuranna
Vittorio Mezzogiorno...........Rocco Giuranna/Young Donato
Andréa Ferréol..Raffaele's Wife
Selected credits
Directed by Francesco Rosi
Written by Tonino Guerra/Francesco Rosi
Produced by Antonio Macri/Giorgio Nocella
Released February 1982
113 mins

CHRISTIANE F
Cast
Natja Brunckhorst...Christiane
Thomas Haustein...Detlev
Jens Kuphal...Axel
Rainer Wolk..Leiche
Selected credits
Directed by Uli Edel
Written by Herman Weigel/Uli Edel
Based on the book by Kai Hermann & Horst Rieck
Produced by Bernd Eichinger/Hans Kaden/Bertram Vetter/
Hans Weth
Released March 1982
131 mins

THE SLUMBER PARTY MASSACRE
Cast
Michele Michaels..Trish
Robin Stille..Valerie
Michael Villella..Russ Thorn
Debra Deliso...Kim
Andree Honore...Jackie
Gina Mari..Diane
Jennifer Meyers...Courtney
Joseph Alan Johnson...Neil
David Millbern..Jeff
Jim Boyce..John Minor
Pamela Roylance...Coach Jana
Brinke Stevens...Linda
Rigg Kennedy...David Contant
Jean Vargas.......................................Te.lephone repairwoman
Anna Patton...Mrs Devereaux
Howard Furgason...Mr Devereaux
Pam Canzaro..Carpenter
Aaron Lipstadt..Pizza boy
Francis Menendez...Paper boy
Selected credits
Directed by Amy Jones
Written by Rita Mae Brown/Amy Jones
Produced by Amy Jones/Aaron Lipstadt
Associate Producer Mark Allan
Music by Ralph Jones
Cinematographer Steve Posey
Edited by Sean Foley
Art Director Francesca Bartoccini
Released March 1982
77 mins

BATTLETRUCK
Cast
Michael Beck..Hunter
Annie McEnroe...Corlie

James Wainwright.......................................Straker
Bruno Lawrence...Willie
John Bach..Bone
Randy Powell...Judd
John Ratzenberger..Rusty
Diana Rowan..Charlene
Kelly Johnson..Alvin
Ross Jolly..Shotgun
Mark Hadlow..Orrin
John Banas...Reuben
Marshall Napier..Driver
Peter Rowell...Feathers
Timothy Lee..Hacker
Oona Menges..Zoe

Selected credits
Directed by Harley Cokliss
Written by Irving Austin/Harley Cokliss/John Beech
Story by Michael Abrams
Produced by Lloyd Phillips/Rob Whitehouse
Music by Kevin Peek
Cinematographer Chris Menges
Edited by Michael Horton
Production Designer Gary Hansen
Art Director Ron Highfield
Second Unit Director Buddy Joe Hooker
Produced August 1981/Released April 1982
91 mins

TAG: THE ASSASINATION GAME

Cast
Robert Carradine................................Alex Marsh
Linda Hamilton.................................Susan Swayze
Kristine DeBell..........................Nancy McCauley
Perry Lang................................Frank English
John Mengatti.........................Randy Simonetti
Michael Winslow.................................Gowdy
Frazer Smith.........................Nick Carpenter
Bruce Abbott..............................Loren Gersh

Xander Berkeley...Connally
Ivan Bonar...Patterson
Scott Dunlop..Wallace
Jim Greenleaf..Swanson
Charlene Nelson...Charlene
Steven Peterman..Schooster
John Anthony Bailey.............................Gowdy's aide
Aaron Scott Bernard.................Racquetball player
Nora Boland............................Cleaning woman
Richard Chudnow..Coach
Isabel Cooley........................Prof Wadsworth
David Mason Daniels...............................Student

Selected credits
Directed/Written by Nick Castle
Produced by Peter Rosten/Dan Rosenthal
Executive Producers Jean Ubaud/Kate Edelman
Associate Producer Karen Siegel
Music by Craig Safan
Cinematographer Willy Kurant
Edited by Tom Walls
Production Designer Peter Politanoff
Art Directors Randy Moore/Craig Stearns
Produced April 1981/Released April 1982
90 mins

FORBIDDEN WORLD
Cast
Jesse Vint...Mike Colby
Dawn Dunlap....................................Tracy Baxter
June Chadwick.........................Dr Barbara Glaser
Linden Chiles...........................Dr Gordon Hauser
Fox Harris...............................Dr Cal Timbergen
Raymond Oliver................................Brian Beale
Scott Paulin.....................................Earl Richards
Michael Bowen.................................Jimmy Swift
Don Olivera.......................................SAM-104

Selected credits
Directed/Edited by Allan Holzman
Written by Tim Curnen
Story by Jim Wynorski/RJ Robertson
Produced by Roger Corman/Mary Ann Fisher
Music by Susan Justin
Cinematographer Tim Suhrstedt
Production Designer Christopher Horner
Art Directors Joe Garrity/Wayne Springfield
Second Unit Director Aaron Lipstadt
Produced February 1982/Released May 1982
82 mins

GALAXY EXPRESS
Voices
B J Ward/Tony Pope/Fay McKay/Booker Bradshaw/Gary
Seegar/Corey Burton/Dicey Adams/Jill Fisher
Selected credits
Directed by Taro Rin

271

Mind Warp

Written by Paul Grogan/Shiro Ishimori
Story by Leiji Matsumoto
Executive Producer Chiaki Imada
Music by Nozomu Aoki
Cinematographers Masatoshi Fukui/Toshio Katayama
Edited by RJ Kizer/Masaahi Hanai/Skip Schoolnik
Production Designers Tadao Kubota/Takamura Mukuo
Released March 1981
91 mins

THE CALLING

Cast

Richard Chamberlain...Nat Bridger
John Houseman..Stanley Markowitz
Sara Botsford..Ridley Taylor
Robin Gammell..Noah Clayton
Gary Reineke..Lt Meara
Barry Morse...Fred Waites
Alan Scarfe...John Websole
James B Douglas...Jack Gilsdorf
Ken Pogue...Fil Thorner
Neil Munro...Winters
Jefferson Mappin..Photographer
Tom Butler...Detective Tamblyn
Colin Fox...Dr Alderman
Luba Goy..Beth Freemantle
Lenore Zann...Connie Lawson
Clare Coulter..Bag lady
George R Robertson..George Lord
Jo-Anne Hannah...Sandra Thorner
Duncan McIntosh..David Misner
Richard Greenblatt...George

Selected credits

Directed by Michael Anderson
Written by Michael Butler/Dennis Shryack/John Kent Harrison
Story by George Armondo/James Whiton/Michael Butler/ Dennis Shryack
Produced by Robert M Cooper/Brian Walker
Executive Producers Gurston Rosenfeld/Michael A Levine/ Stanley Colbert
Associate Producer Michael W Hadley
Music by John Barry
Cinematographer Reginald H Morris
Edited by Martin Pepler
Production Designer Seamus Flannery
Produced August 1980/Released August 1982
79 mins

FITZCARRALDO

Cast

Klaus Kinski...................................Brian Sweeney Fitzgerald
Claudia Cardinale...Molly
Jose Lewgoy...Don Aquilino
Miguel Angel Fuentes......................................Cholo
Paul Hittscher...The Captain
Huerequeque Enrique Bohorquez....................Huerequeque
Grande Othelo.........................Railway station chief
Peter Berling.............................Director of the opera
David Perez Espinosa...........................Campa chief
Milton Nascimento.......................Black attendant
Rui Polanah...Rubber baron
Salvador Godinez............................Old missionary
Dieter Milz....................................Young missionary
Bill Rose...Notary
Leoncio Bueno......................................Prison guard

Selected credits

Directed/Written by Werner Herzog
Produced by Werner Herzog/Lucki Stipetic
Music by Popol Vuh
Cinematographer Thomas Mauch
Edited by Beate Mainka-Jellinghaus

Produced January 1981/Released October 1982
157 mins

THE PERSONALS

Cast

Bill Schoppert...Bill
Karen Landry...Adrienne
Paul Eiding...Paul
Michael Laskin...David
Vicki Dakil...Shelly
Chris Forth...Jennifer
Patrick O'Brien..Jay
Arlene Simon...Party hostess
Barbara Kingsley.................................Reader secretary
Peggy Knapp...............................Bill's pickup at bar
John Lewin..Matchmaker
Char Baehr.............................Punk girl at reader
Claudia Bloch........................Marriage counselor
Emily Schmit-Larkin................................Bill's editor
Sharon O'Brien................................Couple in café
Mark MacDonald..............................Couple in café
James Cada......................................Man in skyway
Jerome Wilson.......................Rollerskating instructor
Deborah Claesgems......................Rollerskater Bill chases
Judith Morkrid...........................Fantasy rollerskater
Vicki Dane.......................................Fantasy date

Selected credits

Directed/Written by Peter Markle
Produced by Patrick Wells
Executive Producers Robert L Melamed/William Melamed
Associate Producers Bill Schoppert/Stephen E Rivkin
Music by Will Sumner
Cinematographers Peter Markle/Greg Cummins
Edited by Stephen E Rivkin
Released October 1982
90 mins

SORCERESS

Cast

Leigh Harris...Mira
Lynette Harris...Mara
Bob Nelson...Erlick
David Millbern...Pando
Bruno Rey..Baldar
Ana De Sade...Delissia
Robert Ballesteros...Traigon
Douglas Sanders..Hunnu
Tony Stevens...Khrakannon
Martin LaSalle..Krona
Silvia Masters...Kanti
William Arnold...Dargon
Teresa Conway...Amaya
Lucy Jensen...Dancer
Michael Fountain...Player
Peter Farmer..Armorer
Charles Rogers...Servant
Phillip Garrigan..Soldier
Mark Arevan...Gambler
Gloria Meister..Nursemaid

Selected credits

Directed/Produced by Jack Hill (as Brian Stuart)
Written by Jim Wynorski/Jack Hill
Cinematographer Álex Phillips Jr
Edited by Larry Bock/Barry Zetlin
Art Director Joe Greenman
Produced October 1981/Released October 1982
83 mins

TIME WALKER

Cast

Ben Murphy...McCadden
Nina Axelrod...Susie

Kevin Brophy...Peter
Robert Random...Parker
James Karen..Rossmore
Sam Chew Jr...Serrano
Melissa Prophet..Jennie
Austin Stoker...Dr Melrose
Gerard Prendergast..Greg
Shari Belafonte-Harper...Linda
Antoinette Bower..Dr Hayworth
Darwin Joston..Plummer
Greta Blackburn..Sherri
John Lavachielli..Bill
Clint Young...Willoughby
Ken Gibbel...Courtney
Gary Dubin..Michael
Greta Stapf...Ellen
Jason Williams..Jeff
Jack Olson...Ankh-Venaris

Selected credits
Directed by Tom Kennedy
Written by Tom Friedman/Karen Levitt
Story by Jason Williams/Tom Friedman
Produced by Dimitri Villard/Jason Williams
Executive Producer Robert A Shaheen
Music by Richard Band
Cinematographer Robbie Greenberg
Edited by/Second Unit Director Skip Schoolnik
Art Directors Robert A Burns/Joe Garrity
Produced March 1982/Released October 1982
86 mins

JIMMY THE KID
Cast
Gary Coleman...Jimmy
Paul Le Mat...John
Ruth Gordon..Bernice
Dee Wallace..May
Cleavon Little..Herb
Fay Hauser..Nina
Pat Morita...Maurice
Avery Schreiber...Dr Stevens
Walter Olkewicz..Kelp
Don Adams..Harry Walker
Robert F Hoy..1st trooper
Steven Chambers...2nd trooper
Sarina C Grant..Pearl
Lew Horn...Kimball
Frank Miller..Cop
Barry Hope..1st neighbour
Stephen Stucker..2nd neighbour
Ed Call..1st agent
Harvey Lewis..Attendant
Jennifer Jacobs..Waitress

Selected credits
Directed by Gary Nelson
Written by Sam Bobrick
Based on the novel by Donald E Westlake
Produced by Ronald Jacobs
Executive Producers Harry Evans Sloan/Lawrence Kuppin
Music by John Cameron
Cinematographer Dennis Dalzell
Edited by Richard C Meyer
Art Director Bill Ross
Produced August 1981/Released November 1982
85 mins

SCREWBALLS
Cast
Peter Keleghan..Rick McKay
Kent Deuters...Brent Van Dusen III
Linda Speciale...Purity Busch
Alan Deveau...Howie Bates

Linda Shayne...Bootsie Goodhead
Jason Warren..Melvin Jerkovski
Jim Coburn..Tim Stevenson
Terrea Foster..Rhonda Rockett
Donnie Bowes..Principal Stuckoff
Kimberly Brooks...Miss Boudoir
Nicky Fylan...Vince the Prince
Paula Farmer...Miss Shivers
Joe Crozier..Ward Busch
Heather Smith..June Busch
Nola Wale...Mrs Roach
Nancy Chambers..Trisha
John Fox...MC
Jan Taylor..Sarah Bellum
Caroline Tweedle..Librarian
John Glossop...Moose Reardon

Selected credits
Directed by Rafal Zielinski
Written by Linda Shayne/Jim Wynorski
Produced by Maurice Smith
Associate Producers Peter McQuillan/Nicky Fylan
Music by Tim McCauley
Cinematographer Miklós Lente
Edited by Brian Ravok
Art Director Sandra Kybartas
Produced October 1982/Released May 1983
80 mins

SPACE RAIDERS
Cast
Vince Edwards..Hawk
David Mendenhall...Peter
Drew Snyder...Aldebarian
Patsy Pease...Amanda
Thom Christopher...Flightplan
Luca Bercovici..Ace
Ray Stewart...Zariatin
George Dickerson...Tracton
Michael Miller..Lou
Virginia Kiser...Janeris
Don Washburn...Jessup
William Boyett...Taggert
Howard Dayton..Elmer
Dick Miller...Crazy Mel
Elizabeth Charlton..Cookie
Claude Johnson...Technician
Suzan Hollis...Space hooker
Laura Coles...Singer
James Mendenhall...1st guard
Patrick Close...2nd guard

Selected credits
Directed/Written by Howard R Cohen
Produced by Roger Corman
Cinematographer Alec Hirschfeld
Edited by RJ Kizer/Anthony Randel

Art Director Wayne Springfield
Second Unit Director Mary Ann Fisher
Released May 1983
84 mins

DEATHSTALKER

Cast

Rick Hill..Deathstalker
Barbi Benton...Codille
Richard Brooker..Oghris
Lana Clarkson...Kaira
Victor Bo..Kang
Bernard Erhard..Munkar
August Larreta..Salmaron
Lillian Ker..Toralva
Marcos Woinsky..Gargit
Adrian De Piero...Nicor
George Sorvic...King Tulak
Boy Olmi...Young man
Horace Marassi...Creature leader
Patrick Duggan..Colobri
Maria Fournery...Anella
Gabriela Rubinstein...Tarra
Sebastián Larreta..Talan
Amalia Marty...Zaptiah
Claude Petty/Rudy Kumze...Guards

Selected credits

Directed by James Sbardellati (as John Watson)
Written by Howard R Cohen
Produced by James Sbardellati/Hector Olivera/Alex Sessa
Associate Producer Frank K Isaac Jr
Music by Óscar Cardozo Ocampo
Cinematographer Leonardo Rodríguez Solís
Edited by John K Adams/Silvia Ripoll
Art Director Emilio Basaldua
Second Unit Director John Buechler
Released September 1983
80 mins

LOVE LETTERS

Cast

Jamie Lee Curtis...Anna Winter
Bonnie Bartlett...Maggie Winter
Matt Clark..Chuck Winter
James Keach...Oliver Andrews
Bud Cort...Danny De Fronso
Amy Madigan...Wendy
Brian Wood..Frank
Phil Coccioletti..Ralph Glass
Larry Cedar...Jake
Michael Villella..Oliver's client
Jeff Doucette..Hippie
Sally Kirkland...Hippie
Betsy Toll..Marcia Newell
Lyman Ward..Morgan Crawford
Shelby Leverington...................................Edith Andrews
Emma Chapman...Emma
Scott Henderson...Paul
Robin Thomas.......................................Girl at radio station
Michelle Cundey...Young Anna
Rance Howard..Joseph Chesley

Selected credits

Directed/Written by Amy Jones
Produced by Roger Corman
Executive Producers Mel Pearl/Don Levin
Associate Producer Charles Skouras III
Music by Ralph Jones
Cinematographer Alec Hirschfeld
Edited by Gwendolyn Greene
Art Director Jeannine Oppewall
Produced January 1983/Released January 1984
98 mins

ANDROID

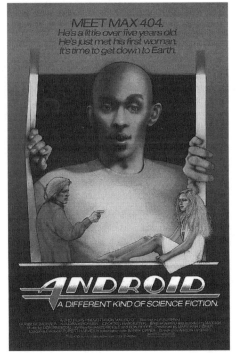

Cast

Klaus Kinski...Dr Daniel
Don Opper..Max 404
Brie Howard..Maggie
Norbert Weisser..Keller
Crofton Hardester...Mendes
Kendra Kirchner...Cassandra
Gary Corarito...Terrapol: Neptune
Mary Ann Fisher..Terrapol: Neptune
Darrell Larson...Terrapol: Neptune
Ian Scheibel...Terrapol: Neptune
Wayne Springfield...Terrapol: Minos
Julia Gibson..Terrapol: Minos
Randy Connor...Terrapol: landing party
Roger Kelton...Terrapol: landing party
Rachel Talalay...Terrapol: landing party
Johanne Todd...Terrapol: landing party

Selected credits.

Directed by Aaron Lipstadt
Written by James Reigle/Don Opper
Story by Will Reigle
Produced by Mary Ann Fisher
Executive Producers Rupert Harvey/Barry Opper
Associate Producer RJ Kizer
Music by Don Preston
Cinematographer Tim Suhrstedt
Edited by Andy Horvitch
Art Directors KC Scheibel/Wayne Springfield
Released February 1984
80 mins

SUBURBIA

Cast

Chris Pedersen..Jack Diddley
Bill Coyne...Evan Johnson
Jennifer Clay...Sheila

Timothy Eric O'Brien...Skinner
Wade Walston...Joe Schmo
Mike B The Flea..Razzle
Maggie Ehrig...Mattie
Grant Miner..Keef
Christina Beck...T'resa
Andrew Pece...Ethan Johnson
Don Allen..Officer William Rennard
Robert Peyton..Jim Tripplett
Jeff Prettyman..Bob Skokes
Dorlinda Griffin..Mother in car
Robert Griffin..Baby
Donna Lamana...Tina Johnson
Anna Schoeller...Anna
André Boutilier...Peg Leg
Nicky Beat...Club owner
Steve Bidrowski.......................................Spotlight operator

Selected credits
Directed by Penelope Spheeris
Written by Penelope Spheeris/Bert Dragin
Produced by Bert Dragin
Executive Producer Roger Corman
Music by Alex Gibson
Cinematographer Tim Suhrstedt
Edited by Ross Albert
Art Director Randy Moore
Released April 1984
94 mins

THE WARRIOR AND THE SORCERESS
Cast
David Carradine...Kain

Luke Askew..Zeg
Maria Socas...Naja
Anthony De Longis...Kief
Harry Townes..Bludge
William Marin..Bal Caz
Arthur Clark..Burgo
Daniel March..Blather
John Overby...Gabble
Richard Paley..Scarface
Mark Welles...Burgo's captain
Cecilia North..Exotic dancer
Dylan Willias...Zeg's guard
Joe Cass...Zeg's guard
Michael Zane...Zeg's guard
Herman Cass...Zeg's guard
Arthur Neal..Zeg's guard
Herman Gere...Zeg's guard
Gus Parker..Zeg's guard
Ned Ivers..Slave
Lillian Cameron..Drowning slave
Eve Adams..Woman at well

Selected credits
Directed/Written by John Broderick
Story by John Broderick/William Stout
Produced by John Broderick/Frank K Issac Jr/Héctor Olivera/Alex Sessa
Music by Luis María Serra (as Louis Saunders)
Cinematographer Leonardo Rodríguez Solís
Edited by Silvia Roberts
Art Director Emmett Baldwin
Released April 1984
81 mins

Hollywood Boulevard (Dick Miller)

bibliography

Roger Corman has been the subject of innumerable articles and interviews over the past 50 years, as well as several books. Two of the best are Corman's own 1990 autobiography, which is both entertaining and insightful, and Beverly Gray's 2000 biography *Roger Corman: An Unauthorised Biography of the Godfather of Indie Filmmaking* (which was revised and retitled in 2004). Gray worked at New World Pictures and at Concorde-New Horizons, and her book is a must for anyone who wants to know what it *really* is like to work for Roger Corman!

Ackerman, Forrest J, ed.
> *Science-Fiction Classics: The Stories That Morphed Into Movies.*
> New York: TV Books, 1999.

Bleiler, Everett F and T E Dikty, eds.
> *Imagination Unlimited.*
> New York: Berkley Books, 1959.

Brown, Rita Mae.
> *Rita Will.*
> New York: Bantam Books, 1997.

Childress, Alice.
> *A Hero Ain't Nothin' But a Sandwich.*
> New York: Puffin Books, 2000.

Corman, Roger with Jim Jerome.
> *How I Made a Hundred Movies in Hollywood and Never Lost a Dime.*
> New York: Da Capo Press, 1998.

Di Franco, J Philip, ed.
> *The Movie World of Roger Corman.*
> New York: Chelsea House, 1979.

Gaspard, John.
> *Fast, Cheap & Written That Way.*
> Studio City: Michael Wiese Productions, 2007.

Gray, Beverly.
> *Roger Corman: Blood-Sucking Vampires, Flesh-Eating Cockroaches, and Driller Killers.*
> New York: Thunder's Mouth Press, 2004.

Green, Hannah.
> *I Never Promised You a Rose Garden.*
> New York: Signet Books, 1964.

Gregory, Mollie.
> *Women Who Run the Show.*
> New York: St. Martin's Press, 2002.

Hillier, Jim and Aaron Lipstadt.
> *Roger Corman's New World.*
> London: British Film Institute, 1981.

Komatsu, Sakyo.
> *Japan Sinks.*
> New York: Harper & Row, 1976.

Mather, Anne.
> *Leopard in the Snow.*
> Toronto: Harlequin Books, 1974.

McGee, Mark Thomas.
> *Roger Corman: The Best of the Cheap Acts.*
> Jefferson: McFarland & Company, 1988.

McGilligan, Patrick.
Backstory 3: Interviews with Screenwriters of the 60s.
Berkeley: University of California Press, 1997.

Moorcock, Michael.
The Final Programme.
New York: Avon, 1968.

Naha, Ed.
The Films of Roger Corman: Brilliance on a Budget.
New York: Arco, 1982.

Norris, Chuck with Ken Abraham.
Against All Odds: My Story.
Nashville: B&H Books, 2006.

Ray, Fred Olen.
The New Poverty Row.
Jefferson: McFarland & Company, 1991.

Segrave, Kerry.
Drive-In Theatres.
Jefferson: McFarland & Company, 1992.

Slater, Ben.
Kinda Hot: The Making of Saint Jack in Singapore.
Singapore: Marshall Cavendish, 2006.

Theroux, Paul.
Saint Jack.
London: Penguin Books, 1976.

Venticinque, Darrin and Tristan Thompson.
The Ilsa Chronicles.
London: Midnight Media, 2000.

Wallace, Edgar.
Blue Hand.
New York: A L Burt Company, 1926.

Weaver, Tom.
Interviews with B Science Fiction and Horror Movie Makers.
Jefferson: McFarland & Company, 1988.

Westlake, Donald E.
Jimmy the Kid.
New York: Walter J Black, 1974.

Willeford, Charles.
Cockfighter.
Berkeley: Black Lizard Books, 1987.

www.hemlockbooks.co.uk

Hemlock Books is an independent publisher specialising in genre-related film titles, with particular emphasis on horror, mystery and the macabre.